Transatlantic Abolitionism in

Transatlantic Abolitionism in the Age of Revolution offers a fresh exploration of anti-slavery debates in the late eighteenth and early nineteenth centuries. It challenges traditional perceptions of early anti-slavery activity as an entirely parochial British, European or American affair, and instead reframes the abolition movement as a broad international network of activists across a range of metropolitan centres and remote outposts.

Interdisciplinary in approach, this book explores the dynamics of transatlantic abolitionism, along with its structure, mechanisms and business methods and, in doing so, highlights the delicate balance that existed between national and international interests in an age of massive political upheaval throughout the Atlantic world. By setting slave-trade debates within a wider international context, J. R. Oldfield reveals how popular abolitionism emerged as a political force in the 1780s and how it adapted itself to the tumultuous events of the late eighteenth and early nineteenth centuries.

J. R. OLDFIELD is Wilberforce Professor of Slavery and Emancipation and Director of the Wilberforce Institute for the study of Slavery and Emancipation (WISE) at the University of Hull. He has written extensively on slavery and abolition in the Atlantic world and has published numerous articles and books in this area. He was formerly Professor of Modern History at the University of Southampton and Director of the Southampton Centre for Eighteenth-Century Studies (2008–10). His research interests include the American South, maritime history and racialised relations in the USA.

Critical Perspectives on Empire

Editors

Professor Catherine Hall
University College London

Professor Mrinalini Sinha
University of Michigan

Professor Kathleen Wilson
State University of New York, Stony Brook

Critical Perspectives on Empire is a major series of ambitious, cross-disciplinary works in the emerging field of critical imperial studies. Books in the series explore the connections, exchanges and mediations at the heart of national and global histories, the contributions of local as well as metropolitan knowledge, and the flows of people, ideas and identities facilitated by colonial contact. To that end, the series not only offers a space for outstanding scholars working at the intersection of several disciplines to bring to wider attention the impact of their work, it also takes a leading role in reconfiguring contemporary historical and critical knowledge, of the past and of ourselves.

A full list of titles published in the series can be found at:
www.cambridge.org/cpempire

Transatlantic Abolitionism in the Age of Revolution

An International History of Anti-slavery, c. 1787–1820

J. R. Oldfield

CAMBRIDGE
UNIVERSITY PRESS

CAMBRIDGE
UNIVERSITY PRESS

University Printing House, Cambridge CB2 8BS, United Kingdom

Cambridge University Press is part of the University of Cambridge.

It furthers the University's mission by disseminating knowledge in the pursuit of education, learning and research at the highest international levels of excellence.

www.cambridge.org
Information on this title: www.cambridge.org/9781107594937

© J. R. Oldfield 2013

First published 2013
First paperback edition 2015

A catalogue record for this publication is available from the British Library

Library of Congress Cataloguing in Publication data
Oldfield, J. R. (John R.)
Transatlantic abolitionism in the age of revolution : an international history of anti-slavery, c. 1787–1820 / J. R. Oldfield.
    pages   cm.
Includes bibliographical references and index.
ISBN 978-1-107-03076-3 (hardback)
1. Antislavery movements–History–18th century.   2. Antislavery movements–History–19th century.   3. Antislavery movements–Great Britain–History.   4. Antislavery movements–France–History.   5. Antislavery movements–United States–History.   I. Title.
HT1025.O54 2013
326′.809033–dc23
2013004683   CIP

ISBN 978-1-107-03076-3 Hardback
ISBN 978-1-107-59493-7 Paperback

For Tom and Matt

Contents

Illustrations

Acknowledgements

In one way or another I have been working on this book for the past ten years, and during that time I have accumulated countless debts of gratitude. Pride of place must go to the many archivists and librarians who have given freely of their time and expertise. In particular, I would like to thank the staffs of the following institutions: the Archives Nationales, Paris; the Bodleian Library, Oxford; the British Library; the Friends House Library, London; the Hartley Library, University of Southampton; the Historical Society of Pennsylvania; the Huntington Library, San Marino, California; the Lewis Walpole Library, Farmington, Connecticut; the New-York Historical Society; the New York Public Library; St John's College, Cambridge; the Whitworth Art Gallery, Manchester; and the William R. Perkins Library, Duke University, Durham, North Carolina.

This book would also not have been possible without the generous support of the Gilder Lehrman Institute for American History, the Historical Society of Pennsylvania (Barra Foundation International Fellowship), the Huntington Library (John Brockway Foundation Fellowship) and the Lewis Walpole Library (Short-Term Fellowship). During the writing-up stage I was also fortunate enough to receive a six-month research fellowship from the Arts and Humanities Research Council. A small grant from the British Academy made possible a short trip to Washington, DC, while the Faculty of Humanities at the University of Southampton very generously funded the cost of illustrations. I am extremely grateful for their assistance.

No less important were the many friends and colleagues who helped with enquiries or at different times took the trouble to discuss this project with me, among them Gillian Dow, Alastair Duke, Colette Gallet, Catherine Hall, Doug Hamilton, Ryan Handley, Kate Hodgson, Richard Huzzey, Cora Kaplan, Christer Petley, Francis Pritchard, Joel Quirk, David Richardson, Joan Tumblety and James Walvin. I would also like to say a big thank you to the staff at the Library Company of

Philadelphia, especially the Director, James Green, and the incomparable Connie King, who must have grown tired of my repeated requests for information. Equally, I have benefited enormously from the extensive comments from the press's two anonymous readers, as well as those from the series editors. These processes can sometimes be painful, but the book is better as a result of their input, although I take full responsibility for the faults that remain. Portions of Chapter 5 have previously appeared in *Imagining Transatlantic Slavery*, edited by Cora Kaplan and John Oldfield, and are reproduced here by kind permission of Palgrave Macmillan.

I have two final acknowledgements to make. The first is to Michael Watson, who commissioned the book, and to all the production staff at Cambridge University Press, particularly my wonderful copy editor, Liz Hudson. The second is to my wife, Veronica, whose loving support, good cheer and endless patience never cease to amaze me. Perhaps we will be able to go out a bit more now? The book is dedicated to our two sons, Tom and Matt. I can only hope that in some small way it repays the pleasure and pride they have given their parents over the past twenty-five years. Many thanks – both of you.

Note on terminology

This book deals with the histories of a number of different countries and uses a range of terms, particularly racial terms, that are specific to each. For instance, the term 'free blacks' is used here to denote those African men and women, North and South, who enjoyed free status in the USA during the eighteenth and nineteenth centuries. According to modern usage, the term is inclusive: the key thing is that these people were non-slaves. By contrast, the terms 'free coloured' and 'free people of colour' have a very specific French Caribbean context and refer to those men and women who were both free and of mixed black and white ancestry (literally *gens de couleur*). The terms 'mulatto', 'quadroon' and 'octoroon' were commonly used in slave societies across the Atlantic world, particularly in the French Caribbean and parts of the American South (Louisiana, for example) and reflected finely grained racial distinctions based on ancestry and hence skin colour. A mulatto was the offspring of one white and one black parent; a quadroon was the offspring of a mulatto and a white parent; octoroon referred to a person with one-eighth African ancestry.

Introduction

As the recent bicentennial of the Abolition Acts of 1807 amply demonstrated, 'abolition' continues to speak to national interests as well
as to specific (national) ways of remembering the past. In Britain, at
least, the 2007 commemorations were seen by many, including government ministers, as an opportunity for Britons to reflect on 'the spirit of
freedom, justice and equality that characterised the efforts of the early
abolitionists' – 'the same spirit that drives our determination to fight
injustice and inequality today'.[1] According to this view, abolition of the
slave trade in 1807 embodied a certain kind of British philanthropy
and – just as important – a certain kind of Britishness.[2] Similarly, in
the USA, abolition has often been seen as a test of the country's democratic values. More recently, Andrew Delbanco has identified abolitionism (broadly defined) as a peculiar 'impulse' in American public life
that links anti-slavery abolitionists of the mid nineteenth century to
women's-rights and gay-rights campaigners in the twentieth century –
and, at the other end of the political spectrum, modern-day pro-life
advocates. As he puts it, such parallels 'should remind us [Americans]
that all holy wars, whether metaphoric or real, from left or right,
bespeak a zeal for combating sin, not tomorrow, not in due time, not,
in Lincoln's phrase, by putting it "in the course of ultimate extinction,"
but *now*'.[3]

---

[1] Government Press Notice, 22 January 2007, quoted in J. R. Oldfield, '2007 Revisited:
Commemoration, Ritual and British Transatlantic Slavery', in David T. Gleeson and
Simon Lewis, eds., *Ambiguous Legacy: The Bicentennial of the International Slave Trade
Bans* (Columbia, SC: University of South Carolina Press, 2012), pp. 192–207, at
p. 195.

[2] For a discussion of these themes and the evolution of a 'culture of abolitionism' in
Britain, see J. R. Oldfield, *'Chords of Freedom': Commemoration, Ritual and British
Transatlantic Slavery* (Manchester University Press, 2007).

[3] Andrew Delbanco, 'The Abolitionist Imagination', in Andrew Delbanco, John
Stauffer, Manisha Sinha, Darryl Pinckney and Wilfred M. McClay, *The Abolitionist
Imagination* (Cambridge, Mass.: Harvard University Press, 2012), pp. 1–55, at
pp. 48–9.

Yet abolition was never entirely a national issue. From the outset, activists on both sides of the Atlantic reached out to each other in a spirit of mutual cooperation. Self-styled 'citizens of the universe', these men (and they were by and large men) were intent on creating a new world order, one in which darkness (including slavery and the slave trade) would progressively give way to enlightenment (liberty, equality, fraternity). Many of the leading figures in these campaigns, among them Granville Sharp, William Wilberforce and Thomas Clarkson, were themselves international celebrities, whose works were circulated and consumed across and within the Atlantic world. Indeed, the early abolitionist movement is best understood as an international movement that rested on dense networks that linked activists in large metropolitan centres such as Paris and London with those in more remote outposts such as Washington, Pennsylvania. In much the same way, activists on both sides of the Atlantic monitored each other's progress, shared ideas and strategies and, as the situation demanded, offered each other support and encouragement. One of the central arguments of this book is that these networks gave abolitionists a distinct advantage over their opponents (it is noticeable, for instance, that pro-slavery advocates, especially those in Britain and in the USA, created no comparable transatlantic connections), even if they did not necessarily guarantee success, at least in the short term.

Historians have long been aware of the international dimensions of abolitionism. One thinks, for instance, of Betty Fladeland's pioneering work on Anglo-American cooperation during the eighteenth and nineteenth centuries. More recently, Seymour Drescher and David Brion Davis, among others, have written major works on slavery and abolition that in different ways draw attention to international perspectives.[4] Yet, in saying this, historians have not always been alert to the 'circum-Atlantic' dimensions of this story – that is, the spaces in

[4] Betty Fladeland, *Men and Brothers: Anglo-American Antislavery Cooperation* (Urbana, Ill.: University of Illinois Press, 1972); Seymour Drescher, *Abolition: A History of Slavery and Antislavery* (Cambridge University Press, 2009); David Brion Davis, *Inhuman Bondage: The Rise and Fall of Slavery in the New World* (Oxford University Press, 2006). See also Robin Blackburn, *The American Crucible: Slavery, Emancipation and Human Rights* (London: Verso, 2011); Derek R. Peterson, ed., *Abolitionism and Imperialism in Britain, Africa, and the Atlantic* (Athens, OH: Ohio University Press, 2010); Robin Blackburn, *The Overthrow of Colonial Slavery, 1776–1848* (London: Verso, 1987); Seymour Drescher, *Capitalism and Antislavery: British Mobilization in Comparative Perspective* (London: Macmillan, 1986); David Brion Davis, *The Problem of Slavery in the Age of Revolution, 1770–1823* (Ithaca, New York: Cornell University Press, 1975).

which abolitionist ideas were circulated and exchanged.[5] Above all else, the early abolitionist movement was about communication. Through their networks, activists circulated a huge amount of material – letters, newspapers, prints, books and pamphlets – that, in turn, was abridged, translated and recycled, depending on local circumstances. Moreover, these 'circuits of knowledge' were multi-directional in the sense that information flowed from east to west and from west to east. Just as importantly, they also encompassed the Caribbean, a region that had a huge impact on slave-trade debates in the eighteenth and nineteenth centuries. Only by excavating these Atlantic spaces, I would argue, can we fully understand the dynamics of international abolitionism, its structure, mechanisms and ways of doing business.

If there is a 'circum-Atlantic' dimension to this study, there is also a comparative or 'trans-Atlantic' dimension to it as well.[6] Part of the intention here is to de-centre Britain. Instead, the approach I have chosen is 'triangular', in the sense that it sets out to compare Britain with two other important centres of abolitionist activity, France and the USA, not as a way of stressing British or American exceptionalism but as a way of explaining why activists made the decisions they did. As we shall see, transatlantic abolitionism moved at different paces, depending on local circumstances. One of the most glaring of these differences was the decision of British and French activists, at a relatively early stage in the campaign, to attack slavery through the slave trade, thereby distancing themselves from American efforts to attack slavery head-on. These subtle distinctions were initially the source of some confusion and misunderstanding. Nevertheless, for all their differences, anti-slavery activists were highly dependent on each other, particularly during periods of crisis. Indeed, international cooperation proved critical in sustaining the Société des Amis des Noirs, probably the most vulnerable of the early abolitionist societies, as well as offering support and encouragement to others, including the London-based Society for Effecting the Abolition of the Slave Trade (SEAST), organised in 1787.

But while at one level the transatlantic history of abolition is about synergies, at another it is about strains and tensions. Indeed, a central

---

[5] I am adopting David Armitage's use of the term 'circum-Atlantic' here. See David Armitage, 'Three Concepts of Atlantic History', in David Armitage and Michael J. Braddick, eds., *The British Atlantic World, 1500–1800* (Basingstoke: Palgrave Macmillan, 2002), pp. 11–27, at pp. 18–20.

[6] Armitage, 'Three Concepts of Atlantic History', pp. 20–3. Rightly, Armitage stresses that 'trans-Atlantic' history can be called international history, not least in the sense that it 'joins states, nations, and regions within an oceanic system' (p. 22).

theme of this book is what might be described as the limits of inter-nationalism. Naively perhaps, early abolitionists saw themselves rid-ing intellectual currents (the American and French revolutions were important here) that would sweep away slavery and the slave trade. The reality was somewhat different. National governments tended to view abolition with suspicion, not least because if acceded to it ran the risk of surrendering an important economic advantage to their competitors. In short, the question became who would make the first move. For this reason, abolition was all too often seen as a plot of some kind, designed to threaten either British or European interests, depending on one's point of view. If anything, the Terror and the Revolutionary war with France (1793–1801) heightened these tensions. As a conservative reac-tion set in, activists on both sides of the Atlantic struggled to make themselves heard. Local societies folded, sympathisers, especially those living in the American South, deserted the cause, and, to all intents and purposes, the flow of abolitionist publications dried up.

Reluctantly, activists were forced to adapt to these changing circum-stances. One approach, that adopted by James Stephen, a key British strategist, was to turn the international situation to their advantage, in effect realigning national and international interests. The French colony of Saint-Domingue was central to these debates. We tend to think of Saint-Domingue as having a negative impact on slave-trade debates, and certainly the revolt of 1791 caused alarm on both sides of the Atlantic, precipitating a reaction that united French planters and merchants, the West India lobby in the British Parliament and slave-holders in the American South in their condemnation of abolitionist activity.[7] Yet, ironically, Saint-Domingue also acted as a stimulus to reform. The unsuccessful French invasion of 1801–4, which resulted in the creation of an independent black republic (Haiti) in the centre of the Caribbean, caused what many activists saw as a new colonial crisis. As I argue here, Saint-Domingue (and the Caribbean region generally) played an important role in the slave-trade debates of 1804–7. Indeed, for many activists, chief among them Henry Brougham, Haiti posed a simple choice: either to give up the slave trade or to risk losing every-thing – slaves, property, livelihoods – in a wave of violence orchestrated

---

[7] David Geggus, 'British Opinion and the Emergence of Haiti, 1791–1805', in James Walvin, ed., *Slavery and British Society, 1776–1846* (London: Macmillan, 1982), pp. 123–49. See also David Geggus, ed., *The Impact of the Haitian Revolution in the Atlantic World* (Columbia, SC: University of South Carolina Press, 2001); Laurent Dubois and John D. Garrigus, *Slave Revolutions in the Caribbean, 1789–1804: A Brief History with Documents* (New York: Palgrave Macmillan, 2006).

by Haiti's military leaders or, at the very least, patterned after their example.

In this sense, the national and the international were in delicate balance with each other, sometimes colliding, at other times coalescing to effect meaningful political change. Abolition proceeded by degrees, nudged forward by war, shifting political alliances and, above all, the prospect of international cooperation. As Philip D. Morgan has recently pointed out, abolition in 1807 was never merely 'a parochial British affair'.[8] On the contrary, British activists were profoundly aware of the international situation not only in the Caribbean (Haiti, Trinidad, Dutch Guiana) but also in the USA. Indeed, as we shall see, they spent a lot of time ascertaining whether Americans would take deliberate action in 1807–8, as the US Constitution seemed to imply they would. It may well have been that government ministers could have carried abolition in 1807 without outside help, but news of Congress's intention to abolish the slave trade, which reached Britain ahead of the crucial debates in the House of Lords, undoubtedly strengthened their hand and made pushing abolition through Parliament that much easier, as did their earlier success in pushing through the Foreign Slave Act (1806), which in many ways should be regarded as a war measure or, at least, one made possible by European war.

One aim of this book, therefore, is to tease out the relationship between the national and the international. After 1807, for instance, British activists set out to make abolition 'universal', partly out of self-interest and partly out of humanitarian zeal. But, here again, as the Congresses of Vienna (1814–15) and Aix-la-Chapelle (1818) demonstrated, there were limits to how far they could push internationalism, particularly if that meant signing up to binding international agreements. Debates around the mutual right of search, a key element of the suppression politics of the early nineteenth century, exposed serious differences of opinion, not only between Britain and Europe but also between Britain and America. Nevertheless, it proved difficult to turn a blind eye to such initiatives or the interests and ideologies that lay behind them. The USA provides an interesting case study. Wary of anything that touched on either their independence or their self-respect, members of Congress instead decided to take matters into their own hands, tightening existing prohibitions against the slave trade, even to the extent of authorising the President to send navy patrols to the west coast of Africa. Of

---

[8] Philip D. Morgan, 'Ending the Slave Trade: A Caribbean and Atlantic Context', in Derek R. Peterson, ed., *Abolitionism and Imperialism in Britain, Africa, and the Atlantic*, pp. 101–28, at pp. 120–1.

course, internal domestic pressures were also important here, but, by the same token, we cannot ignore the international context, or the pressures it brought to bear on nineteenth-century slave-trade debates.

As will already be obvious, in writing this book I have been strongly influenced by recent work on Atlantic history, which in the past twenty years or so has steadily grown in importance.[9] In particular, I have been influenced by David Armitage's 'three concepts of Atlantic history', although, like him, I would want to stress that these concepts ('circum-Atlantic', 'trans-Atlantic' and 'cis-Atlantic') are by no means mutually exclusive.[10] I have also been influenced by the 'new imperial history', which, at the risk of oversimplification, sees metropole and colony as constituent parts of what might be called 'Greater Britain'. As Antoinette Burton puts it, 'Empire was not just a phenomenon "out there," but a fundamental part of English culture and national identity at home.'[11] The slave-trade debates of the eighteenth and nineteenth centuries particularly lend themselves to analysis of this kind. As we shall see, the Caribbean was a constant presence in these debates and not simply because of its strategic importance or the political muscle of the West India lobby. Books, pamphlets, newspapers and prints were all responsible for circulating ideas about the Caribbean – many of them decidedly negative – that had a profound effect on how those in the metropole viewed both colonial planters and the violent and seemingly

---

[9] See, for instance, Jack D. Greene and Philip D. Morgan, eds., *Atlantic History: A Critical Appraisal* (Oxford University Press, 2009); Bernard Bailyn and Patricia L. Denault, eds., *Soundings in Atlantic History: Latent Structures and Intellectual Currents, 1500–1830* (Cambridge, Mass.: Harvard University Press, 2009); Eliga H. Gould, 'Atlantic History and the Literary Turn', *Early American Literature*, 43 (1) (2008): 197–203; Bernard Bailyn, *Atlantic History: Concept and Contours* (Cambridge, Mass.: Harvard University Press, 2005); Nicholas P. Canny, 'Atlantic History: What and Why? *European Review*, 9 (4) (October 2001): 399–411; Nicholas P. Canny, 'Writing Atlantic History; or, Reconfiguring the History of Colonial British America', *Journal of American History*, 86 (3) (1999): 1093–114.

[10] Armitage, 'Three Concepts of Atlantic History', pp. 28–9. Armitage defines 'cis-Atlantic' history, the third of his three concepts, as the 'history of any particular place – a nation, a state, a region, even a specific institution – in relation to the wider Atlantic world' (p. 24).

[11] Antoinette Burton, 'Who Needs the Nation? Interrogating "British" History', in *Empire in Question: Reading, Writing, and Teaching British Imperialism* (Durham, NC: Duke University Press, 2011), pp. 41–55, at p. 43. See also L. Tabili, 'Colony and Metropole: The New Imperial History', *The Historian*, 69 (1) (2007): 84–6; Catherine Hall and Sonya Rose, eds., *At Home with the Empire: Metropolitan Culture and the Imperial World* (Cambridge University Press, 2006); Kathleen Wilson, ed., *A New Imperial History: Culture, Identity and Modernity in Britain and the Empire, 1660–1840* (Cambridge University Press, 2004); David Feldman, 'The New Imperial History', *Journal of Victorian Culture*, 9 (2) (2004): 235–9; Catherine Hall, *Civilising Subjects: Metropole and Colony in the English Imagination, 1830–1867* (Cambridge: Polity Press, 2002).

'un-British' societies they had created under the gaze of the British Empire.

This book is divided into three distinct parts. In the first of these I look at the ways in which activists on both sides of the Atlantic went about creating a transatlantic network that proved remarkably enduring, owing in no small part to a number of key actors, among them James Pemberton, William Dillwyn and Jacques-Pierre Brissot. Almost without exception, these men shared an international vision that transcended narrow national boundaries. In a telling comment, Thomas Clarkson, another important figure in this transatlantic story, said of Brissot that 'he was no patriot in the ordinary acceptation of the word; for he took the habitable globe as his country, and wished to consider every foreigner as his brother.'[12] James Pemberton aspired to the same cosmopolitan ideal, as did Granville Sharp. Indeed, what united British, French and American activists was their sense that their activities had a global reach and significance. Time and shifting political currents would disrupt these associations – and, indeed, it is tempting to see them as a manifestation of the late 1780s, years of revolutionary fervour – nevertheless, they proved highly adaptable, providing activists on both sides of the Atlantic with a ready-made support system.

In Chapter 2, I go on to look at the way activists exploited these networks, using them to circulate abolitionist books and pamphlets, creating in the process an information highway that encompassed Europe, the USA and the Caribbean. As we shall see, activists were tireless letter-writers, picking up their pens on a regular basis to tell each other about their victories and setbacks, to share information and, where necessary, to offer criticisms. But the crucial point is that these 'circuits of knowledge' made transatlantic abolitionism work and gave it purchase. Finally, in Chapter 3, I consider abolitionist strategies, looking in detail at the different positions taken by British, French and American activists. In particular, I have taken trouble to trace the evolving nature of French anti-slavery debates as activists struggled to come to terms with events in Saint-Domingue. The growing importance of free coloured rights, which loomed large in French anti-slavery debates after 1789, is another example of how metropolitan debates were influenced by people at the margins, among them Julien Raimond, a free

---

[12] Thomas Clarkson, *The History of the Rise, Progress, and Accomplishment of the Abolition of the African Slave-Trade by the British Parliament*, 2 vols. (London: Longman, Hurst, Rees & Orme, 1808), vol. II, p. 166.

coloured Saint-Dominguan, whose career as an Atlantic traveller has been reconstructed in painstaking detail by John D. Garrigus.[13]

In Part II, I move on to consider how the international vision of the late 1780s was disrupted first by the French Revolution (particularly the Terror) and then by the 1791 slave revolt in Saint-Domingue. Together, these cataclysmic events provoked a reaction across the Atlantic world as conservative interests sought to protect the institution of slavery, adopting a siege mentality that saw 'outsiders', whether they were free blacks in the American South or black émigrés from Saint-Domingue, as a menace that needed to be checked and controlled. Inevitably, these pressures took their toll. This is perhaps most evident in Britain and France, where organised societies failed during the 1790s, but, as the proceedings of the American Convention demonstrate, in the USA, too, activists were forced onto the defensive. As a result, slave-trade debates during the 1790s were much less expansive in character. In Chapter 5, I explore some of these developments, using newspapers, plays and prints to recreate cultures and mentalities that, if anything, (re)presented abolition as a national impulse or, at least, as one that spoke to national sensibilities.

Part III begins with the slave-trade debates of 1807, which engineered a breakthrough, catapulting Britain and the USA into a new abolitionist era. Chapter 6 examines these debates in detail, building on a lot of existing work to present a more rounded, international history of abolition. Chapter 7 continues this story, looking at British attempts to make abolition universal, a campaign that worked at two distinct levels: the first, diplomatic activity, where activists found themselves working in close cooperation with government ministers; and the second, perhaps less well known, involving attempts to educate Europeans (particularly the French) about slavery and the slave trade. Part of my argument here is that these opinion-building activities deserve much closer attention, not least because they did have an impact, particularly in France, where by 1820 we can see an abolitionist culture starting to take root. The final chapter deals with the related issue of colonisation, related in the sense that the idea of a black nationality, whether in Africa or the Caribbean, was for a long time a key part of abolitionist thinking.[14] Here again

[13] John D. Garrigus, 'The Free Colored Elite of Saint-Domingue: The Case of Julien Raimond, 1774–1801', available online at http://users.ju.edu/jgarrig (accessed 14 June 2011).
[14] See Seymour Drescher, *The Mighty Experiment: Free Labor versus Slavery in British Emancipation* (Oxford University Press, 2002), pp. 88–105; Christopher Leslie Brown, 'Empire without America: British Plans for Africa in the Era of the American Revolution', in Derek R. Peterson, ed., *Abolitionism and Imperialism in Britain, Africa, and the Atlantic* (Athens, OH: Ohio University Press, 2010), pp. 84–100.

colonisation was a common concern, uniting activists on both sides of the Atlantic and creating, in turn, networks that stretched from the USA to Britain and from Britain to Africa and the Caribbean. No less striking is the involvement of blacks in colonisation schemes, among them Paul Cuffe, another remarkable Atlantic traveller. Colonisation, however, was also a contested space, leading many blacks to reject what they saw as 'forced migration', a decision that re-energised abolitionist debates in the USA, forcing them into new and unexpected directions.

The book ends in 1820. At first glance, this might seem like an artificial demarcation. But there is a real sense in which the early 1820s marked the opening of a new chapter in transatlantic abolitionism, one that was much more restless, more uncompromising and concerned, above all, with challenging slavery head-on. Of course, early abolitionists were hardly oblivious to the plight of enslaved Africans, whether in the Caribbean or the USA. Nevertheless, their approach was cautious and, in the main, accommodating. As John Stauffer astutely observes, 'they compromised effectively and worked across sectional, and occasionally racial, divisions'.[15] Above all, they found common cause in the international slave trade. For British activists, in particular, this was the key to everything. Only abolish the slave trade, they argued, and slavery itself would eventually crumble to dust. By the early 1820s, however, this orthodoxy was starting to break down. Britons would go on trying to suppress the international slave trade but increasingly they came to see that their American counterparts were right in focusing their attention on slavery as well. As a result, the 1820s would witness a series of transformations as activists on both sides of the Atlantic adopted increasingly radical positions until by 1832 'immediatism' (that is, the immediate and unconditional abolition of slavery) had become for many, especially younger activists, a new kind of orthodoxy and one that gave transatlantic abolitionism of the 1830s a new and very distinctive character.

---

[15] John Stauffer, 'Fighting the Devil with His Own Fire', in Andrew Delbanco, John Stauffer, Manisha Sinha, Darryl Pinckney and Wilfred M. McClay, *The Abolitionist Imagination* (Cambridge, Mass.: Harvard University Press, 2012), pp. 57–79, at p. 71.

Part I

Building an anti-slavery wall

1 Networks

Properly speaking, the history of organised anti-slavery dates from the 1780s. Of course, there were dissenting voices before this date. In his monumental *The History of the Rise, Progress and Accomplishment of the Abolition of the African Slave-Trade by the British Parliament* (1808), Thomas Clarkson devoted ten chapters to these early pioneers, identifying scores of activists on both sides of the Atlantic, among them Anthony Benezet and John Woolman, two early Quaker propagandists, and Granville Sharp, whose involvement in the Somerset decision of 1772, which set a limit on the ability of masters to take African 'servants' out of Britain against their will, gained him widespread recognition, not least in the USA.[1] Though the work of these men was largely uncoordinated, common concerns did sometimes draw them together. Sharp's growing list of American correspondents, for instance, included not only Anthony Benezet but also Benjamin Rush, a young Philadelphian doctor, who, in 1773, published anonymously *An Address to the Inhabitants of the British Settlements in America, upon Slave-Keeping*, a devastating critique of slavery and slaveholders, as well as white racist attitudes.[2] Similarly, the international Quaker network facilitated the regular exchange of ideas and information. But, important as they were, these stirrings did not as yet represent a coherent movement. That was to come in the years immediately after the American Revolution, with the appearance on both sides of the Atlantic of highly organised, energetic and broad-based abolitionist societies that together formed a vibrant and relatively well-integrated international community.[3]

[1] Clarkson, *History*, vol. I, pp. 1–258.
[2] David Freeman Hawke, *Benjamin Rush: Revolutionary Gadfly* (Indianapolis, Ind.: Bobbs-Merrill, 1971), pp. 104–7. For Sharp's relationship with Benezet, see Drescher, *Abolition*, pp. 107–8.
[3] There is a rich theoretical literature on networks, some of which I draw on below. See, for instance, Martin Kilduff and Wenpin Tsai, *Social Networks and Organizations* (London: Sage, 2006); Alain Degenne and Michel Forse, *Introducing Social Networks*, trans. Arthur Borges (London: Sage, 1999); Stanley Wasserman and Katherine Faust, *Social Network Analysis: Methods and Application* (Cambridge University

The timing of this 'take off' was not entirely accidental. While there were long-term factors involved, including economic development and the growth of compassionate humanitarianism, there is little doubt that the American Revolution changed the terms of the debate.[4] The Declaration of Independence, in particular, raised pressing questions about the nature and extent of liberty, a fact not lost on some British observers, who suspected the Patriots, especially those in the slave South, of insincerity or, worse, hypocrisy. For others, however, the logic of their position was inescapable. As Benjamin Rush put it, 'It would be useless for us to denounce the servitude to which the Parliament of Great Britain wishes to reduce us, while we continue to keep our fellow creatures in slavery just because their colour is different.'[5] In Britain, meanwhile, the American Revolution unleashed a heated debate about political representation that was quite often framed in terms of slavery (disenfranchisement) and freedom (the vote). But of far greater moment was the fact that the conflict effectively divided British America, at the same time halving the number of slaves in the British Empire. Suddenly, the problems of slavery and the slave trade became a good deal more manageable. 'As long as America was ours', Thomas Clarkson conceded in 1788, 'there was no chance that a minister would have attended to

Press, 1994). Historians have also shown a growing interest in networks, particularly trading networks within the Atlantic world. See, for instance, Douglas Hamilton, 'Local Connections, Global Ambitions: Creating a Transoceanic Network in the Eighteenth-Century British Atlantic Empire', *International Journal of Maritime History*, 23 (2) (December 2011): 1–17; Natasha Glaisyer, 'Networking: Trade and Exchange in the Eighteenth-Century British Empire', *Historical Journal*, 47 (2) (2004): 451–76; David Hancock, *Citizens of the World: London Merchants and the Integration of the British Atlantic Community, 1735–1785* (Cambridge University Press, 1995). For two rather different perspectives, stressing the importance of familial and political networks, respectively, see Sarah M. S. Pearsall, *Atlantic Families: Lives and Letters in the Later Eighteenth Century* (Oxford University Press, 2008) and Zoë Laidlaw, *Colonial Connections, 1815–45: Patronage, the Information Revolution and Colonial Government* (Manchester University Press, 2005). Finally, François Furstenberg has recently used the slavery tracts in George Washington's library at Mount Vernon to explore Washington's engagement with international debates on slavery and the slave trade. See François Furstenberg, 'Atlantic Slavery, Atlantic Freedom: George Washington, Slavery, and Transatlantic Abolitionist Networks', *The William and Mary Quarterly*, 3rd series, 68 (April 2011): 247–86. My own emphasis, by contrast, is on the denser networks that involved organised anti-slavery societies on both sides of the Atlantic.

[4] For an overview of some of these issues, see Drescher, *Abolition*, especially p. 110, n. 45; Christopher Leslie Brown, *Moral Capital: Foundations of British Abolitionism* (Chapel Hill, NC: University of North Carolina Press, 2006), pp. 3–22; Davis, *Inhuman Bondage*, pp. 231–49.

[5] Brown, *Moral Capital*, pp. 123–34; Arthur Zilversmit, *The First Emancipation: The Abolition of Slavery in the North* (University of Chicago Press, 1967), pp. 227–8; David Brion Davis, *The Problem of Slavery in Western Culture* (London: Penguin Books, 1970), p. 478 (quotation).

the groans of the sons and daughters of Africa, however he might feel
for their distress.'[6] In short, after 1783, activists found themselves operating in a very different political climate, one in which formal amalgam-
ation, in the shape of abolitionist societies, seemed not only possible but
also highly desirable.

The oldest of these societies was the Pennsylvania Society for
Promoting the Abolition of Slavery and the Relief of Free Negroes
Unlawfully Held in Bondage, usually referred to as the Pennsylvania
Abolition Society (PAS), which was originally organised in 1775 by a
group of Philadelphia Quakers.[7] With a population of around 30,000,
Philadelphia was the second-largest city in what was then still the
British Empire. Commerce drove this thriving seaport. By the early
1770s it is estimated that Philadelphia had about 320 merchants, many
of them Quakers, who dominated the social, economic and political
life of the community. The city was also justifiably proud of its commitment to rational thought and progress; before the Revolution it not
only boasted a library (the first circulating library in America) but also
a college, a hospital and various other literary, philosophical and philanthropic organisations. The heart of the city, however, remained the
crowded wharves jutting out into the Delaware river, where wealthy
merchants mixed with shopkeepers, sailors, slaves (close to 1,500 in
1767) and artisans.[8] It was here, in the Rising Sun Tavern overlooking
the waterfront, that on 14 April Quaker activists took the first steps in
the organisation of what was to become the PAS.

Forced to suspend its operations during the Revolutionary war, in
1784 the PAS was revived, largely at the instigation of Thomas Harrison,
a Quaker tailor. New members were recruited, and, just as important,
the organisation expanded beyond its narrow sectarian base. As Gary
Nash and Jean Soderlund point out, of the thirty-seven men who joined
the PAS between April 1784 and December 1785, only thirteen were
Quakers. Perhaps just as significant, most of these men were artisans,
shopkeepers, manufacturers and lesser merchants.[9] By late 1786, however, Harrison and his colleagues were obviously aware that something

[6] J. R. Oldfield, *Popular Politics and British Anti-Slavery: The Mobilisation of Public Opinion Against the Slave Trade, 1787–1807* (Manchester University Press, 1995), p. 33; Andrew O'Shaughnessy, *An Empire Divided: The American Revolution and the British Caribbean* (Philadelphia, Pa.: University of Pennsylvania Press, 2000), p. 245 (quotation).
[7] The date is sometimes given as 1774, but there is nothing in the handwritten minutes to suggest that the society was active before April 1775.
[8] See Gary B. Nash, *First City: Philadelphia and the Forging of Historical Memory* (Philadelphia, Pa.: University of Pennsylvania Press, 2006), pp. 45–78.
[9] Gary B. Nash and Jean R. Soderlund, *Freedom by Degrees: Emancipation in Pennsylvania and Its Aftermath* (Oxford University Press, 1991), pp. 115–16.

more was needed, particularly if they were to tackle slavery head-on 'rather than rescuing individuals one by one from its snares'.[10] Mindful that a Constitutional Convention was soon to meet in Philadelphia, in April 1787 the PAS underwent further reorganisation. Significantly, among the new recruits were members of Philadelphia's elite, men of considerable wealth and influence, among them Benjamin Rush, Tench Coxe, Caspar Wistar, David Wilson and James Pemberton. Equally telling was the decision to make the veteran politician Benjamin Franklin president of the reorganised society. In other words, by 1787 the PAS had been not only reorganised but also placed on an entirely different social and political footing.[11]

Philadelphia reformers may also have been influenced by developments in New York, where in January 1785 a group of activists organised the New York Manumission Society (NYMS). From its inception, the NYMS attracted some of the state's most prominent statesmen. Its first president, for instance, was John Jay, US Secretary of Foreign Affairs from 1784 to 1789 and, later, one of the co-authors of the *Federalist Papers*. Other members included Alexander Hamilton, formerly George Washington's aide-de-camp and a member of the Continental Congress (1782-3); Revolutionary soldier Matthew Clarkson, who went on to become a member of the New York Assembly (1789–90); and Melancton Smith, a merchant and lawyer, who was also a member of the Continental Congress (1785–8). Like the Pennsylvania society, the NYMS was a 'mixed' organisation. Richard S. Newman estimates that at least up until 1815 over 50 per cent of its members were Quakers, among them the society's long-time treasurer, John Murray, Jnr., a New York merchant and later president of the city's Chamber of Commerce, and John Keese, a New York attorney.[12] The appearance of this new society, led by men of such obvious distinction, set an example for others to follow; hence the decision in April 1787 to reorganise the PAS and hence the decision to make Franklin its new president.

The initial impetus, therefore, came from America. In May 1787, however, another new society appeared, this time on the other side of the Atlantic. Here again, Quakers were an important driving force. In 1783, the London Meeting for Sufferings appointed a special committee

---

[10] Nash and Soderlund, *Freedom by Degrees*, p. 124.

[11] Nash and Soderlund, *Freedom by Degrees*, p. 124. See also Richard S. Newman, *The Transformation of American Abolitionism: Fighting Slavery in the Early Republic* (Chapel Hill, NC: University of North Carolina Press, 2002), esp. pp. 16–22.

[12] Newman, *The Transformation of American Abolitionism*, p. 18. All biographical details have been extracted from the *American National Biography Online*, www.anb.org (accessed 11 March 2011).

to distribute abolitionist books and pamphlets in what may have been a calculated attempt to extend their influence beyond the narrow confines of the Society of Friends.[13] Subsequently, this same group made contact with Thomas Clarkson, largely through the intervention of James Phillips, who had agreed to publish Clarkson's *Essay on the Slavery and Commerce of the Human Species* (1786). But what held British abolitionists back, initially at least, was their lack of political influence, particularly within the British Houses of Parliament. Wilberforce's decision to take up the cause in the House of Commons, however, was the signal for the organisation of the SEAST, which was to prove the most innovative of all the early abolitionist societies. The nucleus of this society was provided by Samuel Hoare, George Harrison, William Dillwyn, John Lloyd and Joseph Woods, who had all been members of the original Quaker committee established in 1783. In all, nine of the twelve founding members were Quakers, the exceptions being Granville Sharp, Phillip Sansom and Clarkson himself. The other significant feature of the original society or, at least, its guiding London Committee, was its middle-class origins in trade and business. Two members were bankers, four were merchants or had some experience of trade, while two, John Barton and James Phillips, were small manufacturers. Unlike the PAS or the NYMS, the SEAST had few, if any, members who were serving politicians (Wilberforce, for example, did not formally become a member until April 1791), even if in Sharp it had a figure of considerable influence, not least among jurists.[14]

The SEAST, in turn, had a direct impact on the organisation of the Société des Amis des Noirs in February 1788.[15] Based in Paris, the French society was led by Jacques-Pierre Brissot de Warville and Etienne Clavière, one a writer and publicist, the other a banker, who drew around them a group of lawyers, academics, legislators and doctors that included M. de Gramagnac, Marie Jean Antoine Nicolas de Caritat, marquis de Condorcet, Jérôme Pétion de Villeneuve, Honoré

---

[13] See Brown, *Moral Capital*, pp. 424–5.
[14] Oldfield, *Popular Politics*, pp. 41–2, 71–3. See also Judith Jennings, *The Business of Abolishing the British Slave Trade, 1783–1807* (London and New York: Routledge, 1997).
[15] Lawrence C. Jennings, *French Anti-Slavery: The Movement for the Abolition of Slavery in France, 1802–1848* (Cambridge University Press, 2000), pp. 1–2; Daniel P. Resnick, 'The Société des Amis des Noirs and the Abolition of Slavery', *French Historical Studies*, 7 (4) (1972): 558–69. The manuscript minutes or 'registre' of the Société des Amis des Noirs, which can be found at the Archives Nationales in Paris, have been published, along with those of the later Société des Amis des Noirs et des Colonies, in a single volume edited by Marcel Dorigny and Bernard Gainot. See Marcel Dorigny and Bernard Gainot, *La Société des Amis des Noirs, 1788–1799: Contribution à l'histoire de l'abolition de l'esclavage* (Paris: UNESCO, 1998).

Gabriel Mirabeau and François Xavier Lanthenas, many of whom would later play a leading part in the French Revolution.[16] But this was never exclusively a metropolitan group. There were corresponding members in other parts of France (Lyon, Chartres and Nantes, for example), as well as in Brussels, Dublin and London. Uniquely among these early societies, the Société des Amis des Noirs also had direct links to colonial slavery in the shape of its free coloured members. As we shall see, the presence of these men, chief among them the Saint-Dominguan planter Julien Raimond, gave the French society a very different focus and direction, particularly after 1789. What is worth stressing at this point, however, is that the Société des Amis des Noirs was the most diverse of all these early abolitionist societies, not just in regard to *gens de couleur* but also in regard to women, who could also become members and, under its constitution, attend some of its meetings, although it is clear from the official minutes that few of them ever did.[17]

In organisational terms, all four of these societies shared striking similarities. For the most part, the real work, meaning decision-making and the formulation of policy, was done by 'general' meetings that met either monthly or quarterly; this was certainly the case with the PAS, the NYMS and the Société des Amis des Noirs.[18] Day-to-day business (that is, business between meetings) was invariably carried out by 'acting' or 'standing' committees, or sometimes secretaries or treasurers. The constitution of the Société des Amis des Noirs, for instance, provided not only for monthly 'general assemblies' but also for an elected committee ('Le Comité') that in practice met three or four times a

---

[16] Dorigny and Gainot, *La Société des Amis des Noirs*, pp. 39–46. Some of these figures had already published works attacking slavery. See, for instance, Marie Jean Antoine Nicolas de Caritat, marquis de Condorcet, *Réflexions sur l'esclavage des nègres* (Neuchâtel: Chez la Société Typographique, 1781). For early slavery debates in France, see Sue Peabody, *'There Are No Slaves in France': The Political Culture of Race and Slavery in the Ancien Régime* (Oxford University Press, 1996).

[17] *Règlement de la Société des Amis des Noirs* (Paris, 1788), p. 21. A membership list published around 1790 included the names of three women: Madame la marquise de Baussans, Madame Poivre and Madame Clavière. See Eloise Ellery, *Brissot de Warville: A Study in the History of the French Revolution* (Boston, Mass.: Houghton Mifflin, 1915), pp. 442–7. It would seem that women were only admitted to special half-yearly assemblies rather than to monthly assemblies, which were reserved for men. See Dorigny and Gainot, *La Société des Amis des Noirs*, pp. 125, nn. 135, 233, 236.

[18] Some of these meetings were quite large. In 1796, for instance, the average attendance at the quarterly meetings of the NYMS was twenty-three and in 1802 thirty-two. Figures extracted from the Quarterly Committee Minutes, 1785–97 and 1798–1814, New York Manumission Society (hereafter NYMS Minutes), NYMS Papers, New-York Historical Society, New York.

month.[19] Some of these societies also had committees of correspondence and even electing or membership committees. By contrast, the SEAST was a much leaner organisation, concentrating all of these different functions into its central London Committee, which met on a much more regular basis, usually once a week. In short, the effectiveness of these societies and, by extension, the effectiveness of the abolitionist network, often depended on the energy and commitment of relatively small numbers of people. Average weekly attendance at the meetings of the London Committee was rarely more than ten, while throughout this period (1787–95) the highest recorded attendance was only seventeen.[20]

By February 1788, therefore, there were four major abolitionist societies, two on either side of the Atlantic. Significantly, none of these societies operated in isolation. One of the first acts of the PAS, following its reorganisation in 1787, was to write to the NYMS, as well as to leading British and European activists, among them Thomas Clarkson, Granville Sharp and the Abbé Raynal. Simultaneously, in July 1787, the London Committee of the SEAST instructed four of its members to prepare a letter to the societies at 'Philadelphia and New York to inform them of the measures this committee are taking for the abolition of the Slave Trade'.[21] The French society was equally quick to make contact with British and American abolitionists. In March 1788, the Société des Amis des Noirs set up a special committee to correspond with the SEAST, while Brissot's visit to the USA later that same year would help to forge important links with both the PAS and the NYMS.[22] This reaching out to each other reinforced a sense that abolitionism transcended narrow national boundaries. Inspired variously by political ideals of freedom and equality and religious notions of benevolence and brotherhood, abolitionists saw themselves as part of an Atlantic world that was at once progressive and enlightened. Greeting the Société des Amis des Noirs in February 1788, SEAST president, Granville Sharp, reminded them that he and his colleagues had not taken up the cause of

---

[19] *Règlement de la Société des Amis des Noirs*, pp. 18–19, 21–8, 36–48. The twenty-one members of La Comité of the Société des Amis des Noirs were elected by the General Assembly at the beginning of each year and served for three years.

[20] Figures extracted from the minutes of the London Committee of the SEAST (hereafter SEAST Minutes), Add. MS 21254, British Library, London. These minutes are arranged in three volumes as follows: Add. MSS 21, 254 (22 May 1787–26 February 1788); Add. MSS 21, 255 (5 March 1788–7 July 1791); and Add. MSS 21, 256 (20 July 1790–1819).

[21] SEAST Minutes, 5 July 1787.

[22] Oldfield, *Popular Politics*, pp. 51–2; Dorigny and Gainot, *La Société des Amis des Noirs*, pp. 72–88 (minutes of meeting of 4 March 1788).

abolition as 'Englishmen' but as 'citizens of the Universe'. 'In truth', he went on, 'we consider our plan as encompassing the whole globe, and we will only consider it complete when violence against the rights of humanity ceases everywhere.'[23]

This was the language of the Enlightenment, of cosmopolitanism and the rights of man. For men such as Sharp, abolition was never solely a national project; rather, it spoke to universal values as well as to sympathetic connections with all humankind.[24] Not by accident, the same language was invoked in the constitution of the PAS. 'It having pleased the Creator of the World to make of one flesh all the Children of men', the preamble began, 'it becomes them to consult and promote each other's happiness as Members of the same family, however diversified they may be by color, situation, religion or different states of Society.'[25] But this was not merely a Christian obligation; those who professed 'to maintain for themselves the rights of human nature' also had a duty 'to use such means as are in their power, to extend the blessings of Freedom to every part of the human race'.[26] The framers were thinking here especially of those enslaved in the USA. Like their counterparts in Britain and France, however, Pennsylvania activists saw themselves as 'citizens of the universe'. With this in mind, the PAS arranged for 1,000 copies of its constitution to be printed and distributed, not just within the USA but overseas as well. The constitution, in effect, became the society's calling card, a written affirmation of its commitment to exporting abolition and to establishing a 'relationship of brotherhood and mutual correspondence' with reformers on both sides of the Atlantic.[27]

Though not all abolitionists were radicals, the heady optimism of the late 1780s (really the period up to 1792) also encouraged them to think of abolition in global terms. This was perhaps most evident in France, where the American Revolution inspired what Durand Echeverria describes as a genuine 'Americanism', that is, a popular movement or sensibility that saw America as 'the hope of the human race'.[28] As Brissot

[23] Quoted in Dorigny and Gainot, *La Société des Amis des Noirs*, p. 86.
[24] For cosmopolitanism, see Michael Scrivener, *The Cosmopolitan Ideal in the Age of Revolution and Reaction, 1776–1832* (London: Pickering & Chatto, 2007).
[25] Minutes of General Meetings, Pennsylvania Abolition Society (hereafter PAS Minutes), 23 April 1787, PAS Papers, Historical Society of Pennsylvania, Philadelphia, microfilm edition, Reel 1.
[26] PAS Minutes, 23 April 1787.
[27] PAS Minutes, 23 April 1787 and 5 January 1789; James Phillips to James Pemberton, 21 July 1787, Pemberton Papers, 48/110, Historical Society of Pennsylvania, Philadelphia. See also James Pemberton to John Pemberton, 30 April 1787, Pemberton Papers, 48/31.
[28] Durand Echeverria, *Mirage in the West: A History of the French Image of American Society to 1815* (Princeton University Press, 1968), pp. 39–78.

told members of the Société des Amis des Noirs, the Revolution had
'impressed upon the minds of most men a respect truly religious for
the cause of liberty; it [had] impressed upon them an aversion, a horror for all tyrannical proceedings, under whatever shape'. 'Unite all
the strength of men of integrity, that it may be directed to a common
end', Brissot went on, stressing the importance of international cooperation. 'Let them make it their constant occupation, and nothing will
resist efforts that are always wisely directed.'[29] If anything, the French
Revolution furthered the development of this idealistic internationalism. Events in France seemed to many to confirm the emergence of
a new democratic era. This, of course, was the wider meaning of the
Declaration of the Rights of Man and the Citizen (26 August 1789),
which significantly was framed in terms not so much of French rights
but of universal human rights, and therefore applicable everywhere.[30]
As we shall see, the legacy of the French Revolution was fraught and
complicated, but, initially at least, activists greeted it with enthusiasm.
There was increasing talk of pushing back the limits of monarchy, of
tyranny and of oppression. Even as late as November 1794, Thomas
Clarkson, who among British abolitionists was perhaps most closely
identified with the French Revolution, was still confident that repub-
licanism would effect widespread social and political change, not least
in Britain itself.[31]

Responding to these trends, organised anti-slavery expanded rapidly
after 1788 until by the mid 1790s it represented a complex network of
groups, some more active than others. In Britain, this expansion was
linked directly to the two petition campaigns that the SEAST organised against the slave trade, the first in 1788 and the second in 1792. Up
and down the country, committees were set up to manage petitions (the
collection of signatures and so on) and to see to it that they eventually
reached the House of Commons. As a result, some of them survived
only a matter of months, or as long as it took to organise petitions.
Others, however, were much more substantial. The Exeter committee,
for instance, met regularly between July 1788 and January 1789 and
seems to have survived more or less intact until the petition campaign of

---

[29] Jacques-Pierre Brissot de Warville, *A Discourse, Upon the Necessity of Establishing at Paris, a Society to Co-operate with Those of America and London, Towards the Abolition of the Trade and Slavery of the Negroes. Delivered the 19th of February 1788, in a Society of a Few Friends, Assembled at Paris, at the Request of the Committee of London* (Philadelphia, Pa.: Francis Bailey, 1788), pp. 146, 156–7.

[30] William Doyle, *The French Revolution: A Very Short Introduction* (Oxford University Press, 2001), p. 16.

[31] See Diaries of Katherine Plymley, 1066/29 (1 December 1794), Shropshire Record Office, Shrewsbury.

1792. Much the same thing was true of the committees at Manchester, Newcastle, Edinburgh and Glasgow. In each case, survival depended on the energy and commitment of local committee members, men such as Thomas Walker in Manchester and William Elford in Plymouth, or else the strength of religious ties and associations. From what we know about the committee system in Britain, an important impetus came from Nonconformists and from Quakers and Unitarians, in particular. To take one example, the driving force behind the Newcastle committee came from the members of the Hanover Square Unitarian Chapel, among them William Baston, a prosperous corn merchant. In Exeter, on the other hand, it was Quakers who took the lead. At least eight members of the local committee were Friends, including Samuel Milford, co-founder of the Exeter City Bank, and Joseph Saunders, a woollen draper, while a further three were dissenting ministers.[32]

There was a similar expansion in the USA. In 1788, a group of Quakers in Dover, led by veteran activist Warner Mifflin, founded the Delaware Society for Promoting the Abolition of Slavery, for Superintending the Cultivation of Young Free Negroes, and for the Relief of Those Who May Be Unlawfully Held in Bondage, and another society began meeting in Wilmington, Delaware, in 1789.[33] Other societies quickly followed: at Providence, Rhode Island; Washington, Pennsylvania; Baltimore, Maryland; New Haven, Connecticut; and Richmond, Virginia.[34] Here again, the impetus came from Quakers and Evangelical Protestants. But PAS members also provided an important lead, encouraging the growth of local societies and providing them with financial support, as well as with books and pamphlets. The Pennsylvania group underwrote the activities of the Wilmington society, for instance, and in July 1792 directed its committee of correspondents to 'take measures for effecting the establishment of abolition societies in New Jersey'.[35] When a

---

[32] Oldfield, *Popular Politics*, pp. 96–105.
[33] T. Stephen Whitman, *Challenging Slavery in the Chesapeake: Black and White Resistance to Human Bondage, 1775–1865* (Baltimore, Md.: Maryland Historical Society, 2007), p. 51; Monte A. Calvert, 'The Abolition Society of Delaware, 1801–1807', *Delaware History*, 10 (4) (1963): 295-320, at pp. 298–9; *Pennsylvania Mercury and Universal Advertiser*, 2 February 1788 (organisation of Wilmington society); *Pennsylvania Packet, and Daily Advertiser*, 22 August 1788 (organisation of Dover society).
[34] *Freeman's Journal*, 25 February 1789, 11 March 1789 and 23 December 1789, 29 September 1790 and 17 November 1790; PAS to SEAST, 24 June 1789, 28 February 1790 and 25 October 1790 Committee of Correspondence, Pennsylvania Abolition Society (hereafter PAS Correspondence), PAS Papers, microfilm edition, Reel 11. For the Rhode Island society, see also Charles Rappleye, *Sons of Providence: The Brown Brothers, the Slave Trade and the American Revolution* (New York: Simon & Schuster, 2006), pp. 259–60, 268–9, 305–9.
[35] PAS Minutes, 2 July 1792.

New Jersey society was finally organised in 1793, PAS vice-president
James Pemberton boasted that 'the chain [was] now complete, from RI
to VA inclusive'.[36] The PAS would go on pressing for further expansion, and, to judge from the proceedings of the American Convention
for Promoting the Abolition of Slavery, they clearly made an impact.
At different times between 1788 and 1800, anti-slavery societies were
organised at Alexandria in Virginia, and at Choptank, Easton and
Chestertown on the eastern shore of Maryland. The PAS even received
enquiries from a group of activists in Augusta, Georgia, although perhaps not surprisingly nothing seems to have come of the idea.[37]

The largest of these societies had hundreds of members. When the
Rhode Island society was formally incorporated in June 1790, the Act
listed 190 names, including sixty-eight from Massachusetts and three
from Connecticut.[38] If anything, the Maryland society was larger still.
A report prepared in 1797 listed over 200 members, roughly 40 per
cent of them from outside the state. The majority, however, came from
Baltimore, led by a group of fifty-seven merchants, among them figures such as Elisha Tyson, John McKim and Richard Lawson. Perhaps
just as striking were the large number of shopkeepers and small manufacturers who were members of the Maryland society. The full membership list included over twenty-five different occupational categories,
ranging from merchants and gentlemen to scriveners, cabinet-makers,
bricklayers, carpenters and saddlers.[39] With a membership of this size,
the society was easily as large as the PAS and the NYMS (202 members in 1797) and in many ways just as influential. Granville Sharp was
an honorary member of the Maryland society, for instance, as were

---

[36] PAS Minutes, 2 July 1792 and 1 October 1792, 1 April 1793 and 2 May 1794; PAS
to SEAST, 21 May 1793 (Pemberton quotation) and PAS to NYMS, 14 March
1793, PAS Correspondence, microfilm edition, Reel 11. For the activities of
the New Jersey Abolition Society, see Minutes of the New Jersey Society for the
Abolition of Slavery, available online at http://triptych.brynmawr.edu/cdm4/docu-
ment.php?CISOROOT=/HC_QuakSlav&CISOPTR=12257&CISOSHOW=12143
(accessed 13 July 2011). The original minutes are deposited in Haverford College
Library, Haverford, Pennsylvania.
[37] *Minutes of the Proceedings of the Fourth Convention of Delegates from the Abolition
Societies Established in Different Parts of the United States, Assembled at Philadelphia, on
the Third Day of May, One Thousand Seven Hundred and Ninety-Seven, and Continued,
by Adjournments, Until the Ninth Day of the Same Month, Inclusive* (Philadelphia, Pa.:
Zachariah Poulson, Junior, 1797), pp. 3–4.
[38] *Providence Gazette and Country Journal*, 14 August 1790.
[39] Maryland Society to the American Convention for Promoting the Abolition of Slavery,
probably May 1797, PAS Papers, microfilm edition, Reel 28, Correspondence relating to the American Convention. The Treasurer of the Maryland Society, David
Brown, was a potter, and among the members of the electing committee were two
cabinet-makers, a silversmith, a painter and a printer.

prominent American activists such as Uriah Tracy (Connecticut) and Warner Mifflin (Delaware). In all, the society had some seventy-five honorary members, a further indication of the scale of its ambitions, as well as its importance in connecting different groups of actors, thereby strengthening the abolitionist network.

Other societies were much smaller and probably only survived through the efforts of a few dedicated activists. Size, however, was no indicator of energy or resolve. One of the most remarkable of these early American societies was that organised in Washington, Pennsylvania, in February 1789.[40] Located some 300 miles west of Philadelphia and close to the Virginia border, Washington was at the crossroads of the internal slave trade. As James Pemberton explained, 'it has been a practice of the cattle drovers of late years to pass through [Washington] and adjacent counties from the frontiers of the Southern states to the back parts of this [and] New Jersey, and there exchange the flesh of beasts for that of mankind'.[41] Finally losing patience, a group of local activists led by Thomas Scott, Absalom Baird and David Redick 'determined to speak out', and over the course of the next five years they waged a protracted battle against local slave traffickers. The Pennsylvania society, in turn, lent them support and even brought their activities to the attention of British and French abolitionists, thereby linking them to the wider international movement.[42] Such gestures created enduring friendships and alliances. When the first American Convention for Promoting the Abolition of Slavery met in 1794, Absalom Baird was one of those who made the trip to Philadelphia, obviously determined to take his place among the delegates at this critical moment in the movement's history.[43]

Equally remarkable, particularly given its geographical location, was the society formed in Richmond, Virginia. A key figure here was Robert Pleasants, a Quaker slaveholder and proprietor of a tobacco-exporting company, who in 1782 freed all his slaves and thereafter devoted his time and energy to persuading others, mainly Quakers, to follow his example.[44] Virginia was hostile territory for abolitionists, but, by the

---

[40] *Pennsylvania Mercury and Universal Advertiser*, 7 March 1789; *Pennsylvania Packet, and Daily Advertiser*, 29 April 1789.

[41] James Pemberton to William Dillwyn, 25 February (possibly 25 April) 1789, Pemberton Papers, 51/182.

[42] See William Dillwyn to James Pemberton, 9 July 1789, Pemberton Papers, 52/129.

[43] *Minutes of the Proceedings of a Convention of Delegates from the Abolition Societies Established in Different Parts of the United States, Assembled at Philadelphia, on the First Day of January, One Thousand Seven Hundred and Ninety Four, and Continued, by Adjournments, Until the Seventh Day of the Same Month, Inclusive* (Philadelphia, Pa.: Zachariah Poulson, Junior, 1794), p. 6.

[44] For Pleasants, see http://trilogy.brynmawr.edu/speccoll/quakersandslavery/commentary/people/pleasants_map.php (accessed 20 May 2011).

late 1780s, Pleasants thought he detected a shift in local opinion. 'It really appears admirable to me', he wrote in 1788, 'that the minds of men should be so changed in the compass of a few years in a matter so generally prevalent', adding that

> although the bulk of the people can't yet give up their views of ease and conse-
> quence in the estimation of the world, so far as to emancipate their slaves, there
> are very few now that undertake to justify the keeping them in that state, on
> any other principle than mere convenience, or policy as they term it.[45]

Pleasants was equally encouraged by the course of events in Europe, particularly the French Revolution. Writing to a friend in September 1789, he predicted that the abolition of the slave trade by the British Parliament, which he thought imminent, would be 'a prelude to Emancipations in the West Indies and indeed the world over; for it seems as if the spirit of liberty in France was not to be restrained by all the efforts of those in power'.[46] Significantly, Pleasants' prophetic imagery was rooted very firmly in his religious faith and in his read-ing of Scripture. If the prevalence of anti-slavery feeling demonstrated anything, he believed, it was that the time was fast approaching when 'righteousness shall cover the Earth, as the Waters cover the Seas'.[47]

By the summer of 1790, activists in Virginia were clearly convinced that the time was right to organise a statewide abolitionist society. Here, again, Pleasants played a significant part, becoming the soci-ety's first president, although initially, at least, the real impetus came from local Methodists; Pleasants, in fact, confessed to being 'a lit-tle mortified to find so much slackness among us [Quakers], when others especially Methodists seem so much more zealous in promot-ing it'.[48] From these small beginnings, the Virginia society expanded until by 1792 it had more than 100 members, most of them from the counties in and around Richmond (New Kent, Charles City, Prince George and Chesterfield).[49] Thanks largely to Pleasants, the Virginia

---

[45] Robert Pleasants to John Townsend, 25 January 1788, Robert Pleasants Letterbook, 1754–97, available online at http://triptych.brynmawr.edu/cdm4/document.php? CISOROOT=/HC_QuakSlav&CISOPTR=11435&REC=10 (accessed 10 February 2011). The original letterbook can be found at Haverford College, Haverford, Pennsylvania.
[46] Robert Pleasants to Jacob Scott, 18 September 1789, Robert Pleasants Letterbook, 1754–97.
[47] Robert Pleasants to Jacob Scott, 9 March 1790, Robert Pleasants Letterbook, 1754–97. See also Robert Pleasants to Charles Carter, 17 August 1790, and Robert Pleasants to James Madison, 6 June 1791.
[48] Robert Pleasants to Samuel Bailey, 23 July 1790, Robert Pleasants Letterbook, 1754–97; *Pennsylvania Mercury and Universal Advertiser*, 17 July 1790.
[49] Robert Pleasants to Dr George Cheeseman, 6 July 1792, Robert Pleasants Letterbook, 1754–97. By 1797 the Virginia society was reported to have 147 members. For details,

society became an important regional hub, forging close links with the PAS as well as with activists in the Carolinas. Like so many Quakers, Pleasants was extremely well connected, both inside and outside the state. Perhaps just as important, his list of correspondents included members of the Virginia establishment, among them Thomas Jefferson and Patrick Henry.[50] An intense and seemingly tireless figure, Pleasants helped to give the Virginia society focus and direction; indeed, it was by no means accidental that his death in 1801 coincided with the demise of the organisation, although, as we shall see, there were other factors involved, too.

Yet it would be a mistake to conclude that abolitionists had everything their own way. In Providence, for instance, slave merchants waged a protracted war against the members of the Rhode Island society, questioning their motives as well as their sincerity.[51] Slaveholders proved equally obdurate. Activists in New Jersey reported that opposition to abolition in the eastern part of the state was 'formidable', and there were similar reports from Maryland, where in 1791 the House of Delegates came within two votes of declaring the state abolition society 'subversive to the rights of our citizens'.[52] Sometimes the levels of resistance were such that organisation proved impossible. David Rice tried repeatedly to organise an abolition society in Kentucky but found it difficult to 'get any number of weighty influential characters to engage in [the] business'.[53] Even many churchmen, he discovered, opposed abolition. 'The rich hold the slaves, and the rich make the laws' was Rice's frank assessment of the situation.[54] While Rice remained hopeful that an abolitionist society would eventually be organised in Kentucky, he

---

see Joseph Anthony to the American Convention for Promoting the Abolition of Slavery, probably May 1797, PAS Papers, microfilm edition, Reel 28.

[50] Robert Pleasants to Patrick Henry, 1 September 1790 and 21 July 1792; and Robert Pleasants to Thomas Jefferson, 1 June 1796 and 8 February 1797, Robert Pleasants Letterbook, 1754–97. For Pleasants' contacts with activists in the Carolinas, see Robert Pleasants to Exum Newby, 30 July 1795.

[51] *Providence Gazette and Country Journal*, 14 (28) February 1789; Moses Brown to James Pemberton, 8 March 1789, Pemberton Papers, 52/4; Rappleye, *Sons of Providence*, pp. 260–7.

[52] *Minutes of the Proceedings of the Seventh Convention of Delegates from the Abolition Societies Established in Different Parts of the United States, Assembled at Philadelphia, on the Third Day of June, One Thousand Eight Hundred and One and Continued, by Adjournments, Until the Sixth Day of the Same Month, Inclusive* (Philadelphia, Pa.: Zachariah Poulson, Junior, 1801), p. 11; Ira Berlin, *Slaves Without Masters: The Free Negro in the Antebellum South* (Oxford University Press, 1974), p. 81.

[53] David Rice to William Rodgers, 4 November 1794, PAS correspondence, Reel 11.

[54] Rice to Rodgers, 4 November 1794.

was equally convinced that to be successful he would need the support of others. 'If such a Society shall be formed', he conceded, 'I shall esteem it an honour and a great advantage to be favoured with a correspondence with other societies, who have in the main the same object in view.'[55]

By the mid 1790s, therefore, the transatlantic abolitionist network had grown to some sixteen societies (more if we include the provincial British committees) that spanned the Atlantic world, from Paris to Washington, Pennsylvania; from London to Richmond, Virginia. The backbone of the network, however, remained the old historic centres. In the USA, many of the newer societies, especially those in Washington, Richmond and Providence, clearly looked to the Pennsylvania society for support and encouragement. The PAS, in turn, provided these groups with an important link with the outside world. Very few American societies had direct contact with European abolitionists; instead, ideas and information tended to be channelled through Philadelphia or, occasionally, New York. In short, the effectiveness of the abolitionist network depended less on integration across the full network than on intensive integration through network cliques.[56] At an international level, for instance, there were particularly strong links between London, Paris and Philadelphia. By contrast, the links between New York, London and Paris – and between New York and some of the other American societies – were comparatively weak.[57] An important factor here was the transatlantic Quaker community. As we shall see, there were close personal and business ties between Quakers in London and Philadelphia, and the same thing was true at the domestic level, where again Quaker networks helped to foster close cooperation between activists in Philadelphia, Richmond and Providence.

Ultimately, however, the effectiveness of the transatlantic abolitionist network depended on individual resolve and endeavour. Particularly important here were a number of key actors, men who occupied a central position within their own specific groups or societies but who also acted as critical links between other groups within the network.[58] An important example was set by figures such as Granville Sharp, president

---

[55] Rice to Rodgers, 4 November 1794. A society was eventually organised in Kentucky in 1808. See Carter Tanant to John Thomas, 27 May 1809, PAS Correspondence, microfilm edition, Reel 11.

[56] Kilduff and Tsai, *Social Networks and Organizations*, pp. 45–7.

[57] It is revealing, for instance, that when the NYMS first broached the subject of what would become the American Convention for Promoting the Abolition of Slavery in March 1793, they directed letters meant for the societies at Dover, Baltimore and Richmond through the Pennsylvania society. See PAS to NYMS, no date given but definitely 1793, PAS Correspondence, microfilm edition, Reel 11.

[58] Kilduff and Tsai, *Social Networks and Organisations*, pp. 29–30, 132–4.

of the SEAST, whose list of correspondents included James Pemberton, Benjamin Rush, the marquis de Lafayette and François Lanthenas. As his papers reveal, Sharp was a compulsive letter-writer and one who was not afraid to use his influence to chide and encourage fellow activists, even at the risk of causing them offence.[59] But, more than that, he lent the international abolitionist movement a certain kind of celebrity status, dragging others along with him. To an extent, the same thing was true of Benjamin Rush, another figure whose writings and research, principally in medicine and science, had earned him an international reputation. Rush made no secret of his abolitionist sympathies. As vice-president and later president of the PAS, he corresponded with activists on both sides of the Atlantic, helping in the process to locate abolitionism within a wider Enlightenment culture that shone 'just as brightly on the far side of the Atlantic as on the banks of the Seine and the Thames'.[60]

Not as well known perhaps but no less important were figures such as James Phillips. A Cornishman by birth, Phillips moved to London during the 1760s. He next appears in 1775 when he bought a printing business from Mary Hine, another Quaker, in George Yard, Lombard Street.[61] At first, Phillips seems to have concentrated on religious works. But from 1783, the same year that the London Meeting for Sufferings appointed a special committee to distribute abolitionist books and pamphlets, he began to publish an increasing amount of literature devoted to slavery and the slave trade. Phillips announced himself with two important works: Anthony Benezet's *The Case of the Oppressed Africans* (1783) and David Cooper's *Serious Address to the Rulers of America, on the Inconsistency of their Conduct respecting Slavery* (1783). The following year he reprinted Benezet's *Caution to Great Britain and Her Colonies* and published two works by James Ramsay, including his influential *Essay on the Treatment and Conversion of African Slaves in the British Colonies*. In 1785 and 1786 he published two more books by Ramsay, but, of greater significance, certainly in terms of the history of the early abolitionist movement, was his decision to publish Clarkson's prize-winning *Essay on the Slavery and Commerce of the Human Species* (1786). In other words, by the time the SEAST was organised in May 1787, Phillips had

---

[59] Granville Sharp, for instance, was highly critical of the newly adopted US Constitution, particularly those clauses relating to slavery and the slave trade, which he thought were 'so clearly null and void by their iniquity that it should be even a crime to regard them as law'. See Granville Sharp to Benjamin Franklin, 10 January 1788, Pemberton Papers, 49/56.

[60] Echeverria, *Mirage in the West*, p. 26.

[61] Biographical files, Friends House Library, London.

already earned himself a reputation as a leading publisher of specialist (abolitionist) literature.[62]

For obvious reasons, Phillips' business expanded rapidly after 1787. As the SEAST's official printer, he was responsible for all of its reports and circular letters, as well as for most of the books and pamphlets the London Committee approved at its various meetings. But this was not all. When the committee sat down in July 1787 to draw up a list of contacts through which it could distribute its publications, Phillips provided over half of the 132 names. His contacts in thirty-four English counties included George Croker Fox, Josiah Wedgwood and the Manchester radical Thomas Walker.[63] Phillips also had a large number of American correspondents, among them James Pemberton. Phillips was certainly doing business with Pemberton by 1783, probably before, and, through him, was in touch with a number of Philadelphia booksellers, including Joseph Cruikshank. Furthermore, Phillips had close kinship ties with the Griffitts and Fisher families, who, like the Pembertons, were influential in Quaker circles in Philadelphia, and he seems to have kept up a regular correspondence with both James Pemberton and Miers Fisher.[64] It was undoubtedly for this reason that in July 1787 he was made an honorary member of the PAS, along with Granville Sharp and Thomas Clarkson. Energetic, resourceful and well connected, James Phillips occupied a central position in the transatlantic abolitionist network that emerged in the late 1780s, both in terms of 'degree' (that is, having many ties to other actors) and 'betweenness' (that is, connecting different groups of actors).[65]

If anything, James Pemberton (see Fig. 1.1) was more energetic still. Some years older than Phillips, Pemberton was a member of an important Philadelphia Quaker dynasty. His father and grandfather were both merchants, and he and his brothers John and Israel were also involved in the shipping trade. It was in pursuit of these interests that in 1748 he visited Britain, where he established many of the contacts that would

---

[62] All of these details about Phillips' publishing business are extracted from the online version of the *English Short-Title Catalogue*, http://est.bl.uk (accessed 9 May 2011).

[63] SEAST Minutes, 17 July 1787.

[64] James Pemberton to John Pemberton, 1 January 1783, Pemberton Papers, 38/7/1; James Pemberton's Account with James Phillips, 1783, Pemberton Papers, 48/48; James Phillips to James Pemberton, 28 February 1788, Pemberton Papers, 49/125; James Phillips to Miers Fisher, 23 July 1791, 7 July 1792 and 7 February 1793, Fisher Family Papers, Box 11, Folders 4, 5 and 6, Historical Society of Pennsylvania; James Phillips to Samuel Griffitts, 30 May 1796 and 8 August 1796, Dreer Collection, Historical Society of Pennsylvania.

[65] PAS Minutes, 2 July 1787; Kilduff and Tsai, *Social Networks and Organisations*, pp. 132–3.

Figure 1.1 David McNeely Stauffer, *James Pemberton*, *c.* 1893, based
on an original portrait by John F. Watson. Courtesy of the Historical
Society of Pennsylvania, David McNeely Stauffer Collection on
Westcott's *History of Philadelphia*.

survive the American Revolution. As befitted a man of his wealth
and station, Pemberton played an important role within the Society
of Friends. He was a leading member of the Philadelphia Meeting for
Sufferings from its organisation in 1756 until 1808, and, together with
his brother Israel, was one of the trustees of the Friendly Association for

Regaining and Preserving Peace with the Indians by Pacific Measures. He also took an active interest in the political life of the colony, serving two terms as a member of the Pennsylvania Assembly, first in 1756 and then again in 1765–9. Pemberton, therefore, was part of the Philadelphia elite. He and his family lived at 'Evergreen', a country house near 23rd and South Streets, to the west of the city, and by 1800 he was listed in the City Directory as a 'gentleman'.[66]

Nevertheless, Pemberton was no stranger to hardship or misfortune. Like many Quakers, he supported the Patriot cause during the American Revolution but stopped short of bearing arms against the British. Naturally, this stance (there were even rumours that some Philadelphia Quakers had colluded with the enemy) aroused suspicion, so much so that in September 1777 he and nineteen other men, mostly Quakers, were charged by the US Congress with 'evincing a disposition inimical to the cause of America' and detained in the Masons' Lodge.[67] Led out of Philadelphia under armed guard, Pemberton and his fellow prisoners, who included his two brothers, John and Israel Pemberton, as well as his brother-in-law Samuel Pleasants, older brother of Robert Pleasants, were subsequently escorted to Winchester, Virginia, where they endured an exile of eight months. As Pemberton's journal makes clear, throughout this difficult period he and his friends tried to go on much as before, meeting and praying together, while all the time protesting their innocence. But there is little doubt that the experience was traumatic or that it engendered a lingering sense of injustice. At no time either before or during their exile were the prisoners allowed to answer the charges made against them, and even after their release in April 1778 they were politely warned against pursuing the matter any further, for fear of causing more distress and aggravation.[68]

Following his return to Philadelphia, Pemberton gave up all active interest in politics, devoting himself instead to his various reform interests, which included health (he was a member of the first board of managers of the Pennsylvania Hospital) and education. Following its reorganisation in 1787, he was also invited to become a member of the PAS, assuming the role of vice-president and, after 1790, president. Grateful for this opportunity to take a lead once again in public affairs,

[66] *American National Biography Online*, www.anb.org (accessed 9 May 2011); *Friends' Miscellany*, 7 (2) (1835): 49–95; Pemberton Papers, Miscellaneous Items, Box 3; *Philadelphia City Directory*, 1800.
[67] Thomas Gilpin, *Exiles in Virginia with Observations on the Conduct of the Society of Friends During the Revolutionary War, Comprising the Official Papers of the Government Relating to That Period, 1777–1778* (Philadelphia, Pa: Published for the Subscribers, 1848), p. 71.
[68] See Gilpin, *Exiles in Virginia*.

Pemberton threw himself into the work of the new society, going out of his way to create close working relationships with abolitionists on both sides of the Atlantic. Letters and letter-writing were vital to this process. Pemberton not only put groups into contact with each other, as he did in February 1789 when he encouraged the society newly established in Providence, Rhode Island, to open a correspondence with the SEAST, but he also circulated news and information, as well as books and artefacts, through these different channels.[69] However, Pemberton was more than a go-between. Steeled by his experiences in Virginia, he brought to the early abolitionist movement great patience, as well as great fortitude; indeed, it became Pemberton's peculiar role to rouse others, including British abolitionists, when their energies flagged or, more often, when they became dispirited or disillusioned.

Another key actor in the international abolitionist network was Jacques-Pierre Brissot de Warville (see Fig. 1.2). Unlike Phillips and Pemberton, however, Brissot's activism was shaped not so much by his religious beliefs (Brissot was nominally a deist) but by Enlightenment thinkers, men such as Rousseau, Voltaire and Diderot; indeed, if there is a consistent theme in his rich and varied life it is his commitment to the Enlightenment principles of liberty, equality and sovereignty of the people. Seemingly destined for a legal career, Brissot became better known as a writer. During the 1780s he wrote a number of books on ethics and philosophy and, for a time, worked on the *Mercure de France* and the *Courier de l'Europe*. These activities were part of a more ambitious project, however, namely to promulgate ideas of political and legal reform. From an early stage, Brissot encouraged close collaboration between European intellectuals (at one point, he even proposed setting up a *lycée*, really a kind of 'philosophic club', with its own journal, based in London) and later, with Etienne Clavière, founded a Franco-American society, which was designed to promote commercial relations between the two nations. Like many young Frenchmen of his generation, Brissot was clearly inspired by the American Revolution, both as an idea and as an event. America, with its free institutions, became his ideal republic and, just as important, a model for others, including France, to follow.[70]

---

[69] James Pemberton to William Dillwyn, 25 February (or possibly 25 April) 1789, Pemberton Papers, 51/182; James Pemberton to Edward Miller, 18 June 1789, Pemberton Papers, 52/98; John Murray to James Pemberton, 29 June 1789, Pemberton Papers, 52/112.

[70] See Ellery, *Brissot de Warville*, pp. 4–40; Jacques-Pierre Brissot de Warville, *New Travels in the United States of America, 1788*, ed. Durand Echeverria (Cambridge, Mass.: The Belknap Press of Harvard University, 1964), pp. xi–xvi.

B R I S S O T,

DÉPUTÉ À LA CONVENTION NATIONALE,

Décapité le 31 octobre 1793.

Figure 1.2 Charles François Gabriel Levachez, *Jacques-Pierre Brissot,*
c. 1805. Author's own collection.

Brissot's abolitionism was all of a piece with his progressive thinking. Inspired by the example of British abolitionists, some of whom he
already knew, in August 1787 he contacted the London Committee
of the SEAST with an offer to act as their agent, along with his close
friend Clavière. As Clarkson later explained: 'He purposed to translate
and circulate through France, such publications as they might send him

from time to time, and to appoint bankers in Paris, who might receive subscriptions and remit them to London for the good of their common cause.'[71] Brissot also raised the possibility of setting up a similar society in France, but only if 'his own countrymen should be found to take an interest in this great cause'.[72] The London Committee was clearly intrigued by this approach, so much so that on 27 August it called a special meeting to discuss Brissot's offer. The outcome was a polite rebuff. Not surprisingly, the committee declined the offer of 'pecuniary aid' (perhaps because they feared an adverse reaction from their British supporters), but, while doing so, they encouraged Brissot to do everything in his power to set up a French society and to join them in making common cause against the slave trade. In a gesture of solidarity, they also made Brissot and Clavière honorary members of the SEAST. If Brissot was disappointed, he did not show it. On the contrary, the London Committee's carefully worded response seems to have been just the stimulus he was looking for, so much so that it was pasted into the minutes of the first formal meeting of the Société des Amis des Noirs, thereby becoming an essential part of its history as well as its memory.[73]

As luck would have it, the following year Brissot visited the USA. Although this was meant to be a business trip and designed primarily to obtain information for Clavière, who was about to speculate on the American domestic debt, it was no accident that Brissot carried with him letters of introduction from both the Société des Amis des Noirs and the SEAST, or that he used this opportunity to make contact with American abolitionists. Brissot seems to have presented his credentials to the NYMS in August 1788 and to the PAS in September. Both groups welcomed these overtures and, with them, the prospect of opening a correspondence with French abolitionists. Both groups also set up temporary committees to help him with his 'enquiries' while he was in America.[74] Brissot established especially close ties with the members of the PAS, who, at a meeting in October, made him one of their honorary members. He spent a lot of time with James Pemberton, on one occasion accompanying him to the funeral of Thomas Howell, one of the elders of the Society of Friends, and formed particularly close ties with Miers Fisher and his family. As his account of his visit to the USA

---

[71] Clarkson, *History*, vol. I, p. 446.
[72] Clarkson, *History*, vol. I, p. 447; Ellery, *Brissot de Warville*, p. 183.
[73] Clarkson, *History*, vol. I, p. 447; SEAST Minutes, 27 August 1787; Dorigny and Gainot, *La Société des Amis des Noirs*, p. 63.
[74] Brissot, *New Travels*, pp. xix–xx; NYMS Minutes, 21 August 1788; PAS Minutes, 3 September 1788 (for letters of introduction) and 19 January 1789.

makes clear, Brissot warmed to the Quakers, in whom he discovered what he regarded as simple republican virtues.[75] Here, it seemed, was the potential for meaningful international cooperation; in fact, it is possible that Brissot found in transatlantic abolitionism a substitute for the kind of collaboration he had envisaged in the *lycée*.

Brissot finally left the USA on 3 December 1788. By this stage he was keen to get back to France, where a meeting of the Estates-General had been called for early the following year, but it is also clear that he was under increasing surveillance. Edmund Prior in New York reported that 'the French Minister here watched all his movements & conducts in such a manner as rendered his stay unpleasant'.[76] Significantly, Brissot returned to Paris via London, where he attended a meeting of the London Committee on 20 January 1789. These visits gave him a unique vantage point. He was, if you will, the public face of transatlantic abolitionism, as well as being a key figure in the emerging alliance between French and American activists.[77] Over the course of the next five years, until his death in 1793, Brissot would keep up a regular correspondence with American abolitionists, among them Pemberton and Fisher. On another front, he also corresponded with James Phillips and Thomas Clarkson; indeed, the number of his contacts underscored his centrality to the emerging abolitionist network. Brissot's contribution was important in another way, too. A prolific author, between 1788 and 1790 he produced a range of abolitionist texts that enjoyed a wide circulation not only in Europe but also in the USA. As we shall see, Brissot was one of the few French (abolitionist) authors who penetrated America during the 1780s, a feat that in a European context, at least, was equalled only by his friend Thomas Clarkson.

All of these figures stand out because in each case they linked together three different parts of the abolitionist network: Britain, France and the USA. Others, however, were part of much smaller cliques or subsets, sometimes involving only two different parts of the network. A case in point is the Quaker William Dillwyn (Fig. 1.3). An American by birth, Dillwyn was educated at the public school in Philadelphia, where he fell under the influence of Anthony Benezet. The experience changed his

---

[75] Brissot, *New Travels*, pp. 168–72, 240, n. 18, 298–335. James Phillips later told James Pemberton that Brissot 'seemed quite delighted with the reception he met with in America particularly amongst friends [Quakers] & mentioned thy name in such terms as bespoke his gratitude for thy favourable attention'. See James Phillips to James Pemberton, 10 March 1789, Pemberton Papers, 52/6.

[76] Ellery, *Brissot de Warville*, p. 85; Edmund Prior to James Pemberton, 29 January 1789, Pemberton Papers, 51/137.

[77] SEAST Minutes, 20 January 1789. See also William Dillwyn to James Pemberton, 3 March 1789, Pemberton Papers, 51/190.

Figure 1.3 C. R. Leslie, *William Dillwyn*, 1815. Courtesy of the Library of the Religious Society of Friends in Britain.

life. In 1772, he visited South Carolina, seemingly at Benezet's suggestion, and the following year produced, with Richard Smith and Daniel Wells, *Brief Considerations on Slavery and the Expediency of Its Abolition*. Around 1777, Dillwyn moved to Britain, where he remarried and put down roots in Walthamstow, Essex. Here he continued to involve himself in abolitionist activity. In 1783, he became a member of the London Meeting for Sufferings on the Slave Trade, and the same year he co-wrote *The Case of Our Fellow-Citizens, the Oppressed Africans*, one of the earliest abolitionist tracts published in Britain. Four years later, he joined Thomas Clarkson, John Lloyd, James Phillips and others in the organisation of the SEAST, and he would remain a member of the society's London Committee until 1807.[78]

As these few details suggest, Dillwyn was an important link between British and American abolitionists, at both a personal and an intellectual level; Clarkson went so far as to suggest that he was the 'great medium' whereby the various classes of 'forerunners and coadjutors up to 1787' were brought together and unified.[79] But Dillwyn's influence did not end there. Though he never returned to the USA, he retained strong links with Philadelphia Quakers, chief among them his brother, George, and his cousin, James Pemberton. Dillwyn and Pemberton were especially close. As we shall see, the two men corresponded regularly, at least once a month, and came to rely on each other for ideas and information. Dillwyn also took a keen interest in the welfare of James's brother, John Pemberton, who was in Europe during the greater part of the 1780s and 1790s, and accompanied him on his visit to the Netherlands and Germany in 1795.[80] As even a cursory glance at Pemberton's papers suggests, the Dillwyn–Pemberton nexus was one of the most important strands or 'spurs' of the abolitionist network, not least because of the levels of trust that existed between the various parties, John Pemberton included. Theirs was a special relationship that in drawing activists in London and Philadelphia closer together underscored the importance of transatlantic abolitionism during the 1780s.

By contrast, Thomas Clarkson's interests and sympathies turned eastward. Obsessive and indefatigable, Clarkson (Fig. 1.4) not only popularised abolition through his various books and pamphlets, but also, as the SEAST's travelling agent, provided a vital link between London and the provinces. In 1787 he visited the major slave ports. This was followed in 1788 by a tour of the south coast of England; in 1790 by a tour of Scotland and the north of England; and in 1791 by a tour of Shropshire and the north of England. Clarkson, as a result, built up a huge network of local and regional correspondents, many of whom he was in contact with on a regular basis, particularly during the petition campaigns of 1788 and 1792.[81] He also established important links

[78] Biographical files, Friends House Library, London.
[79] Clarkson, *History*, vol. I, p. 202.
[80] Biographical files, Friends House Library, London.
[81] Oldfield, *Popular Politics*, pp. 74–7.

Figure 1.4 Carl Frederick von Breda, *Thomas Clarkson*, 1789.
Courtesy of the National Portrait Gallery, London.

with French abolitionists. In July 1789 he visited Paris at the London
Committee's request and quickly immersed himself in the activities of
the Société des Amis des Noirs. He was a regular presence at meetings (twelve, in all, between 21 August 1789 and 29 January 1790) and,
armed with a French translation of his *Essay on the Impolicy of the Slave
Trade* and copies of the plan and sections of the slave ship *Brookes*, even
lobbied members of the French Constituent Assembly to take up the
question of the slave trade.[82] During this visit Clarkson also befriended
figures such as Brissot and Honoré Gabriel Mirabeau, many of whom
would become his lifelong friends; indeed, Clarkson's correspondence
with Mirabeau testifies to the enduring friendships that existed between
British and French activists.[83]

Clarkson also had an impact in the USA. He was certainly held in
high esteem by American abolitionists, and, as we shall see, his books
and pamphlets enjoyed a wide readership.[84] Yet, strangely, he seems to
have made little effort to cultivate American abolitionists. Pemberton's
papers, for instance, contain only a few letters from Clarkson, and most
of these date from after 1807. One reason for this was that Clarkson
was something of an outsider. Unlike Brissot, he was not person-
ally known to American abolitionists and neither did he have many
American contacts. (Dillwyn, on the other hand, was deeply embedded in the transatlantic Quaker community and could count men such
as Pemberton among his close personal acquaintances.) And yet there
were undoubtedly other factors at work here, too. Clarkson considered
himself a 'Democrat', and, if anything, his visit to Paris in 1789 reinforced his identification with the French Revolution. Many of the members of the Société des Amis des Noirs, including Brissot, Mirabeau
and Condorcet, were themselves deeply involved in the revolutionary
movement in France, and, much to the dismay of some of his colleagues, Clarkson was quick to lend them his support.[85] By contrast,
if his surviving correspondence is anything to go by, Clarkson showed
little interest in America or in the potential of American abolitionism.
Put a different way, his perspective was European rather than transatlantic, and it was this outlook, as much as kinship, religion or, indeed,
familiarity, that helped to shape his allegiances.

---

[82] Clarkson, *History*, vol. I, pp. 122–66; Dorigny and Gainot, *La Société des Amis des
Noirs*, pp. 239–70: Ellen Gibson Wilson, *Thomas Clarkson: A Biography* (London and
New York: Macmillan, 1990), pp. 53–9.
[83] For Clarkson's correspondence with Mirabeau, see Thomas Clarkson Papers,
CN36–40, Huntington Library, San Marino, California.
[84] See Chapter 2.
[85] Oldfield, *Popular Politics*, pp. 80–1.

Wilberforce, for his part, stood both inside and outside these networks. As the chief parliamentary supporter of abolition, Wilberforce was widely applauded, not least in the USA where groups such as the NYMS made him one of their honorary members.[86] But Wilberforce did not cultivate American contacts – partly because he was not actively involved in the opinion-building activities of the SEAST and partly because, like Clarkson, he attached more significance to France, although his interests here were strategic rather than ideological. (Wilberforce had no time for the political ideals of French revolutionaries.) If anything, Wilberforce preferred to work through his own networks, which revolved around fellow Evangelicals (Hannah More, Henry Thornton, Bishop Beilby Porteous) whose aim was nothing less than a total revolution in British manners.[87] Wilberforce's relationship with the SEAST was, as a result, complex. While Wilberforce clearly looked to the London Committee for support, he did not formally become a member of the society until April 1791, on the eve of the second petition campaign. Theirs was in many ways a marriage of convenience, shaped as much by political necessity as it was by close personal, religious or kinship ties. Indeed, if William Allen is to be believed, Wilberforce had serious doubts about the religious convictions of Quakers, even if 'continued association seemed in a degree to soften down those prejudices'.[88]

The 1780s, therefore, witnessed the emergence of an abolitionist network that spanned the Atlantic world, connecting places as far afield as London, Paris, New York, Baltimore, Richmond and Philadelphia. Wherever they were, activists seem to have reached out to each other. They were frequently members of societies in a number of different countries (this was particularly true of Sharp, Clarkson and Brissot); they corresponded with each other on a regular basis; and they freely exchanged ideas and strategies. Put a different way, this was a genuinely transatlantic community, a network of like-minded reformers that was cosmopolitan in both its outlook and composition. As we have seen, the nature and extent of these relationships – some of them quite complex, others relatively simple – depended on a variety of factors: kinship ties, business and religious contacts, personal recommendations and

---

[86] PAS Minutes, 29 December 1794.
[87] For Wilberforce and Evangelicals, see Ford K. Brown, *Fathers of the Victorians: The Age of Wilberforce* (Cambridge University Press, 1961); R.J. Hind, 'Wilberforce and Perceptions of the British People', *Historical Research*, 60 (143) (1987): 321–35; G. F. A. Best, 'The Evangelicals and the Established Church in the Early Nineteenth Century', *Journal of Theological Studies*, new series, 10 (April 1959): 68–78.
[88] (Anon.), *Life of William Allen, with Selections from His Correspondence* (Philadelphia, Pa.: Henry Longstreth, 1847), vol. I, pp. 133–4.

face-to-face meetings and visits. There was no simple formula and no guarantee of success; indeed, some parts of the international abolitionist network clearly worked better than others. A lot, however, depended on the willingness of those involved to make these relationships work. This is why figures such as Granville Sharp, Benjamin Rush, James Phillips, Brissot, James Pemberton, William Dillwyn and Thomas Clarkson were so important. Through their patience and perseverance, these men not only sustained the early abolitionist movement but they also ensured that it remained a potent international force.

2   Circuits of knowledge

The abolitionist network that emerged in the late eighteenth century was first and foremost a communication network that stretched across vast distances and involved a number of interactions, some of them formal (in the sense that they involved printed texts), others informal. Along its lines, activists circulated a variety of media and genres – letters, books, pamphlets, newspapers, prints and artefacts – that overlapped and intersected in a number of different milieux: coffee shops, taverns, bookshops, wharves, salons and private parlours. As we shall see, information often originated from different points and travelled in different directions, from east to west and west to east. But, as Robert Darnton rightly points out, 'the crucial question does not concern the origin of a message but its amplification and assimilation – the way it reverberated through society and became meaningful to the public'.[1] This process of assimilation, which involved copying, adapting and recycling abolitionist material, is what concerns me here. Abolitionism, as it emerged in the late 1780s, relied heavily on the exchange of ideas and information, creating in the process its own (universal) language and motifs. Mapping these modes of communication offers us an important insight into how activists hoped to build a constituency for abolition, not just within narrow national boundaries but also across and within the Atlantic world.

Despite the distances that often separated them, activists kept in contact with each other through letters and letter-writing; letters, in fact, were the essential glue that held the abolitionist network together.[2]

---

[1] Robert Darnton, *The Forbidden Best-Sellers of Pre-Revolutionary France* (New York and London: W. W. Norton, 1995), p. 190. What follows draws heavily on Darnton's ideas about communication networks. See also Robert Darnton, 'An Early Information Society: News and Media in Eighteenth-Century Paris', *American Historical Review*, 105 (February 2000), pp. 1–35.

[2] For letters and letter-writing in an Atlantic context, see especially Pearsall, *Atlantic Families*; Ian K. Steele, *The English Atlantic, 1675–1740: An Exploration of Communication and Community* (Oxford University Press, 1986); Toby L. Ditz, 'Formative Ventures: Eighteenth-Century Commercial Letters and the Articulation of Experience', in

Many of these letters were formal, in the sense that they were official or semi-official letters, usually written from one society to another. This correspondence had its own tempo, which was only partly determined by winds and currents and the speed and efficiency of eighteenth-century travel. A lot also depended on the regularity of meetings, since formal letters were often discussed in committee, even though they were invariably written and signed by named individuals, either presidents (Granville Sharp, for instance), secretaries or sometimes even treasurers. As a result, communication was often sluggish or, at least, intermittent. This was particularly true of transatlantic correspondence, where there might be an interval of five or six months between sending a letter and receiving a reply. The Pennsylvania society was particularly conscientious about keeping up its correspondence but managed only two letters to the SEAST in 1788, three in 1789, four in 1790 and one in 1791. Letters between Philadelphia and Paris were, if anything, more intermittent still. The PAS–SEAST correspondence is probably the most extensive formal correspondence that has survived, and yet it seems unlikely that the total number of letters written in the ten-year period 1787–97 ever exceeded twenty-five, representing something like two to three letters a year.[3]

Important as these formal letters were, not least in reinforcing a common set of values, the real work was done by the much larger number of private letters that circulated across and within the Atlantic world. For obvious reasons, this correspondence had a very different tempo. To take one example, William Dillwyn wrote to James Pemberton at least once a month throughout the 1780s and 1790s, while James's brother, John, often wrote once a week, sometimes more.[4] At different times, it is also possible to identify similar patterns of letter-writing between Brissot and Thomas Clarkson, for instance, or James Phillips and Miers Fisher.[5] Mapping the full extent of this private correspondence is extremely difficult. What is clear, however, is that personal letters, more than any others, helped to build friendships and to sustain a wider sense of community. We get an insight into this from Pemberton's voluminous papers. Although Pemberton carried considerable weight as

Rebecca Earle, ed., *Epistolary Selves: Letters and Letter-Writers, 1600–1945* (Aldershot: Ashgate, 1999), pp. 59–78.
[3] These figures are based on a close analysis of the PAS–SEAST correspondence, which can be found in the minutes and correspondence of the PAS. See PAS Papers, Reels 1 and 11.
[4] See Pemberton Papers, Historical Society of Pennsylvania.
[5] For Brissot and Clarkson, see Thomas Clarkson Papers, St John's College, Cambridge. For Fisher and Brissot, see PAS Correspondence, microfilm edition, Reel 20.

president of the PAS, it is his private correspondence, as opposed to his official letters, that reveal the true extent of his activities. While the distinction between 'private' and 'public' was often hazy and indeterminate (Pemberton himself may not have recognised it), there is little doubt that Pemberton relied heavily on his personal contacts, or that he took it upon himself, rather than leaving it to others, including the society's committee of correspondence, to forge links between abolitionists, distribute books and otherwise promote interest in the movement.

In common with other activists, Pemberton operated in two different and overlapping spheres. To judge from his papers, he spent as much time writing to his domestic correspondents, from Rhode Island to South Carolina, as he did cultivating his foreign contacts; one activity, in effect, informed the other. Moses Brown and Robert Pleasants were no less assiduous in using their personal contacts, usually Quakers, to build local and regional alliances, and much the same thing was true of Clarkson (in Britain) and Brissot (in France).[6] What we are dealing with here, in other words, is a complex web of associations that functioned at a number of different levels. For those at the periphery, such as the Virginia society, letters, whether formal or informal, were important lifelines. Not only did they provide contact with the outside world, itself important, but they also helped to reframe abolitionism, setting it in a wider political context. Robert Pleasants hinted at this in 1791 when he wrote to thank James Pemberton and, through him, the London Committee of the SEAST, for a parcel of books that he had sent the Virginia society.[7] Such gestures – and the care and thought that lay behind them – bound abolitionists together, in the process making the local national and the national international.

All letters perform for an audience, and these letters were no exception.[8] One of their principal functions was to provide information and commentary. Throughout the 1780s, James Phillips, John Pemberton and William Dillwyn all wrote to James Pemberton on a regular basis, offering him a blow-by-blow account of the work of the SEAST as well as the proceedings in the British House of Commons. Part of the intention here was to impress. To take an example, in March 1788 Dillwyn

---

[6] For Moses Brown, see PAS Correspondence, Reel 11. For Pleasants, see Robert Pleasants Letterbook, 1754–97.

[7] Robert Pleasants and Gressett Davis to James Pemberton, 4 January 1791, PAS Correspondence, microfilm edition, Reel 11.

[8] Pearsall notes that 'when people wrote letters, they may have fashioned a self, but they were generally at least as interested in fashioning others'. See Pearsall, *Atlantic Families*, p. 14. This was especially true of 'abolitionist' letters, which by turn were intended to impress, encourage and offer constructive criticism.

gave Pemberton the following update on the progress of the British campaign:

Thomas Clarkson is very forward with a new Edition of his Essay with a considerable addition of new Matter, particularly on the Impolicy of the Trade. James Ramsay has also a new pamphlet in the press on the latter point. The Evidence of two Eye Witnesses of the Cruelties of the Traffic (Newton a Clergyman & Falconbridge a Surgeon) has been lately separately published. And then a new Edition of Anthony Benezet's Historical Account of Guinea is now finished with a few Additions. All of which are intended for Distribution among our Legislators and the People at large.[9]

Brissot provided American abolitionists with similar reports on the French campaign, assuring Miers Fisher in June 1790 that 'the liberality of sentiments is spreading more and more, & that many people are now ashamed of the hellish trade of Negroes'.[10] Information also flowed in the other direction, from west to east, again largely through the intervention of people such as Pemberton and Fisher. Formal letters, those between abolitionist societies, provided a further level of commentary on tactics and organisation, as well as details of new initiatives (the Sierra Leone experiment, for instance, or, in the case of the PAS, the organisation of schools for free blacks).[11] Occasionally, too, activists on both sides of the Atlantic helped each other with specific requests for information. In October 1787, for instance, the quarterly meeting of the PAS spent several weeks collecting 'certificates' attesting to the progress made by manumitted slaves in the USA, thereby enabling the SEAST to rebut charges that blacks were incapable of enjoying 'the blessings of freedom and civilisation'.[12] In the same way, the London Committee helped the Pennsylvania society with enquiries relating to free blacks, usually transatlantic travellers, who had been kidnapped and sold back into slavery.[13]

Another function of these letters was to offer support and encouragement. As close analysis of the PAS–SEAST correspondence reveals, Pemberton and his colleagues seem to have slipped easily into this role. 'We hope you will not be put off your guard by sanguine Expectations, nor discouraged & cast down by Disappointment', they gravely warned

[9] William Dillwyn to James Pemberton, 23 March 1788, Pemberton Papers, 49/159.
[10] Jacques-Pierre Brissot de Warville to Miers Fisher, June 1790, PAS Correspondence, microfilm edition, Reel 20.
[11] SEAST to PAS, 3 March 1789; PAS to SEAST, 24 June 1789; and PAS to SEAST, 3 (possibly 8) May 1790, PAS Correspondence, microfilm edition, Reel 11.
[12] SEAST to PAS, 28 February 1788, PAS Correspondence, microfilm edition, Reel 11.
[13] PAS Minutes, 1 October 1787, 17 October 1787, 20 October 1787; PAS to SEAST, not dated but definitely 1791, and Granville Sharp to James Pemberton, 24 November 1794, PAS Correspondence, microfilm edition, Reel 11.

the London Committee in November 1788. 'You know the Cause is just & of the greatest moment, what then remains but to proceed in a modest yet firm & steady Application to the Reason & Feelings of those who have it in their power to complete this desirable work.'[14] When the British movement reached a low point in 1796, Pennsylvania activists again intervened, this time to remind the London Committee that it was 'the duty of a good man to continue his efforts for promoting the cause of righteousness, and to make a momentary stop only when he cannot clearly see his way out'. 'It is not for us to point out your line of duty', they added, 'but we cannot help encouraging you not to quit the obvious path.'[15] Letters and letter-writing, therefore, were always about more than the exchange of ideas and information. As Pemberton succinctly put it, 'although there may be nothing very important to communicate, yet we believe you will agree with us that it is proper to keep up a regular correspondence – the strength and encouragement afforded thereby are too sensibly felt not to be acknowledged'.[16]

PAS members could say these things because they rightly assumed that a degree of trust existed between the two societies. Research suggests that successful inter-organisational collaboration relies heavily on trust, as well as the development of what are called 'reciprocity norms'. That is to say, in balanced relationships, both partners are prepared to make commitments, just as they are both prepared to take risks.[17] Given the impersonal nature of the international abolitionist network, letters were an important and often indispensable way of building trust; crucially, they brought partners together, in the process creating denser links between them. (This is another reason why collaboration between the PAS and the SEAST was so successful, and why the activities of the SEAST and the NYMS were, by comparison, less well integrated.) Clearly, PAS members felt no qualms about criticising their British counterparts, or about offering them advice, and the reverse was also the case. Passage of the US Foreign Slave Trade Act in 1794, for instance, prompted a robust response from the London Committee, highlighting what they regarded as the major flaws in the legislation.[18] Trust made these exchanges possible. Both societies seem to have been only too willing to share each other's disappointments, venting their frustration in long and sometimes detailed accounts of the duplicity

---

[14] PAS to SEAST, 12 (possibly 15) November 1788, PAS Minutes (minutes of meeting of 19 January, 1789).
[15] PAS to SEAST, 29 February 1796, PAS Correspondence, microfilm edition, Reel 11.
[16] PAS to SEAST, 6 May 1794, PAS Correspondence, microfilm edition, Reel 11.
[17] Kilduff and Tsai, *Social Networks and Organizations*, p. 44.
[18] SEAST to PAS, 10 July 1794, PAS Correspondence, microfilm edition, Reel 11.

of their opponents. Such confidences were signifiers of alliance and friendship, epistolary gestures that bound together reformers on both sides of the Atlantic.

Yet, at the same time, these letters also underscored a preferred or ideal model of activism. Clearly, the view from Philadelphia was that British abolitionists were too impatient and, if anything, too prone to despondency. Strong interests, the PAS argued, were not to be overcome 'in an Instant'.[19] On the contrary, what was needed was 'patience and perseverance'.[20] 'You are perhaps planting seeds for the next generation', they counselled the British society in 1787, 'but your labour is absolutely necessary to secure a harvest to your posterity.'[21] In saying this, Pemberton and his colleagues could not help turning to their own history, pointing out that 'it was not until they had made many fruitless exertions, that our Predecessors in this business were able to effect one thing in favour of the unfortunate Africans'.[22] 'The history of our Cause', they went on, 'shews that whatever may be the power of Self Interest, Truth and Humanity will prevail, if their suit be urged with firmness and perseverance.'[23] Not content with claiming precedence over their British counterparts, therefore, the PAS offered the London Committee a model of activism that reflected their own sense of themselves as leaders in this transatlantic movement.

From what we can gather, most of these letters would have been read aloud at meetings or else circulated among society members. The nearest thing to instant communication, they complemented and extended the many face-to-face conversations that went on between abolitionists on both sides of the Atlantic, whether in coffee shops, committee rooms or private parlours. Simultaneously, their contents were often copied and recycled, thereby ensuring that they received a much wider audience. 'The intelligence thou has kindly taken pains to give me is very obliging', James Pemberton wrote to William Dillwyn in October 1789, 'and has been acceptable to divers of our Associates of the Abolition Society to whom I have imparted such paragraphs as most immediately related to the Subject in which they continue to be engaged.'[24] Pemberton seems to have regularly recycled information in this way,

---

[19] PAS to SEAST, 28 February 1790, PAS Correspondence, microfilm edition, Reel 11.
[20] PAS to SEAST, 1791.
[21] PAS to SEAST, 20 October 1787, PAS Minutes (minutes of meeting of 20 October 1787).
[22] PAS to SEAST, 1791.   [23] PAS to SEAST, 1791.
[24] James Pemberton to William Dillwyn, 20 October 1789, Pemberton Papers, 52/104. See also James Pemberton to Edmund Prior, 20 October 1787, Pemberton Papers, 48/175, and James Pemberton to Thomas Collins, 2 May 1788, Pemberton Papers, 50/24.

using it to encourage fellow activists. We also know that he passed on extracts from his private correspondence to local newspapers, again with the intention of giving them as wide a circulation as possible. In the same way, Brissot arranged for Clarkson's correspondence to be published in *Le Patriote Français*.[25] As a result, some of these letters (we do not know how many) entered a very different domain, helping to shape public debates about slavery and the slave trade.

Just as important as the letters themselves was what accompanied them. Many letters contained enclosures, whether reports, circulars, newspapers or copies of statutes and petitions. All of the evidence suggests that there was a steady flow of this type of information back and forth across the Atlantic. Writing to the London Committee in June 1789, the PAS enclosed 'a copy of the association formed [at Washington, Pennsylvania], together with the letter which accompanies it and also a copy of the Constitution of a Society lately established at Providence in Rhode Island'.[26] Abolitionists on both sides of the Atlantic clearly valued these exchanges. 'We shall herewith send you copies of this committee's report to our society at large', the SEAST wrote to the PAS in February 1788, 'and also such other of the tracts lately published here, on the subject, as we can collect – some of these you may think it proper to republish. And we shall feel obliged by any returns of the same kind you may be able to make.'[27] Several months later, the London Committee wrote to the Pennsylvania society again, this time enclosing copies of the Slave Limitation (or Middle Passage) Act, recently passed by the British Houses of Parliament, 'together with what other Publications have lately occurred'.[28] In short, letters were part of a much more extensive exchange of ideas and information that not only encouraged 'reciprocity' but also helped to create a transatlantic abolitionist culture.

Letters were also sometimes accompanied by gifts of books, although here a more unusual pattern emerges. Initially, British abolitionists looked to America for inspiration. Many of the titles that Phillips printed between 1783 and 1784 were American imprints, principally works by Anthony Benezet and David Cooper.[29] From 1784 onwards, however, it is possible to identify a shift, as more and more British imprints

---

[25] *Le Patriote Français*, 10 September 1789, 17 September 1789 and 13 February 1790. See also Dorigny and Gainot, *La Société des Amis des Noirs*, p. 264.

[26] PAS to SEAST, 24 June 1789, PAS Correspondence, microfilm edition, Reel 11.

[27] *Pennsylvania Packet*, 22 May 1788.

[28] SEAST to PAS, 30 July 1788, PAS Minutes (minutes of meeting of 6 October 1788).

[29] For details of Phillips' publications, see the online version of the *English Short-Title Catalogue*, http://estc.bl.uk (accessed 5 May 2011).

appeared, many of which found their way across the Atlantic. By contrast, American publications dried up. The NYMS repeatedly tried to encourage local (American) publications, and even published several of them, including Samuel Hopkins' *Dialogue Concerning the Slavery of the Africans* (1785), but very few of these works seem to have had much of an impact.[30] By 1788 British imprints already predominated and would continue to hold sway until the mid 1790s. The key to this transformation was Clarkson's *Essay on the Slavery and Commerce of the Human Species*, which was published by James Phillips in 1786. Quickly spotting its potential, Joseph Cruikshank of Philadelphia published an American edition that same year, and a second edition followed in 1787. American abolitionists exploited the *Essay* to the full. In April 1787, for instance, the PAS ordered copies to be sent to each of the governors of the thirteen states in the USA. Copies were also distributed by the NYMS and helped to galvanise anti-slavery activity up and down the eastern seaboard. James Pemberton reported to his brother in March 1787 that Clarkson's *Essay* had 'greatly contributed' to the passage of a new state law in Delaware that prohibited the 'exportation' of slaves.[31]

As a result, Clarkson became an object of intense interest to American abolitionists and, for the moment at least, the public face of the British movement. Letters from London to Philadelphia minutely documented Clarkson's activities throughout the spring and summer of 1787, in the process helping to create a mystique around this seemingly indefatigable figure. Part of the fascination here, of course, was in trying to place Clarkson – for obvious reasons, Pemberton wanted to know whether or not he was a Quaker – but there is no mistaking his growing international reputation or his increasing importance to the cause.[32] Such was Clarkson's influence that the Pennsylvania society lost no time in raising a subscription to print an American edition of his second major work, his *Essay on the Impolicy of the Slave Trade* (1788). The book was advertised extensively in the Philadelphia newspapers throughout the

---

[30] NYMS Minutes, 10 November 1785, 9 November 1786, 15 February 1787, 19 February 1794, 19 May 1794, 19 August 1794, 21 March 1797, 16 April 1797, 16 May 1797. The society arranged for the printing of 2,000 copies of Hopkins' address, which had originally been printed in 1776. See NYMS Minutes, 10 November 1785.

[31] PAS Minutes, 23 April 1787; NYMS Minutes, 9 November 1786; James Pemberton to John Pemberton, 29 March 1787, Pemberton Papers, 47/188. See also Edmund Prior to James Pemberton, 7 February 1787, Pemberton Papers, 47/130.

[32] See, for instance, William Dillwyn to John Pemberton, 15 February 1787, Pemberton Papers, 47/137; John Pemberton to James Pemberton, 31 March 1787, Pemberton Papers, 48/2; John Pemberton to James Pemberton, 3 June 1787, Pemberton Papers, 48/63; and John Pemberton to James Pemberton, 26 July 1787, Pemberton Papers, 48/116.

autumn of 1788, together with an endorsement from Dr Richard Price, who predicted that it would give 'the finishing blow to this diabolical traffic'.[33] The response was enthusiastic: the NYMS, for instance, ordered 300 copies, some of which they arranged to be distributed among the members of the New York State legislature, but just as significant was the fact that Clarkson's essay was issued together with an English translation of Brissot's *Discours sur la nécessité d'établir à Paris une société pour l'abolition de la traite*, the whole making a bound volume, 'stitched in blue', of about 160 pages.[34] There was perhaps no better demonstration of how abolitionism fashioned itself as a genuinely international or transatlantic movement: an American imprint containing works by an Englishman and a Frenchman.

If Clarkson helped to engineer a breakthrough, he was, in fact, part of a much wider phenomenon. Estimates vary, but it seems likely that James Phillips published over forty abolitionist titles up to 1798, including works by James Ramsay, Alexander Falconbridge, William Dickson and, of course, Clarkson himself. Many of these works were published expressly for the SEAST. We know from its minutes that the London Committee bought up copyrights, as in the case of Charles Wadstrom's *Observations on the Slave Trade* (1789), just as it commissioned new titles and reprinted old ones (Benezet's *Some Historical Account of Guinea*, for instance).[35] Some of these works, moreover, ran into second and third editions. To take one example, no fewer than four editions of the Dean of Middleham's *Letter to the Treasurer of the Society Instituted for the Purpose of Effecting the Abolition of the Slave Trade* appeared in 1788, each of them longer and more substantial than the last. Phillips was also responsible for the hugely successful engraving of the slave ship *Brookes*, which first appeared in the spring of 1789. Here again, the initial print run was in excess of 8,000 copies, and a further 1,000 copies of the engraving were published early in 1791, to coincide with the debate in the House of Commons. Sadly, the accounts are incomplete, but it is conceivable that between 1787 and 1792 Phillips printed, in all, about 125,000 books and pamphlets for the London Committee.[36]

In France, too, abolitionists spent large amounts of money on books and printing. From an early stage, the Société des Amis des Noirs began the work of translating and publishing English works, chief

[33] *Freeman's Journal*, 17 September 1788 and 1 October 1788; *Pennsylvania Mercury and Universal Advertiser*, 6 September 1788.
[34] NYMS Minutes, 24 September 1788; *Freeman's Journal*, 17 September 1788.
[35] Oldfield, *Popular Politics*, pp. 43–4.
[36] All of these details about Phillips' business are extracted from the online version of the *English Short-Title Catalogue*, http://est.bl.uk (accessed 5 May 2011).

among them Clarkson's *Essay on the Impolicy of the Slave Trade*. The society also published its own texts, some of which, such as its *Seconde adresse à l'Assemblée Nationale* (1790), were printed in-house by Brissot's newspaper *Le Patriote Français*.[37] But such official publications were only the tip of the iceberg. Many other writers and publishers quickly produced abolitionist titles, eager to capitalise on what was rapidly becoming an expanding market; indeed, we may never know the precise number of these texts, especially if we take into account the scores of novels, plays and poems that dealt directly or indirectly with abolitionist themes. Neither was this exclusively a male preserve. Many women also took up their pens against the slave trade, among them Hannah More, Ann Yearsley, Helen Maria Williams and Anna Laetitia Barbauld.[38] Similarly, on the other side of the Channel, Madame de Staël and Olympe de Gouges both attacked slavery or sought to elicit sympathy for those who (as they saw it) were oppressed by violence and injustice. As Doris Kadish points out, slavery was widely perceived to be a 'women's issue', a circumstance that enabled them to acquire 'a voice in the public sphere they would undoubtedly not otherwise have had'.[39]

Internal evidence suggests that most official publications (that is, those either published or approved by organised abolitionist societies) were distributed freely among fellow activists, both at home and abroad. In 1788, for instance, at a very early stage in the French campaign, the SEAST sent the Société des Amis des Noirs a box of ninety books, made up of some twenty-three different titles, among them multiple copies of works by Ramsay, Wesley and Falconbridge.[40] Similar gifts were made to abolitionists in the USA. James Phillips regularly sent

---

[37] Dorigny and Gainot, *La Société des Amis des Noirs*, pp. 105–6 (meeting of 18 March 1788) and p. 190 (meeting of 13 January 1789). See also Edward Derbyshire Seeber, *Anti-Slavery Opinion in France during the Second Half of the Eighteenth Century* (New York: Burt Franklin, 1971), p. 161. In April 1790, *Le Patriote Français* published a list of twenty-five French titles relating to slavery and the slave trade that were available for consultation at the offices of the Société des Amis des Noirs in Paris. Some of these titles were undoubtedly published by and for the society, while others, such as Benjamin Frossard's *La cause des esclaves nègres et des habitants de la Guinée, portée au tribunal de la justice, de la religion, de la politique*, 2 vols. (Lyon, 1789) were published independently. For the full list, see *Le Patriote Français*, 4 April 1790, and Seeber, *Anti-Slavery Opinion in France*, pp. 197–9.

[38] Clare Midgley, *Women Against Slavery: The British Campaigns, 1780–1870* (London and New York: Routledge, 1994), pp. 29–35. See also Moira Ferguson, *Subject to Others: British Women Writers and Colonial Slavery, 1670–1834* (London and New York: Routledge, 1992).

[39] Doris Y. Kadish, 'The Black Terror: Women's Responses to Slave Revolts in Haiti', *French Review*, 68 (4) (1995), 668-90, at p.679.

[40] See Dorigny and Gainot, *La Société des Amis des Noirs*, pp. 102–4 (minutes of meeting of 18 March 1788).

James Pemberton boxes of books, as did William Dillwyn and Robert Barclay. Brissot, for his part, chose to distribute the publications of the Société des Amis des Noirs through his close friend Miers Fisher.[41] Alternatively, books were sent directly to many American abolitionist societies. In September 1788, the NYMS reported that it had received a 'box of pamphlets from London', presumably from the SEAST, which it agreed to inspect with a view to distributing some of them to the speaker of the Assembly of Connecticut, which was then in session.[42] It is impossible to say how many books reached America through these different channels, but the numbers were certainly large enough to cause American abolitionists to rethink their strategies. In May 1787, the PAS set up a committee to collect together 'the opinions of the wise & virtuous at various times and in different countries against the practice of holding slaves', with a view to publishing them under the auspices of the society.[43] Eighteen months later the committee reported back and asked to be dismissed. The reason, they explained, was that 'the numerous, full and excellent treatises, which have been written in England upon the subject of Slavery and the Slave Trade have superseded the necessity of such a compilation as that proposed by the Society'.[44]

What did American abolitionists do with all of these books? Many of them were distributed through abolitionist networks. James Pemberton provided some insight into the thinking behind this strategy in a letter to William Dillwyn of October 1789. 'Of the Publications last sent per Apollo', he explained,

I have already forwarded one of each to a Society lately formed at Baltimore, and to New York & purpose to embrace the first opportunity of supplying that at Washington as desired in thy letter, also to Dover, Wilmington & the Eastern Shore of Maryland where a Society is also lately instituted, and purpose to send a few to Rhode Island lest those which your Committee entered for them should not soon arrive.[45]

In other words, Pemberton used these books to forge alliances and, where appropriate, to raise flagging spirits, their 'ardor and unabated

---

[41] See James Phillips to James Pemberton, 28 February 1788, Pemberton Papers, 49/125, and James Phillips to James Pemberton, 20 July 1790, Pemberton Papers, 52/144; William Dillwyn to James Pemberton, 9 July 1789, Pemberton Papers, 52/129; Jacques-Pierre Brissot de Warville to Miers Fisher, June 1790, PAS Correspondence, microfilm edition, Reel 20; Jacques-Pierre Brissot de Warville to James Pemberton, 26 November 1790 and 6 July 1791, PAS Correspondence, microfilm edition, Reel 11.

[42] NYMS Minutes, 24 September 1788. In the same way, Brissot and Clavière sometimes sent gifts of books directly to the PAS. See, for example, PAS Minutes, 6 July 1789 and 5 July 1790.

[43] PAS Minutes, 3 May 1787.   [44] PAS Minutes, 6 October 1788.

[45] James Pemberton to William Dillwyn, 20 October 1789, Pemberton Papers, 52/104.

firmness' providing an example for American societies to follow.[46] As we have seen, European texts were also used as part of more ambitious opinion-building activities, which included putting pressure on state governors and legislators. Others were made available to the public at large, or else deposited in local libraries. When the members of the Providence society received a box of books from London in 1790 they immediately put an advertisement in one of the local newspapers so that anyone who had 'a Desire of further Information upon the Subject [might] have an Opportunity of perusing them'.[47] The PAS, meanwhile, regularly made gifts of books to the Library Company of Philadelphia, thereby ensuring that they were readily accessible to readers.[48]

Interestingly, another way in which British and French texts were circulated was through American newspapers. On both sides of the Atlantic, the eighteenth century witnessed a rapid increase in the number of newspapers and, with it, the growing importance of the press. By 1780 there were probably fifty or more provincial newspapers in Britain alone. Several towns had more than one newspaper, while for a time Newcastle and Manchester boasted as many as three.[49] There was a similar expansion in the USA. Jeffrey Pasley estimates that there were over 100 American newspapers by 1790 and over 250 by 1800.[50] Usually no more than four closely printed pages, these newspapers were a vital source of information about domestic and foreign affairs, fashion, gossip and the changing fortunes of trade and business. Certainly up to the 1790s, editorial comment was uncommon. Heavily dependent on subscribers, very few printers could afford to alienate their customers, and those that did, such as Benjamin Franklin Bache of the Philadelphia *General Advertiser*, quickly ran into difficulties. As one discerning reader put it: 'Printers ought never to come to view in their own papers, unless they are soliciting arrears from their subscribers, & they get little of good by abuse of their brother printers.'[51]

---

[46] See PAS to the Washington Society, 25 October 1790, PAS Correspondence, microfilm edition, Reel 11.
[47] *Providence Gazette and Country Journal*, 20 March 1790.
[48] PAS Minutes, 6 October 1788, 6 July 1789, 19 October 1789.
[49] G. A. Cranfield, *The Development of the Provincial Newspaper, 1700–1760* (Oxford University Press, 1962), p. 173.
[50] Jeffrey L. Pasley, *'The Tyranny of Printers': Newspaper Politics in the Early American Republic* (Charlottesville, Va.: University of Virginia Press, 2001), pp. 33, 403–4.
[51] Thomas Evans to Miers Fisher, 16 February 1795, Fisher Family Papers, Box 12, Folder 2. As Pasley argues, this was rapidly becoming an outdated view, at least in the USA. The 1790s, he suggests, witnessed the emergence of an increasingly partisan press dominated by a new breed of printers and editors who were closely identified with the emerging party system. For British perspectives, see Hannah Barker,

For the most part, newspapers in Britain and the USA were open and democratic. The situation in France, however, was very different. Here, newspapers were relatively late to emerge. The first French daily newspaper, *Le Journal de Paris*, did not appear until 1777. More to the point, the French press was tightly regulated. To quote Robert Darnton: 'Official journals – notably the *Gazette de France*, *Mercure*, and *Journal des Savants* – possessed royal privileges for the coverage of certain subjects, and no new periodical could be established without paying them for a share in their turf.'[52] All of this would change, of course, with the storming of the Bastille and the Declaration of the Rights of Man and the Citizen, which significantly allowed for the freedom of the press. As a result, many aspiring editors and printers rushed forward to establish their own newspapers, among them Brissot, who in July 1789 published the first edition of *Le Patriote Français*, a new journal that proclaimed itself to be 'free, impartial and national'.[53] While, as Darnton notes, it is possible to exaggerate the servility of the press under the Old Regime, there is little doubt that the Revolution established newspapers (and, through newspapers, public opinion) as a noisy, competitive and highly contentious force in French politics.

Abolitionists needed no prompting in exploiting the potential of eighteenth-century newspapers. Gaining access to them, however, invariably meant having the right connections. This was particularly the case in France where throughout 1788–9 the members of the Société des Amis des Noirs relied heavily on Mirabeau and Condorcet to gain access to *L'Analyse des papiers anglais* and *Le Journal de Paris*, respectively, which both enjoyed royal privileges. Through these channels, French activists were able to disseminate details about the SEAST as well as the progress of the British campaign. Early in 1788, Mirabeau even proposed publishing extracts from British texts (Clarkson's essays, for instance) as supplements to *L'Analyse des papiers anglais*, although, as far as we know, nothing seems to have come of the idea.[54] The real breakthrough, however, came after 1789. Brissot's *Le Patriote Français*

Newspapers, Politics and Public Opinion in Late Eighteenth-Century England (Oxford: Clarendon Press, 1998).

[52] Darnton, 'An Early Information Society', p. 6.

[53] The first issue of *Le Patriote Français* was published on 28 July 1789. For the proliferation of a free press during the Revolution, see Hugh Gough, *The Newspaper Press in the French Revolution* (London and New York: Routledge, 1988); Claude Belanger, Jacques Godechot, Pierre Guiral and Fernand Terrou, eds., *Histoire générale de la presse français* (Paris: Presses Universitaires de France, 1969–76), vol. I: *Des origines à 1814*.

[54] Valerie Quinney, 'Decisions on Slavery, the Slave Trade and Civil Rights for Negroes', *Journal of Negro History*, 55 (2) (April 1970): 118-27, at pp. 120-1; Dorigny and Gainot, *La Société des Amis des Noirs*, pp. 72–85.

gave French activists what amounted to open access to the press, being in effect an in-house journal. The newspaper carried regular reports on the British and American campaigns, as well as notices of the meetings of the Société des Amis des Noirs. In the same spirit, Brissot opened the pages of *Le Patriote Français* to Thomas Clarkson during his visit to Paris in 1789–90 and used it to promote the interests of *gens de couleur* in the French colonies.[55] Though its primary focus was the proceedings of the National Assembly, which it recorded in minute detail, *Le Patriote Français* was the nearest thing to an abolitionist newspaper during this period. Very much a reflection of Brissot's own interests, it provided French activists with a cheap, reliable and highly effective mouthpiece, right up until Brissot's arrest and execution in 1793.

By contrast, British abolitionists used newspapers only sparingly. Part of the problem here was expense. Some printers, such as William Woodfall, editor of *Woodfall's Diary*, were prepared to offer abolitionists special rates, and others, we know, subscribed to local societies. But the costs involved could still be daunting, even for the SEAST. 'The little use we have made of [newspapers]', William Dillwyn confessed in March 1789, 'has cost a very considerable Sum, and the present State of our Fund, with the uncertainty of further Demands on it, force us to an Economy we reluctantly submit to, on many Temptations to deviate from it'.[56] At a rough estimate, the London Committee spent over £100 on advertising in its first year and slightly less than that (£77) in 1788–9, after which the accounts are incomplete. A lot of this money was spent on notices of the SEAST's own activities, mainly reports and subscription lists, but interspersed among them were items of foreign news, usually carefully selected to throw down a challenge to Britons. In October 1787, for instance, the SEAST arranged for the London papers to carry the memorial of the PAS to the Convention of Delegates sitting in Philadelphia and thereafter would see to it that other American news items, particularly those relating to individual state action against the slave trade, were given equal prominence in the British press.[57] Occasionally, too, the society would place anonymous letters in the London newspapers. Dillwyn revealed to James Pemberton in August 1789 that William Dickson 'devotes all his time to writing on

---

[55] See, for example, *Le Patriote Français*, 5 August 1789, 18 August 1789, 24 August 1789, 1 September 1789, 4 September 1789, 10 September 1789, 17 September 1789, 28 September, 9 October 1789, 23 October 1789, 11 November 1789, 26 November 1789, 3 December 1789, 24 December 1789 and 14 January 1790.
[56] Oldfield, *Popular Politics*, pp. 131–2; William Dillwyn to James Pemberton, 3 March 1789, Pemberton Papers, 51/190.
[57] SEAST Minutes, 2 October 1787, 20 May 1788, 1 July 1788, 12 August 1788, 21 October 1788, 14 April 1789, 28 July 1789.

[the slave trade], and answering the Essays etc of our Adversaries in the Daily Papers, under the control of a Sub-Committee, who approve previous to publication'. 'Writing under different Signatures', Dillwyn continued, barely disguising his delight, 'the Cause has Credit for so many different Advocates, and hitherto he [Dickson] has supported it with Credit & Effect.'[58]

Nevertheless, Dillwyn clearly felt that British abolitionists worked under significant constraints, certainly when compared to their American counterparts. 'If this Channel to public Notice was as accessible as with you', he wrote to Pemberton, 'we could use it very beneficially to the Cause.'[59] The Pennsylvania society seems to have enjoyed particularly close links with local newspapers. Part of the reason for this is that some editors, such as Francis Bailey, were themselves activists. Others probably mixed in the same religious and business circles as abolitionists, or else relied on their custom. Whatever the reason, Philadelphia editors were only too willing to accommodate abolitionists and, just as important, to waive their fees. James Pemberton claimed that 'the publishers of our Newspapers are in general very disposed to insert the occurrences we hand them on the Subject, at the same time that they serve themselves, they also become instrumental in promoting the cause of humanity & the Society is relieved from a considerable expence in printing'.[60] And what was true of Philadelphia seems to have been true of other American cities, certainly those in the New England and Middle Atlantic states. Here again, the amount of attention devoted to foreign news is striking. Prompted by activists such as Pemberton, American newspapers paid close attention to British abolitionist activity, particularly during the early part of 1788, when the first petition campaign was in full flow. Besides the SEAST's annual reports, circular letters and notices of meetings, many newspapers also printed copies of petitions as well as extracts from the debates in the House of Commons. Most newspapers during the critical first phase of the movement (1787–92) carried some news from Britain and, with it, some further indication of the strength of international feeling against the slave trade.[61]

[58] William Dillwyn to James Pemberton, 7 August 1789, Pemberton Papers, 52/165.
[59] William Dillwyn to James Pemberton, 3 March 1789, Pemberton Papers, 51/190.
[60] James Pemberton to William Dillwyn, November 1789, Pemberton Papers, 53/49.
[61] See, for example, *Freeman's Journal*, 16 April 1788, 3 September 1788, 10 September 1788, 17 September 1788, 24 September 1788 and 10 December 1788, 3 August 1791 and 10 August 1791; *Providence Gazette and Country Journal*, 24 May 1788 and 6 December 1788, 12 September 1789, 19 September 1789, 26 September 1789, 3 October 1789 and 14 November 1789, 16 July 1791, 23 July 1791, 13 August 1791,

Space was also given to abolitionist activity in France. The organisation of the Société des Amis des Noirs was announced in many American newspapers; Bailey's *Freeman's Journal* even went so far as to print the names of all seventy-one of its founding members. Others printed details of the debates in the National Assembly and, after 1791, of events in Saint-Domingue, but by and large British news tended to predominate.[62] Most of these items would have been passed to newspaper printers in much the same way as Pemberton described. The process was straightforward, even if it was not always transparent (at least, to readers). To take one example, many of the supposedly anonymous letters printed by the *Freeman's Journal* were really letters that had been sent to James Pemberton by his English correspondents, among them William Dillwyn and his own brother, John. Pemberton's voluminous papers reveal that he regularly copied out extracts from his correspondence, evidently with the intention of passing them to one or other of the Philadelphia printers. Some of these letters enjoyed a wide circulation. In April 1788, for instance, extracts from one of John Pemberton's letters, together with copies of two petitions he had sent from Northampton and Kendal, appeared in the *Freeman's Journal*, the *Pennsylvania Mercury and Universal Advertiser* and the New York *Independent Journal; or, General Advertiser*. Information was regularly recycled in this manner. Close analysis of John Carter's *Providence Gazette and Country Journal* suggests that he frequently copied material from other newspapers; indeed, copying or recycling was the only way most printers could survive, particularly given the constraints on their time and finances. But, by the same token, many items in the *Providence Gazette* were clearly printed at the specific request of activists (helpfully, Carter usually indicated when this was the case), even if, for the most part, they remained anonymous.[63]

Besides letters and reports, many editors were also willing to reprint abolitionist books and pamphlets, and here the difference between Europe and America is most strikingly evident. A case in point is Daniel Humphreys, editor of the *Pennsylvania Mercury and Universal Advertiser*.

---

20 August 1791, 27 August 1791 and 10 September 1791, 28 April 1792, 16 June 1792, 23 June 1792, 30 June 1792 and 1 September 1792; New York *Independent Journal*, 19 April 1788; *Pennsylvania Mercury and Universal Advertiser*, 15 April 1788, 19 April 1788, 18 November 1788 and 2 June 1789.

[62] *Freeman's Journal*, 8 October 1788, 8 April 1789, 12 April 1789, 23 November 1791; *Pennsylvania Gazette*, 27 June 1792.

[63] See, for example, *Providence Gazette and Country Journal*, 14 June 1788, 13 September 1788, 20 June 1789 and 13 March 1790. Carter was not a member of the Rhode Island society, although he seemingly had abolitionist sympathies, having freed his two slaves in 1789. See Rappleye, *Sons of Providence*, p. 260.

Between January and August 1788 Humphreys printed in their entirety Clarkson's *Summary View of the Slave Trade*, the Dean of Middleham's *Letter*, Newton's *Thoughts Upon the African Slave Trade*, and James Stanfield's *Observations on a Guinea Voyage*.[64] During the same period (May–June 1788), the *Pennsylvania Packet, and Daily Advertiser* printed the full text of *Remarks on the Slave Trade, and the Slavery of the Negroes, in a Series of Letters* by 'Africanus', and followed this up in 1789 with *The Speech of Mr Beaufoy, Tuesday 18 June, in a Committee of the Whole House, on a Bill for Regulating the Conveyance of Negroes from Africa to the West Indies, to Which Are Added, Observations on the Evidence Adduced Against the Bill*.[65] Similarly, in Providence, Carter printed Stanfield's *Observations on a Guinea Voyage* in six parts between September and November 1788, and the following year he also printed extracts from Newton's *Thoughts Upon the African Slave Trade*.[66] One further example will suffice. In 1788, when the Connecticut Assembly was discussing a Bill to 'prevent' the slave trade, the *New-Haven Gazette* published the Dean of Middleham's *Letter*, together with extracts from Newton, William Cowper (*The Negro's Complaint*) and Isaac Bickerstaffe (*The Padlock*). Here again the timing was important, but equally revealing was the reliance on European texts to make the case against American slavery.[67]

American newspapers also printed French texts, although the language barrier posed obvious problems. In July 1789, for instance, the *Pennsylvania Packet, and Daily Advertiser* published an English translation of Condorcet's *Lettre aux bailliages*, probably the same one published by James Phillips earlier in the year, noting with satisfaction that 'many Bailliages had adopted their proposal, and have recommended the matter [i.e. abolition of the slave trade] to the States General.'[68]

---

[64] *Pennsylvania Mercury and Universal Advertiser*, 5 January 1788, 8 January 1788, 21 February 1788, 13 May 1788, 15 May 1788, 17 May 1788, 20 May 1788 and 7 August 1788, 9 August 1788, 12 August 1788, 16 August 1788, 19 August 1788, 21 August 1788.

[65] *Pennsylvania Packet, and Daily Advertiser*, 20 May 1788, 28 May 1788, 5 June 1788, 19 June 1788, 21 June 1788, 23 June 1788, 24 June 1788 and 3 August 1789, 4 August 1789, 6 August 1789 and 17 August 1789.

[66] *Providence Gazette and Country Journal*, 13 September 1788, 20 September 1788, 27 September 1788, 11 October 1788, 1 November 1788, 8 November 1788 and 20 June 1789. Again, Pemberton's influence is evident here. Writing to William Dillwyn in November 1788, he notes that 'Stanfield's letters also have been published in one of our [Philadelphia] newspapers, as also in Rhode Island as Moses Brown writes me, to whom I sent a copy of them.' See James Pemberton to William Dillwyn, 15 November 1788, Pemberton Papers, 51/75.

[67] *New-Haven Gazette, and the Connecticut Magazine*, 16 October 1788, 22 October 1788, 13 November 1788 and 27 November 1788.

[68] *Pennsylvania Packet, and Daily Advertiser*, 6 July 1789.

Not to be outdone, in March and April of 1790 the *Providence Gazette* devoted two issues to an English translation of the introductory address that accompanied the *Règlement de la Société des Amis des Noirs*, originally published in 1788, while later that year the *Pennsylvania Mercury* published three extracts from Benjamin Frossard's *La Cause des esclaves nègres* (1788) – but there is little doubt that British texts made the greater impact, if only because they were more readily accessible.[69] Such details provide important insights into how abolitionist ideas were transmitted during the Age of Revolution. Clearly, one of the reasons why more British and French abolitionist books and pamphlets were not published in the USA (and we should not be misled by this) was that they could be printed more cheaply, and arguably reach a much wider audience, by being printed, usually in parts, in local newspapers. If we assume that the circulation of an average American newspaper during this period was between 2,000 and 3,000 copies, then we can see how newspapers not only provided American abolitionists with greater flexibility but also offered them the ability to penetrate local markets at relatively low cost.[70]

It was not only books and pamphlets that circulated across and within the Atlantic world. Abolitionism early acquired its own visual culture, a culture that was at once dynamic, immediate and malleable. No one perhaps understood the commercial value of abolition better than the Staffordshire potter Josiah Wedgwood, who in August 1787 became an active member of the SEAST. Wedgwood's influence is discernible, above all, in the design of the London Committee's seal, adopted in October 1787, depicting a kneeling slave together with the motto 'Am I Not a Man and a Brother?' Not content with this, Wedgwood subsequently produced a black-and-white jasperware medallion incorporating the same design. Cameos were already fashionable consumer goods; Wedgwood's catalogue of 1779 advertised a range of designs 'fit for rings, buttons, lockets and bracelets; and especially for inlaying in fine Cabinets, Writing Tables, Bookcases, etc.'. Here, in other words, was an important marketing opportunity. It comes as no surprise to learn that some gentlemen had Wedgwood's slave medallion 'inlaid in gold on the lid of their snuff-boxes', or that 'of the Ladies, several wore them in bracelets and others had them fitted up in an ornamental manner as pins for their hair'.[71] Wedgwood's achievement, therefore, was to make

---

[69] *Providence Gazette and Country Journal*, 13 March and 3 April 1790; *Pennsylvania Mercury and Universal Advertiser*, 16 September 1790, 18 September 1790 and 30 September 1790.
[70] Pasley, *'The Tyranny of Printers'*, pp. 7–8, 203–4.
[71] Clarkson, *History*, vol. II, pp. 191–2.

abolition fashionable at a period when emulative spending already had a powerful hold over the lives of many middle-class men and women.[72]

The first of these cameos were probably produced early in 1788, and almost immediately some were shipped to the USA. In February of that year, James Phillips sent a box of books to Ben Franklin and with it a small box meant for James Pemberton 'containing some cameos or impressions from our Seal made by Josiah Wedgwood which he gave me for my friends in your city'.[73] Phillips even provided Pemberton with a 'list of those to whom I wish to have them presented'.[74] But the cameo never really seems to have caught on, perhaps because Pemberton and his colleagues saw it as a form of ostentation and display. They were much more excited, however, by the engraving of the slave ship *Brookes*, which first reached them in April 1789. As we now know, this engraving was originally devised and printed by the local Plymouth committee in December 1788 and reprinted with improvements by the SEAST the following year.[75] James Phillips was so pleased with the results that he presented the PAS with a framed and glazed copy of the enlarged print in July 1789, pointing out that while the original Plymouth engraving had been 'a happy thought', it had not been 'correctly executed'. 'The slaves which ought to be 6 feet long', he explained, 'i.e. the men, in some parts are not above 3 – unless others may be supposed to be 10 or 12. This new plan cost some, indeed a good deal of trouble & I hope is exact & correct – it was examined by Capt Seer surveyor of the Navy.'[76] What Phillips was describing here was the 'improved' plan, which not only contained a view of the lower deck but also longitudinal and cross sections of the whole vessel, rendered with an exactitude that, as Marcus Wood has pointed out, owed a great deal to navigational and ship drawing.[77]

The members of the London Committee set great store by such details. If Phillips' nervousness hinted at the vulnerability of British abolitionists and their sensitivity to criticism, it also hinted at something else, namely their insistence on empirical inquiry. Being exact, rather like being 'respectable', another favourite word in the abolitionists' vocabulary, was part of a broad Enlightenment inquiry that privileged

[72] Oldfield, *Popular Politics*, pp. 155–9.
[73] James Phillips to James Pemberton, 28 February 1788, Pemberton Papers, 49/125.
[74] Phillips to Pemberton, 28 February 1788.
[75] Oldfield, *Popular Politics*, pp. 163–4.
[76] James Phillips to James Pemberton, 20 July 1789, Pemberton Papers, 52/144.
[77] Marcus Wood, *Blind Memory: Visual Representations of Slavery in England and America, 1780–1865* (Manchester University Press, 2000), pp. 16–36.

observation and experience over bigotry and received opinion. Phillips' gift came too late, however. Almost as soon as they received the original Plymouth engraving, the Pennsylvania society arranged for 6,000 copies of it to be printed, 3,000 of which were subsequently inserted in the *American Museum* for May 1789.[78] Pemberton reported on 20 October that the print had been 'fix[ed] up thro the City & Country in places of public resort & many of them dispersed thro several States from New Hampshire to Georgia & some sent to the West India Islands'.[79] This was no exaggeration. Thomas Arnold, secretary of the Providence society, wrote in September to ask for '200 more of the Ship's Deck, if they are to be spared, as it was thought they might be very usefully distributed'.[80] And copies certainly reached the South. John Kirk of Charleston, South Carolina, judged the engraving 'a very striking description of the oppressed Africans in their Transportation from their native Country' and hoped that its distribution might prove 'useful in exposing the iniquity of that cruel, unrighteous indeed inhuman Traffick'.[81] Copies were even sent to Britain. In August 1789, William Dillwyn thanked Pemberton for 'another of *your* engraved Sketches of a Slave Ship', which he had sent in a packet, together with other publications testifying to the progress of the movement in the USA.[82]

By 1790 there were actually four versions of the *Brookes* in circulation: the original Plymouth version; the Philadelphia version, copied from the Plymouth engraving; the 'improved' London version, which was published in two variants, one a woodcut, the other a more expensive copperplate engraving; and, finally, a French version, based on the London engraving, which was published by the Société des Amis des Noirs and bound together with a fourteen-page 'description'.[83]

---

[78] James Pemberton to William Dillwyn, 1 June 1789 and 20 October 1789, Pemberton Papers, 52/83 and 52/104; PAS Minutes, 6 July 1789. See also Cheryl Finlay, 'Committed to Memory: The Slave Ship Icon in the Black Atlantic Imagination', unpublished Ph.D. thesis, Yale University, 2002, p. 94, n. 119. In addition, the Pennsylvania society printed a further 1,500 copies of the engraving in July 1789, making 7,500 copies in all. See PAS Minutes, 6 July 1789 and 20 July 1789.
[79] James Pemberton to William Dillwyn, 20 October 1789, Pemberton Papers, 52/104.
[80] Thomas Arnold to James Pemberton, 7 September 1789, Pemberton Papers, 52/187.
[81] John Kirk to James Pemberton, 22 September 1789, Pemberton Papers, 53/5.
[82] William Dillwyn to James Pemberton, 7 August 1789, Pemberton Papers, 52/165.
[83] Finlay, 'Committed to Memory', p. 94, n. 119; Dorigny and Gainot, *La Société des Amis des Noirs*, p. 224 (meeting of 19 May 1789), p. 227 (meeting of 9 June 1789) and p. 261 (meeting of 8 January 1790). Reading between the lines, it is clear that the cost of producing this engraving, *Description d'un navire négrier* (1789), put the finances of the French society under severe strain, so much so that it was forced to turn to the SEAST for help. See Jacques-Pierre Brissot de Warville to Thomas Clarkson, 29 March 1790, 25 April 1790 and 27 May 1790, Thomas Clarkson Papers, St John's College, Cambridge.

In all, the total number of engravings published on both sides of the Atlantic likely ran into the tens of thousands. The London Committee alone printed 9,700 copies up to 1791, in addition to which Clarkson reported that 'above a thousand' of the French version were distributed among the Société des Amis des Noirs and the members of the National Assembly.[84] When we add to this the 1,500 engravings printed by the Plymouth committee, as well as those published in Philadelphia, the final figure was probably close to 20,000, making it one of the most widely circulated of all abolitionist texts and images. Whatever the weaknesses of the original engraving, the plan and description of the slave ship *Brookes* rapidly became one of the most effective pieces of abolitionist propaganda, a visual cue or shorthand whose ability to shock and provoke helped to make abolition a matter of pressing international concern.

Perhaps the most striking part of Pemberton's letter of 20 October was the revelation that copies of the *Brookes* had been sent to the Caribbean. After 1791, it became customary in some quarters to blame abolitionists for destabilising the Caribbean and fanning the flames of slave insurrection. In his *Historical Survey of the Island of Saint Domingo, Together with an Account of the Maroon Negroes in the Island of Jamaica; and a History of the War in the West Indies, in 1793 and 1794*, originally published in 1796, the Jamaican planter Bryan Edwards accused the SEAST of distributing

at a prodigious expence throughout the colonies, tracts and pamphlets without number, the direct tendency of which was to render the white inhabitants odious and contemptible in the eyes of their own slaves, and excite in the latter such ideas of their natural rights and equality of condition, as should lead them to a general struggle for freedom through rebellion and bloodshed.[85]

The exiled French planter Felix Carteau echoed these sentiments. The Société des Amis des Noirs, he claimed, was guilty of disseminating 'among the Negroes of the colony [of Saint-Domingue] many books that showed pity for their fate, and many similar engravings'.[86] In fact, it seems more likely that the real culprits were the Americans. Certainly, there is nothing to suggest that British abolitionists targeted

[84] Clarkson, *History*, vol. II, p. 151.
[85] Bryan Edwards, *An Historical Survey of the Island of Saint Domingo, Together with an Account of the Maroon Negroes in the Island of Jamaica; and a History of the War in the West Indies, in 1793 and 1794* (London: John Stockdale, 1801), p. 109.
[86] Quoted in Laurent Dubois, *A Colony of Citizens: Revolution and Slave Emancipation in the French Caribbean, 1787–1804* (Chapel Hill, NC: University of North Carolina Press, 2004), p. 105. Carteau also claimed that he had seen abolitionist texts, including works by the Abbé Raynal, 'among the hands of some Negroes'.

the Caribbean in any deliberate way, a charge they vigorously denied, and the same holds true for the Société des Amis des Noirs, although it is possible some of its members may have distributed abolitionist propaganda in the Caribbean in an individual capacity.[87]

Edwards and Carteau were right about one thing, however: abolitionist ideas and rumours about emancipation circulated freely throughout the Caribbean region. In large part, this was a reflection of the Caribbean's importance in terms of transatlantic trade. By the late 1780s, hundreds of American and European ships were entering and clearing Caribbean ports each year.[88] Most of these ships brought with them news of the outside world in the shape of letters, pamphlets and newspapers, which, in turn, encouraged discussion about issues such as slavery and the slave trade. According to Julius Sherrard Scott III, 'both public and private channels carried accounts of the building sentiment for abolition. In Barbados, newspapers appearing in early April [1788] reported the growing interest in Britain and throughout Europe in the "iniquitous and inhuman traffic"'.[89] Just as important was the presence in the Caribbean of large numbers of foreign sailors, who mixed freely with slaves and free blacks in bars and so-called 'white markets' that occurred on Sundays and public holidays. Again, these face-to-face contacts complemented and extended debates about 'slavery' and 'freedom'. Scott argues persuasively that seamen working on slave ships may have been a vital source of information for Caribbean blacks, not least because 'European seafarers had long recognised the striking parallels between life before the mast and life on the plantation.' 'Seamen subject to rigid and arbitrary discipline, to the absolute power of ships' masters, to press gangs and the lash', he goes on, 'found an appropriate analogy for their lives in the slave experience.'[90]

News and speculation spread quickly through the Caribbean, thanks in no small part to the inter-island trade and the movements of runaways, free blacks and deserters from military service.[91] As a result, Caribbean

---

[87] For the London Committee's response to Edwards' claims, see SEAST Minutes, 29 March 1797. There is no reason to suspect they were not telling the truth.
[88] See Julius Sherrard Scott III, 'The Common Wind: Currents of Afro-American Communication in the Era of the Haitian Revolution', unpublished Ph.D. thesis, Duke University, 1987, pp. 60, 82, 128. Scott estimates that in 1788 Jamaica's trade alone 'employed close to 500 ships and well over 9,000 seamen' (p. 60).
[89] Scott, 'The Common Wind', p. 127.
[90] Scott, 'The Common Wind', pp. 66–8, 134–43. See also Paul A. Gilje, *Liberty on the Waterfront: American Maritime Culture in the Age of Revolution* (Philadelphia, Pa.: University of Pennsylvania Press, 2004), pp. 69, 138.
[91] See W. Jeffrey Bolster, *Black Jacks: African American Seamen in the Age of Sail* (Cambridge, Mass.: Harvard University Press, 1997), pp. 17–21, 40–1.

blacks were remarkably well informed about events in Britain and France, much to the dismay of white planters, who vented their frustration on groups such as the SEAST or the Société des Amis des Noirs. The process could also work the other way. After 1791, American ships trading with Saint-Domingue supplied vital news about the course of the slave insurrection, which was disseminated throughout the Americas.[92] Events in Saint-Domingue also brought with them other dislocations, which impacted on the lives of Americans, both black and white. Between 1791 and 1794, thousands of French émigrés left the island, among them some 3,000 who took passage for Philadelphia.[93] Most of these refugees were white, but some planters also brought with them as many slaves as they could control. Gary Nash estimates that of the 3,000 French émigrés who settled in Philadelphia during this period, over 25 per cent (848) were black. Though the vast majority of black Saint-Dominguans were only teenagers when they arrived in the USA, their presence in the city, together with fresh reports of slave rebellion throughout the Caribbean, undoubtedly helped to politicise Philadelphia blacks. Perhaps the best example of this growing black assertiveness was the decision of a group of them in September 1793 to draft a letter to the 'French National Convention', thanking its members for 'breaking our chains' with 'the immortal Decree [of August 1793] wiping out all traces of slavery in the French colonies'.[94]

The emergence of black activists in the USA mirrored developments on the other side of the Atlantic. To judge from newspaper reports, a group of twenty or more blacks (Sons of Africa) were active in and around London during the late eighteenth century. Meanwhile, in Paris the city's free black community organised its own Society of American Colonists, which sought 'to use the Revolution to rid the colonies of the disabilities which free nonwhites suffered, and which had increased in intensity since the 1770s'.[95] Though these different groups were not in contact with each other, they were almost certainly

---

[92] Scott, 'The Common Wind', pp. 203–6.

[93] French émigrés also sought refuge in other American cities, among them Norfolk, Charleston and Baltimore. See Scott, 'The Common Wind', pp. 274–7.

[94] Gary B. Nash, 'Reverberations of Haiti in the American North: Black Saint Dominguans in Philadelphia', *Pennsylvania History*, 65 (5) (1998): 44–73; Scott, 'The Common Wind', p. 282 (quotation). Unbeknown to Philadelphia blacks, the decree in question had actually been issued by the French commissioners in Saint-Domingue rather than by the National Convention. See Chapter 4.

[95] Oldfield, *Popular Politics*, p. 126; Scott, 'The Common Wind' (quotation), p. 161.

aware of each other's existence. Here again, newspapers were import-
ant channels of communication. In October 1788, for instance, the
Philadelphia *Freeman's Journal* reprinted from the London *Morning
Chronicle* three letters from a group of six blacks, among them Quobna
Ottobah Cugoano and Olaudah Equiano, thanking Sir William Dolben,
William Pitt, and Charles James Fox, respectively, for their support of
Dolben's Slave Limitation Bill. Describing themselves as 'persons of
colour, happily released from the common calamity', the group identified themselves with those 'who will not (as we understand) longer
suffer the rights of humanity to be confounded with ordinary commod-
ities, and passed from hand to hand, as an article of trade', a plea that
thanks to the *Freeman's Journal* echoed across the Atlantic.[96] Similarly,
a year later the *Providence Gazette* printed what purported to be 'A
Letter of a Negro', originally published in Manchester, that attacked
both the damaging effects of slavery on black 'character' and the hypocrisy of those whites who condemned blacks for resisting 'tyranny'.[97]
In this way, blacks on both sides of the Atlantic were made aware of
each other's concerns and anxieties, just as they were made aware of
rising black consciousness.

Equally significant was the emergence of influential black 'voices',
among them those of Cugoano and Equiano. In his *Thoughts and
Sentiments on the Evil of Slavery*, originally published in 1787, Cugoano
produced what Vincent Carretta has described as the 'most overt and
extended challenge to slavery ever made by an English-speaking person of African descent'.[98] A second and shorter version of the book
was published in 1791, and, significantly, a French edition appeared
in 1788.[99] Equiano's *Interesting Narrative* was, if anything, more influential still. Originally published in 1789, the autobiography went
through nine British editions, including editions printed in Dublin and
Edinburgh, in little more than five years, making it probably 'one of the
best-selling new books of that half decade'.[100] During the same period,
the *Interesting Narrative* was also translated into Dutch (1790), German

---

[96] *Freeman's Journal*, 8 October 1788.
[97] *Providence Gazette and Country Journal*, 7 March 1789. Again, the source for this letter was probably James Pemberton. See Pemberton Papers, 49/85.
[98] Quobna Ottobah Cugoano, *Thoughts and Sentiments on the Evil of Slavery*, ed. Vincent
Carretta (1787; rpt. London: Penguin Books, 1999), p. i. The reference to the French
translation can be found on p. xxxii.
[99] Seeber, *Anti-Slavery Opinion in France*, p. 198.
[100] James Green, 'The Publishing History of Olaudah Equiano's *Interesting Narrative*',
Slavery and Abolition, 16 (3) (1995): 362–75, at p. 363.

(1792) and Russian (1794), and an American edition of perhaps 1,000 copies appeared in 1791.[101] In France, meanwhile, Julien Raimond, an influential free man of colour, produced a series of works dealing with the specific political claims of free non-whites in the French colonies, among them his *Observations sur l'origine et les progrès du préjugé des colons blancs contre les hommes de couleur* (1791).[102] Finally, in America, two black ministers, Richard Allen, a Methodist, and Absalom Jones, an Episcopalian, co-authored *A Narrative of the Proceedings of the Black People, During the Late Awful Calamity in Philadelphia, in the Year 1793* (1794), which contained 'an explicit attack on slavery, the first penned by black Americans after the ratification of the Constitution'.[103] Taken together, these works signalled the emergence of a 'Black Atlantic', a wider community of writers and activists that served as a counterpoint to slave insurrection in the Caribbean.

In these different ways, abolitionist propaganda spilled out across the Atlantic world, from east to west and from west to east. If a lot of this work was done by printed texts, letters and oral communication also helped to extend debates about slavery and the slave trade; in fact, each fed off the other and formed part of the same process of cultural transmission. What we are dealing with here, in other words, is a dense communication network involving a variety of media and genres. Of course, there was a practical dimension to all of this activity. As Brissot explained to the members of the Société des Amis des Noirs, 'mutual correspondence' was beneficial for a number of reasons. Not only did it extend knowledge but it also saved time and effort.[104] Yet the real significance of the international abolitionist network (that is, viewed as a communication network) was its role in shaping public opinion. Admittedly, this was never a one-way process; as it turned out, many people strongly opposed abolitionist ideas and principles. Nevertheless, the flow of information back and forth across the Atlantic – and, just as important, the rapid assimilation of a lot of this information – helped to create a wider constituency for abolition, enabling it to transcend

---

[101] Green, 'Publishing History', pp. 371, 373–4.

[102] Julien Raimond, *Observations sur l'origine et les progrès du préjugé des colons blancs contre les hommes de couleur* (Paris: Belin, Desenne & Bailly, 1791). Two years previously Raimond had published *Observations adressée a l'Assemblée Nationale par un député des colons américains* (Paris, 1789).

[103] Absalom Jones and Richard Allen, *A Narrative of the Proceedings of the Black People, During the Late Awful Calamity in Philadelphia, in the Year 1793: and a Refutation of Some Censures Thrown Upon Them in Some Late Publications* (Philadelphia, Pa.: William W. Woodward, 1794): Nash, 'Reverberations of Haiti', p. 64.

[104] Brissot, *A Discourse, Upon the Necessity*, p. 154.

national boundaries. The effort that activists put into developing and sustaining these exchanges speaks for itself. Energetic and resourceful, they succeeded in bridging the gap between the national and the international, in the process nurturing sympathetic connections that, for the moment at least, gave abolition an urgent moral force.

3   Strategies

Creating what in effect was an information highway turned out to be relatively straightforward. More difficult was deciding how best to put pressure on governments to take action against slavery, what to aim for and what not. Here, for the most part, activists were guided by their sense of what was possible, whether that meant 'abolition' or 'emancipation', 'gradualism' or 'immediatism'. Priorities could also change to fit local circumstances, as was the case in France where, as we shall see, the impact of the French Revolution, particularly in the Caribbean, led members of the Société des Amis des Noirs to take up the issue of free coloured rights, eventually privileging it over their attempts to abolish the slave trade. National and imperial agendas, in other words, pressed heavily on these debates. Yet, at the same time, figures such as Brissot, Sharp and Pemberton clearly saw themselves as part of a wider Atlantic community. Despite the distances between them, they instinctively reached out to each other, not simply for ideas and information but also for support and encouragement. In the same way, activists on both sides of the Atlantic spent a lot of time monitoring each other's progress, conscious that what happened in one country, whether it was Britain, France or America, had an important bearing on what happened in another. As a result, these different groups achieved a high level of interdependence, evident, above all, in the international struggle against the slave trade.

Significantly, activists in Britain, France and America started from very different positions, some more advanced than others. The pioneers, certainly in the early years, were the Americans. Here, the related questions of slavery and the slave trade had been debated intensively since at least the 1760s, largely thanks to figures such as Anthony Benezet who led the fight to rid the Society of Friends of slaveholding or, indeed, any connection with slavery.[1] Not content with this, by the early 1770s Benezet was calling for the abolition of slavery and the slave trade

---

[1] See Brown, *Moral Capital*, pp. 394–402.

throughout the British Empire. It was these ambitions that led him to make contact with Granville Sharp, whose involvement in the Somerset case of 1772 had already provoked widespread discussion about the meaning and limits of black freedom 'from one end of the Continental colonies to the other'.[2] Up to this point, Benezet's preferred strategy had been to organise petitions in the colonies urging Parliament to suspend slave imports. Under Sharp's influence, however, Benezet came to see that individual colonial assemblies might have the authority to take action against the slave trade without applying for parliamentary relief. Indeed, Sharp's clear advice was that the colonies should direct their petitions to the king, George III, thereby signalling not only their loyalty but also their independence of both Houses of Parliament.[3]

For obvious reasons, the American Revolution (1775–83) intensified these debates about the future of slavery, particularly in a nation vociferously committed to the natural rights of mankind. The contradictions inherent in this position eventually led some states to take action against the slave trade. Between 1774 and 1783, no fewer than seven states banned the importation of slaves, either permanently or temporarily.[4] Moreover, several states, including Vermont, Massachusetts and Pennsylvania, went further by abolishing slavery itself, a movement that accelerated even more rapidly after 1783.[5] Most states, however, stopped short of immediate emancipation, favouring gradual emancipation laws that in freeing newborn children tied them to terms of service, often until they were into their twenties. In economic terms, gradualism, as it was sometimes called, offered owners obvious benefits, but, at the same time, it also reflected a widespread belief that blacks (ex-slaves) needed to be prepared for freedom.[6] Very few people, it seemed, believed in the wisdom or utility of immediate emancipation. In short, the American Revolution greatly expanded the realm of black freedom, at the same time popularising 'among blacks as well as whites [a] belief in individual freedom and inalienable natural rights'.[7] Ironically, too, the British offered patriotic blacks their freedom, eventually evacuating tens of thousands of fugitives from the Southern states, many of whom ended up in Nova Scotia, Canada, the Bahamas and, later, Sierra Leone.[8]

[2] Drescher, *Abolition*, pp. 99–107.
[3] Drescher, *Abolition*, pp. 107–8.
[4] W. E. B. Du Bois, *The Suppression of the African Slave-Trade to the United States of America, 1638–1870* (1896; rpt. New York: Library of America, 1986), pp. 224–9.
[5] Davis, *Inhuman Bondage*, p. 152; Leon F. Litwack, *North of Slavery: The Negro in the Free States, 1790–1860* (University of Chicago Press, 1961), p. 3.
[6] Davis, *Inhuman Bondage*, pp. 152–3.
[7] Davis, *Inhuman Bondage*, p. 156.
[8] Davis, *Inhuman Bondage*, pp. 149–52; Maya Jasanoff, *Liberty's Exiles: The Loss of America and the Remaking of the British Empire* (London: HarperCollins, 2011).

By the time groups such as the PAS and the NYMS were organised, therefore, abolition – at least in legislative terms – was already well advanced in the USA, certainly when compared to Britain and France. As a result, from the outset American activism was multifaceted and concerned as much with securing the legislative gains of the 1770s and 1780s as with winning new freedoms, important though these freedoms were. Most societies, for example, devoted a lot of their time and energy to so-called freedom suits, that is, legal cases involving blacks who had been wrongfully kidnapped or re-enslaved, slaveholders who ignored gradual emancipation laws or who broke indenture agreements, migrants caught up in the domestic and international slave trade and, after 1793, black émigrés from Saint-Domingue whose masters refused to emancipate them or tried to sell them into slavery.[9] In short, these societies provided blacks with what Richard S. Newman describes as 'a legal aid system'.[10] The PAS dealt with literally hundreds of cases of this kind, probably more than any other American society, but all of them, from Rhode Island to Virginia, had large caseloads of freedom suits, many of which dragged on for years.[11] Robert Pleasants reported in 1791 that the Virginia society then had under its care 'several suits depending in different courts, wherein the freedom of several hundred are concerned'.[12] This was costly and potentially dangerous work, particularly in the South, and yet Pleasants and his colleagues remained determined, he said, 'to aid and assist' all those who might appear to them to have a legal right to their liberty.[13]

Besides freedom suits, American activists also devoted a lot of time to the condition of free blacks, whose moral and religious progress became an important test of their faith in black capabilities. In the years immediately following the American Revolution, thousands of blacks, many of them fugitives, migrated to Northern cities. To take one example, the black population of New York trebled between 1790 and 1810, while that of Philadelphia doubled during the 1780s and more than

---

[9] For an excellent discussion of these various activities, see Newman, *The Transformation of American Abolitionism*, pp. 60–85. See also Whitman, *Challenging Slavery in the Chesapeake*, pp. 80–2.
[10] Newman, *The Transformation of American Abolitionism*, p. 62.
[11] Newman, *The Transformation of American Abolitionism*, p. 63. For further details, see NYMS Papers, Standing Committee Minutes, 1791–1807, vol. VII, New-York Historical Society, New York; PAS Minutes, 1787–1824; Robert Pleasants Letterbook, 1754–97.
[12] Robert Pleasants to Robert Carter, 8 October 1791, Robert Pleasants Letterbook, 1754–1797.
[13] Pleasants to Carter, 8 October 1791.

tripled – from about 2,000 to more than 6,500 – over the next two decades.[14] The transition from slavery to freedom brought other tensions
besides overcrowding, among them fears (often exaggerated) about
black crime, drunkenness, indecency and general unruliness.[15] In
response, American activists sought to temper black 'boisterousness' by
instilling in their fellow citizens the middle-class virtues of hard work,
sobriety and settled family life. Both the PAS and the NYMS periodically issued addresses to free blacks reminding them of their responsibilities in this regard and, on occasion, met with black leaders and
visited black homes. In October 1789, for instance, the PAS adopted
an ambitious plan 'for improving the condition of Free-Blacks' that
involved the creation of four subcommittees, including a 'committee of
inspection', whose task it was to 'superintend the morals, general conduct, and ordinary situation of Free-Blacks, and afford them advice and
instruction, protection from wrongs, and other friendly offices', and a
'committee of employ', which, as its name implies, was designed to find
employment for those men and women who were able to work.[16]

In a related move, the 1789 plan also set up a 'committee of education'. American activists were in no doubt about the value of black
education – it was simply a case of providing the right sort of opportunities. While many of the smaller American societies struggled
with this problem and were only able to address it on an ad-hoc basis,
groups such as the PAS and the NYMS were able to come up with
more permanent or semi-permanent solutions. In the case of the PAS,
the 1789 initiative rapidly gained momentum, so much so that in May
1793 James Pemberton was able to report that 'the schools heretofore
held in the winter of evenings and in the summer on first-days chiefly
for grown persons are kept up and have been not only beneficial to
many of those who attend them in point of school learning but also
in respect of morals and conduct'.[17] There were similar initiatives in
New York. As early as 1787, the NYMS set up the African Free School

---

[14] Shane White, *Stories of Freedom in Black New York* (Cambridge, Mass.: Harvard
University Press, 2002), p. 29; Nash, 'Reverberations of Haiti', p. 62.
[15] See White, *Stories of Freedom in Black New York*, pp. 38–67.
[16] PAS Minutes, 5 October 1789, 19 October 1789; *Freeman's Journal*, 25 November
1789.
[17] PAS to SEAST, 21 May 1793, PAS Correspondence, microfilm edition Reel 11. In the
same letter, Pemberton reported that the society had also lately purchased 'a house
and lot of ground and [engaged] a proper teacher to instruct the black children', but
in fact it was not until 1798/9 that a school building was finally erected. See *Minutes of
the Proceedings of the Fifth Convention of Delegates from the Abolition Societies Established
in Different Parts of the United States, Assembled at Philadelphia on the First Day of June,
One Thousand Seven Hundred and Ninety-Eight, and Continued, by Adjournments, Until*

where children of both sexes were taught reading, writing and arithmetic.[18] Provision elsewhere was patchy at best, but, as the proceedings of the American Convention for Promoting the Abolition of Slavery attest, education would remain a vital concern of American activists, not least because in their minds there was a clear link between education and 'virtuous habits'.[19]

Nevertheless, it would be misleading to see these societies merely as relief organisations. Simultaneously, they fought to protect rights and, where possible, to extend them – although, here again, many of these activities had a specific, domestic context. Activists in Pennsylvania, for instance, worked tirelessly to defend the state's gradual abolition act from assault, petitioning the state legislature against possible infringements by French émigrés (1793) and, ironically, members of the US Congress.[20] Starting from a very different base, activists in Virginia petitioned the Virginia Assembly in 1791 and again in 1797 to adopt a gradual abolition law, and there were similar campaigns in Maryland and New Jersey. As Newman notes, most of these petitions were carefully worded and designed, above all, 'to persuade subtly, not to demand dogmatically'.[21] Similarly, most American societies eschewed mass petitioning, preferring instead to appeal to state legislatures in their own right, that is, as independent and, in some cases, legally incorporated bodies. And yet, some of these petitions did bear a popular stamp. Robert Pleasants reported in May 1797 that the Virginia petition had been signed by 'about 500 people, divers of whom are very respectable slaveholders'.[22] Moreover, it is clear that in Virginia, at least, petitions were circulated or left open for signatures. Either way, many more people signed the 1797 petition than were ever paid-up members of the Virginia society.[23]

These different activities gave American abolitionism its own distinctive character, a character that for obvious reasons set it apart from

the Sixth Day of the Same Month, Inclusive (Philadelphia, Pa.: Zachariah Poulson, Junoir, 1798), p. 10.

[18] For the history of the African Free School, see Minutes of the Proceedings of the Eighth Convention of Delegates from the Abolition Societies Established in Different Parts of the United States, Assembled at Philadelphia, on the Tenth Day of January, One Thousand Eight Hundred and Three, and Continued, by Adjournments, Until the Fourteenth Day of the Same Month, Inclusive (Philadelphia, Pa.: Zachariah Poulson, Junior 1803), pp. 6–7.

[19] Minutes of the Proceedings of the Eighth Convention of Delegates, pp. 6–7.

[20] Newman, The Transformation of American Abolitionism, pp. 45–6.

[21] Newman, The Transformation of American Abolitionism, p. 39.

[22] Robert Pleasants to St. George Tucker, 30 May 1797, Robert Pleasants Letterbook, 1754–97.

[23] Something similar seems to have gone on in New Jersey. See Minutes of the New Jersey Abolition Society, 7 September 1795 and 4 September 1797.

abolitionism in Britain and France. But, at the same time, there were common interests that bound together activists on both sides of the Atlantic. One of these was the slave trade. While it is true that American states had already made progress in suppressing if not abolishing the slave trade, the purpose of a lot of the legislation passed in the 1770s and 1780s had been to ban the importation of slaves, whether by land or sea, rather than to criminalise involvement in the Atlantic slave trade. Two states, moreover, South Carolina and Delaware, had agreed only to ban imports temporarily.[24] From the late 1780s, therefore, American activists sought to close these loopholes, which in practice meant lobbying state legislatures to pass new, more comprehensive laws designed to 'prohibit' the slave trade *tout court*. At the same time, they hoped to put pressure on the Federal Government to rescind the decision of the Constitutional Convention of 1787 to leave the slave trade intact until 1808. How this proposal had come to be adopted, first at Philadelphia and later by the state ratifying conventions, bewildered many British activists. 'After all their repeated respect to the natural and unalienable rights of mankind', George Dillwyn wrote to John Pemberton in January 1788, 'how can such a provision be considered otherwise, than as a designed sanction to every crime that trade involves.'[25] Weakly, American activists tried to respond, but privately they accepted the inescapable logic of these arguments, as well as the need to do something about them. National pride and honour demanded nothing less.

Between 1788 and 1792, American activists waged a concerted campaign against US participation in the slave trade that operated on a number of different levels. One of these involved lobbying state legislatures. A key part of this strategy was the distribution of books and pamphlets, many of them British texts which were assiduously circulated by groups such as the PAS. As we have seen, copies of these books, including Clarkson's essays, were sent to state governors and legislators; others were serialised by newspapers, usually at the instigation of local activists.[26] The size and scale of this campaign was impressive. American activists are sometimes criticised for being conservative, deferential and elitist – and this was certainly true when it came to things such as radical petitioning tactics – but they proved remarkably astute in building a constituency for abolition, both inside and outside state legislatures.[27] Indeed, as even a cursory glance at many local newspapers suggests, it

---

[24] For details, see Du Bois, *The Suppression of the African Slave-Trade*, pp. 48–9, 57, 223–33.
[25] George Dillwyn to John Pemberton, 2 January 1788, Pemberton Papers, 49/45.
[26] See Chapter 2.
[27] See Newman, *The Transformation of American Abolitionism*, pp. 26–8, 31, 39, 44–9.

would have been difficult to ignore abolition between 1788 and 1790, so pervasive was the press coverage, particularly in the New England and Middle Atlantic states. The fact that this campaign was led, by and large, by British books was also significant. Pointedly, American activists threw down a challenge to state legislatures by suggesting, mistakenly or not, that the British were poised to take a lead in what was now clearly a flourishing international movement. Comparisons were inevitable. As a correspondent in the *Providence Gazette* put it, citing the number of prominent women who were members of the Société des Amis des Noirs, 'if gentlemen of France learnt the principles of liberty in America, let the ladies of this country look up to those of France – they have given an example'.[28] 'Blush, O Americans', echoed a correspondent in the *New-Haven Gazette*, 'to be outdone by Britain in humanity.'[29]

The momentum generated by American activists seems to have paid off. Between 1788 and 1790, six states passed revised slave-trade laws that not only banned the importation of slaves but also – in most cases – prohibited involvement in the 'nefarious traffic'. The Massachusetts Act of 1788, for instance, made it a crime for any citizen of the state, either as master, factor, supercargo, owner or hirer, 'to buy, sell, or receive on board his or their vessel, with intent to be imported or transported, any of the inhabitants of any state or kingdom, in that part of the world called Africa, as slaves, or as servants for term of years'.[30] Similarly, the Delaware Act of 1789 set down a penalty of £500 for anyone who fitted out, equipped, manned or otherwise prepared any ship or vessel 'for the purpose of carrying on a trade or traffic in slaves, to, from, or between Europe, Asia, Africa or America'.[31] Activists such as James Pemberton were in no doubt that British influence – or, to be more precise, British testimony – had helped to secure these legislative reforms. In turn, British activists were able to use America's example as a stick to beat their own legislators, urging them to follow suit. Put a different way, there was an obvious synergy between these two campaigns, just as there was between the campaigns in France and in the USA; in effect, each relied on the other, a point reinforced by the constant stream of correspondence that spilled out across the Atlantic world.

American activists had to come to terms with one disappointment, however, and that concerned the Federal Government and the slave

---

[28] *Providence Gazette and Country Journal*, 13 March 1790.
[29] *New-Haven Gazette, and the Connecticut Magazine*, 15 May 1788.
[30] Du Bois, *The Suppression of the African Slave-Trade*, p. 235.
[31] Du Bois, *The Suppression of the African Slave-Trade*, pp. 238–9.

trade. When the first US Congress met in New York in 1790, the PAS took this opportunity to present a petition against the slave trade (a second petition, this time from Quakers in New York, Pennsylvania and Virginia, was also presented at the same session). Predictably, the Pennsylvania society based its protest on humanitarian and religious grounds, urging Congress to ban the slave trade outright. Not content with that, the petition also asked the Federal Government 'to ignore its constitutional limitation by "promoting the abolition of slavery" throughout America'.[32] Why the PAS chose to take this stance, effectively linking the slave trade to the broader question of domestic slavery, is unclear. But there is little doubt that the manoeuvre lost it vital support. Quick to defend their interests, Southern Congressmen vigorously opposed the proposal, arguing that those who were not interested ought not to interfere.[33] Eventually, after intense debate, the House of Representatives affirmed that it could neither ban the slave trade, at least not before 1808, nor take any action effecting the emancipation of slaves. The Constitution, in other words, meant exactly what it said.[34] Try as they might to put on a brave face, pointing to the action already taken by the individual states against the slave trade, the decision came as a grave disappointment to American activists, who had wanted the Federal Government to put its mark on abolition, not least as a way of reaffirming its commitment to the revolutionary principles that lay at the heart of the country's struggle with the British.

After 1790, American activists were forced to change tack, focusing their efforts at the federal level on alleviating or regulating the slave trade, a plan of action that British activists or, at least, the London Committee of the SEAST, explicitly rejected.[35] Nevertheless, both groups cooperated over efforts to curb the foreign slave trade, which, by common consent, the US Congress did have power to do something about. American activists took a keen interest in this issue, orchestrating a nationwide petition campaign, involving the societies in New York, Pennsylvania, Virginia, Rhode Island, Connecticut and Maryland, which would eventually bear fruit in the Foreign Slave Trade Act of 1794.[36] The news, when it came, gave renewed impetus to British activists, who 'had

---

[32] Newman, *The Transformation of American Abolitionism*, p. 48.
[33] *Freeman's Journal*, 8 March 1790.
[34] Oldfield, *Popular Politics*, p. 53.
[35] Newman, *The Transformation of American Abolitionism*, p. 49.
[36] These petitions, which were drafted between December 1790 and November 1791, were later collected together and published as a separate volume. See *Memorials Presented to the Congress of the United States of America by the Different Societies Instituted for Promoting the Abolition of Slavery, Etc. in the States of Rhode-Island, Connecticut,*

been waiting with some anxiety, having had information that attempts would be made towards that object'.[37] As Granville Sharp explained to James Pemberton, not least of the benefits was that the American legislation would remove an argument frequently raised by their opponents, namely 'that if England were to discontinue the traffic in slaves, America in particular would engage in those branches of it which the former would relinquish'.[38] Yet, once again, events conspired against them. A Foreign Slave Bill passed the House of Commons in 1794 but was put off by the Lords who, at the time, were still hearing evidence for and against the slave trade. And there the matter rested until 1806 when the British Parliament finally passed a Foreign Slave Trade Act, a good twelve years after the Americans.[39]

The slave trade would continue to provide a point of mutual interest up to 1807/8 and beyond. Moreover, these synergies provided a stimulus to others, which were to prove equally important. For one thing, British activists took a close interest in American efforts to educate free blacks, some of them (Samuel Hoare and David Barclay, for example) even sending the PAS gifts of money.[40] French activists, too, gave prominence to black education, seeing it as yet further evidence of a universal belief in black capabilities.[41] Africa was another area where there seemed to be the potential for mutual cooperation, although, as James Pemberton was quick to point out, 'the means of support being more easily attained in America than in Europe, we rather suppose the [Sierra Leone] settlement must derive its principal supply from you'.[42] Nevertheless, Pemberton and his colleagues eagerly sought news about Sierra Leone, just as they came to recognise its strategic importance, not least in terms of suppressing the Atlantic slave trade.[43] While they had their own priorities, therefore, chief among them the abolition of slavery, American activists were never content to go it alone. On the

---

New-York, Pennsylvania, Maryland, and Virginia. Published by Order of the 'Pennsylvania Society for Promoting the Abolition of Slavery, and the Relief of Free Negroes Unlawfully Held in Bondage, and for Improving the Condition of the African Race' (Philadelphia, Pa.: Francis Bailey, 1792).

[37] SEAST to PAS, 10 July 1794, PAS Correspondence, microfilm edition, Reel 11.

[38] SEAST to PAS, 10 July 1794.

[39] Roger Anstey, *The Atlantic Slave Trade and British Abolition, 1760–1810* (London: Macmillan, 1975), p. 279.

[40] SEAST to PAS, 20 February 1790 and 20 July 1790 PAS Correspondence, microfilm edition, Reel 11; PAS Minutes, 5 July 1790; William Dillwyn to James Pemberton, 9 July 1789, Pemberton Papers, 52/129.

[41] *Le Patriote Français*, 14 January 1790.

[42] PAS to SEAST, 24 June 1789, PAS Correspondence, microfilm edition, Reel 11.

[43] PAS Minutes, 6 July 1795 and 6 August 1795; Minutes of the New Jersey Abolition Society, 7 September 1795 and 5 September 1796.

contrary, they relied heavily on their counterparts in Britain and France. More than that, and James Pemberton's correspondence is again significant here, they obviously saw themselves as leaders in this international movement, as a kind of advance guard whose peculiar role it was to provide others with support, encouragement and – perhaps most important of all – inspiration.

Initially at least, many British activists seem to have been prepared to follow America's lead. As late as February 1787, James Phillips was pressing James Pemberton for evidence supporting the benefits of free labour over slavery, keen, as he put it, to prove that 'slaveholding' was 'not only wicked but impolitic'.[44] But attacking slavery head-on carried with it enormous risks, particularly given the strength of the West India lobby. As a result – and following discussions with William Wilberforce – the London Committee of the SEAST chose to concentrate its early campaigning efforts on ending British involvement in the transatlantic slave trade, convinced that such a plan of action would ultimately lead to the abolition of British colonial slavery, preferably through a process of gradual emancipation. To avoid any confusion, Phillips assured James Pemberton in July 1787 that

the present state of the country and its commerce, colonies and revenue is likely to render any attempt to effect the absolute destruction of the system of slavery, which has been so long established, hopeless and therefore our views are yet extended no farther than to put a stop to [the] exportation of Negroes from Africa.[45]

Over the years, this strategy – attacking slavery through the slave trade – would become a British orthodoxy. The problem was that it was open to misinterpretation, deliberate or otherwise. As Granville Sharp readily conceded, British activists were frequently forced to defend themselves against the charge that their 'endeavours went not only to abolition but emancipation; an impression of little consequence to us individually considered, but big with mischief to the cause in which we are engaged'.[46] Even many American activists were initially confused by the distinction the SEAST drew between 'abolition' and 'emancipation'. Keen to set the record straight, in July 1788 Sharp politely informed the members of the PAS that 'emancipation' was 'entirely beyond the business of our Society, the sole purpose of whose institution is the abolition

---

[44] James Phillips to James Pemberton, 17 February 1787, Pemberton Papers, 47/139–40. See also James Pemberton to John Pemberton, 29 March 1787, Pemberton Papers, 47/188.

[45] James Phillips to James Pemberton, 21 July 1787, Pemberton Papers, 48/110.

[46] SEAST to PAS, 30 July 1788, PAS Minutes (minutes of meeting of 6 October 1788).

of the African slave trade'.[47] In short, from the outset there were clear differences between the British and American campaigns, not least in terms of objectives. Whereas groups such as the PAS and the NYMS saw slavery as a domestic problem that demanded their closest attention, the SEAST regarded it as a colonial question that, in Sharp's words, could 'only be effected by such gradual and temporal means, as the different colonial Assemblies may adopt'.[48]

The other crucial difference concerned tactics and organisation. As Newman points out, American activists tended to adopt a conservative approach, characterised by a particular mode of 'dispassionate reform'.[49] By contrast, British activists were much less circumspect. Starting from a very different base, they used a variety of different techniques – cheap disposable literature, subscription lists, advertising and inertia selling – to create a constituency for abolition. The result was two hugely successful petition campaigns, the first in 1788 when over 100 petitions dealing with the slave trade were presented to the House of Commons, the second in 1792 when a further 519 petitions were tabled for discussion, 'the largest number ever submitted to the House on a single subject or in a single session'.[50] Significantly, these were not 'official' petitions, in the sense that they were presented by or on behalf of the SEAST or any one of the regional committees; rather, they were what we would now describe as mass petitions. In 1792, for instance, 3,865 people signed the Edinburgh petition 'on the spot at different tables, all with the most admirable decorum'.[51] The final figure was 10,885, exceeded only by the 15,000 to 20,000 reported to have signed the Manchester petition. In all, 400,000 people may have put their names to petitions in 1792, representing about 13 per cent of the adult male population of England, Scotland and Wales (assuming, of course, that most petitioners were males over the age of fifteen).[52] Nothing like this ever happened in the USA, certainly not before the 1830s. Put another way, British activists were responsible for a form of popular politics that was quite alien to the experience of groups such as the PAS.

British abolitionism, however, was never a monolithic structure. While many, including Wilberforce, Clarkson and Sharp, favoured immediate abolition of the slave trade, others favoured a more moderate

---

[47] SEAST to PAS, 30 July 1788.
[48] SEAST to PAS, 30 July 1788.
[49] Newman, *The Transformation of American Abolitionism*, p. 4.
[50] Oldfield, *Popular Politics*, pp. 45–50, 58–61; Drescher, *Capitalism and Antislavery*, p. 80 (quotation).
[51] Oldfield, *Popular Politics*, p. 114.
[52] Oldfield, *Popular Politics*, pp. 113–14.

approach. John Barton, a founding member of the SEAST, confessed in March 1788 that he saw 'very plainly that many mischiefs would attend the *immediate* abolition of the Slave Trade, which need not be feared if that abolition took place *gradually*; and am further convinced that if it takes place at all, the latter and not the former, will be the mode adopted'.[53] Others, such as Barton's friend William Roscoe proposed not only a sliding scale of duties on slave imports, leading to a total ban after January 1800, but also the imposition of slaves-per-ton ratios on all slave ships clearing British ports.[54] In the same way, many of the petitions presented to the House of Commons in 1788 called for regulation of the slave trade. Wary of compromising their principles, however, Wilberforce and the London Committee stood firm, thereby alienating Barton, who later resigned over the issue. But if some argued that regulation assumed approbation of the slave trade, others recognised that agitation of the question had 'a tendency to strengthen the cause of humanity'.[55] When Sir William Dolben introduced his Slave Limitation (or Middle Passage) Bill in the House of Commons in May 1788, Granville Sharp noted that 'even the interested evidence, which was brought against the measure, tended to confirm the truth of those cruelties which this bill is designed to obviate'.[56]

Regulation provided many legislators with an easy and convenient way of avoiding the 'general question' of the slave trade. It came as no surprise, therefore, that while both Houses approved Dolben's Bill, Pitt's motion for an early end to the slave trade was deferred until the next session.[57] Some sense of the choices facing British activists, and the concerns that beset them, is revealed in James Phillips' correspondence with James Pemberton. Phillips' assessment of the situation in March 1789 was that the House of Commons would vote for 'immediate and absolute' abolition of the slave trade. Yet he was forced to admit that some members of the SEAST, as opposed to its guiding London Committee, feared that 'by aiming at so much we shall obtain nothing and wish the proposition may be a *gradual* abolition'.[58] Phillips also conceded that he had grave doubts about the Lords, 'that House

[53] John Barton to William Roscoe, 6 March 1788, William Roscoe Papers, 920 ROS/243, Liverpool Record Office, Liverpool.
[54] Roscoe's ideas on regulation of the slave trade are outlined in his *General View of the African Slave-Trade, Demonstrating Its Injustice and Impolicy: With Hints Towards a Bill for Its Abolition* (London: R. Faulder, 1788). Clarkson published a response in his *Essay on the Comparative Efficiency of Regulation or Abolition, As Applied to the Slave Trade* (London: James Phillips, 1789).
[55] William Dillwyn to James Pemberton, 27 June 1788, Pemberton Papers, 50/86.
[56] SEAST to PAS, 30 July 1788, PAS Minutes (minutes of meeting of 6 October 1788).
[57] Oldfield, *Popular Politics*, pp. 50–1.
[58] James Phillips to James Pemberton, 10 March 1789, Pemberton Papers, 52/6.

being in almost all cases less favourable to questions of general liberty and justice than the Commons'.[59] In short, Wilberforce and the
London Committee were playing for high stakes. Equally revealing is
the admission that 'gradualism' (that is, the position favoured by figures such as Roscoe) still pressed heavily on these debates. Whether a
gradual abolition Bill would have won favour in 1789 is open to question. What is more interesting is that the option was openly canvassed
in abolitionist circles, even though it was firmly rejected by the London
Committee.[60]

These were not the only challenges facing British activists. As
Srividhya Swaminathan has recently argued, the slave-trade debates
of the late 1780s were dynamic and evolving.[61] Accordingly, activists
had to be constantly alert to the arguments put forward by their opponents. William Dillwyn noted in March 1788 that the pro-slavery lobby
had abandoned its efforts to justify the slave trade 'on the principles of
justice and morality', shifting its attention to the value of the trade to
Britain's national interests.[62] It was a 'melancholy reflection', he went
on, 'that abolition should [now] appear to depend on adducing incontrovertible proof that the nation will *lose nothing* by adopting the measure'.[63] This question of the 'impolicy' of the slave trade nagged at many
British activists. In November 1789, for instance, the *Pennsylvania
Mercury* reprinted a letter from 'Leicestrensis' to the SEAST, warning it against moving the debate away from religion and morality to
questions of political expediency. To his mind, this was merely a diver-
sion. 'Every man knows the slave trade is criminal', he pointed out,
'but not every one perceives that it is impolitic.'[64] Put a different way,
activists were in danger of being drawn into a debate they could not
possibly win. 'Why should the friends of humanity be ashamed of that
religion, which teaches the most extensive and refined compassion?'
'Leicestrensis' wanted to know. 'Why should [they] descend to the level
of abjects, who are stickling for a practice, which disclaims all sacred
obligation, and defies the bolts of heaven!'[65]

---

[59] Phillips to Pemberton, 10 March 1789.
[60] See SEAST to PAS, 28 February 1788, *Pennsylvania Packet*, 22 May 1788; SEAST to
PAS, 30 July 1788, PAS Minutes (minutes of meeting of 6 October 1788).
[61] Srividhya Swaminathan, *Debating the Slave Trade: Rhetoric of British National Identity,
1759–1815* (Farnham: Ashgate, 2009), pp. 5–7.
[62] William Dillwyn to James Pemberton, 23 March 1788, Pemberton Papers, 49/159.
[63] Dillwyn to Pemberton, 23 March 1788.
[64] *Pennsylvania Mercury and Universal Advertiser*, 25 November 1789. The original letter
was dated 20 April 1789 and probably copied from one of the London papers.
[65] *Pennsylvania Mercury and Universal Advertiser*, 25 November 1789.

But the truth was that activists could ill afford to ignore their adversaries or their arguments. By mid 1788 the SEAST was deeply embroiled in the impolicy issue. 'To this point, the endeavours of our Committee are now principally directed', Dillwyn reported, 'and many are with us and convinced that policy, no less than humanity, strongly suggests the necessity of suppressing the wicked commerce.'[66] New publications rolled off the presses, among them Clarkson's *Essay on the Impolicy of the Slave Trade* (1788), originally planned as an addendum to his *Essay on the Slavery and Commerce of the Human Species*. Sensitive to the charge that abolition of the slave trade might seriously put the nation at risk, British activists also showed an increasing interest in Africa. Clarkson's 'Africa box', containing examples of African produce (cotton, spices, gum rubber and different kinds of wood), became yet another propaganda tool, designed to convince sceptics that there was, after all, an alternative to the slave trade. The Sierra Leone experiment – the abortive expedition in 1787 and, later, the colonisation scheme managed by the government-sponsored Sierra Leone Company – was part of the same wider strategy.[67] In these different ways, activists sought to present themselves not only as patriots ('true Britons') but also as men fully attuned to the nation's commercial and imperial interests.

British activists also drew inspiration from the USA. Theirs was in many ways a reciprocal relationship. Just as activists on the other side of the Atlantic used British books and pamphlets to make the case against American slavery, so British activists used the American example to win over potential converts. In this sense, what happened in America did have an impact on debates in Britain, and vice versa. To take an example, in October 1787 the SEAST arranged for the *Morning Chronicle* to carry the memorial of the Pennsylvania society to the Convention of Delegates sitting in Philadelphia. This was followed in May 1788 by the report of the Pennsylvania Assembly relating to the slave trade and in July by details of the legislation passed against the slave trade by the states of Rhode Island and Massachusetts.[68] Undoubtedly, all of these items were chosen because they gave abolition an important

---

[66] William Dillwyn to James Pemberton, 23 March 1788.
[67] For Clarkson's 'Africa box', see Marcus Wood, 'Packaging Liberty and Marketing the Gift of Freedom: 1807 and the Legacy of Clarkson's Chest', in James Walvin, Melanie Unwin and Stephen Farrell, eds., *The British Slave Trade: Abolition, Parliament and People* (Edinburgh University Press, 2007), pp. 203–23. For Sierra Leone, see Simon Schama, *Rough Crossings: Britain, the Slaves and the American Revolution* (London: BBC Books, 2005); Drescher, *The Mighty Experiment*, pp. 88–105; Stephen J. Braidwood, *Black Poor and White Philanthropists: London's Blacks and the Foundation of the Sierra Leone Settlement, 1786–1791* (Liverpool University Press, 1994).
[68] SEAST Minutes, 2 October 1787, 20 May 1788 and 1 July 1788.

international dimension, setting it in a very different political context. Perhaps just as important, they also thrust Britons into a competitive humanitarian market that identified abolition with progress and a belief in benevolent Christianity. Recent events – principally the loss of the American colonies – gave these debates a highly partisan character. Here, in other words, was an opportunity for the nation to redeem itself and at the same time to assert its national superiority.

All of this activity was by way of a prelude to what activists hoped would be a Commons victory in 1789. For nearly a year the Privy Council had been looking into the slave trade, and, in the meantime, the SEAST had published countless books and pamphlets, among them the key speeches in the debates on Sir William Dolben's Slave Limitation Bill. They had also struck upon a novel propaganda tool in the shape of the plan and sections of the slave ship *Brookes*. First published in its enlarged or improved form in 1789, copies were sent 'to the Members of both Houses of Parliament & to such other persons as may be thought expedient by the Committee of Distribution', the intention being to lobby MPs before Wilberforce's motion came before the House of Commons on 11 May.[69] But far from being willing to act on the report of the Privy Council, or even to discuss Wilberforce's proposals for an early abolition of the slave trade, the Commons resolved to hear evidence at its own bar, a compromise measure that left activists playing a dangerous waiting game. Dillwyn was in no doubt that the West India lobby was behind these manoeuvres. Their aim, he believed, was to discourage the 'friends of humanity by additional trouble and expence', trusting that in the meantime 'the spirit of the nation in favour of abolition [would] gradually subside'.[70] Yet the members of the London Committee remained upbeat. 'Thou wilt have heard that the determination of the question is deferred to the next session', Phillips wrote to James Pemberton in July. 'We hope no public misfortune will then as it did last year happen to procrastinate the business – we have great hopes of succeeding. In the Commons we have no doubt of success.'[71]

Sadly, he was to prove mistaken. In the event, the hearings in the House of Commons dragged on throughout 1790 and would not conclude until February 1791. American activists monitored these events closely. By mid 1790 they had obviously concluded that the British movement was becalmed. Accordingly, they began to look to French activists to take a lead. In a revealing letter, James Pemberton confessed

[69] SEAST Minutes, 17 March 1789 and 21 April 1789.
[70] William Dillwyn to James Pemberton, 9 July 1789, Pemberton Papers, 52/129.
[71] James Phillips to James Pemberton, 20 July 1789, Pemberton Papers, 52/144.

to Brissot in August 1790 that 'it is on the benevolent exertions of your nation that we at present rely for the first decisive steps in Europe towards the Abolition of the Slave Trade'.[72] Pemberton returned to the same theme almost a year later. 'Although our hopes are sanguine as to the success of the cause [in Britain]', he wrote insistently, 'yet we shall be greatly disappointed if it does not make a still more rapid and decided progress in yours.'[73] Pemberton was reacting in part to Brissot's own optimistic accounts of the progress of French anti-slavery. But behind his comments there was also a conviction that the French Revolution had shifted the terms of the debate, offering activists an opportunity to press home their advantage. What Pemberton did not realise until much later was that his optimism was misplaced.

As we have seen, the Société des Amis des Noirs was created very much in the image of the SEAST. Mindful that the success of the movement at home depended on international support and cooperation, British activists did all they could to encourage the new society. They also worked hard to integrate it into the wider transatlantic movement. Writing to James Pemberton in February 1788, Granville Sharp made a point of drawing his attention to the Société des Amis des Noirs, adding that 'it may perhaps be in your power to assist our views of thus extending the sphere of action'.[74] As usual, Pemberton was quick to take the hint. By November, the Pennsylvania society was already in contact with Brissot and his colleagues, having sent them 'copies of our constitution and of the laws passed by the legislature of this state in favor of the Blacks and requesting their co-operation with us'.[75] Pemberton was no less assiduous in introducing the Société des Amis des Noirs to the other American societies, citing its appearance as further evidence of the progress of 'the principles of justice and sound policy' in different parts of the world.[76] Activists on both sides of the Atlantic drew obvious comfort from these signs of 'general reformation'.[77] Reflecting on the 'consequences of small *beginnings* in a matter which infinite wisdom seems remarkably to have blessed within a few years', William Dillwyn

---

[72] PAS (Pemberton) to Société des Amis des Noirs at Paris, 30 (possibly 20) August 1790, PAS Correspondence, microfilm edition, Reel 20.
[73] PAS (Pemberton) to Société des Amis des Noirs, 29 August 1791, PAS Correspondence, microfilm edition, Reel 20.
[74] SEAST to PAS, 28 February 1788, *Pennsylvania Packet*, 22 May 1788.
[75] PAS to SEAST, 12 (possibly 15) November 1788, PAS Minutes (minutes of meeting of 19 January 1789).
[76] James Pemberton to Thomas Scott, 20 April 1789, PAS Correspondence, microfilm edition, Reel 11. Scott was president of the newly established society in Washington, Pennsylvania.
[77] William Dillwyn to James Pemberton, 23 March 1788, Pemberton Papers, 49/159.

could not help feeling that there was 'encouragement at least to attempt them, and persevere through every difficulty, which interest or prejudice may throw in our way'.[78]

In its early years, at least, the Société des Amis des Noirs was content to align itself with British activists. A key part of this strategy was the reprinting, distribution and in some cases the abridgement of British books and pamphlets, chief among them Clarkson's *Essay on the Slavery and Commerce of the Human Species*. The members of the Société des Amis des Noirs also used what limited access they had to the French press – principally the *Journal de Paris* and *L'Analyse des papiers anglais* – to publicise the British movement.[79] The similarities did not end there. Like their British counterparts, French activists drew a sharp distinction between 'emancipation' and 'abolition'. Emancipation, they stressed repeatedly, 'would not only be fatal to the French colonies, but also to the Blacks themselves, given the abject state to which cupidity had reduced them'.[80] Rather, what French activists wanted and campaigned for was the total and immediate abolition of the slave trade. This emphasis was reflected in the address or petition that the Société des Amis des Noirs presented to the French General Assembly in 1790, a remarkable document that in many ways encapsulated European thinking about the slave trade at this period, whether considered as a moral question or as a matter of political expediency. In short, there was a community of interests between French and British abolitionists that, despite appearances to the contrary, set them apart from activists on the other side of the Atlantic.

Yet, at the same time, French activists laboured under a number of obvious difficulties. Crucially, there was no infrastructure. French anti-slavery never really penetrated deep into the provinces, and even in Paris it was handicapped by poor communications, notably the lack of a free press. More to the point, the members of the Société des Amis des Noirs faced mounting opposition from pro-slavery forces, made up principally of slave merchants, planters and colonial interests.[81] For all of these reasons, the society found it difficult to exert any real pressure on the French Government or, indeed, to build up any kind of momentum – that is, until Jacques Necker, Louis XVI's minister of finances, announced in August 1788 that the Estates-General, the nearest

---

[78] Dillwyn to Pemberton, 23 March 1788.
[79] Dorigny and Gainot, *La Société des Amis des Noirs*, pp. 234–44.
[80] *Adresse à l'Assemblée Nationale pour l'abolition de la traite des noirs par la Société des Amis des Noirs de Paris* (Paris: L. Poitier de Lille, 1790), p. 3. See also *Le Patriote Français*, 24 August 1789.
[81] Quinney, 'Decisions on Slavery', p. 124; Jennings, *French Anti-Slavery*, pp. 1–3.

French equivalent to the British Parliament, would meet in 1789 for the first time in nearly 175 years. Here, at last, an opening seemed to present itself. Certainly, this was the view of the SEAST, which seized this opportunity to lobby Necker, urging him (and, through him, the Estates-General) to take up the question of the slave trade. Necker's response was suitably diplomatic. 'Such an enterprise throws a new lustre on your nation', he acknowledged, but it was 'not yet a national object in France', whose colonies were 'much more considerable' than Britain's. Yet, in saying this, he conceded that 'the moment perhaps may come', adding – and this was the note of encouragement that the SEAST had been looking for – that 'I shall think myself happy in preparing the way.'[82] True to his word, Necker referred to the slave trade in his long opening address to the Estates-General in May 1789, hinting that 'some middle line' (code for regulation) might indeed be appropriate.[83]

The SEAST clearly felt that it could do business with Necker. But then events in France took an unexpected turn. Necker's abrupt dismissal on 12 July and the storming of the Bastille two days later initially caught many British activists off guard. If some feared that a lot of good work might be undone by the 'unparalleled revolution', others predicted it would hand France an important advantage, thereby 'robbing' Britain of 'the honour of leading the way' in the slave-trade struggle.[84] The members of the SEAST were in agreement about one thing, however: they could not let this opportunity pass. So it was that Wilberforce and the SEAST prevailed upon Clarkson to visit Paris, with a view to offering the Société des Amis des Noirs any assistance they required in pushing forward the question of the slave trade in the French National Assembly (later the National Constituent Assembly), which had proclaimed national sovereignty on 17 June. In many ways, Clarkson was an unlikely choice for a mission of this kind. He had very little French, very few contacts and – perhaps of greater concern – could often appear brusque and overbearing. Nevertheless, what he lacked in social graces Clarkson more than made up for in energy, determination and sheer bloody-mindedness. In this sense, at least, he was the perfect man for the job.

What Clarkson discovered on his arrival in Paris was that the political situation was less encouraging and certainly more complex than British activists had imagined. To all intents and purposes, the Société des Amis

---

[82] As quoted in William Dillwyn to James Pemberton, 3 March 1789, Pemberton Papers, 51/90.
[83] Dillwyn to Pemberton, 3 March 1789.
[84] James Phillips to James Pemberton, 20 July 1789, Pemberton Papers, 52/144, and William Dillwyn to James Pemberton, 7 August 1789, Pemberton Papers, 52/165.

des Noirs had suspended its operations (it met only three times between 30 June and 21 August 1789 and was inactive again between September and November 1789), and many of its leading members, including Brissot and Condorcet, were embroiled in the political events then engulfing the nation, not least the framing of a new constitution.[85] When the slave trade was mentioned at all, it could still arouse deep antagonism. Dillwyn reported that the 'most absurd reports' were 'industriously propagated' to discredit the French society, among them one that 'our London Committee had sent 10,000 stand of arms to encourage the slaves of St Domingo to assert their natural rights'.[86] Sometimes these tensions escalated into open violence. In August 1789, for instance, the meeting rooms of the Société des Amis des Noirs were ransacked by an angry mob, and Clarkson later claimed that he was openly threatened with assassination during his visit to Paris.[87] Characteristically, Clarkson brushed these threats aside, but, ironically, his very presence in France seemed to confirm what many already suspected: that abolition was a British conspiracy and, as such, something to be resisted.

It did not help, either, that Clarkson and the Société des Amis des Noirs became deeply involved in another issue, free coloured rights, that again raised the suspicion of their opponents. No sooner had the Estates-General reconvened than white planters in the French colonies demanded representation in the new Assembly.[88] If in theory it was difficult to refuse this request, critics such as Mirabeau could not help pointing out that whites represented only a relatively small proportion of the population of the French colonies. Besides hundreds of thousands of slaves, there was also a large number of free coloureds (*gens de couleur*), over 27,000 in Saint-Domingue alone in 1788, roughly the same number as whites.[89] Many of these men were wealthy slaveholders, who, in economic terms at least, enjoyed considerable influence, even if they were denied social mobility. Since the 1760s, impoverished white immigrants, so-called *petits blancs*, had helped prepare 'an avalanche of special restrictions' directed at segregating free men of colour.[90] For

---

[85] See Dorigny and Gainot, *La Société des Amis des Noirs*, pp. 234–44.
[86] William Dillwyn to James Pemberton, 8 October 1789, Pemberton Papers, 53/22.
[87] *Le Patriote Français*, 24 August 1789; Clarkson, *History*, vol. II, pp. 130–1, 154.
[88] C. L. R. James, *Black Jacobins: Toussaint L'Ouverture and the San Domingo Revolution* (1938; rpt. London: Virgin Publishing, 1991), pp. 59–60.
[89] Garrigus, 'The Free Colored Elite of Saint-Domingue', p. 3. See also Dubois, *A Colony of Citizens*, p. 75. Dubois notes that 'in Martinique *gens de couleur* comprised a population 50 per cent as large as that of the whites; in Guiana, 40 per cent' (p. 75). In Guadeloupe, by contrast, *gens de couleur* were a substantial minority.
[90] John D. Garrigus, *Before Haiti: Race and Citizenship in French Saint-Domingue* (Basingstoke: Palgrave Macmillan, 2006), p. 168.

instance, they were not allowed to ride in coaches, could not dine with whites and, perhaps most onerous of all, could not fill responsible civil offices.[91] Yet, as tax-payers, Mirabeau insisted that free coloureds were every bit as deserving of recognition as whites. As for the slaves, either they were men or they were not. 'If the colonists consider them to be men', he went on, 'let them free them and make them electors and eligible for seats; if the contrary is the case, have we, in apportioning deputies according to the population of France, taken into consideration the number of our horses and our mules?'[92]

Mirabeau eventually had to concede defeat, but from this moment (mid 1789), the issue of free coloured rights would loom large in French anti-slavery debates.[93] A key figure here was Julien Raimond, a wealthy coloured proprietor from the southern peninsula of Saint-Domingue, who in 1784 moved with his wife to Angoulême in France.[94] Raimond, it should be stressed, was not an abolitionist, at least not in the strict sense of the term. Rather, he was a proponent of free coloured rights and, first and foremost, of the rights of wealthy slaveholders such as himself, that is, those 'who could count two generations of legitimacy from white European fathers'.[95] It was really only after 1789 that he began to work for the extension of full civil rights to all free persons. In short, 'what Raimond sought for himself and those like him, and what he claimed would eventually come to less-successful free coloreds, was a rank in society that matched their accomplishments'.[96] Raimond set all this out in a series of letters or remonstrances to the colonial minister at Versailles who was interested enough to forward Raimond's modest proposals to Port-au-Prince for review. But then the French Revolution intervened. By August 1789, Raimond was in Paris, having in the meantime transferred his powers as a free coloured 'representative' to a sympathetic nobleman, the Count de Jarnac, who had undertaken to raise the question of free coloured rights in the French National Assembly on his behalf.[97]

No sooner had he arrived in Paris than Raimond made contact with another wealthy Saint-Dominguan quadroon, Vincent Ogé, and, together with Ogé, joined forces with The Society of American

[91] Garrigus, *Before Haiti*, p. 169.
[92] Quoted in James, *Black Jacobins*, p. 60.
[93] The Assembly eventually agreed to admit twelve white colonial deputies from the French Caribbean, including six from Saint-Domingue. See Dorigny and Gainot, *La Société des Amis des Noirs*, pp. 229–30, n. 403, p. 235, n. 422.
[94] Biographical details for Raimond can be found in Garrigus, *Before Haiti*, pp. 1–2.
[95] Garrigus, 'The Free Colored Elite of Saint-Domingue', p. 16.
[96] Garrigus, 'The Free Colored Elite of Saint-Domingue', pp. 25–6.
[97] Garrigus, *Before Haiti*, p. 236.

Colonists, a group of free men of colour who had started meeting at the offices of Etienne-Louis Hector de Joly, a white barrister. At last, on 22 October, de Joly was allowed to address the National Assembly, assuring the delegates that free people of colour were French citizens and, as such, entitled to full civil rights, including representation in the National Assembly. To underline his point, de Joly also repeated free coloured readiness to donate 6 million livres to the Revolution as 'a patriotic gift'.[98] Around the same time, Raimond made contact with members of the Société des Amis des Noirs. The precise details are unclear, but Raimond seems to have had little difficulty winning over French activists to his cause. By early October 1789, Brissot's *Le Patriote Français* was already carrying regular reports on the campaign to win free coloured representation, and over the coming months the two groups were in regular contact with each other.[99] Another convert was the Abbé Henri Grégoire, constitutional bishop of Blois and a leading figure in the French Revolution. At this date, Grégoire was still not officially a member of the Société des Amis des Noirs, but, as his *Memorandum in Favour of the People of Colour or Mixed-Bloods of Sierra Leone and the Other French Islands of America* (1789) made clear, he was in no doubt that free coloured delegates should be admitted to the National Assembly. Grégoire, in fact, went further, predicting the end of the slave trade and raising the possibility of slave revolt in the French Caribbean.[100]

The growing alliance between French activists and free men of colour became fully apparent in November 1789, when Brissot introduced de Joly, Raimond, Ogé and three other 'deputies' to members of the Société des Amis des Noirs. After a short address from de Joly setting out the details of their case, the meeting proceeded to adopt a resolution supporting the claims of free coloured citizens before the National Assembly.[101] Someone else present at this meeting was Clarkson, who had already met Raimond and Ogé through the marquis de Lafayette. Clarkson was clearly persuaded by what he heard. Once free coloured deputies had taken their seats in the Assembly, he was assured, they would 'propose an immediate abolition of the slave trade, and an immediate amelioration of the state of slavery also, with

[98] Garrigus, *Before Haiti*, p. 240.
[99] *Le Patriote Français*, 9 October 1789, 23 October 1789, 10 November 1789, 11 November 1789, 24 November 1789, 3 December 1789, 5 December 1789 and 7 December 1789.
[100] Garrigus, *Before Haiti*, p. 241.
[101] Dorigny and Gainot, *La Société des Amis des Noirs*, pp. 244–8 (minutes of meeting of 24 November 1789).

a view to its final abolition in fifteen years'.[102] But Clarkson would also
have known that their first priority was free coloured rights. Raimond
made this very clear at another meeting of the Société des Amis des
Noirs on 11 December, at which Clarkson was again present. When
Grégoire proposed asking the president of the National Assembly for
immediate permission to raise the question of the slave trade once 'the
affair of the citizens of colour' had been concluded, Raimond objected
on the grounds that linking the two issues at this stage 'would be harmful to each and weaken both'.[103] Far better, he argued, to deal with the
question of free coloured representation first. Aware that many of those
he represented were slaveholders, Raimond baulked at the idea of supporting abolition, at least for the moment. Perhaps more surprisingly,
the Société des Amis des Noirs agreed to do as he suggested, thereby
making it very clear where its own priorities now lay.[104]

By the end of 1789, therefore, French activists had significantly reor-
dered their strategic objectives. One of the consequences was that the
distinction between 'abolition' and 'emancipation' became blurred and
indistinct. Though many members of the Société des Amis des Noirs
may have thought there was nothing inconsistent in the position they
had adopted, it was only too easy for their critics to jump to the opposite
conclusion. To them, the campaign for free coloured rights looked like
interference in colonial affairs, the first step in a social and economic
revolution that ultimately would lead to the destruction of the French
colonies (this, of course, was the logic of Grégoire's *Memorandum*).
Naively perhaps, French activists clung to the idea that the strategy
would work – that the National Assembly would eventually accede
to free coloured demands – but the omens were not good. Clarkson
later reported that 'the deputies had been flattered by the prospect of
[another] hearing no less than six times; and, when the day arrived,
something had constantly occurred to prevent it'.[105] Ominously, some
of them began to talk of taking matters into their own hands, a threat
that Clarkson said he sought to defuse, for fear that it 'might not only
ruin their own cause in France, but bring indescribable misery upon
their native land'.[106]

---

[102] Clarkson, *History*, vol. II, p. 134.
[103] Dorigny and Gainot, *La Société des Amis des Noirs*, p. 254 (minutes of meeting of 11
December 1789).
[104] Dorigny and Gainot, *La Société des Amis des Noirs*, pp. 251–4 (minutes of meeting of
11 December 1789).
[105] Clarkson, *History*, vol. II, p. 149.
[106] Clarkson, *History*, vol. II, p. 151.

Clarkson would go on working closely with the members of the Société des Amis des Noirs. He was a constant presence at meetings between November 1789 and January 1790 and took a keen interest in the society's proceedings, at one point even accompanying de Joly to meet those members of the National Assembly who were also members of the Société des Amis des Noirs (whether the SEAST was aware of these activities is unclear).[107] Meanwhile, armed with the engraving of the slave ship *Brookes*, Clarkson tried to lobby as many people as he could, among them the Bishop of Chartres, the Duc de la Rochefoucauld, Pétion de Villeneuve and the Archbishop of Aix. To Clarkson's mind, the choices facing the French were straightforward. Sooner or later, he predicted, revolutions would take place in the French colonies. Far better, then, to abolish the slave trade immediately and to press for some kind of amelioration of colonial slavery. That way,

the minds of the Negroes [would] be calmed, they [would] see that France, in the midst of her struggle, [had] not forgotten their cause ... the proprietors ... would preserve their estates for themselves and their dependents, and France [would] preserve her islands, with an accumulation of treasure to be derived from thence in a quantity hitherto unknown.[108]

Besides, France's honour and reputation were also at stake. If France continued the slave trade, Clarkson went on, 'the principles on which she [had] brought about the revolution [would] be justly considered to have flowed from a polluted source, her Declaration of the Bill of Rights [would] be considered as the Declaration of Hypocrites ... and France [would] become the Derision of Europe'.[109] In other words, France 'must abolish the slave trade, whether any other nation [did] or not'.[110] But, here again, such sentiments (and such activities) only aroused suspicion. According to his own account, later published in his *History*, Clarkson was frequently 'denounced as a spy and as one sent by the English minister to bribe members in the Assembly to do that in a time of public agitation, which in the settled state of France they could never have been prevailed upon to accomplish'.[111] By the beginning of 1790, it was clear that he had made little headway. The sticking point, as Clarkson saw it, was French distrust of Britain's motives. 'If France were to give up [the slave trade], and Britain to continue it', he

---

[107] Dorigny and Gainot, *La Société des Amis des Noirs*, p. 247.
[108] Thomas Clarkson to Auguste Jean Baptiste Bouvet de Cressé, 1 December 1789, Thomas Clarkson Papers, CN 53, Huntington Library, San Marino, California.
[109] Clarkson to Bouvet de Cressé, 1 December 1789.
[110] Clarkson to Bouvet de Cressé, 1 December 1789.
[111] Clarkson, *History*, vol. II, p. 154.

was asked time and time again, 'how would humanity be the gainer?'[112] But, as Clarkson understood only too well, it was impossible to give the French the assurances they demanded. The result was stalemate.[113]

Clarkson finally left Paris at the end of January, just as the French movement entered what was to prove its most critical phase. Crucially, the question of free coloured rights still remained unresolved. In desperation, in February 1790 de Joly and Raimond, aided by the Société des Amis des Noirs, started lobbying the representatives of the Paris Commune, hoping they might intervene with the National Assembly on their behalf.[114] Simultaneously, after months of delay, French activists finally decided to present their address against the slave trade. 'It came out in time', Brissot wrote to Clarkson on 14 February, 'for a violent storm gathered against us, especially at Bordeaux. The patriotic army of [that] city is furious against our society. Addresses pour in against the abolition of the slave trade. However, we are putting on a brave face and making converts.'[115] Brissot was clearly shaken. Anxiously, he kept a close eye on events in Britain. Was it true, he wanted to know, 'that your government has recently concluded a treaty with the Spanish government in order to supply the Spanish islands with Blacks?' Had the treaty been approved by Parliament? When was it due to end? As this suggests, Brissot saw British and French interests as being inextricably linked. 'The account of the progress of your business has been communicated to the society here and has caused great satisfaction', he wrote again in March. 'Indeed we long for the decision. If the trade is abolished in the House of Commons, that blow will revive the spirits in our National Assembly.'[116]

The feverish pace of Brissot's correspondence with Clarkson during these crucial months testifies to the enduring significance of international abolitionism, not just in terms of ideas and information but also in terms of policies and coordination. Ideally, what activists on both sides of the Atlantic were looking for was a way of moving the movement forward that rose above narrow national interests. The problem, however, was that neither Britain nor France (nor the USA, for that matter) was willing to give ground. Put a different way, there was always a tension in these debates between the national or imperial and

[112] Clarkson, *History*, vol. II, p. 158.
[113] Clarkson, *History*, vol. II, pp. 135–66.
[114] *Le Patriote Français*, 5 February 1790.
[115] Jacques-Pierre Brissot de Warville to Thomas Clarkson, 14 February 1790, Thomas Clarkson Papers, St John's College, Cambridge.
[116] Jacques-Pierre Brissot de Warville to Thomas Clarkson, 9 March 1790, Thomas Clarkson Papers, St John's College, Cambridge.

the international. That much became apparent when on 8 March the National Assembly – or, to be more precise, the Assembly's Colonial Committee – finally pronounced on the related questions of the slave trade and free coloured representation. Bowing to pressure from white planters, the committee proposed what John D. Garrigus describes as 'a loose constitutional relationship between the colonies and the metropole', whereby '"freely" elected Colonial assemblies would write local laws and supply delegates to the French National Assembly'.[117] But, significantly, the report said nothing about whether qualified men of colour would be allowed to vote. In effect, the Colonial Committee devolved the issue of free coloured rights to the colonial assemblies, granting them 'the lee-way to decide the fate of all blacks and men of color on the islands'.[118]

This still left the question of the slave trade. Here, the committee upheld the right of the National Assembly to make the final decisions on commercial arrangements but, in doing so, made it very clear that it had never been its intention 'to *innovate* in any branch of commerce either direct or indirect of France with its colonies'.[119] In other words, the slave trade remained intact. But this was not all. In what was for French activists the final indignity, the decree of 8 March criminalised all activity aimed at exciting 'revolts' (*soulèvements*) against white colonists.[120] The members of the Société des Amis des Noirs could hardly have suffered a more resounding defeat. While it seems unlikely that the National Assembly would have entertained abolition, particularly without British cooperation, the campaign for free coloured rights undoubtedly proved a strategic mistake, handing pro-slavery advocates an important advantage. Perhaps more to the point, French activists had been beaten at their own game. Valerie Quinney goes so far as to suggest that the campaign to *preserve* the slave trade was 'one of the most clear-cut examples of pressure politics in the early French Revolution'.[121] Between mid January and March 1790, at least twenty-four pro-slavery petitions had been presented to the National Assembly, reflecting widespread condemnation of the proposals put forward by the Société des Amis des Noirs. By contrast, 'not a single petition from a French city in these months asked for the slave trade to be abolished or even that the conditions of the slaves be ameliorated'.[122]

---

[117] Garrigus, *Before Haiti*, p. 243.
[118] Quinney, 'Decisions on Slavery', p. 127.
[119] Quinney, 'Decisions on Slavery', p. 125. My emphasis.
[120] *Seconde adresse a l'Assemblée Nationale, par la Société des Amis des Noirs, établie à Paris* (Paris: De l'Imprimerie du Patriote Français, 1790), p. 5.
[121] Quinney, 'Decisions on Slavery', p. 125.
[122] Quinney, 'Decisions on Slavery', p. 124.

Angry and humiliated, the members of the Société des Amis des Noirs fought back. In April, they presented a second address to the National Assembly, this time protesting against the 'misconstructions' placed upon their activities.[123] In the meantime, Grégoire and others tried to clarify the meaning of the clause relating to colonial rights. Under mounting pressure, the Colonial Committee drafted an 'Instruction' to the colonies (28 March) that in its final form enfranchised 'all persons twenty-five years old at least, owners of property, or if not propertied, domiciled in the parish for two years and paying tax'.[124] Brissot, at least, took 'persons' to include qualified men of colour, which partly explains why he thought now was the time for the Société des Amis des Noirs to press home its advantage.[125] On 25 March, he reported to Clarkson that the French society had been put on 'another footing more liberal and more extensive', presumably a reference to the election of Pétion de Villeneuve, a member of the National Assembly and later mayor of Paris, as president earlier that month.[126] New publications rolled off the presses. 'The speech of Pétion [against the 8 March decree] is printing now and shall be out next Saturday', Brissot went on. 'We are also to print Mirabeau's speech. I believe it will make everywhere the deepest impression. As soon as they shall be out we shall send copies to you.'[127] Brissot's mood remained unfailingly upbeat (and this is undoubtedly what led James Pemberton to put so much faith in the progress of the French movement). Writing to Clarkson on 25 April, he confidently predicted that 'at the next legislature and perhaps sooner we will succeed and chiefly if England takes some determination against that infamous traffic'.[128]

That same month, Brissot introduced a new plan that involved five members of the Société des Amis des Noirs dividing 'amongst themselves all the researches to be made on the trade and on slavery'.[129] Yet in so far as the French society remained a force at all, free coloured rights continued to take up most, if not all, of its time and energy. By

---

[123] See Jacques-Pierre Brissot de Warville to Thomas Clarkson, 25 April 1790, Thomas Clarkson Papers, St John's College, Cambridge.

[124] Quinney, 'Decisions on Slavery', p. 126.

[125] Jacques-Pierre Brissot de Warville to Thomas Clarkson, 29 March 1790, Thomas Clarkson Papers, St John's College, Cambridge; Garrigus, *Before Haiti*, p. 244.

[126] Jacques-Pierre Brissot de Warville to Thomas Clarkson, 25 March 1790, Thomas Clarkson Papers, St John's College, Cambridge. See also Dorigny and Gainot, *La Société des Amis des Noirs*, p. 280 (minutes of meeting of 15 March 1790).

[127] Brissot to Clarkson, 25 March 1790.

[128] Jacques-Pierre Brissot de Warville to Thomas Clarkson, 25 April 1790, Thomas Clarkson Papers, St John's College, Cambridge.

[129] Brissot to Clarkson, 25 April 1790. See also Dorigny and Gainot, *La Société des Amis des Noirs*, pp. 283–4 (minutes of meeting of 23 April 1790).

May 1790 it was already clear that white colonists had no intention of surrendering political power to their opponents; that same month, the Colonial Assembly of Saint-Domingue 'voted to exclude all men of African ancestry from full citizenship, including whites who had married women of colour'.[130] In response, free coloured citizens began to organise protest meetings. Tensions escalated still further when Vincent Ogé returned to Saint-Domingue in October, having previously spent time in Britain. At first, Ogé demanded that the Governor, Philibert Blanchelande, allow qualified men of colour to vote. When that did not work, he roused what in effect became a free coloured uprising, a force of some 300 followers that gathered in the south of the island and eventually fled across the Spanish border to escape a large force of royal troops. White reprisals were swift and brutal. In January 1791, Ogé and twenty-three others were extradited and executed in Cap-Français's main square, 'their corpses publicly displayed like those of rebel slaves'.[131]

The Ogé uprising caused widespread alarm and consternation, not least in Paris, where many opponents of abolition laid the blame firmly on French activists. (A further uprising, this time a slave conspiracy in Port Salut parish in January 1791, gave further credence to the connection between 'abolition' and 'rebellion'.[132]) There were also claims by some that Clarkson or the SEAST were behind the uprising. The fact that Ogé had spent time in Britain before returning to Saint-Domingue naturally aroused suspicion, as did the fact that the SEAST was obviously subsidising the French society's publication programme; indeed, it is possible that these two things were confused in the minds of many commentators, fuelling conspiracy theories around the true intentions of French activists.[133] Yet, at the same time, the Ogé uprising – and particularly the brutal treatment of the rebels – undoubtedly aroused sympathy among some members of the National Assembly, who now began to see free coloured citizens as potential allies. Certainly, the metropolitan campaign showed no signs of abating. In December, Brissot published a pamphlet attacking the Revolution's colonial policies, and the following March, Raimond and others again demanded

[130] Garrigus, *Before Haiti*, p. 244.
[131] Garrigus, *Before Haiti*, pp. 247–9.
[132] Garrigus, *Before Haiti*, pp. 250–1, 254.
[133] For British involvement in the Ogé uprising, see James, *Black Jacobins*, pp. 73–4; Ruth F. Necheles, *The Abbé Grégoire, 1787–1831: The Odyssey of an Egalitarian* (Westport, Conn.: Greenwood, 1971), p. 76. For the SEAST and the French society's publication programme, see Jacques-Pierre Brissot de Warville to Thomas Clarkson, 9 March 1790, 25 March 1790, 29 March 1790, 25 April 1790 and 27 May 1790, Thomas Clarkson Papers, St John's College, Cambridge.

their full civil rights, as laid down in Article 4 of the 'Instruction' of 28 March 1790.[134]

As Garrigus points out, by the spring of 1791, 'Raimond's argument that free men of color were virtuous Frenchmen while colonial whites were bad fathers and brothers began to bear fruit.'[135] On 15 May, the National Assembly finally approved a 'compromise decree', which enfranchised tax-paying adult sons of free coloured parents in the French Caribbean, in effect some 1,000 voters.[136] This was not the comprehensive reform that Raimond and Brissot had been looking for. Nevertheless, it represented an important victory for French activists. The decree, Grégoire declared in his *Lettre aux citoyens de couleur* (1791), had removed a stain from the French Constitution and repaid a painful debt. But, in saying this, Grégoire raised the very prospect that many opponents of abolition had feared all along. Free coloured rights, it transpired, were not an end but a beginning. 'We have alleviated your pains', Grégoire told free coloured citizens in the final part of his letter. '[Now] alleviate those of the unhappy victims of avarice who soak your fields with their sweat and often their tears; that existence for slaves will no longer be a torment; by your kindness to their regard, expiate the crimes of Europe.'[137] This was hardly a representative view (Raimond, for instance, consistently argued that free coloured rights would actually reinforce slavery); rather, it exposed the confusion among French activists, their indiscipline and their inability to control their message.

As it turned out, the decree of 15 May was never implemented. Angry free men of colour again organised protest meetings; others took up arms, determined to fight for their equality. Then, on 22 August 1791, slaves began to revolt around Cap-Français in what was to prove the opening salvo in a protracted struggle that would eventually lead to Haitian independence in 1804.[138] Almost overnight, the dynamics of the situation in Saint-Domingue changed dramatically. Now there were three parties to this dispute, a scenario that witnessed the emergence of shifting alliances, as each side sought to steal an advantage over its rivals. In the meantime, French activists were left to ponder the wider significance of the slave rebellion. On the surface, it seemed that they had two choices; either to embrace the rebellion, thereby risking

---

[134] Garrigus, *Before Haiti*, pp. 253–7.
[135] Garrigus, *Before Haiti*, p. 254.   [136] Garrigus, *Before Haiti*, p. 258.
[137] *Lettre aux citoyens de couleur et nègres libres de Saint-Domingue, et des autres isles françoises de l'Amérique. Par M. Grégoire, député à l'Assemblée Nationale, evêque du Département de Loir [sic] et Cher* (Paris: De L'Imprimerie du Patriote Français, 1791), pp. 2, 13.
[138] Garrigus, *Before Haiti*, p. 260.

a vicious white backlash, or to reject it, a strategy that in the circum-stances was equally fraught with difficulties, especially given some of Grégoire's more ill-advised comments. Instinctively, many members of the Société des Amis des Noirs tried to distance themselves from violence or, indeed, the threat of violence. The reality, however, was that French activists were too deeply implicated in the events unfolding in Saint-Domingue, not least through their support of free coloured demands, to effect any kind of tactical withdrawal. Increasingly dis-tracted and bedevilled by mounting debts, all that they could realisti-cally do was to wait and try to ride out the crisis.

Not surprisingly, the slave rebellion in Saint-Domingue reframed debates about slavery and the slave trade, setting them in a very dif-ferent context. In Britain, at least, the timing of the revolt was critical. Here, Parliament had been hearing evidence both for and against the slave trade for almost two years. Finally, in February 1791, the hearings drew to a close. Almost immediately, Wilberforce and others set about preparing a digest or abridgement of the evidence, which reached mem-bers of the House of Commons just in time for the Commons debate on 18 April. Hopes ran high. Once again, however, Wilberforce's motion for an immediate end to the slave trade was defeated, this time by 163 votes to eighty-eight.[139] The size of this defeat prompted Wilberforce to propose launching another petition campaign but this time on a much larger scale. Everything indicated that public support for abolition was still strong. Help also came from an unexpected quarter in the shape of William Fox's *Address to the People of Great Britain, on the Propriety of Abstaining from West India Sugar and Rum* (1790). This short address, published at a time of soaring sugar prices, proved an immediate suc-cess. Estimates vary, but it is thought that 70,000 copies were printed in only four months, running through some fourteen or fifteen impres-sions. Perhaps more to the point, Fox's pamphlet, and a host of pirated versions, inspired a nationwide boycott of West Indian sugar that at its peak involved some 300,000 families from 'all ranks and parties', rich and poor, churchmen and Dissenters.[140]

Clarkson, for one, clearly saw non-consumption, as it was sometimes called, as a direct stimulus to petitioning, but it is a measure of how tense the political situation had become by 1791 that some members of the SEAST feared it might actually harm the cause by linking abo-lition with popular agitation and the spectre of the mob.[141] These fears

---

[139] John Pollock, *Wilberforce* (1977; rpt. London: Lion Publishing, 1986), pp. 102–8.
[140] Oldfield, *Popular Politics*, pp. 56–7, 139–40.
[141] Oldfield, *Popular Politics*, p. 58.

became all the more evident once news of the events in Saint-Domingue started to reach Britain. For many – and this was as true of the USA as it was of Britain – the rebellion made explicit the connection between abolition and slave unrest (one, in effect, led to the other). But overlaid with this perception was another: that abolition was a French invention or, at least, associated with the excesses of the French Revolution. Already there were signs that a reaction was setting in. On his tour of Scotland in 1792, William Dickson found that one local resident, while sympathetic to abolition, was 'terrified for insurrections'.[142] Others expressed similar misgivings. In some quarters, the petition campaign itself was looked upon as nothing more than a calculated ploy, a 'pretence' to disguise the 'deep designs' of men dismissively referred to as 'the JACOBINS of ENGLAND'.[143]

Reacting swiftly, the SEAST moved to dampen these rumours by placing advertisements in the London and provincial papers restating its original aim and purpose, namely the 'Abolition of the Trade to the Coast of Africa for Slaves'.[144] Clarkson also set to, publishing a more direct refutation of the charges laid against abolitionists in the wake of the Saint-Domingue slave revolt. To his mind, the cause of the insurrection was not so much abolitionist activity but 'the pride and obstinacy of the whites who drove them [blacks] to their fate, by an impolitic and foolish dissention with the mulattoes, and with each other'.[145] Saint-Domingue, in other words, was a special case. Clarkson denied that abolition of the slave trade would lead to similar insurrections in the British Caribbean, a distinction that was easier to maintain, given the SEAST's much narrower strategic focus. Determined to give such views as wide a circulation as possible, in February 1792 the SEAST printed and distributed 1,000 copies of Clarkson's *Inquiry into the Causes of the Insurrection of Negroes in the Island of St Domingo*. In a related move, the following July the PAS arranged to reprint 500 copies of the same essay, further evidence of the way in which the rebellion galvanised abolitionist activity on both sides of the Atlantic.[146]

These tactics seem to have worked. Certainly, there is little to suggest that the slave rebellion in Saint-Domingue adversely affected the

---

[142] Oldfield, *Popular Politics*, p. 60.
[143] Oldfield, *Popular Politics*, p. 60.
[144] SEAST Minutes, 31 January 1792 and 14 February 1792.
[145] [Thomas Clarkson], *An Inquiry into the Causes of the Insurrection of Negroes in the Island of St Domingo. To Which Are Added, Observations of M. Garron-Coulon on the Same Subject* (London: J. Johnson, 1792), p. 25.
[146] SEAST Minutes, 31 January 1792 and 14 February 1792; PAS Minutes, 2 July 1792. The American edition was printed by Joseph Cruikshank of Philadelphia.

petition campaign of 1792. On the contrary, the campaign was an unqualified success. While the industrial north continued to provide the most vocal support for abolition, every English county was represented, in addition to which Scotland made a massive contribution, thanks largely to Dickson's efforts. But just as important as the size of the campaign (over 500 petitions, in all) was its range and diversity. In Northumberland, for instance, even market towns such as Belford (400 signatures), Woolner (400 signatures) and Alnick (600 signatures) organised petitions, adding their voices to the gentlemen and shipowners of North and South Shields.[147] Petitioning on this scale was always likely to cause alarm in the minds of men with one eye on events in France. Nevertheless, the campaign could not be ignored, and it undoubtedly exerted considerable leverage in the ensuing parliamentary debate, which saw the House of Commons resolve by 230 votes to eighty-five that the slave trade ought to be *gradually* abolished. The only remaining question was by what date. Some, such as Henry Dundas, favoured postponing abolition until 1800; others, however, proposed that the date should be brought forward to 1 January 1793. Eventually, after further debate, the House compromised on 1 January 1796 by a narrow majority of just nineteen votes.[148]

Important as this victory was, it fell some way short of the 'immediate and utter abolition' that Wilberforce and the SEAST had been looking for.[149] Despite these misgivings, however, the London Committee moved quickly to capitalise on the Commons' vote. On 8 May 1792, after a long silence, contact was re-established with the Société des Amis des Noirs in Paris. Three weeks later, it was agreed to go further and prepare a French translation of the 1791 debate on Wilberforce's motion against the slave trade, with a view to giving it as wide a circulation as possible.[150] But this sense of euphoria was to prove short-lived. The following month, the Lords rejected the Commons' resolution and voted to postpone the business until the next session, when it proposed to hear its own evidence for and against the slave trade. Breaking the news to the PAS, Sharp conceded that these delaying tactics 'must be a source of regret with all good men'.[151] Yet, at the same time, he and his colleagues remained confident that 'their Lordships [would] finally accede to the resolution of the House of Commons and unite in purging

[147] Oldfield, *Popular Politics*, pp. 61, 114.
[148] Pollock, *Wilberforce*, pp. 115–16; SEAST to PAS, 9 June 1792, PAS Correspondence, microfilm edition, Reel 11.
[149] SEAST Minutes, 19 June 1792.
[150] SEAST Minutes, 8 May 1792 and 29 May 1792.
[151] SEAST to PAS, 9 June 1792 PAS Correspondence, microfilm edition, Reel 11.

this nation from its foulest stain'.[152] Whatever happened, Sharp went on, he and his colleagues could 'console themselves in the reflection that their utmost endeavours [had] been exerted to promote a more speedy termination of the evil'.[153] Nevertheless, there was no getting away from the fact that the Lords' decision represented a significant defeat. British activists suffered a further setback in 1793 when the House of Commons refused to revive the question of the slave trade, thus effectively reversing the 1792 vote in favour of gradualism.[154]

These early years exposed both the strengths and weaknesses of international anti-slavery. While activists were able to forge alliances across huge distances and to create synergies where none had existed before, they found it much more difficult to overcome the 'long habits and strong interests' – specifically national interests – that opposed them.[155] They also sometimes found it hard to retain their focus, although, as we have seen, even the most disciplined campaigns could run into difficulties. The sad reality was that after five years of collective endeavour activists were still some way short of the total reformation they had been looking for. Perhaps more to the point, they had suffered some serious setbacks, particularly during 1789–90 when the international movement had seemed in danger of losing momentum. By 1791, the strains in the transatlantic alliance were already becoming apparent, perhaps nowhere more so than in France where the Société des Amis des Noirs seemed to be in danger of imploding. Increasingly, activists on both sides of the Atlantic found themselves on the defensive as growing numbers began to question the utility of the kind of idealistic internationalism that had dominated anti-slavery debates in the late 1780s. In retrospect, 1792 was to prove the high-water mark of the early abolitionist movement, certainly in Britain – an important reference point but also a reminder of how much had changed, not least in terms of personnel and organisation.

---

[152] SEAST to PAS, 9 June 1792.
[153] SEAST to PAS, 9 June 1792.
[154] Pollock, *Wilberforce*, pp. 122–3; Clarkson, *History*, vol. II, pp. 461–3.
[155] PAS to SEAST, 28 February 1790, PAS Correspondence, microfilm edition, Reel 11.

Part II

Abolitionism in a cold climate

4   Rupture and fragmentation

Between 1788 and 1792, activists on both sides of the Atlantic worked together in close cooperation, confident that theirs was a universal struggle that transcended political and national boundaries. After 1793, however, they faced increasing challenges, which would see the movement fragment and, in some cases, go into reverse. If truth be told, cracks were evident in the anti-slavery wall before this date, but the radicalisation of the French Revolution, together with the outbreak of war between Britain and France (February 1793), presaged the emergence of a narrow, coercive mood that made international cooperation much more difficult. War, repression and nationalistic rivalries shattered the optimism of the 1780s and, with it, the cosmopolitanism that had seemed to mark the opening of a new democratic era. On both sides of the Atlantic activists struggled to come to terms with these new realities, which created in their wake a greater sense of caution. Some, such as Thomas Clarkson, were forced into political exile. Others retreated back into their own spheres of influence (this was perhaps most evident in the USA), although, as we shall see, the idealistic internationalism of the 1780s never entirely faded away.

French activists were among the first to feel the full force of these dislocations. Widely suspected of being British 'agents', the members of the Société des Amis des Noirs had always invited suspicion, not least among colonial interests, and their identification with free coloured ambitions in the French Caribbean had done little to win them friends. But even more damaging was the loss of some of the leading members, notably Brissot. From an early stage, Brissot had identified himself with the wider, international aims of the Revolution, including open-ended war against France's enemies, which he felt should be conducted without compromising the Revolution's original and representative principles at home. This stance, however, antagonised not only the Paris mob but also radicals such as Robespierre, who mistook Brissot's conservative tendencies (especially his respect for the rule of

law) for dishonesty or, worse, treachery. As the revolutionary struggle within France intensified, Brissot's party, the so-called Girondins,
faced mounting opposition. In June 1793, twenty-nine of them, including Brissot, were arrested and subsequently shot or guillotined. Clavière
suffered a similar fate; Condorcet, another prominent Girondin, committed suicide in prison. In reality, there was no way back from these
catastrophic events. Robbed of some of their most effective leaders, the
members of the Société des Amis des Noirs dispersed and the society
was dissolved.[1]

Meanwhile, the crisis in Saint-Domingue continued to escalate.
Hoping to contain the slave revolt, in April 1792 France had extended
citizenship to all free men of colour and, in pursuit of this controversial policy, had sent a civil commission to Saint-Domingue, led by
Léger-Félicité Sonthonax, a right-wing Jacobin who was also a friend
of Brissot.[2] But, as the commissioners discovered, the policy proved
unworkable. Confronted by rebellious slaves, discontented whites
and the threat of an invasion from the Spanish-held part of the island
(Santo Domingo), on 31 October 1793 they bowed to the inevitable
and issued a decree declaring the end of slavery. In many ways it was
an act of desperation and one unconnected with either the Société
des Amis des Noirs or, for that matter, humanitarian sentiment. Keen
to win over blacks to the newly established French Republic and to
restore some kind of order in Saint-Domingue, the commissioners
gave them their liberty, thereby 'formalizing a fait accompli brought
about by the Saint-Domingue slave uprising'.[3] The decree was ratified
by the National Convention and extended to all the French colonies on
4 February 1794. One newspaper reported that 'a Negress who heard
[it], fainted away, and did not recover but by the noise of acclamation,
and the shout of Vive la République'.[4] Just as telling, Georges Danton
was said to have declared that the decree would 'kill' Pitt, a recognition of its wider bearing on France's ongoing conflict with both Britain
and Spain.[5]

Not surprisingly, responses to the decree were mixed, even hostile.
What caught many British activists off guard was the extremism of the
measure. As we have seen, most members of the SEAST studiously

---

[1] M. J. Sydenham, *The Girondins* (London: The Athlone Press, 1961), pp. 101–4, 107, 118, 121–2, 173–9; Jennings, *French Anti-Slavery*, pp. 2–3.
[2] Garrigus, *Before Haiti*, p. 268; James, *Black Jacobins*, pp. 118–19.
[3] James, *Black Jacobins*, pp. 128–9; Jennings, *French Anti-Slavery*, p. 3 (quotation). There had been earlier decrees in August and September 1793.
[4] Dubois, *A Colony of Citizens*, p. 172.
[5] *Lloyd's Evening Post*, 19 February 1794.

avoided the issue of emancipation, and, in so far as they thought about it at all, favoured a gradualist approach.[6] American activists were equally sceptical about the French decree. To their way of thinking, a 'sudden' emancipation of this kind was likely to lead only to 'individual distress and general commotion'.[7] In saying this, they could not help pointing to the soundness of their own gradualist approach, as adopted in the Northern (New England) states, where slavery was 'nearly abolished', and the Middle states where 'the work of emancipation had made great progress'.[8] What was needed in such cases, they believed, was some kind of training or preparation for freedom, hence the importance of education, an overriding concern for American activists. In short, the French decree seemed to many British and American activists to represent a flawed experiment, a dangerous counter-example that flew in the face of everything they held most dear. The fact remained, however, that the French had quite spectacularly stolen a march on their rivals, opening up the British, in particular, to the charge of hypocrisy.[9]

If the debates in the British Parliament are anything to go by, France's example only stiffened opposition to abolition, fuelling widespread fears of bloody revolution. As Sir William Young put it, in the Commons debate on the second reading of the Foreign Slave Bill (25 February 1794), 'the circumstances of the question were entirely changed since the abolition of colonial slavery by the French Convention, and the measures lately pursued in the French islands'.[10] Others went further. In the Upper House, Lord Abingdon dismissed abolition of the slave trade as 'a French proposition', arguing that it was 'grounded in and founded upon French principles: it means neither more nor less, than liberty and Equality: it has Tom Paine's Rights of Man for its chief and best support'.[11] If Britain adopted such principles, Abingdon predicted, there would only be one outcome: 'insubordination, anarchy, confusion, murder, havoc, devastation and ruin'.[12] The French Revolutionary War gave these debates a

---

[6] There were some British activists who supported the decree, however, among them William Fox. See his *A Defence of the Decree of the National Convention of France, for Emancipating the Slaves in the West Indies* (London, 1794).

[7] Draft of a letter from the American Convention for Promoting the Abolition of Slavery to the Société des Amis des Noirs et des Colonies, (month unknown) 1797, PAS Papers, microfilm edition, Reel 28.

[8] Draft of a letter from the American Convention for Promoting the Abolition of Slavery to the Société des Amis des Noirs et des Colonies, (month unknown) 1797.

[9] James Stephen, among others, was particularly alert to this point. See his *The Danger of the Country; by the Author of War in Disguise* (London: J. Butterworth & J. Hatchard, 1807), pp. 171–2.

[10] *Cobbett's Parliamentary History*, 30 (1792–4), p. 1445.

[11] *Cobbett's Parliamentary History*, 31 (1794–5), p. 467.

[12] *Cobbett's Parliamentary History*, 31 (1794–5), p. 467.

highly partisan character. In September 1793, British forces had landed in Saint-Domingue from Jamaica at the express invitation of white planters, who were keen to restore the *ancien régime* in the colony, 'slavery, mulatto discrimination, and all'.[13] It was to prove an ill-fated campaign but one whose wider significance was not lost on British activists. War in the Caribbean pitted two rival colonial systems against each other. This is what Pitt had in mind when he described the French decree as 'wild and improvident'.[14] Far better, he implied, to do things the British way, even if that meant deferring emancipation until some later date.[15]

In the end, the association between abolition and revolution proved the SEAST's undoing. Still smarting from the Commons defeat of 1793, activists suffered a further setback in 1795 when the House of Commons voted down Wilberforce's motion for the total abolition of the slave trade by 1796.[16] The London society was 'entirely at a loss how to proceed'.[17] 'Since the commencement of our correspondence', Samuel Hoare wrote disconsolately to the PAS in August 1795, 'we have never addressed you under circumstances of greater discouragement, as to the attainment of the object of our institution, than at present.'[18] Characteristically, James Pemberton urged the members of the SEAST to press on, reminding them it was the duty of a good man 'to make a momentary stop only when he cannot clearly see his way pointed out', but for once his words fell on deaf ears.[19] Faced by growing hostility both inside and outside Parliament, the London Committee deemed 'any further public measure' inadvisable 'at the present juncture'.[20] Instead, it belatedly endorsed a boycott of 'West India produce', thereby leaving it to 'the serious consideration of every individual what

---

[13] James, *Black Jacobins*, p. 134. For the British campaign in Saint-Domingue, see David Geggus, *Slavery, War and Revolution: The British Occupation of Saint Domingue, 1793–1798* (Oxford: Clarendon Press, 1982).

[14] *Cobbett's Parliamentary History*, 30 (1792–4), p. 1448.

[15] *Cobbett's Parliamentary History*, 30 (1792–4), p. 1448. Pitt was speaking here in support of the Foreign Slave Bill, a measure that he believed would prevent a second Saint-Domingue in the British Caribbean, since 'it was acknowledged that those that were recently imported were the most likely to rebel'. The following year, in the debate on the abolition of the slave trade, Pitt went on to draw a sharp distinction between the 'wild, spurious and imaginary tenets of the Rights of Man and the general principles of practical justice and rational liberty', but all to no avail. See *Cobbett's Parliamentary History*, 31 (1794–5), pp. 1342–3.

[16] Anstey, *The Atlantic Slave Trade*, pp. 280–1.

[17] Samuel Hoare to PAS, 14 August 1795, PAS Correspondence, microfilm edition, Reel 11.

[18] Hoare to PAS, 14 August 1795.

[19] James Pemberton to Granville Sharp, 29 February 1796, PAS Correspondence, microfilm edition, Reel 11.

[20] London Committee Report, 26 June 1795, PAS Correspondence, microfilm edition, Reel 11.

measures to take in order to sap the foundation of this enormous mass of iniquity'.[21] Rendered increasingly ineffectual, in March 1795 the London Committee of the SEAST decided to discontinue its regular weekly meetings and to give up its office in the Old Jewry. Thereafter, the Committee met only intermittently – twice in 1796 and twice again in 1797 – before ceasing operations altogether.[22]

The reverses of 1793–5 left the members of the SEAST thoroughly demoralised. One of those most visibly affected was Thomas Clarkson. For five long years, Clarkson had poured all his energies into the abolition of the slave trade. It had been a superhuman effort, but eventually the tours, the long hours and the constant anxiety began to take their toll. When Clarkson visited his old friends Joseph and Katherine Plymley in Longnor, Shropshire, in October 1791, he was already showing signs of strain.[23] By the spring of 1793 he was on the verge of complete nervous and physical collapse. 'I am suddenly seized with Giddiness and Cramps', he wrote to a parliamentary friend. 'I feel unpleasant Ringing in my Ears. My hands frequently tremble. Cold Sweats suddenly come upon Me. My Appetite becomes all at once ravenous, & if I am not almost immediately gratified, I am ready to faint.'[24] Increasingly, Clarkson's thoughts turned towards retirement. In September 1794 he spent two months boarding with Thomas Wilkinson, a 'plain sensible' Quaker, who owned a farm in the Lake District. Here, he 'attended entirely to his heath', 'dining at half past 12 or 1 o'clock & taking constant gentle exercise with [Wilkinson], such as mowing, reaping, & the like'.[25] The regimen clearly did him good. When Clarkson visited Longnor again in November 1794, Katherine noted that although he looked 'rather thinner his countenance [had] a much more healthy appearance'.[26]

Another change had come over Clarkson: he had fallen in love with the Lake District. At Longnor, he talked of nothing else, often introducing the subject into conversation abruptly, 'in a way that proved how much his thoughts dwell on it'.[27] Clarkson was so taken with the Lake District, in fact, that in 1794 he bought a plot of land at the far end of Ullswater, where he proposed to build a cottage and turn his attention

---

[21] London Committee Report, 26 June 1795.
[22] William Dillwyn to James Pemberton, 12 March 1795, PAS Correspondence, microfilm edition, Reel 11. See also SEAST Minutes, 1795–7.
[23] Diary of Katherine Plymley, 1066/2 (21–2 October 1791).
[24] Thomas Clarkson to Matthew Montagu, 28 August 1793, Elizabeth Montagu Papers, MO710, Huntington Library, San Marino, California.
[25] Diary of Katherine Plymley, 1066/28–9 (14 July–1 December 1794), entry for 17 November.
[26] Plymley diary, entry for 1 December 1794.
[27] Plymley diary, entry for 1 December 1794.

to the gentler pursuits of a gentleman farmer. Much to the Plymleys' surprise, he also talked of getting married, although he was careful not to mention any names. Even now, many of Clarkson's closest friends refused to believe that he meant to retire from the slave-trade agitation. James Phillips told Katherine Plymley that whatever Clarkson might fancy, he 'cannot give up politics'.[28] But Katherine recognised only too well that Clarkson needed a rest from his labours, if only temporarily. A keen observer of Clarkson's shifting moods, she noted that 'he endeavoured to remove gloomy thoughts from his mind', for fear they might overwhelm him.[29] His mind was made up. 'Once I had other views in life beside the Abolition', Clarkson told her. 'Now my mind and body are exhausted, & rest appears to me the most desirable object, to rest my thoughts constantly turn.'[30]

While Clarkson was clearly in poor health in 1793–4, it is also possible to see his decision to move to the Lake District as a political retreat. The 1790s were testing times for radicals, particularly those sympathetic to the principles of the French Revolution. With the outbreak of hostilities with France, Pitt's government commenced a vicious crackdown on alleged 'seditious' activities that culminated in November 1794 in the treason trials of Thomas Hardy, Horne Tooke and John Thelwall.[31] The cases against all three men were weak and unsubstantiated (the Government found it well nigh impossible to prove that any of them had actually advocated the use of armed force, all but essential to support a charge of high treason), but more worrying to Clarkson, at least, was the presumption that 'you were answerable for such letters as may be found in your possession ... though perhaps you may disapprove the sentiments contained therein'.[32] Clarkson almost certainly had contact with radical clubs and societies. Even if, as he claimed, he had never replied to any of their invitations, the logic of the cases presented against Hardy, Tooke and Thelwall was inescapable. Significantly, Clarkson claimed that 'had Tooke been pronounced guilty he would have left this country & settled in America'.[33] Others (Joseph Priestley, for instance) had already turned their thoughts in the same direction. Utopian visions of a better life in America would continue to preoccupy

---

[28] Diary of Katherine Plymley, 1066/41–2 (22 January–17 February 1796), entry for 17 February 1796.
[29] Plymley diary, entry for 1 December 1794.
[30] Plymley diary, entry for 1 December 1794.
[31] Edward Royle, *Revolutionary Britannia? Reflections on the Threat of Revolution in Britain, 1789–1848* (Manchester University Press, 2000), pp. 17–18; John Cannon, *Parliamentary Reform, 1640–1832* (Cambridge University Press, 1973), pp. 129–31.
[32] Plymley diary, entry for 1 December 1794.
[33] Plymley diary, entry for 1 December 1794.

British radicals into the late 1790s and beyond. So, too, would utopian visions of a simple rural life, ideally spent in the company of like-minded individuals.[34]

Clarkson had good reason to fear that the net might be tightening round him. In April 1794, his friend Thomas Walker, a leading member of the Manchester abolition society, had been tried and subsequently acquitted of conspiring to overthrow the government, and others he either knew or had worked with, among them William Frend, were clearly being watched.[35] Government spies were everywhere. Small wonder, then, that Clarkson felt increasingly vulnerable or that he was looking for some means of escape. Asked about his immediate plans, he confessed to the Plymleys in 1794 that he intended to be in London 'as little as possible'. 'Such is the spirit of the times', he went on, 'it is almost dangerous to go into company, an unguarded expression may send you to the Tower.'[36] Viewed in this light, Clarkson's decision to seek refuge in the Lake District was always about more than his health. It was also a political reflex, an act of self-preservation as much as it was a tactical retreat; indeed, in retrospect it is easy to see that the treason trials and the emergence of what E. P. Thompson describes as a 'loyal consensus' in Britain effectively silenced radicals such as Clarkson, forcing them into political exile.[37]

In the USA, too, the fallout from the French Revolution seriously disrupted abolitionist activity. At first, Americans had greeted news of the storming of the Bastille in July and the promulgation of the Declaration of the Rights of Man and the Citizen in August 1789 with enthusiasm. Events in France seemed to echo their own revolutionary struggle. Certainly, this was the view of Thomas Jefferson, probably the leading American Francophile, but many Federalists, too, initially supported the French Revolution.[38] Equally striking were the hundreds of American parades and festivals staged in honour of the French. If many of these rituals bore a distinctly partisan (that is, Democratic Republican) character, there was no mistaking popular support for the French Revolution, at least until

---

[34] See Richard Holmes, *Coleridge: Early Visions* (London: Penguin Books, 1990), pp. 59–88; E. P. Thompson, *The Romantics: England in a Revolutionary Age* (The New York Press, 1997), pp. 173–5. For Priestley and America, see Jenny Graham, 'Revolutionary in Exile: The Emigration of Joseph Priestley to America, 1794–1804', *Transactions of the American Philosophical Society*, 85 (2) (1995) 1–213, at pp. 21–41.

[35] Frida Knight, *The Strange Case of Thomas Walker* (London: Lawrence & Wishart, 1957), pp. 122–40.

[36] Plymley diary, entry for 1 December 1794.

[37] Thompson, *The Romantics*, p. 156.

[38] Gordon S. Wood, *Empire of Liberty: A History of the Early Republic, 1789–1815* (Oxford University Press, 2009), pp. 174–7, 179–81.

1792.[39] Thereafter, the mood began to change. The execution of Louis XVI in January 1793 shocked many Americans, turning them against the Revolution. While Republicans, led by Jefferson, continued to applaud the French, their Federalist opponents began to see Jacobinism as a serious threat to American democracy. The outbreak of war between Britain and France further polarised Americans, forcing them to take sides. Inserting abolitionism into this frenzied debate would prove increasingly difficult. But more ominous still were the signs of growing repression, as state legislatures moved to clamp down on the circulation of potentially subversive individuals and information (and here the parallels with what was happening in Britain are particularly striking).[40]

Little of this was immediately apparent, however. On the contrary, 1794 started on a note of renewed optimism. In January of that year, twenty-six delegates from nine abolition societies met in the City Hall in Philadelphia to discuss the merits of collective action.[41] The 'convention', as it was called, marked a new phase in the history of American abolitionism. Up to this point, most state societies had acted independently, although in practice groups such as the PAS had offered some kind of leadership, if only because they were better resourced and better connected. But clearly many activists now felt that something more was needed, particularly if they were to exert pressure on legislators to take further action against slavery and the slave trade. It was with this in mind that the NYMS had originally suggested the idea of a convention.[42] The response was enthusiastic. While the largest delegations were from Delaware and Pennsylvania, nearly all of the societies were represented at Philadelphia in 1794, the obvious exceptions being Virginia and Rhode Island. Maryland, for instance, sent four delegates, including Samuel Sterett, a former member of the State Senate who had also served one term in the US House of Representatives. Uriah Tracy, another former Congressman, came from Connecticut, mixing on the convention floor with the veteran abolitionist Warner Mifflin (Delaware) and Benjamin Rush from Philadelphia.[43] The sense of excitement was

[39] See Simon P. Newman, *Parades and the Politics of the Street: Festive Culture in the Early American Republic* (Philadelphia, Pa.: University of Pennsylvania Press, 1997), pp. 120–51.
[40] Wood, *Empire of Liberty*, pp. 177, 181–5.
[41] The nine societies represented were Chestertown, Maryland; New Haven, Connecticut; Dover, Delaware; Maryland; New Jersey; New York; Pennsylvania; Washington, Pennsylvania; and Wilmington, Delaware.
[42] John Rogers (NYMS) to PAS, 14 March 1794, PAS Correspondence, microfilm edition, Reel 11.
[43] *Minutes of the Proceedings of a Convention of Delegates* (1794), pp. 4–6; *American National Biography Online*, www.anb.org (accessed 20 April 2011); *Biographical Directory of the United States Congress*, http://bioguide.congress.gov (accessed 9 May 2011).

palpable. Aware of the responsibilities resting on their shoulders, over the course of the next seven days the delegates hammered out a set of clear objectives for the Convention, which significantly included agreeing to meet the following year.

First and foremost, the Convention resolved to submit a memorial to Congress calling for legislation to prohibit US citizens from supplying slaves to foreign nations – a matter of growing concern to many activists, North and South. Not content with that, the delegates also drafted memorials to those state legislatures that had yet to take decisive action against either slavery or the slave trade, urging them to do so. Simultaneously, the Convention endorsed efforts to educate free blacks, so as to prepare them 'for becoming useful citizens of the United States'.[44] As these few details suggest, the tone of the proceedings was confident, expansive and optimistic, so optimistic in fact that the delegates decided to issue an address to the citizens of the USA, calling on them 'to refrain immediately from that species of rapine and murder which has improperly been softened with the name of the African trade'.[45] Slavery, they argued, was not only 'inconsistent with sound policy, in exposing the states which permit it, to all those evils which insurrection and the most resentful war [had] introduced into one of the richest islands of the West Indies [Saint-Domingue]'; it was also 'unfriendly to the present exertions of the inhabitants of Europe in favour of liberty'.[46] 'In vain has the tyranny of kings been rejected', they went on, 'while we permit in our country a domestic despotism, which involves, in its nature, most of the vices and miseries that we have endeavoured to avoid.'[47]

It is difficult to know which was more striking: the scale of the delegates' ambitions or their commitment to a form of idealistic internationalism that was fast becoming more and more difficult to defend, certainly in public. Undeterred, the Convention ordered 1,500 copies of its proceedings to be printed, with a view to giving them as wide a circulation as possible (copies reached London, for instance, as early as July 1794).[48] Given the political situation in the USA, this experiment might have gone horribly wrong. But, remarkably, the Convention almost immediately won an important victory. On

---

[44] *Minutes of the Proceedings of a Convention of Delegates*, pp. 8–10.
[45] *Minutes of the Proceedings of a Convention of Delegates*, p. 25.
[46] *Minutes of the Proceedings of a Convention of Delegates*, p. 23.
[47] *Minutes of the Proceedings of a Convention of Delegates*, p. 23.
[48] *Minutes of the Proceedings of a Convention of Delegates*, p. 28; SEAST to PAS, 10 July 1794, PAS Correspondence, microfilm edition, Reel 11.

22 March 1794, after lengthy deliberation, the US Congress passed a law banning the foreign slave trade. The legislation was not perfect (as the London Committee pointed out, it contained some significant flaws), and it was probably an exaggeration to suggest that it had been the Convention's doing (there were undoubtedly other issues involved, too, not least of which were the events unfolding in Europe and the Caribbean).[49] Nevertheless, the 'Act to prohibit the carrying on the Slave Trade from the United States to any foreign place or country' gave the Convention a significant boost, lending it a credibility that belied its relative organisational weakness.[50] For the moment, at least, it seemed as if collective action might well effect meaningful change in the USA, although arguably the real test was whether the various state legislatures, particularly those in the South, would respond positively to the Convention's calls for reform.

At the outset, enthusiasm, novelty and no small degree of success sustained the American Convention. Over half of the delegates returned for the second convention in 1795, and there was a similar continuity between the second and third conventions; in fact, only about a third of those present in 1796 were attending their first convention. What this meant was that during these early years the delegates were familiar figures to one another. As one might expect, there was a sizeable representation from the Pennsylvania society. Benjamin Rush, for instance, attended the first five conventions, his colleague Samuel Coates the first four, and Samuel Griffitts, William Rawle and James Todd three out of the first four. But other delegates were equally conscientious about attending the Convention and came back time and time again, among them the playwright William Dunlap from New York and Joseph Bloomfield, a former state attorney general who would later go on to become Governor of New Jersey (1801–12). Men such as Rush and Bloomfield dominated the proceedings of these early Conventions (Bloomfield served as president four times between 1794 and 1800), providing much-needed continuity both inside and outside the convention hall. By contrast, the New York society had a relatively high turnover of delegates, twelve in five years. Only William Dunlap attended

---

[49] Rappleye, *Sons of Providence*, pp. 289–300; SEAST to PAS, 10 July 1794; *Minutes of the Proceedings of the Second Convention of Delegates from the Abolition Societies Established in Different Parts of the United States, Assembled at Philadelphia, on the Seventh Day of January, One Thousand Seven Hundred and Ninety-Five, and Continued, by Adjournments, Until the Fourteenth Day of the Same Month, Inclusive* (Philadelphia, Pa.: Zachariah Poulson, Junior, 1795), p. 13.

[50] Du Bois, *The Suppression of the African Slave-Trade*, p. 242.

more than two conventions before 1800, while the vast majority (ten in all) attended only once.[51]

The optimism of these early years, however, soon gave way to increasing concerns about the strength and unity of the movement. Between 1794 and 1797, no fewer than four societies seem to have failed, namely those in New Haven (Connecticut), Dover (Delaware), Washington (Pennsylvania) and Chestertown (Maryland). It is true that new societies at Richmond (Virginia), Alexandria (Virginia) and Choptank (Maryland) emerged to take their place, but there was no mistaking the signs of decay and disintegration.[52] The situation in Delaware was a particular cause of concern. By all accounts, the Dover-based Delaware Society for Promoting the Abolition of Slavery had dissolved in 1795, and there were similar problems in Wilmington, where a society had been established in 1789.[53] By 1797, the situation had become so serious that the PAS delegated four of its members to visit the Wilmington society, with a view to offering it financial assistance, £100 spread over two years in quarterly instalments. For whatever reason, the proposed meeting did not take place until November 1800, by which date the society had been temporarily suspended. Undeterred, the PAS delegation pressed the case for perseverance, at the same time renewing their offer of financial assistance. Their efforts seem to have paid off. The following month the Wilmington society was relaunched as the Delaware Society for the Abolition of Slavery and for Relief and Protection of Free Blacks and People of Colour, Unlawfully Held in Bondage or Otherwise Oppressed.[54] The association had been saved but largely (and this is the crucial point) because the members of the PAS had seen fit to intervene.

Finance was only part of the issue here. For many, the slave rebellion in Saint-Domingue had brought home the wider implications of French revolutionary principles, fuelling fears of further uprisings across the Americas. That threat became all the more apparent after

---

[51] All of these details are extracted from the published proceedings of the American Convention, 1794–6. For Bloomfield, see *Biographical Directory of the United States Congress*, available online at http://bioguide.congress.gov (accessed 9 May 2011). There was also a social dimension to these occasions, which, in Dunlap's case, involved dinners and theatregoing. See William Dunlap, *A History of the American Theatre from Its Origins to 1832* (1832; rpt. Urbana, Ill.: University of Illinois Press, 2005), pp. 172–3.

[52] *Minutes of the Proceedings of the Fourth Convention of Delegates* (1797), pp. 4–5. See also PAS to SEAST, 2 March 1795, PAS Correspondence, Reel 11.

[53] Calvert, 'The Abolition Society of Delaware', 295–320, at pp. 299–300.

[54] PAS Minutes, 3 July 1797, 17 July 1797, 13 November 1797, 1 January 1798, 6 January 1800.

1792, with the arrival in the USA of thousands of French émigrés from Saint-Domingue, many of them accompanied by their slaves. While some of these immigrants settled in the North, large numbers disembarked in Southern ports. By the end of July 1793, residents of Norfolk, Virginia, reported that the town was 'crowded with Frenchmen … [and] too many [French] Negroes', and there were similar reports from Baltimore and Charleston. If many southerners sympathised with the plight of these émigrés, many more viewed them with suspicion. Black immigrants were a special cause of concern. Tainted by the excesses of the French Revolution, they were widely suspected of being troublemakers; even their very presence in the South was thought by some whites to have a harmful influence on the slave population. In response, many Southern states passed laws prohibiting black immigration from the Caribbean. Georgia already had such a law by 1793, and South Carolina and North Carolina followed suit in 1794 and 1795 respectively. Even where such laws did not exist (Virginia is a case in point), there were concerted efforts to restrict black immigration from the Caribbean, simply by refusing landing rights to vessels suspected of having 'French Negroes' on board.[55]

In a related move, many Southern state legislatures also began to restrict the mobility of free blacks. In 1795, for instance, North Carolina passed a law requiring free blacks entering the state to post a bond of £200. Other states simply banned free black entry, effectively prohibiting interstate migration. Simultaneously, the laws requiring free blacks to carry freedom papers were tightened up. Registers were introduced, which had to be renewed annually so as to prevent abuses. Some states even required free blacks to wear identifying marks – shoulder patches, for instance. The cumulative effect of this legislation was devastating. As Ira Berlin puts it: 'By the beginning of the nineteenth century, the freedmen's liberty was precarious indeed. At any time, any white could demand proof of a free Negro's status; even if his papers were in order, an unemployed free Negro could be jailed and enslaved and his children bound out to strangers.'[56] Part of the intention, of course, was to keep free blacks away from slaves. Penalties for harbouring runaways were severe, as they were for forging freedom papers. In some states, free blacks could be prosecuted and fined for 'entertaining slaves, meeting in groups of more than seven, attending school, or holding church meetings'.[57] Like black immigrants from the Caribbean, free blacks

[55] Scott, 'The Common Wind', pp. 274–82.
[56] Berlin, *Slaves Without Masters*, p. 95.
[57] Berlin, *Slaves Without Masters*, p. 96.

were seen as subversives and therefore as threats to the peace and security of the slave system. Consequently they needed to be controlled.

Abolitionists, too, came under increasing attack. In 1791, for instance, the Maryland House of Delegates condemned the state abolition society and, eager to press home its advantage, began to attack abolitionist-supported freedom suits.[58] Activists in Virginia faced similar repression. In 1795, Elisha Dick, a local doctor, disrupted one of the early meetings of the Alexandria society, warning its members of 'the dangerous consequences which might result from the establishment of such a Society, by infusing into the slaves a spirit of insurrection and rebellion, which might eventually destroy the tranquillity of the State'.[59] Not content with that, pro-slavery forces organised a remonstrance against the Alexandria society, which resulted in a new state law designed to censure abolitionists and, at the same time, to limit their involvement in freedom suits.[60] As if that were not enough, in the same session, the Virginia General Assembly narrowly defeated a proposal for the gradual abolition of slavery. The events of 1795 left Virginia activists thoroughly demoralised. Joseph Anthony of the Richmond society reported to the American Convention in 1797 that the overall effect had been to 'slacken the exertions of many of our members, so that we can have but little of a pleasing nature at this time to communicate'.[61]

Even in Pennsylvania there were unmistakable signs of decline and retrenchment. The society in Washington, for instance, saw its numbers diminish between 1788 and 1790, not only because of the 'unpopularity of the association' but also because of the 'intemperate zeal' of some of its members. More worryingly still, others began to have serious doubts about the value of the whole enterprise. 'This is not the worst', Alexander Addison confided to James Pemberton in 1790, 'for we find with regret that though we restore slaves to freedom we cannot

---

[58] Berlin, *Slaves Without Masters*, p. 81. Complaints against the Maryland society for 'improper interference' in freedom suits reached the General Assembly again in 1792. See *Providence Gazette and Country Journal*, 17 March 1792, 24 March 1792 and 31 March 1792.

[59] See Archibald McClean to William Roger, 15 February 1796, PAS Correspondence, microfilm edition, Reel 11.

[60] McClean to Roger, 15 February 1796.

[61] *Minutes of the Proceedings of the Third Convention of Delegates from the Abolition Societies Established in Different Parts of the United States, Assembled at Philadelphia, on the First Day of January, One Thousand Seven Hundred and Ninety-Six, and Continued, by Adjournments, Until the Seventh Day of the Same Month, Inclusive* (Philadelphia, Pa.: Zachariah Poulson, Junior, 1796), p. 10; Berlin, *Slaves Without Masters*, pp. 80, 84; Joseph Anthony to the American Convention for Promoting the Abolition of Slavery, probably May but definitely 1797, PAS Papers, microfilm edition, Reel 28.

transform them to virtue'.[62] Addison's point was simple: that without adequate resources abolitionists in Washington were powerless to effect meaningful change.[63] His words were to prove prophetic. By 1795 the Washington society had been disbanded. Some members, among them David Redick, subsequently joined the PAS, but to all intents and purposes they worked alone. Redick more than once found himself 'singly engaged' against armed gangs who entered the town in broad daylight and attempted to 'force [free Blacks] down the [Ohio] River to be sold into slavery'.[64] Surrounded by unsympathetic townspeople and duplicitous lawyers, Redick felt increasingly vulnerable. 'The Washington society is of no importance', he wrote to Pemberton in May 1795, '[and] as a member of your Society, I have considered myself just a Man in these exertions, for as I have not had it in my power to have your counsel nor instructions, I almost feel out of the reach of succour.'[65] This was not self-pity. On the contrary, Redick's plight in many ways exemplified the predicament that scores of state activists found themselves in as they struggled to come to terms with the narrow, repressive and increasingly partisan mood of the late 1790s.

By 1796 it was already clear that the movement had become becalmed and that in some states it was actually in retreat. The progress of the Convention's various memorials to state legislatures told their own story. Society after society reported that these memorials had either not been submitted or had been brought in and lost. Equally revealing were some of the reasons given. The Rhode Island society, for instance, deemed that it had not been 'expedient' to present their memorial against slavery. Similarly, the Maryland society reported that it had twice forwarded its memorial to the State Assembly but that 'those persons who undertook to present it were of opinion, it was not a proper time to deliver it in, and therefore returned it to the society again'.[66] By tacit agreement, these various memorials seem to have been set aside and forgotten. When the American Convention met again in May 1797, attention shifted to continued abuses of the legislation against the slave trade (specifically, infringements of the Foreign Slave Trade Act of 1794), to the education of free blacks and a proposal to publish a 'general history of slavery in the United States'.[67] In short, this was a much more muted gathering

---

[62] Alexander Addison to James Pemberton, 6 December 1790, PAS Correspondence, microfilm edition, Reel 11.
[63] Addison to Pemberton, 6 December 1790.
[64] David Redick to James Pemberton, 24 May 1795, PAS Correspondence, microfilm edition, Reel 11.
[65] Redick to Pemberton, 24 May 1795.
[66] *Minutes of the Proceedings of the Third Convention of Delegates* (1796), pp. 9–11.
[67] *Minutes of the Proceedings of the Fourth Convention of Delegates* (1797), pp. 7–13.

and one that was clearly intent on proceeding cautiously. Everything indicated that the resolve of the delegates remained as firm as ever. Nevertheless, there is no denying the fact that after 1797 they found themselves operating in a much more hostile environment.

It did not help, either, that the international situation appeared so unpromising. News of the imminent demise of the SEAST stunned many American activists. 'We are sensible of the many difficulties you labour under', James Pemberton wrote to Granville Sharp in February 1796, 'but cannot conclude without expressing an earnest wish that you will not be discouraged from continuing your correspondence.'[68] Britain remained a key strategic partner. As Pemberton conceded, one of the charges most commonly levelled against British abolitionists was that if Britain gave up the slave trade then America would profit as a result. 'We see the force of it', he went on, 'and are sorry to say, it is not without an appearance of foundation.'[69] Common interests, therefore, brought the two nations together, which is why between 1795 and 1797 the NYMS cooperated with the Court and Directors of the Sierra Leone Company to apprehend and prosecute violators of the US Foreign Slave Act.[70] Yet somehow the fire had gone out of the old Anglo-American alliance. The PAS–SEAST correspondence, for so long a measure of the strength of international cooperation, broke down after 1797. Persistent to the last, James Pemberton urged British activists to carry on ('as the way is pointed out', he argued, 'we cannot be wrong whomsoever we may offend'[71]), but after a time even he was forced to concede defeat.

France, on the other hand, posed a different set of challenges. In 1796, a group of activists led by Henri Grégoire, François Xavier Lanthenas, Benjamin Frossard and the Swedish abolitionist Charles Wadstrom relaunched the Société des Amis des Noirs, now renamed the Société des Amis des Noirs et des Colonies.[72] As the change in its

---

[68] James Pemberton to Granville Sharp, 29 February 1796, PAS Correspondence, microfilm edition, Reel 11.

[69] James Pemberton to SEAST, 26 April 1797, PAS Correspondence, microfilm edition, Reel 11.

[70] NYMS Minutes, 2 June 1795, 17 November 1795, 15 November 1796, 17 January 1797 and 16 May 1797.

[71] James Pemberton to SEAST, 26 April 1797.

[72] The extant minutes of the revived society date from 30 November 1797, although the members were almost certainly meeting before that date, if only informally. See Dorigny and Gainot, *La Société des Amis des Noirs*, pp. 308–10; Necheles, *The Abbé Grégoire*, pp. 159–60. Alexandre Giroud (see below) claimed that the society had been revived in March 1796. What happened in 1797, therefore, may have been a 'reunion of the friends of the blacks and colonies', a view shared by Necheles, who claims that the new society was largely inactive during the first year of its existence. See also

title implied, the aim of the new society was to encourage the social, political and economic development of the French colonies through educational initiatives, the transfer of new technologies and the creation of model farms that would demonstrate the advantages of colonies founded on the principles of liberty. In short, the aim of the society was to aid the transition from slavery to emancipation, but, significantly, to do so within the context of French colonial rule.[73] Like its predecessor, the new society was keen to reach out to fellow activists. In January 1796, for instance, Lanthenas approached Clarkson with a view to publishing a French edition of the evidence presented against the slave trade to the British Parliament, together with a 'summary of the work of our two societies'.[74] There is also a suggestion that the French society hoped to use Wadstrom, who was well known to the members of the SEAST, to forge closer links with British activists.[75]

More intriguing still were the activities of Alexandre Giroud, a mining engineer from Grenoble, who in March 1796 left for Saint-Domingue as part of a five-man commission (the Third Civil Commission) that also included Léger-Félicité Sonthonax, Julien Raimond and Philippe Roume de St Laurent. Specifically tasked by the French Directory to keep free coloured ambitions in check, the commission worked tirelessly to promote the welfare of ex-slaves, at the same time instilling in them the necessity of labour. Devastated plantations were rebuilt, schools established, legal restraints on blacks suspended and all forms of coercion (whipping, for instance) outlawed.[76] It was with these concerns in mind that early the following year Giroud visited the USA, where he met the corresponding committee of the PAS on 14 January. Presenting himself as a member of the new French society, which he claimed had been revived in March 1796, Giroud set out the purpose of his visit, which was to interest American activists in forming 'settlements' in Saint-Domingue. Conditions in the colony, he insisted, were ripe for such an enterprise. The ancient prejudices were daily wearing away, and peace and 'good understanding' reigned 'between the Whites, Blacks and men of colour, between the proprietors and cultivators, and

Samuel Griffitts to James Pemberton, 20 October 1798, Etting Collection, No. 30, Physicians, Historical Society of Pennsylvania; PAS Minutes, 20 November 1798.
[73] Necheles, *The Abbé Grégoire*, pp. 159–64; Dorigny and Gainot, *La Société des Amis des Noirs*, pp. 301–27; Jennings, *French Anti-Slavery*, p. 3.
[74] François Xavier Lanthenas to Clarkson, 16 January 1796, Thomas Clarkson Papers, St John's College, Cambridge.
[75] François Xavier Lanthenas to Thomas Clarkson, 16 January 1796, Thomas Clarkson Papers, St John's College, Cambridge; Necheles, *The Abbé Grégoire*, p. 159. Necheles claims that this was Grégoire's idea but that Wadstrom refused to cooperate.
[76] James, *Black Jacobins*, pp. 174–5; Garrigus, *Before Haiti*, pp. 290, 304, 309.

between the citizens and the government'.[77] Moreover, as he could vouch from personal experience, the commissioners were 'continually' letting out plantations belonging to the republic, which required nothing more than 'some advances to yield a very advantageous produce'.[78] But, rather than take his word for all this, Giroud insisted that the committee come and see for themselves. If they were to nominate one or two deputies, he guaranteed that the French Government at Saint-Domingue would receive them as 'sincere friends of France, and of the principles of humanity, liberty and equality, upon which basis her colonial system will rest for the time to come'.[79]

Giroud, it should be stressed, was not suggesting that the PAS should throw its weight behind attempts to colonise American blacks in Saint-Domingue, although this may have been at the back of his mind; rather, what he seems to have been proposing was a form of economic aid, whereby the PAS would rent or purchase land in Saint-Domingue and have oversight of its cultivation, working in cooperation with free blacks.[80] The PAS undoubtedly saw the merits of such a scheme. What Giroud was offering, in effect, was an opportunity to contribute to the success of Saint-Domingue as a free labour experiment. Strategically, therefore, the proposal made a lot of sense. Yet, at the same time, it carried enormous risks, not least because of the possible political ramifications. Saint-Domingue was a divisive issue. While Republicans tended to side with the French colonial regime, Federalists encouraged the independence of Saint-Domingue, if only as a means of monopolising the colony's trade.[81] Giroud clearly knew all this. As his subsequent actions revealed, he was not only intent on drawing the USA and France closer together but was also prepared to play on Republican sympathies in order to achieve his ends.[82] This was a dangerous game. The activities in America

---

[77] Alexandre Giroud to PAS, 17 January 1797, PAS Correspondence, microfilm edition, Reel 11.

[78] Giroud to PAS, 17 January 1797.

[79] Alexandre Giroud to Samuel Griffitts, 23 January 1797, PAS Correspondence, Reel 20; James Alexander Dun, 'Philadelphia Not Philanthropolis: The Limits of Pennsylvanian Antislavery in the Era of the Haitian Revolution', *The Pennsylvania Magazine of History and Biography*, 145 (1) (2011): 73–102.

[80] Alexandre Giroud to PAS, 9 April 1797, PAS Correspondence, microfilm edition, Reel 11.

[81] Tim Matthewson, 'Jefferson and Haiti', *Journal of Southern History*, 61 (May 1995): 209–48, at pp. 213, 216; Peter P. Hill, *French Perceptions of the Early American Republic, 1783–1793* (Philadelphia, Pa.: University of Pennsylvania Press, 1988), p. 79.

[82] The following year, for instance, Giroud presented Jefferson with a present of some rare breadfruit seeds. See Alexandre Giroud to Thomas Jefferson, 9 April 1797, *The Papers of Thomas Jefferson Digital Edition*, ed. Barbara B. Oberg and J. Jefferson Looney, available online at http://rotunda.upress.virginia.edu/founders/TSJN-01-29-02-0273 (accessed 20 March 2011).

of the French minister Citizen Charles Genet had already alerted many Federalists to the political dangers posed by French 'agents'. If exposed, Giroud (and the PAS) ran the risk of similar censure.[83]

Wisely, the PAS stepped back from committing itself to Giroud's ambitious plans for Saint-Domingue, but not before it had made him and three other members of the Third Civil Commission (Raimond, Sonthonax and Henri Pascal) honorary members of the Pennsylvania society.[84] How much the 1797 Convention knew about these overtures is unclear. But the delegates certainly knew enough to appreciate that something was stirring on the other side of the Atlantic. In a carefully worded letter, the president, Joseph Bloomfield, welcomed the revival of the Société des Amis des Noirs, congratulating it on the efforts it was taking to 'improve the condition of the oppressed Africans [in the French colonies], and extend to them the privileges of equal liberty and citizenship'.[85] In doing so, however, he stressed the importance of education in rebuilding post-emancipation societies. 'Convinced that good education is essential to good citizenship', he explained,

this Convention, and the societies in the different states represented in it, endeavour to increase the number of useful schools for the instruction of the Africans and their children. By instilling into their minds the benefits of knowledge, and by training them up in regular and economical habits, they are enabled to form a true estimate of the nature of liberty to respect the rights of other men, as well as their own, in short, they are instructed to be industrious and to be honest.[86]

Bloomfield's cautious approach spoke volumes about the preoccupations of American abolitionists at the turn of the century. Faced by mounting opposition at home, they were increasingly inclined to take the path of least resistance, particularly where international cooperation was concerned.

Given the worsening political situation, the Convention's moderate stance was perfectly understandable. By the middle of 1797, relations between the USA and France had deteriorated to the point where war seemed a real possibility. At first, President John Adams attempted conciliation, but when agents of Talleyrand and the Directory demanded what amounted to a bribe, Adams was forced to inform Congress

[83] Wood, *Empire of Liberty*, pp. 185–9.
[84] PAS Minutes, 3 April 1797, 24 April 1797, 5 June 1797; Léger-Félicité Sonthonax to PAS, 9 April 1797, Julien Raimond to PAS, 10 April 1797, Henri Pascal to PAS, 10 April 1797, PAS Correspondence, Reel 1; Dun, 'Philadelphia Not Philanthropolis', pp. 74–8.
[85] Quoted in Dorigny and Gainot, *La Société des Amis des Noirs*, p. 370.
[86] Quoted in Dorigny and Gainot, *La Société des Amis des Noirs*, p. 370.

that the diplomatic mission had been a failure. The result was not only growing distrust of the French but also of all those, principally Republicans, suspected of being Jacobins. In May 1798, riots broke out in Philadelphia 'between supporters of Britain and those of France, and mobs attacked Republican newspaper editors'.[87] As partisan feeling increased, Federalists looked to check Jacobin influence through new repressive legislation, principally the Naturalisation Act of 18 June, which required all those seeking citizenship to pledge allegiance to the US Constitution; the Aliens Act of 25 June, which gave the President authority to deport those suspected of being 'dangerous to the peace and safety of the United States'; and, perhaps most contentious of all, the Sedition Act of 14 July, which made it a crime to 'write, print, utter or publish ... any false, scandalous, and malicious writing against the Government of the United States, or either Houses of the Congress of the United States, with intent to defame the said government'. Simultaneously, both the army and the navy were enlarged, as the Adams administration sought to bolster home defences against what many feared was the possibility of a French invasion.[88]

The 1798 Convention, therefore, met at a time of escalating tensions. Diligently, the fifteen delegates present went through the business of the Convention, but there was no mistaking the fact that events outside the hall dominated their proceedings. The point was well made by the Committee of Arrangements on the third day of the Convention. 'The situation of public affairs', it concluded,

renders the present time unsuitable for the adoption of any new measures of importance. In many of the United States a peculiar degree of caution in the management of this business becomes necessary; and on this ground it is deemed more prudent to persevere in the steps which have already been so judiciously taken, than to attempt, at this juncture, any material variation or extension of them.[89]

Some delegates went further. Joseph Anthony and Tarlton Pleasants of the Virginia society reported that in the opinion of their 'friends' in the General Assembly, '*any* step' to raise the question of abolition 'at this particular moment would tend to injure the cause it was intended to serve'.[90] The Convention, as a result, counselled 'quiet submission', not least on the part of those who were enslaved. In the circumstances,

[87] Wood, *Empire of Liberty*, p. 245.
[88] Wood, *Empire of Liberty*, pp. 247–60.
[89] *Minutes of the Proceedings of the Fifth Convention of Delegates* (1798), p. 11.
[90] Joseph Anthony and Tarlton Pleasants to Samuel Stansbury, 22 March 1798, PAS Correspondence, microfilm edition, Reel 12. My emphasis.

all that abolitionists could do was to bide their time and look to the future. Once the 'storms' had passed, the Convention address reassured activists, then the

light of truth [would] break through the dark gloom of oppression – cruelty and justice [would] not only hear, but obey, the voice of reason and religion; and in these United States the practice of the people [would] be conformable to their declaration, 'That all men are born equally free and have an unalienable right to Liberty'.[91]

It is a measure of just how tense the situation was in 1798 that the delegates decided to defer the next meeting of the Convention until 1800, thereby breaking a pattern that had been established since 1794. For the next two years the movement in the USA languished. In France, meanwhile, activists found themselves facing two irresistible forces: on the one hand, a reactionary trend that would lead in 1799 to the adoption of a new constitution that invested Napoleon Bonaparte with practically limitless powers as First Consul of the Republic; and, on the other, the course of events in Saint-Domingue. By November 1798, the Société des Amis des Noirs et des Colonies had over sixty members, among them colonial officials such as Sonthonax, the black deputy Pierre Thomany, the economist J. B. Say and a small group of English exiles living in Paris that included the novelist Helen Maria Williams.[92] The society had also grown in confidence. Plans were put forward to print both its own debates and 'scholarly treatises concerning colonial problems', the idea being that such a programme might 'forestall or destroy the prejudices which might arise against us in one part of the public and perhaps among members of the administration and the government'.[93] Reflecting this growing confidence, Sonthonax exhorted a public meeting in February 1799 to fight for complete black freedom so that France's example would spread to the rest of the world. 'You are still the [blacks'] brothers and their friends', he told them, 'even though they are now free.'[94]

Yet, increasingly, such talk began to seem rash, even unpatriotic. Since 1794 France had followed a pro-black policy in Saint-Domingue, culminating in the appointment of Toussaint L'Ouverture as Lieutenant-Governor (May 1796). Up to a point, this policy worked, but then in 1797 things took a turn for the worse, at least from a French perspective. Toussaint's abrupt dismissal of first Sonthonax and then

[91] *Minutes of the Proceedings of the Fifth Convention of Delegates* (1798), pp. 18–19.
[92] Necheles, *The Abbé Grégoire*, p. 162; Dorigny and Gainot, *La Société des Amis des Noirs*, pp. 313–14.
[93] Necheles, *The Abbé Grégoire*, p. 162.
[94] Quoted in Necheles, *The Abbé Grégoire*, p. 163.

General Hedouville, who in July 1797 had been appointed sole agent for Saint-Domingue by the French Directory, left him in effective control of the colony, except for the 'mulatto state' in the south controlled by his one-time ally, André Rigaud. By the beginning of 1799 the colony was on the verge of civil war, which finally broke out in April when Rigaud recklessly launched an offensive against Toussaint.[95] These events severely compromised the members of the Société des Amis des Noirs et des Colonies, who, as a result, found themselves defending interests now considered inimical to France. Gamely, the society struggled on, but in November 1799 it was suppressed when Napoleon came to power.[96] Not for the first time, national interests (in this case, the compelling need to restore 'order' in Saint-Domingue) thwarted the ambitions of reformers committed to the realisation of a new world order based on the principles of liberty, equality and peaceful commerce.

By 1800, therefore, the international movement had reached its nadir. Activity in Britain and France had ground to a halt, while in the USA there were unmistakable signs of disintegration and decay. Just how serious this decline was became apparent when the American Convention met again in June 1800. In all, twelve delegates assembled in the City Hall in Philadelphia, most of them newcomers. Only three delegates had any previous experience of conventions, and, of these, only Joseph Bloomfield from New Jersey could describe himself as a veteran. There were also some important absences, among them figures such as Benjamin Rush, William Dunlap and Samuel Coates. More significant, however, than this break in continuity was the fact that all of the delegates came from just three states: New Jersey (three), Pennsylvania (five) and Virginia (four). Some societies, such as those in Rhode Island and Alexandria, clearly decided to stay away; the NYMS, for its part, sent a report but did not attend.[97] Even so, there was no

---

[95] James, *Black Jacobins*, pp. 186–223.
[96] Jennings, *French Anti-Slavery*, p. 3. Manuscript minutes survive for the Société des Amis des Noirs et des Colonies up to 30 March 1799. See Dorigny and Gainot, *La Société des Amis des Noirs*, pp. 362–3. As Necheles notes, the society was also adversely affected by the deaths of both Lanthenas and Wadstrom in 1799.
[97] See *Minutes of the Proceedings of the Sixth Convention of Delegates from the Abolition Societies Established in Different Parts of the United States, Assembled at Philadelphia, on the Fourth Day of June, One Thousand Eight Hundred, and Continued, by Adjournments, Until the Sixth Day of the Same Month, Inclusive* (Philadelphia, Pa.: Zachariah Poulson, Junior, 1800), pp. 2–4, 13–17. Though it was active into the nineteenth century, the Rhode Island society did not send delegates to the American Convention after 1798. Part of the reason was undoubtedly finance (at once stage the Convention even contemplated defraying delegates' expenses) but there may have been other factors involved, too, among them local political conditions. For his part, Moses Brown, a leading figure in the Rhode Island society, seems to have withdrawn from the field after 1803. See Rappleye, *Sons of Providence*, pp. 336–7.

denying the fact that the movement had lost momentum between 1798 and 1800, or that the 1800 Convention represented the start of a new and very different phase in the history of American abolitionism.

Undeterred, the delegates set about the task of breathing new life into the organisation. Many clearly felt that one way of doing this was through the adoption of a formal written constitution, the idea being that such a document would give the Convention 'energy and stability', not least through the establishment of an acting committee to deal with business between the annual meetings of the Convention. There was also a proposal for the creation of a 'fighting fund', effectively a levy on some of the wealthier societies that would help those (Virginia, for example) that had 'much business to engage their attention but were weak in pecuniary resources'.[98] Union was considered 'indispensable'. As the delegates put it in their final address: 'The societies should never be found in the pursuit of incongruous measures, but act in concert; and this cannot perhaps be better accomplished than by a free and liberal interchange of opinions, and knowledge and experience.' 'The convention', they went on, 'should be the rallying point of information, whence useful knowledge should diverge to each society, communicating life, energy, and consistency to the whole.'[99] This was all very well in theory. The problem was that the effectiveness of the American Convention depended on the strength of the individual societies and their willingness or ability to cooperate. Without adequate resources, the delegates were unable to encourage expansion or to do much to counter white resistance, particularly in the South. In truth, it was as much as the Convention could do to sustain established societies, and, as time went on, even that was to prove increasingly difficult.

These problems were brought sharply into focus when in 1800 authorities in Virginia uncovered a plot led by Gabriel, a twenty-four-year-old enslaved blacksmith, to seize the state armoury in Richmond and capture or kill the Governor and as many legislators as possible. This was no small-scale affair. Some 500 or 600 blacks were involved in the plot, which appears to have been carefully planned over a period of six to eight months and to have aroused little or no suspicion among whites (particularly ironic, given the siege mentality that had been developing in the South during the 1790s).[100] Gabriel and twenty-six of his

---

[98] *Minutes of the Proceedings of the Sixth Convention of Delegates* (1800), pp. 17–18.
[99] *Minutes of the Proceedings of the Sixth Convention of Delegates* (1800), pp. 21–3.
[100] For the Gabriel slave revolt, see Douglas R. Egerton, *Gabriel's Rebellion: The Virginia Slave Conspiracies of 1800–1802* (Chapel Hill, NC: University of North Carolina Press, 1993); James Sidbury, *Ploughshares into Swords: Race, Rebellion, and Identity in Gabriel's Virginia, 1730–1810* (Cambridge University Press, 1997).

co-conspirators were subsequently hanged, but the reverberations did not end there. The size and scale of the plot, not to mention the open defiance of the conspirators (what John Randolph referred to as their 'contempt of danger'), gave many whites pause for thought.[101] Some pointed the finger at free blacks, even though the vast majority of Gabriel's followers were slaves. Others, such as George Tucker, concluded that the real meaning of the plot was that blacks would 'never rest satisfied with anything short of perfect equality'.[102] This being the case, the only solution, he believed, was colonisation; that is, to emancipate the slaves and to relocate them, either to the western territories of the USA (Tucker's preferred destination) or, failing that, to Africa or the Caribbean.[103]

Abolitionists, too, came in for their fair share of blame. In Alexandria, for instance, progress had been made in establishing a school for free blacks, which members of the society ran, each taking their turn to teach the pupils. In the wake of Gabriel's plot, however, the 'school committee was cautioned that it would be prudent to discontinue the school for a time; that however praiseworthy the object might be, such collections of black people could not be admitted'.[104] Sensibly, the committee complied, but their decision proved fatal. Lacking any real focus for their activities, the Alexandria society declined and finally dissolved. Looking back on this course of events in 1804, George Drinker attributed the demise of the society to three factors: the initial decision to admit slaveholders as members, the 'anti-abolition' law of 1795 and, finally, Gabriel's rebellion. Revival was clearly out of the question. 'We are in fact dead', Drinker concluded, 'and I may say, I have no hope of reanimation.'[105] It was the same thing in Richmond. Here, activists had managed to regroup after 1795 but by 1801 the society was reported to be in a 'languid and critical' state, largely because many of those 'who were once hearty in the cause of emancipation, taking a retrospect view of the recent plot which threatened our internal tranquillity with a revolutionary convulsion, have now thought proper to abandon

---

[101] Whitman, *Challenging Slavery in the Chesapeake*, p. 89 (quotation).
[102] Whitman, *Challenging Slavery in the Chesapeake*, p. 90.
[103] Whitman, *Challenging Slavery in the Chesapeake*, pp. 89–91. For more on black colonisation, see Chapter 8.
[104] *Minutes of the Proceedings of the Tenth American Convention for Promoting the Abolition of Slavery, and Improving the Condition of the African Race: Assembled at Philadelphia, on the Fourteenth Day of January, One Thousand Eight Hundred and Five, and Continued by Adjournments Until the Seventeenth Day of the Same Month, Inclusive* (Philadelphia, Pa.: Kimber, Conrad & Co., 1805), p. 23.
[105] *Minutes of the Proceedings of the Tenth American Convention for Promoting the Abolition of Slavery* (1805), pp. 21–6.

it as dangerous to the well-being of society'.[106] Though it managed to send a delegate to the 1801 Convention, the Richmond society seems to have collapsed soon thereafter, effectively ending anti-slavery activity in Virginia, at least at an organised level.

As a result, the American Convention became a much more truncated organisation after 1801, being largely made up of delegates from the old historic centres of Pennsylvania, New York, New Jersey and Delaware. Representation was even more geographically circumscribed than this might suggest. Uniquely among American societies, the New Jersey society was highly decentralised, consisting of four county meetings, each with its own officers. Two of these meetings, those in Salem and Gloucester, were just across the Delaware river from Wilmington, the third, in Burlington, was within striking distance of Philadelphia, and the fourth, in Middlesex, was close to Trenton, where a separate society was organised in 1801.[107] Put a different way, most of these delegates (including those from Delaware) came from within a forty-mile radius of Philadelphia. Lacking any real representation from the South, or from New England, for that matter, the American Convention increasingly became a local or regional association designed to bolster the fortunes of a movement that by 1801 was facing a crisis not just in terms of numbers but also in terms of its ability to influence public debates on slavery and the slave trade.

The charge increasingly made against American abolitionists, especially after the Gabriel revolt, was that their activities were subversive and therefore un-American. The Convention addressed some of these concerns in its 1801 address to the citizens of the USA. It was true, the delegates conceded, that they contemplated the abolition of slavery, 'sooner or later, by such means as your humanity and the wisdom of our rulers may suggest'.[108] Yet, at the same time, they disavowed any wish to contravene existing state laws (or, indeed, the laws of the USA) while they remained in force, 'or to hazard the peace and safety of the community by the adoption of ill advised and precipitate measures'.[109] Simultaneously, they deplored the recent attempts at insurrection by some of the slaves in the Southern states. But, in saying this, they

[106] *Minutes of the Proceedings of the Seventh Convention of Delegates* (1801), p. 22.
[107] 'List of the Officers and the Members of the New Jersey Abolition Society, 1801', PAS Papers, Reel 28; Robert Smith to the American Convention, 6 September 1802, PAS Papers, Reel 28. Originally there had been ten of these county meetings, including two, Hunterdon and Sussex, in the northern part of the state, but no more than six were ever represented at the society's annual general meetings, and by 1800 the number was down to four. See Minutes of the New Jersey Abolition Society, 1793–1809.
[108] *Minutes of the Proceedings of the Seventh Convention of Delegates* (1801), p. 37.
[109] *Minutes of the Proceedings of the Seventh Convention of Delegates* (1801), p. 38.

could not help drawing what to them seemed the obvious conclusion: that to avoid similar insurrections in the future some remedial action needed to be taken, namely 'an amelioration of the present situation of the slaves, and the adoption of a system of gradual emancipation'.[110] 'If the severity of their treatment was lessened', the address went on, 'and the hope of freedom for them or their property were held forth as the reward for good behaviour, the slaves would be bound by personal interest to be civil, orderly and industrious'.[111] Neatly turning the tables on their opponents, the Convention advanced emancipation as a safe option that far from inciting rebellion would benefit slaves and slave-holders alike.

These were difficult times for American activists. Mindful of their responsibilities, they endeavoured – as far as possible – to move with 'circumspection'. The 1804 Convention even went so far as to suggest that care should be taken over the selection of (state) acting committees – 'to fill them with discreet men, in order that no useless umbrage may be given to our opponents, nor suits undertaken with too much precipitation, which for want of this prudent line of conduct have sometimes ended in injury to prosecutors, and been attended with heavy expence'.[112] For the same reasons, in 1803 the Convention decided against petitioning the North Carolina legislature to repeal a law that forbade individuals from emancipating their slaves, judging that 'at the present time' such an application would be 'unpropitious'.[113] Nevertheless, it would be wrong to conclude that the Convention had lost impetus or that it had become moribund. Throughout this period (1801–4), activists were repeatedly urged to promote the work of gradual emancipation, particularly in those states where no such laws existed; to stamp out the 'enormous evil' of kidnapping; and to do all that they could to ensure that state and federal laws against the slave trade were rigorously enforced. Perhaps more to the point, new initiatives were launched. In 1804, for instance, the Convention presented a memorial to the US Congress calling upon it to ban the importation of slaves into the territory of Louisiana, which had recently been ceded to the USA.[114]

---

[110] *Minutes of the Proceedings of the Seventh Convention of Delegates* (1801), p. 38.
[111] *Minutes of the Proceedings of the Seventh Convention of Delegates* (1801), pp. 37–9.
[112] *Minutes of the Proceedings of the Ninth American Convention for Promoting the Abolition of Slavery, and Improving the Condition of the African Race: Assembled at Philadelphia, on the Ninth Day of January, One Thousand Eight Hundred and Four, and Continued, by Adjournments, Until the Thirteenth Day of the Same Month, Inclusive* (Philadelphia, Pa.: Solomon W. Conrad, 1804), pp. 19, 37.
[113] *Minutes of the Proceedings of the Eighth Convention of Delegates* (1803), pp. 27–8.
[114] *Minutes of the Proceedings of the Ninth American Convention for Promoting the Abolition of Slavery* (1804), pp. 40–2.

The problem was not so much a lack of direction from above but the inability of local societies to respond, at least with any degree of consistency. Take education. While the PAS and the NYMS supported flourishing schools for blacks (the African Free School in New York had over 130 pupils in 1801), the picture elsewhere was very different. The Delaware society reported in 1803 that it had 'no school established for the education of children and people of colour', although some teaching was provided on an ad-hoc basis.[115] Arguably, more progress had been made in New Jersey, but in 1801 it was reported that the schools at Burlington, Salem and Trenton had been forced to close, presumably because of a lack of funds.[116] It was the same thing with many of the Convention's other injunctions. The New Jersey society complained that its 'scattered situation' caused many 'embarrassments and difficulties, of which societies that are more compact, have no experience'. 'Those members who contribute the acting committees are often so far apart', they went on, 'as to render it impracticable for them to act in concert in cases of emergency, and are obliged to content themselves with convening but three or four times a year.'[117] What this meant was that societies often had to set their own priorities. To judge from the reports they made to the American Convention, freedom suits continued to take up the greater part of their labours. As a result, they often had little time or energy to devote to new initiatives or, indeed, to respond to the Convention's many calls for information, the planned history of slavery being an obvious case in point.

To some extent, American activists were also victims of their own success. By 1804, all of the New England and Middle Atlantic states had abolished slavery, either by judicial decision (Massachusetts) or by gradual Abolition Acts.[118] Slowly but surely, slavery was on the decline. According to Zilversmit, by 1830 there were only 2,780 enslaved Africans in the Northern states, most of them in New Jersey.[119] Elsewhere (Pennsylvania, for instance), the numbers probably ran

[115] *Minutes of the Proceedings of the Eighth Convention of Delegates* (1803), p. 17.
[116] *Minutes of the Proceedings of the Seventh Convention of Delegates* (1801), pp. 7, 12–13; *Minutes of the Proceedings of the Eighth Convention of Delegates* (1803), p. 17.
[117] *Minutes of the Proceedings of the Seventh Convention of Delegates* (1801), pp. 8–9.
[118] Litwack, *North of Slavery*, p. 3. The struggle was particularly bitter in New Jersey, where gradual Abolition Bills were defeated by narrow majorities in 1794 and 1798, largely owing to opposition from slaveholders in the eastern part of the state. The New Jersey legislature finally passed a gradual abolition law in 1804, thereby marking what Zilversmit describes as 'the triumph of gradual abolition'. See Zilversmit, *The First Emancipation*, pp. 169–200; Minutes of the New Jersey Abolition Society, 2 May 1793, 1 September 1794, 7 September 1795, 5 September 1796, 4 September 1797, 7 September 1801 and 26 September 1804.
[119] Zilversmit, *The First Emancipation*, p. 222. Pennsylvania material on p. 207.

into the hundreds. Of course, kidnapping and other abuses remained perennial problems, but to all intents and purposes the real struggle was over in the North, leading some activists to question the utility of further action. This is why in 1804 and again in 1805 the American Convention attempted to re-establish contact with the societies in Baltimore, Richmond and Alexandria, where slavery remained as firmly entrenched as ever. By taking the struggle to the South, many delegates hoped to re-energise the movement, but, as we have seen, such optimism proved misplaced.[120] The inescapable conclusion was that abolition in the USA was increasingly becoming a sectional issue, one that did not so much define the nation as define it against itself.

The decade 1793–1803, therefore, saw a steady fragmentation of the international abolitionist network. The keys to this transformation were the French and Haitian revolutions. On both sides of the Atlantic, revolution – or, to be more precise, reaction against revolution – created a much harsher climate in which national agendas increasingly took precedence over universal values and principles. This was perhaps most evident in Britain and France, but in the USA, too, fragmentation was noticeable, principally with the decline of activism in the South and the emergence of an emotionally charged nationalism that seriously con-strained the activities of American abolitionists, with the result that the effectiveness of groups such as the PAS came to be 'less related to [their] position in a global revolution against slavery than to [their] distinctive success in dealing with slavery in [their] own area'.[121] Everywhere, there were signs that abolitionism was in retreat or, more accurately, that it was being forced to adapt itself to new realities. Another way of look-ing at this decade, therefore, is to see it as a period of readjustment. Abolitionism did not so much perish as find other modes of expression, and to appreciate this fact fully we need to look again at its ecology, particularly as it evolved during the 1790s.

---

[120] *Minutes of the Proceedings of the Ninth American Convention for Promoting the Abolition of Slavery* (1804), p. 20; *Minutes of the Proceedings of the Tenth American Convention for Promoting the Abolition of Slavery* (1805), p. 29.
[121] Dun, 'Philadelphia Not Philanthropolis', p. 99.

5   Retrenchment

After 1793, international abolitionism seemed to lose momentum. Key figures died or retired from the cause, anti-slavery societies dissolved or became dormant, and the flow of books and pamphlets started to dry up.[1] Yet, as we shall see, abolition was still discussed, even if it took on an increasingly nationalistic hue. To some extent, of course, this had always been the case. Activists on both sides of the Atlantic were often at pains to stress that abolition was not incompatible with patriotism (this was particularly the case in France), and they frequently stressed the specific national benefits of programmes that sought to put an end to slavery and the slave trade, just as they played shamelessly on nationalistic rivalries, using them as a stick to encourage governments to act. Nevertheless, as international tensions increased after 1793, abolitionist discourse reacted accordingly, flowing into channels which were increasingly nationalistic in character. What follows traces the development of these national perspectives, principally in Britain and in the USA, by looking at a range of different sources – newspapers, travel accounts, prints and plays – and considering a range of different actors, among them American blacks.

In Britain at least, a critical voice in these emerging debates was Benjamin Flower, editor of the *Cambridge Intelligencer*, an opposition newspaper established in 1792. Against all odds, Flower made a huge success of this venture. By 1790, most provincial newspapers tended to have 'compact circulation areas which they covered very thoroughly'.[2] The *Intelligencer*, on the other hand, could rightly claim to be a national

---

[1] James Phillips, for instance, published very few abolitionist books and pamphlets after 1793, with the exception of the various reports of the Sierra Leone Company, while in France, Brissot's death interrupted the flow of French abolitionist publications. The rise of a partisan press, particularly in the USA, also seems to have hampered abolitionists, or at least made it much more difficult for them to gain access to newspapers. See Pasley, *'The Tyranny of Printers'*, pp. 3–10.

[2] John Feather, 'Cross-Channel Currents: Historical Bibliography and *l'histoire du livre*', *The Library*, 6th series, 2 (March 1980): 1–15, at p. 11.

newspaper with agents in towns as far afield as York, Dartmouth, Carmarthen and Glasgow.[3] As John Feather points out, the success of the *Intelligencer* needs to be set in the context of increasing government repression and, with it, the virtual silencing of radical opinion. Flower survived, he suggests, in part because the *Intelligencer* was a country newspaper and therefore considered of little national importance, in part because he followed the usual (country) practice of distributing his paper through newsmen and agents, thereby avoiding the Post Office and the threat of government censorship.[4] But politics played a part, too. Fiercely independent – he liked to say that he belonged to no political party – Flower was in favour of parliamentary reform, religious toleration and peace with France. Yet, at the same time, he distanced himself from groups such as the London Corresponding Society, which he considered too extreme, and believed that 'the true spirit of liberty [was] a spirit of order, a strict observance of the laws and a peaceable conduct'.[5] For obvious reasons, this was a delicate balancing act but one that seems to have paid dividends. Significantly, only once did Flower fall foul of the authorities, and that was in 1799 when he was sentenced to six months' imprisonment in Newgate for calling Richard Watson, who was then Bishop of Llandaff, 'an apostate and timeserver'.[6]

Flower's interests ranged widely, but from an early stage he used the *Intelligencer* to speak out against the transatlantic slave trade and to keep the question of abolition before the British public. Like many Dissenters (his family were nominally Unitarians), Flower was an ardent abolitionist.[7] The *Intelligencer* regularly carried reports of the parliamentary debates on the slave trade as well as abolitionist poems, news stories and editorials connected with transatlantic slavery. At a rough estimate, between 1793 and 1803 Flower wrote over thirty editorials on the slave trade, some of them one or even two columns in length. Many other editorials either refer to the subject, usually in the context of 'national sins', or deal with slavery-related themes (the Maroon

---

[3] Feather, 'Cross-Channel Currents', pp. 12–13. See also Michael J. Murphy, *Cambridge Newspapers and Opinion, 1780–1850* (Cambridge: The Oleander Press, 1977), pp. 29–30.

[4] Feather, 'Cross-Channel Currents', pp. 12–13.

[5] Quoted in Murphy, *Cambridge Newspapers and Opinion*, p. 34. See also *Cambridge Intelligencer*, 23 July 1793.

[6] For details of this case, see Benjamin Flower, *The Proceedings of the House of Lords in the Case of Benjamin Flower, Printer of the Cambridge Intelligencer, for a Supposed Libel on the Bishop of Llandaff* (Cambridge: Printed by and for B. Flower, 1800); *Journals of the House of Lords*, vol. XLII (1799–1800), pp. 177, 181–2. Flower later appealed against his sentence to the Court of King's Bench but all to no avail.

[7] Flower discusses his religious ideas in his correspondence with his wife, Eliza, which can be found among the Benjamin Flower Papers at the National Library of Wales, Aberystwyth.

Wars, for instance). So, in reality, we are dealing here with a much larger body of material. Equally striking is the consistency of Flower's attacks on the British Atlantic slave trade. For ten years he pursued the abolition of the slave trade with a dogged determination, pushing and prodding his readers, pouring scorn on the inactivity of both Houses of Parliament, and reserving some of his bitterest criticism, significantly, for figures such as William Wilberforce.

As one might expect, Flower's abolitionism was typically uncompromising. His attacks on the slave trade were conceived not in terms of universal human rights (that is, the rights of those enslaved) but of individual and national wrongdoing on the part of those who were responsible for 'this traffic in the flesh and blood of our fellow-creatures'.[8] Put simply, slavery was a sin. In language that evoked William Fox's pamphlet against the consumption of slave-grown produce (1791) and that anticipated Garrisonian rhetoric of the 1830s, Flower consistently dismissed slave merchants and their accomplices as 'blood suckers', 'murderers' and 'flesh dealers'.[9] Similarly, in his view, the hands of those members of the House of Commons who had resisted calls for the abolition of the slave trade were 'crimsoned with blood'.[10] Flower would return time and time again to these Old Testament images of sin and retribution. Condemning the inactivity of the House of Lords in 1794, he cited the 'awful address of the Almighty Avenger of the oppressed [Genesis 4:10] – What has thou done? The voice of thy brother's blood crieth unto me from the ground. Though ye make many prayers, I will not hear you – Your hands are full of blood!'[11]

Flower was convinced that if left unchecked such 'villainy' would only end in national ruin. Crises in the Caribbean – the ill-fated British invasion of Saint-Domingue (1793–8), the delay of the West India fleet in 1796 – were all seen as signs of impending disaster. 'Calamities thicken in the West Indies', Flower told his readers in 1795, 'and till the infernal SLAVE TRADE is abolished, we can hardly wish them to cease. Desperate measures require desperate remedies.'[12] As this language suggests, Flower was not above encouraging or looking forward to such disasters. More controversially, he also invoked the possibility

---

[8] *Cambridge Intelligencer*, 7 March 1795.
[9] *Cambridge Intelligencer*, 10 May 1794, 4 July 1795, 9 March 1799, 13 April 1799, 5 October 1799, 15 February 1800 and 18 December 1802. For Garrison, see Henry Mayer, *All On Fire: William Lloyd Garrison and the Abolition of Slavery* (New York: St Martin's Press, 1998), especially pp. 69–70, 103, 131, 370.
[10] *Cambridge Intelligencer*, 9 March 1799.
[11] *Cambridge Intelligencer*, 15 February 1794.
[12] *Cambridge Intelligencer*, 1 August 1795.

of slave revolution and resistance. 'Rather than that the system of slavery should continue as it has done, both in the French and the English West India islands for centuries past, we confess we had much rather the whole system were completely revolutionised', he wrote gloomily in December 1801. 'And if statesmen are resolved to persevere in their infernal system of slavery we most sincerely hope that the Almighty Avenger will enable the oppressed to "break their chains over the heads of their oppressors"!'[13]

What was at stake here was not only Britain's national well-being but also the fate of its empire. Reflecting in December 1798 on the 'crimes' committed by Britons in Africa and the West Indies, as well as 'the numerous millions massacred and famished in the East Indies', Flower concluded that 'perseverance in such a course must end in destruction, such an empire must fall, to the astonishment and warning of surrounding empires contemplating the MIGHTY RUIN!'[14] Interestingly, Flower returned to this same theme in one of the last editorials he wrote for the *Intelligencer* in 1803. His mood was characteristically downbeat. But decline, he seemed to suggest, was not inevitable or irreversible. 'In the present moral state of the nation', he lamented,

we have little hopes of national prosperity: should even the clouds which now hang over our political hemisphere be dispersed, we have little doubt but that fresh clouds will soon arise; we have at present all the marks of a falling empire upon us, and unless effectual reformation takes place, we may rest assured that the doom of all the corrupt nations of antiquity will be ours![15]

For Flower, in other words, slavery was inextricably linked to debates surrounding the morality and purpose of empire, and his apocalyptic visions were clearly intended to rouse Britons, or, at least, their political masters, into action. But here again he was to be disappointed. 'Thus is the Public trifled with, and thus is Heaven insulted, by our perseverance in a trade, which no one ought to vindicate, but a *devil incarnate*', he wrote in February 1794, following another defeat for Wilberforce and his supporters. 'If any thing can add to our national guilt, it must be our *fasting* and *praying*, while we continue in this course of villainy.'[16] For Flower, fast days were important dates in the religious calendar, moments of reflection and quiet contemplation. But fasting, he argued,

---

[13] *Cambridge Intelligencer*, 22 December 1801. See also *Cambridge Intelligencer*, 15 August 1795, 19 March 1796 and 15 February 1800.
[14] *Cambridge Intelligencer*, 8 December 1798.
[15] *Cambridge Intelligencer*, 2 April 1803.
[16] *Cambridge Intelligencer*, 15 February 1794.

was only meaningful if it led to something positive, preferably acts of atonement.[17] This is why Flower was so intemperate in his attacks on what he saw as the hypocrisy of both Houses of Parliament. As he pointed out in March 1795, after the House of Commons had again rejected Wilberforce's motion to introduce a Slave Trade Bill, 'this was the *first* vote of the House after the day of *public fasting and humiliation*! The members returned as they went, with their hands full of blood, and immediately set Heaven at defiance, and dared its vengeance!' It was the same thing in 1796. 'The impious aggravation of last year's vote has been repeated', he complained bitterly, barely disguising his frustration. 'A fresh sanction has been given to the trade just after the day of fasting and prayer. We have again defied Heaven, and insulted the Almighty to his face!'[18]

Impatient for success, Flower was frankly bemused by the inaction of the imperial Parliament. If the House of Lords proceeded 'as expeditiously as hitherto in the examination of evidence on the Slave Trade', he observed in 1794, 'they will *only* be TEN YEARS longer before they have finished, when it is expected they will be able to determine whether the trade is *unjust*, *cruel*, and *murderous*, or *just*, *benevolent*, and *humane*.'[19] Similarly, as time went on, Flower came to regard Wilberforce's annual motions against the slave trade as 'tragic-comic farces' whose various Acts followed an all-too-predictable path. 'The bill will, between lukewarm friends, and determined opponents, by some means or other be lost', he wrote in April 1799; 'injustice, oppression, villainy, and cruelty the most atrocious will complete her triumph; while the House of Commons, and the nation at large, are too much engaged fighting for religion to attend to the subject'.[20] Yet Flower always gave space to Wilberforce's motions in the Commons, just as he always took the trouble to remind his readers of the decision taken by the House in 1792 to abolish the slave trade gradually (that is, by 1796). In these and other ways, he kept the subject before the British public, repeatedly drawing

---

[17] For Flower's preoccupation with fasting and national sins, see his *National Sins Considered, in Two Letters to the Rev. Thomas Robinson, Vicar of St Mary's, Leicester, on His Serious Exhortation to the Inhabitants of Great Britain, with Reference to the Fast* (Cambridge, 1796), which also contains another condemnation of the transatlantic slave trade (pp. 23–7).

[18] *Cambridge Intelligencer*, 7 March 1795 and 19 March 1796.

[19] *Cambridge Intelligencer*, 1 March 1794. Charles James Fox and Samuel Whitbread, among others, made this same point in the House of Commons. Whitbread claimed that the Lords had devoted just six days to the examination of witnesses for and against the slave trade in 1793, five in 1794 and only three in 1795. See *The London Chronicle*, 6–8 February 1794 and 26–8 February 1795.

[20] *Cambridge Intelligencer*, 13 April 1799.

attention to the massive public support for abolition, as evidenced by the 500 petitions presented to the Commons in 1792.

Unsparing in his criticism of both Houses of Parliament, Flower took particular delight in mocking the pretensions of Pitt and Wilberforce. He was in no doubt that Pitt had deserted his former principles, or that he simply refused to put his full weight behind abolition of the slave trade. 'What a minister has most at heart he will use his utmost endeavours to accomplish', Flower observed in March 1796.

Mr Pitt since he has been in the Cabinet, has [had] his party squabbles for power and patronage, and on these occasions (his quarrel with the late Lord Chancellor it was generally understood) he had adopted the Resolution – Aut Caesar, aut nullat. The consequence was, Lord Thurlow was turned out. But, respecting the Slave Trade, the abolition of which has always been 'the grand object nearest the heart' of this *virtuous, patriotic, sincere, consistent* minister, he has gone on from year to year, suffering his 'righteous soul to be vexed' at the constant rejection of every measure brought into the house for the purpose.[21]

Flower struggled to comprehend Pitt's actions on the abolition question, just as he struggled to comprehend Pitt's domestic and foreign policies; indeed, it was perhaps inevitable that he should have viewed Pitt's record on abolition through the prism of his (Pitt's) war with France. As Flower put it: 'The indisputable truth is – if Mr Pitt had felt a small part of that sincerity, which has accompanied his endeavours to kindle Europe into a blaze, and vitiate the spirit, and destroy the liberties of his countrymen, the Slave Trade would have been long abolished.'[22]

In short, Flower viewed Pitt as an apostate or, worse, as a hypocrite. 'This wretch was for a long time thought sincere in his wishes for its abolition', he wrote in January 1798. 'He once declared that, "He had rather all our West India possessions were buried in the ocean, than that they should be preserved by such a traffic".'[23] Flower, of course, knew better. It was not just that he thought Pitt was unsound on abolition. He also believed that he connived at the conduct of his minions in the House of Commons and was guilty of encouraging foreigners, 'although at war with us', to continue the slave trade.[24] 'Thus this infernal traffic, this scandal on the nation is to be continued, without even an effort on the part of the minister, who has so frequently and so solemnly professed himself the champion of justice and humanity, for its abolition', Flower observed in June 1800, after Pitt had, at the

[21] *Cambridge Intelligencer*, 19 March 1796.
[22] *Cambridge Intelligencer*, 19 March 1796.
[23] *Cambridge Intelligencer*, 27 January 1798.
[24] *Cambridge Intelligencer*, 27 January 1798.

last minute, decided against introducing a motion on the slave trade.[25] 'Let us however do the minister justice', he added contemptuously. 'We believe him equally sincere in his professions respecting the abolition of the slave trade, as in those respecting the interests of religion, social order, and parliamentary reform.'[26]

Flower's responses to Wilberforce were more complex but no less damning. On the one hand, Flower condemned Wilberforce because he was too close to Pitt and, by extension, the Government. As he put it in 1797, 'the close attachment shewn by Mr Wilberforce to an abandoned apostate, on account of early friendship, affords an awful lesson to more respectable characters, how they suffer themselves to be deluded, or to place confidence and penegyrise men whose public conduct they cannot but condemn'.[27] It was this same delusion, Flower surmised, that had led Wilberforce to support Pitt's scheme of oppression at home, what Flower pointedly referred to as 'Mr Pitt's SLAVE BILLS' (that is, the Treason and Sedition Bills of 1795). To Flower, such conduct naturally smacked of hypocrisy, and he lost no opportunity to remind Wilberforce of the fact. 'Must we call it affectation, or a wish for popularity, that induces Mr Wilberforce to plead the cause of the Africans, while he forges chains and fetters for his own Countrymen', he demanded in February 1796. 'Such persons deserve no support: such inconsistency unfits them for being the Champions of Liberty, nor can its sacred cause thrive in such hands!'[28]

This might not have mattered quite so much, save for Wilberforce's professed piety. This was the real sticking point. For Flower, living a Christian life meant being consistent in thought as well as action. Wilberforce, by contrast, struck him as being flighty and insincere. Flower took particular delight in comparing Wilberforce's record in the House of Commons, where he had not only supported Pitt's 'Slave Bills' but also war with France, with the principles set out in his *Practical Christianity*, published in 1797.[29] Flower went further, claiming that Wilberforce's 'practical conduct' had done 'more towards the DAMNATION OF MILLIONS OF MORTALS! – than his book on practical Christianity can do towards saving them, were it to pass through not only five, but five hundred editions'.[30] Even Wilberforce's

[25] *Cambridge Intelligencer*, 14 June 1800.
[26] *Cambridge Intelligencer*, 14 June 1800.
[27] *Cambridge Intelligencer*, 15 April 1797.
[28] *Cambridge Intelligencer*, 13 February 1796.
[29] William Wilberforce, *A Practical View of the Religious System of Professed Christians Contrasted with Real Christianity* (London: T. Cadell & W. Davies, 1797). The book was an immediate success and went through fourteen editions before 1817.
[30] *Cambridge Intelligencer*, 11 November 1797.

hands, it seemed, were 'crimsoned with blood'. 'Let men talk or write about VITAL CHRISTIANITY as much as they please', Flower wrote in January 1799.

> While their conduct as legislators, for a long series of years, proclaims them persecutors, enemies to the rights of mankind, friends to corruption, offensive war, and to the destruction of the human species, we will never cease to affirm they are either hypocrites, or deplorably ignorant of the nature and spirit of true Christianity.[31]

Flower, therefore, was prepared to engage with Wilberforce on his own terms, questioning his sincerity, a key concept for British Evangelicals, and exposing what he saw as Wilberforce's lack of conviction (predictably, Flower had no time for the 'art' of politics or for political expediency). Flower instinctively came to think the worst of Wilberforce. 'Whatever he professes', he wrote in 1797, 'his [Wilberforce's] uniform support of war, bloodshed, and corruption, too evidently shews, that his religion is not the pure and peaceable religion of Jesus'.[32] Flower was equally critical of the other members of the Clapham Sect, noting bitterly that 'nothing is more common than for Saints of a certain class, to practice those liberties which they deny to every one but themselves, and to raise a most dismal outcry when any one follows their example'.[33] 'When we consider the conduct of these gentlemen', he despaired in November 1795, 'who have with their pretensions to superior piety, supported almost every species of corruption and wickedness for years past, we cannot but help exclaiming with the poet, "Curse on their virtues, they've undone their country!"'[34]

Flower kept up this barrage of criticism for ten years until, in the summer of 1803, he and his backers were forced to wind up the *Intelligencer*.[35] By this date, circulation had dropped to about 1,350, and advertising had started to fall away dramatically. Flower claimed that in the twelve-month period up to June 1803 the average number of advertisements had not exceeded sixteen weekly. To compound these problems, it had also become more difficult to collect small debts and

---

[31] *Cambridge Intelligencer*, 12 January 1799.
[32] *Cambridge Intelligencer*, 25 March 1797.
[33] *Cambridge Intelligencer*, 3 February 1798.
[34] *Cambridge Intelligencer*, 7 November 1795. Flower is here quoting Joseph Addison's *Cato*, Act IV, Scene 1 ('Curse on his virtues! They've undone his country. / Such popular humanity is treason').
[35] Flower left Cambridge in 1804 and later set up a printing business in Harlow. In 1807 he established another newspaper, *Flower's Political Review and Monthly Register*, which ceased publication in 1810. Soon after, Flower and his two daughters moved to Dalston in Greater London, where he died in 1829. See Murphy, *Cambridge Newspapers and Opinion*, pp. 40–1.

to guard the newspaper against bad debts. Flower put all of this down to the impact of Pitt's additional tax of three halfpence on newspapers, introduced in 1797, which, he claimed, had affected the sale of every print in the kingdom.[36] But there were other factors involved, too, one of them being Flower's imprisonment for libel in 1799. Miraculously, Flower had kept the newspaper going, even from his prison cell, but the whole incident caused him and the *Intelligencer* irreparable damage. It also made those around him more cautious. His wife, Eliza, for one, became increasingly anxious that he give up the editorship of the *Intelligencer*, not least because she feared his safety might be compromised by 'a very persecuting Administration'.[37] Less easy to assess is the impact of Cobbett's *Political Register*, established in 1802. Although it initially adopted an anti-Jacobin stance, the *Register* rapidly became a leading opposition paper, filling the void left by Flower's *Intelligencer*.

Despite its untimely demise, the *Intelligencer* remains an important source for historians of British anti-slavery. Through its pages we enter an important eighteenth-century world, a world in which slavery pressed heavily on notions of guilt, just as it pressed heavily on notions of sin and retribution. As we have seen, Flower had no time for half measures and poured scorn on those who prevaricated or stressed the importance of political expediency. This is why he was so unstinting in his criticisms of figures such as Pitt and Wilberforce. If his attacks sometimes appear intemperate, this is because he believed so much was at stake. It made no sense, Flower argued, to criticise the French, or to draw attention to French enormities.[38] To his mind, Britain's crimes were much greater. In saying this, Flower consistently returned to the question of the slave trade. As he put it in his *National Sins Considered* (1796), 'it is impossible for me to use language sufficient to convey any adequate idea of the enormity of our national guilt, in resolutely persevering in such a traffic, after its atrocities have been repeatedly exposed to view'.[39] Slavery, he insisted, was one of the nation's 'principal crimes'. It followed, therefore, that Britons needed to make amends; either that, or they risked losing everything to their enemies.[40]

---

[36] *Cambridge Intelligencer*, 18 June 1803; Murphy, *Cambridge Newspapers and Opinion*, p. 29.
[37] Eliza Gould Flower to Benjamin Flower, 20 November 1802, Benjamin Flower Papers, National Library of Wales, Aberystwyth.
[38] This was a consistent theme of Flower's editorials during the early 1790s. See, for instance, *Cambridge Intelligencer*, 11 January 1794, 3 May 1794 and 19 July 1794.
[39] Flower, *National Sins Considered*, p. 24.
[40] Flower, *National Sins Considered*, pp. 24–7.

Abolition, as a result, became a test of the nation's resolve, as well as its political future. Flower, it should be stressed, was hardly alone in thinking and writing about slavery in these terms. Granville Sharp, Joseph Priestley and John Newton – to name but three – all shared the same preoccupations and, for the most part, evoked the same language and imagery. Jane Bliss's research on eighteenth-century sermons has also stressed the influence of theories of providential design, of sin and retribution, on abolitionist thinking, both among Dissenting and Anglican clergy.[41] But there is little doubt that war with France, and the nationalistic sensibilities that accompanied it, gave Flower's editorials added resonance and meaning. He unashamedly played on these anxieties, linking abolition to the fate of the nation (and the empire) at the very moment that Britain was struggling to assert itself against France and its allies. Part of Flower's genius, therefore, was to make abolition relevant by (re)shaping it into a nationalistic agenda. But just as remarkable was his success in popularising these ideas, reaching out to people the length and breadth of the country (with some justification, Flower could claim that his paper was read 'from the Highlands of Scotland to the lands-end of Cornwall'[42]), thereby ensuring that his uncompromising and, to some, controversial views reached as wide an audience as possible.

The same nationalistic preoccupations were evident in public debates about the Caribbean, which became a matter of absorbing interest to many Britons, particularly after 1791. In part, this development was linked to the slave rebellion in Saint-Domingue, in part to the huge losses that the country incurred as a result of its involvement in the region. Estimates vary, but it seems likely that over 34,000 troops died in the Caribbean between 1793 and 1798, as well as around 10,000 British seamen, largely as a result of the yellow fever whose pathology became a matter of increasing concern to both the Army and the Royal Navy.[43] The speed with which the yellow fever struck its victims and

[41] Jane Bliss, 'The Idea of Providence in Eighteenth-Century Abolitionist Discourse and Its Impact on the British Campaign to Abolish the Slave Trade', unpublished M.Res. thesis, University of Southampton, 2004, pp. 83–94. For Sharp, see Granville Sharp, *The Law of Retribution; or, A Serious Warning to Great Britain and Her Colonies, Founded on Unquestionable Examples of God's Temporal Vengeance Against Tyrants, Slaveholders, and Oppressors* (London: B. White & E. and C. Dilly, 1776).

[42] *Cambridge Intelligencer*, 18 June 1803.

[43] David Geggus, 'The Cost of Pitt's Caribbean Campaigns, 1793–1798', *The Historical Journal*, 26 (September 1983): 699–706, at pp. 702–4. For the yellow fever, see William Lemprière, *Practical Observations on the Diseases of the Army in Jamaica* (London: Longmans, 1799); Leonard Gillespie, *Advice to the Commanders and Officers of His Majesty's Fleet Serving in the West Indies, on the Preservation of the Health of Seamen* (London: J. Cutrell, 1798); James Clark, *A Treatise on Yellow Fever, As It Appeared*

the inability of doctors to treat it left an indelible mark on the public's perceptions of the West Indies. When army surgeon George Pinckard visited Southampton in 1795 to inspect the troops about to embark for the Caribbean under General Robert Abercrombie he noted that

a degree of horror seems to have overspread the nation from the late destructive effects of the yellow-fever, or, what the multitude denominate the West India plague; insomuch that a sense of terror attaches to the very name of the West Indies – many, even, considering it synonymous with the grave; and, perhaps it were not too much to say, that all, who have friends in the expedition, apprehend more from disease than the sword.[44]

They had good reason to be fearful. Newspapers carried regular reports of fatalities, helping to bring home the true enormity of what was happening in the Caribbean. The numbers involved, it was reported, 'filled the minds of everyone with terror and astonishment'.[45]

Negative perceptions of the Caribbean were hardly novel. As Trevor Burnard and others have pointed out, abolitionist propaganda of the late 1780s had proved remarkably effective in demonising the planter class, putting the region and its people under increasing scrutiny.[46] The Revolutionary and Napoleonic Wars, however, gave these debates a very different complexion. Many of those who served in the Caribbean, whether as naval or military officers, set pen to paper, or else recorded their impressions in drawings and watercolours, as did many non-combatants who took this opportunity to travel through the region. Some of these accounts were subsequently published, among them Daniel McKinnen's *A Tour through the British West Indies, in the Years 1802 and 1803* (1804), dedicated to Lieutenant-General George Nugent, Commander-in-Chief of His Majesty's forces in Jamaica, and George Pinckard's *Notes on the West Indies, Written During the Expedition*

---

in the Island of Dominica, 1793–6 (London: J. Murray & S. Highley, 1797); Stewart Henderson, *A Letter to the Officers of the Army under Orders for, or That May Hereinafter Be Sent, to the West Indies, on the Means of Preserving Health, and Preventing That Fatal Disease the Yellow Fever* (London: John Stockdale, 1795).

[44] George Pinckard, *Notes on the West Indies, Written During the Expedition under the Command of the Late General Sir R. Abercrombie, Including Observations on the Island of Barbadoes, and the Settlements Captured by the British Troops, Upon the Coast of Guiana; Likewise Remarks Relating to the Creoles and Slaves of the Western Colonies, and the Indians of South America; with Occasional Hints, Regarding the Seasoning or Yellow Fever of Hot Climates* (London: Longman, Hurst, Rees & Orme, 1806), vol. I, p. 15.

[45] Quoted in Geggus, 'The Cost of Pitt's Caribbean Campaigns', p. 700.

[46] Trevor Burnard, 'Powerless Masters: The Curious Decline of the Jamaican Sugar Planters in the Foundational Period of British Abolitionism', *Slavery and Abolition*, 32 (June 2011): 185–98; Swaminathan, *Debating the Slave Trade*, pp. 191–203. See also Christer Petley, 'Gluttony, Excess and the Fall of the Planter Class in the British Caribbean', *Atlantic Studies*, 9 (1) (2012): 85–106.

under the Command of the Late General Sir R. Abercrombie (1806). These
convoluted titles tell their own story. According to Charles Batten,
eighteenth- and early nineteenth-century readers tended to distrust
the impressions of those who appeared to travel too quickly, favouring descriptions 'collected over relatively long periods of time'.[47] Put
a different way, McKinnen's and Pinckard's accounts aspired to be
'authentic'; indeed, Pinckard made great play of his objectivity, leaving
it to others to form 'a just opinion' of the character and habits of white
Creole society.[48]

The problem for British travellers was that the Caribbean defied easy
categorisation. Pinckard put it well:

The houses, the streets, the people, the fruit, the fish, and vegetables, the trees,
the fields, every thing before us, was new. The very means of labour and amuse-
ment were novel, and all combined to indicate the change we had made – all
bespake our removal from a northern to a tropical latitude.[49]

Nevertheless, comparisons were inevitable. McKinnen thought
Bridgetown a 'disagreeable' town, its streets 'in a great measure
unpaved', the exteriors of the wooden houses 'decayed and warped' and
the fronts of the brick buildings 'dirty and unfinished', with 'smutty
timbers and staggering piazzas'.[50] Kingston, Jamaica, was hardly better.
Indeed, McKinnen was forced to admit that 'setting aside that hospitality of which they partake in common with the country', there was very
little in British West Indian towns 'to excite admiration'.[51] More to the
point, he fancied that the local obstacles – the extremes of temperature,
the 'strong exhalations and mingled odours of the streets' – were not
insurmountable, and here he pointed to the example of the French, 'who
generally fixed their abodes in the colonies for life, [and] could boast of
some handsome towns'.[52] In other words, the problem was not so much
the climate as British absenteeism, or, at least, a tendency to view the
Caribbean as a temporary abode rather than as a 'home' in the proper
sense of the term. Like others after him, McKinnen thought French
towns much superior to those of the British, a damning judgement that

---

[47] Charles L. Batten Jnr., *Pleasurable Instruction: Form and Convention in Eighteenth-Century Travel Literature* (Los Angeles: University of California Press, 1978), pp. 66–8.
[48] Pinckard, *Notes on the West Indies*, vol. I, pp. viii–ix, 261.
[49] Pinckard, *Notes on the West Indies*, vol. I, p. 226.
[50] Daniel McKinnen, *A Tour through the British West Indies, in the Years 1802 and 1803, Giving a Particular Account of the Bahama Islands* (London: J. White, 1804), p. 14.
[51] McKinnen, *A Tour through the British West Indies*, p. 84.
[52] McKinnen, *A Tour through the British West Indies*, p. 85.

raised awkward questions about the British presence in the Caribbean, just as it raised awkward questions about national character.[53]

For some, the spectacular scenery more than made up for the disappointment of Caribbean towns. An enthusiastic tourist, Pinckard described parts of Barbados, particularly the area around Scotland, as 'uncommonly picturesque', combining 'the gentle but lively variety of the soft and flowing surface of England' with 'wide views of the encircling ocean, the shipping at sea and in the harbour, and all the rich luxuriance of tropical vegetation'.[54] McKinnen concurred, although he was quick to add that after the rains the roads were 'scarcely passable'.[55] Nor were there any inns or taverns, meaning that travellers had to rely on private hospitality. But these obstacles were as nothing compared to the 'unfavourable' climate.[56] 'After the first exertions in walking', McKinnen complained, '[the traveller] is overcome by debility and perspiration.'[57] The night air and dews were as formidable as the heat of the day, 'so that it is only at the moment of sun-rise or sun-set that, with any prudence, one can venture abroad'.[58] To McKinnen's mind, the Caribbean climate conspired against the traveller, discouraging exploration.[59] Pinckard was less easily put off, however. He suffered no inconvenience, he said, from 'habits of exercise' and thought nothing of taking excursions into the country, even if it meant being accompanied by slaves as 'running footmen', a custom he found 'painfully annoying'.[60]

Slavery was an absorbing concern of British travellers. So, too, was the state of colonial society. White West Indians were familiar yet strangely different. To McKinnen's mind, their 'meagre and sallow appearance, their sunken eyes, relaxed countenances and languid motions' were conclusive proof that the Caribbean was 'irreconcilable' with the 'constitution' of the British 'race'.[61] The climate seemed to sap their energies. Pinckard agreed. Creoles, he claimed, had a 'degree of languor and lassitude' about them, which rendered them 'inactive and less capable of exertion than others'.[62] This languor seemed to pervade all ranks:

[53] See, for instance, Henry Nelson Coleridge, *Six Months in the West Indies in 1825* (London: John Murray, 1826), pp. 131–3, and Anthony Trollope, *The West Indies and the Spanish Main* (1860; rpt. New York: Carroll & Graf, 1999), pp. 96–7.
[54] Pinckard, *Notes on the West Indies*, vol. I, pp. 295–6.
[55] McKinnen, *A Tour through the British West Indies*, p. 18.
[56] McKinnen, *A Tour through the British West Indies*, p. 17.
[57] McKinnen, *A Tour through the British West Indies*, p. 17.
[58] McKinnen, *A Tour through the British West Indies*, p. 17.
[59] McKinnen, *A Tour through the British West Indies*, pp. 17–18.
[60] Pinckard, *Notes on the West Indies*, vol. I, pp. 255, 281–2.
[61] McKinnen, *A Tour through the British West Indies*, p. 31.
[62] Pinckard, *Notes on the West Indies*, vol. III, p. 259.

You meet in the roads and avenues of the town riders in loose linen dresses and broad-brimmed umbrella hats, their horses gently ambling or pacing; a black footman, perhaps with his hand twisted in the horse's tail, following; and a distance of twelve or fourteen miles is a journey of no inconsiderable exertion for the day.[63]

It was the same thing with agricultural labour. Here again, 'all its operations were necessarily slothful and expensive'.[64] Such debility frustrated British travellers, reinforcing a belief that the climate, 'and perhaps their association with blacks', had 'not a little relaxed in [whites] the strength and integrity of the British moral character'.[65] Even the West Indian drawl was likely to cause offence. Pinckard was typically blunt: 'To convey to you, by pen, any idea of their manner of speaking is utterly impossible: to be comprehended, it must be heard.'[66] In short, white West Indians were not simply different; they were also by implication inferior, a luxuriant but tragically blighted offshoot of British nationhood.

It did not escape the notice of British travellers that West Indians were often most animated when enjoying the pleasures of the table. With some justification, Creoles prided themselves on their hospitality. According to Pinckard, dinners

not infrequently [consisted] of different kinds of fish – a variety of soups – a young kid – a whole lamb, or half a sheep – several dishes of beef, or mutton – a turkey – a large ham – Guinea fowls – and a pigeon pie, with various kinds of pudding; a profusion of vegetables; and multitudes of sweets.[67]

No meal was complete, moreover, without 'free libations of good liquors': Madeira, claret, punch, sangria, porter and cider.[68] But, here again, comparisons were inevitable. Pinckard felt that, in general, white West Indians tended to overdo things. 'That delicacy of arrangement now studied in England, under the term economy of the table', he explained, 'is here deemed a less perfection than a substantial plenty. Liberality is more esteemed than neatness in the supply; and solids are, sometimes, heaped upon the table in a crowded abundance that might make a London fine lady faint.'[69] Pinckard's evident disquiet (he thought some of the dishes set before him 'unseemly') accentuated the cultural distance between metropole and colony.[70] West Indians, he implied, were

[63] McKinnen, *A Tour through the British West Indies*, p. 30.
[64] McKinnen, *A Tour through the British West Indies*, p. 28.
[65] McKinnen, *A Tour through the British West Indies*, p. 31.
[66] Pinckard, *Notes on the West Indies*, vol. II, pp. 107–8.
[67] Pinckard, *Notes on the West Indies*, vol. II, p. 99.
[68] Pinckard, *Notes on the West Indies*, vol. II, p. 98.
[69] Pinckard, *Notes on the West Indies*, vol. II, p. 100.
[70] Pinckard, *Notes on the West Indies*, vol. II, p. 100.

provincials in matters of taste and decorum: untamed, unsophisticated and, what was worse, seemingly unable or unwilling to acknowledge their shortcomings or to do anything about them.

More disquieting still was the moral indifference of white West Indians, particularly when it came to the treatment of their slaves. On one of his excursions into the country around Bridgetown, Pinckard came across four black women, all of them 'almost naked', working in a cane field, supervised by 'a stout robust-looking man, apparently white', who was 'following them, holding a whip at their backs'.[71] Clearly affronted that the man did nothing to help the four women, Pinckard intervened, only to be told 'that it was not his business – that he had only to keep the women at work, and to make them feel the weight of the whip if they grew idle, or relaxed from their labour'.[72] The incident gave Pinckard pause for thought. 'I confess that I must remain long in a land of slavery', he wrote, barely concealing his frustration, 'before I can witness such a scene, without feeling a strong impulse to take the whip from the fellow's hand, and lay the lash across his shoulders, until he shall relieve the women, by, at least, partaking of their toil.'[73] Pinckard was equally concerned for the welfare of the 'running foot-men' who accompanied him on his excursions and whose only duty, it appeared, was 'to travel as fast as we did, and to be in readiness to hold the bridles, or stand at the horses' heads, at any spot where we might chance to alight, or to pause'.[74] Again, he raised his concerns with his hosts, but to his surprise he found that they only 'smiled at our European tenderness, and assured us that so far from it being a fatigue or hardship to them, [the men] always hailed such an excursion as a holiday, and much preferred it to remaining quietly at home'.[75] This objectification of blacks (particularly women) as simple, childlike crea-tures unworthy of any regard or, indeed, protection would become a theme of Pinckard's journals, leading him to conclude that slavery was demeaning, both for whites and for blacks. The institution seemed to blunt Creole sensibilities, creating a 'type' that, to Pinckard's mind, at least, was the antithesis of the 'true Briton'.

Such perceptions were further reinforced by the visual culture of the period, particularly satirical prints. By 1800 London had replaced Paris as the centre of the European print trade. The most fashionable retailers were usually to be found in London's West End and tended

---

[71] Pinckard, *Notes on the West Indies*, vol. I, p. 283.
[72] Pinckard, *Notes on the West Indies*, vol. I, p. 283.
[73] Pinckard, *Notes on the West Indies*, vol. I, p. 284.
[74] Pinckard, *Notes on the West Indies*, vol. I, p. 282.
[75] Pinckard, *Notes on the West Indies*, vol. I, p. 282.

to specialise in engravings of Old Masters and contemporary artists such as Reynolds and Gainsborough. Satirical prints were also popular, thanks largely to William Hogarth, whose social commentaries captured the imagination of an increasingly leisured middle class and spawned a host of imitators, among them James Gillray and Thomas Rowlandson.[76] Most retailers sold political prints, but, as time went on, specialists started to emerge. One of these was William Holland, who, in 1782, opened a print shop in Drury Lane and over the next two decades established close working relationships with James Gillray, Isaac Cruikshank and, later, Richard Newton, who produced over 300 satirical prints for Holland between 1790 and 1798. Described by *The Times* as a 'Jacobin publisher', in 1793 Holland was sentenced to twelve months in Newgate Prison, ostensibly for selling Tom Paine's *Letter Addressed to the Addressers* (1792). Undeterred, he resumed his business in 1794 and would go on publishing prints until his death in 1816.[77]

As far as we know, Holland was not an active abolitionist but in 1803 he published a series of 'West India Prints' that undoubtedly influenced the slave-trade debates then resurfacing in Britain. Here again, Holland was aided by the Revolutionary and Napoleonic Wars and the experience of those who had had some direct contact with the Caribbean, in this case Abraham James, an ensign in the 67th Regiment, which was stationed in Jamaica until November 1801.[78] In 1803, Holland published no fewer than five of James's caricatures, the most graphic of which was *The Torrid Zone; or, Blessings of Jamaica* (Fig. 5.1). Here, a planter and his wife balance precariously on a huge scythe, enjoying what seems to be a carefree existence. Above them, however, is a blazing sun and a wizened angel clutching a bottle of rum, while below them rages the yellow fever, portrayed here as a frightening pot-bellied creature with strange webbed feet, its skull-like head belching out yellow, orange and black flames, and its elongated left hand holding an hourglass, which in visual terms echoes the bottle of rum above. At the bottom of the print are two human figures in the throes of yellow fever, to the left a man with a scorpion at his throat ('Sore Throat'), to the right another who digs his hand relentlessly into his right side ('Dry Gripe'). The whole scene, moreover, is set against a washed black-and-grey background

---

[76] David Alexander, *Richard Newton and English Caricature in the 1790s* (Manchester University Press, 1998), pp. 14–18, 24–8.

[77] John Barrell, 'Radicalism, Visual Culture, and Spectacle in the 1790s', *Romanticism on the Net*, 46 (May 2007), available online at www.erudit.org/revue/ron/2007/v/n46/01613ar.html (accessed 16 August 2011).

[78] Roger N. Buckley, 'The Frontier in the Jamaican Caricatures of Abraham James', *Yale University Library Gazette*, 58 (April 1984): 152–62, at p. 153.

Figure 5.1 Abraham James, *The Torrid Zone; or, Blessings of Jamaica*, 1803. Courtesy of the Lewis Walpole Library, Yale University.

populated by diabolical figures – insects, scorpions, snakes, grotesque hissing monsters – the whole representing a horrendous world of disease, delirium and death.[79]

These, then, are the 'blessings' of Jamaica. The Caribbean is depicted as being inhospitable, deathly and dangerous. Equally suggestive are the references in the print to time and to the passing of time. Colonial society is portrayed as stale and decrepit. Though fashionably dressed, the planter and his wife lounge in attitudes of idleness; their poses are slack and loose-limbed. The planter, moreover, seems old beyond his years. When he is not at rest, either smoking or reading the newspaper, he appears bent and carries a stick, as if the Caribbean climate has sapped his manly energies. The implication is clear. Jamaica's climate is inhospitable and without question debilitating, yet whites spend what little time they have frittering it away. The hourglass, the visual layout of the figures, which detail the different stages of the daily routine,

[79] See Tim Barringer, Gillian Forrester and Barbara Martínez-Ruíz, *Art and Emancipation in Jamaica: Isaac Belisario and His Worlds* (London and New Haven, Conn.: Yale Center for British Art in association with Yale University Press, 2007), p. 335.

from morning to night, in a sort of rolling dial, all reinforce this point.[80] Brilliantly conceived, *The Torrid Zone* not only illustrated the inherent dangers of life in Jamaica, thereby echoing many metropolitan anxieties, but also held up white-planter society to scrutiny, caricaturing its idleness and dissipation.

James returned to the unhealthiness of the Caribbean in *Johnny Newcome in the Island of Jamaica*, also published in October 1803. Johnny Newcome was a stock figure in English literature, personifying in a West Indian context the parvenu or sexual adventurer.[81] James's vision was altogether more chilling, however. His print recounted Johnny's fatal adventure in a series of twenty-one separate images. The story is easily told. On his arrival in Jamaica, Johnny quickly falls ill, 'blasts the country and regrets he came out'. But he quickly recovers and starts to assimilate, adopting the lifestyle of the white-planter elite, which involves a good deal of dissipation. In the tenth image, entitled 'Johnny creolizes and puffs sickness away', Johnny lounges in a chair smoking, his left leg up on a table, in what was rapidly becoming an instantly recognisable Creole pose. Johnny hunts, attends dances and even beats his slave. But then he falls ill again. The last nine images chart Johnny's speedy decline as the yellow fever takes hold. He grows weak and emaciated, his delirium frightens his slaves (in fact, it becomes so bad that he has to be restrained), and eventually he dies. The final image, 'Hic Jacet Joannes Newcome', depicts a priest, a coffin and an open grave.[82] Unlike many later Newcome prints, there was no mention here of interracial relationships. Instead, James presented a story of decay, decline and premature death, which was all of a piece with *The Torrid Zone*.

In three other prints, James extended his critique of planter society. Perhaps the most damning of these was *Segar Smoking Society in Jamaica!* (Fig. 5.2), which depicted the interior of a private club or hostel. The scene is dominated by a large table containing outsized glasses and bottles of sangria, a recurring image in James's prints. Around the edge of the room are arranged the smokers, who sit facing four large windows. Soldiers, planters, a parson and at least six women socialise on the easiest of terms. The scene is one of disorder. Most of the smokers, including some of the women, have their legs up against the wall, while others strike what to metropolitan eyes, at least, would have seemed undignified or unladylike poses. To the right a young women leans back

---

[80] Barringer *et al.*, *Art and Emancipation in Jamaica*, p. 335.
[81] Barringer *et al.*, *Art and Emancipation in Jamaica*, p. 338.
[82] Abraham James, *Johnny Newcome in the Island of Jamaica* (London: William Holland, 1803), Lewis Walpole Library, Yale University, Farmington, Connecticut.

Figure 5.2 Abraham James, *Segar Smoking Society in Jamaica!*, 1802.
Courtesy of the Lewis Walpole Library, Yale University.

provocatively in her chair, one leg crossed over the other, as she puffs
enthusiastically on a cigar; another has a leg up on her neighbour's chair;
a third flirts with an officer who shares with her a glass of sangria.[83]
White Creole society was not only dissolute, James seemed to suggest,
but also unsophisticated and lacking in decorum. Their very 'otherness'
set them apart, accentuating the distance between metropolitan and
colonial elites, to the obvious detriment of the latter. James made the
same point in *A Grand Jamaican Ball* (1803). Here, again, white West
Indians are seen at play, but the large glasses of sangria, the exaggerated
and undignified poses of many of the dancers and the obvious disorder
on the balcony at the back of the room all hint at the dissoluteness of
Jamaican planter society, its lack of sophistication and its complete dis-
regard for social convention.[84]

Equally damning was James's depiction of the West Indian militia.
Martial Law in Jamaica (Fig. 5.3) consisted of seventeen separate images
on a single sheet, which ridiculed the pretensions of the planter elite, their
lack of training and their military incompetence. The militia was hard

[83] Barringer *et al.*, *Art and Emancipation in Jamaica*, p. 337.
[84] Barringer *et al.*, *Art and Emancipation in Jamaica*, p. 336; Petley, 'Gluttony, Excess
and the Fall of the Planter Class in the British Caribbean', pp. 96–7.

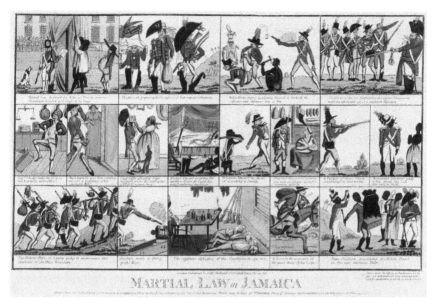

Figure 5.3 Abraham James, *Martial Law in Jamaica*, 1803. Courtesy of the Lewis Walpole Library, Yale University.

to rouse and harder still to press into effective service. 'Ensign Caveat' sleeps while his slave sits with a watch waiting to get him up; 'Volunteer Spruce' walks in an exaggerated way, imitating a march, but declines to carry his gun and ammunition (he has a slave to do that for him); another volunteer advances with his gun upside down. Manoeuvres are chaotic. In 'The flower of the Isle performing the eighteen Manoeuvres under the experienced eye of a creolized Adjutant', six figures march in a disorderly line, all in slightly different uniforms. One clutches at a rifle that has slipped from his shoulder; three others seem more or less in control of their weapons but are tightly squeezed together, as if for protection. The implication is that Creoles are not simply weak, ill-disciplined and vain, but also unmanly. They need black women to dress and prepare them or require the assistance of slaves to get them to parades. These men are made to look foolish, and their 'generals' are no better. James implies that many have divided loyalties (the second image depicts a 'general' split in two, his left side in military uniform, his right in planter dress) or seem more concerned about their wealth than they do about defending Jamaica. The humour here betrayed a growing unease about the ability and willingness of colonial elites to defend themselves, and this at a time when Britons were only too aware of the cost (both financial and human) of protecting their Caribbean possessions.[85]

Taken together, Holland's 1803 'West India Prints' discredited the planter class and, by implication, the institution of slavery, in the process placing it and them beyond the pale of 'civilisation'. Increasingly, the 'West Indian' became a recognisable type, just like the 'Scotsman' and the 'Irishman', two other groups mercilessly lampooned by eighteenth-century caricaturists: the planter's yellow broad-brimmed hat, blue coat, yellow trousers and white stockings would all become familiar tropes during the early nineteenth century. But it was the lifestyle of white West Indians that invited most scrutiny. Crude though some of them were, James's drawings – rather like the works of Pinckard and McKinnen – highlighted the dissipation of planter society, its idleness and lack of sophistication. James's depiction of Creole women was particularly suggestive. The loose-limbed Creole woman, who smoked and drank in public, her legs more often than not up on a chair or table, seemed to be symptomatic of a society that had lost its moral bearings. As Tim Barringer notes perceptively, 'Back in London, these images of colonial bacchanalia forged and accredited the perception of a corrupt lifestyle.'[86] In doing so, they inevitably raised awkward questions about slave societies in the British Caribbean, just as they raised awkward questions about Britain's role in supporting them.

Turning to the USA, here again abolition was frequently (re)cast in nationalistic terms. We can see this in some of the drama of the period, whether original plays or, perhaps more revealing still, American adaptations of British productions. As Heather S. Nathans has recently pointed out, American theatre during the 1790s reflected 'a deep sense of unease about the political and cultural development of the new nation'.[87] Every aspect of theatregoing, she argues, 'from seating arrangements, to musical interludes, to script choice, to performance became a potentially problematic declaration of allegiance to a particular political, economic, or social agenda'.[88] The theatre, in other words,

[85] Abraham James, *Martial Law in Jamaica* (London: William Holland, 1803), Lewis Walpole Library, Yale University, Farmington, Conneticut. Geggus estimates that Pitt's government spent roughly £16 million on its Caribbean campaigns, although, as he points out, 'a large part of this sum would have been expended, whether the government had mounted a Caribbean offensive or not'. See Geggus, 'The Cost of Pitt's Caribbean Campaigns', p. 705.

[86] Barringer *et al.*, *Art and Emancipation in Jamaica*, p. 337.

[87] Heather S. Nathans, *Early American Theatre from the Revolution to Thomas Jefferson: Into the Hands of the People* (Cambridge University Press, 2003), p. 1.

[88] Nathans, *Early American Theatre*, p. 77.

was a highly contested space. What this meant in practice was that for-eign works, the staple fare of most American companies, often had to be heavily revised or adapted to suit American tastes. Pro- or anti-French songs were cut, new prologues and afterpieces added – everything, in fact, was done to ensure that these adaptations appealed 'simultaneously to American patriotic sentiment ... while at the same time permitting them to take a cosmopolitan pride in the fact that their theatres were producing the latest European plays'.[89] Similarly, the few American plays written during the 1790s invariably trumpeted American values, particularly American democratic values, in a manner that was una-shamedly nationalistic, inviting audiences to see the young republic as not only different but also exceptional.

One of those who took up the challenge of writing about contempo-rary American society was John Murdock, a Philadelphia hairdresser. Between 1794 and 1800 Murdock wrote three plays, none of which enjoyed particular success.[90] Nevertheless, his was an important voice, not least because of its engagement with a wide variety of issues, includ-ing, interestingly enough, abolition. In *The Triumphs of Love* (1795), for instance, Murdock dealt with life in Philadelphia, as viewed through the conflicting interests and behaviour of two generations of Quakers: Jacob Friendly, who represents the old Revolutionary generation that remains inflexible in its attachment to Quaker customs, and his son, George Friendly, who is reckless and impetuous but essentially good-hearted. While it deals only tangentially with slavery, the play is chiefly remarkable for including a scene in which George Friendly frees his slave Sambo, after he overhears him ruminating on his predica-ment, thus:

Sometime he tink dis way – he got bess massa in e world. He gib him fine clothes for dress – he gib him plenty money for pend; and for a little while, he tink himself berry happy. Afterward he tink anoder way. He pose massa George die; den he sold to some oder massa. May be he no use him well. When Sambo tink so, it most broke he heart.[91]

[89] Nathans, *Early American Theatre*, p. 87. See also Jason Shaffer, *Performing Patriotism: National Identity in the Colonial and Revolutionary American Theater* (Philadelphia, Pa.: University of Pennsylvania Press, 2007), especially pp. 166–78.
[90] Of these plays, only *The Triumphs of Love* was performed on the Philadelphia stage and that only once. Murdock put this down to bad faith and a preference on the part of theatre managers for foreign plays. See John Murdock, *The Beau Metamorphized; or, The Generous Maid* (Philadelphia, Pa.: Printed by Joseph C. Charles for the Author, 1800), pp. iv–x.
[91] John Murdock, *The Triumphs of Love; or, Happy Reconciliation. A Comedy in Four Acts. Written by an American and a Citizen of Philadelphia. Acted at the New Theatre, Philadelphia* (Philadelphia, Pa.: R. Fowell, 1795), p. 52.

George is clearly affected by this soliloquy; indeed, he admits that it has more sensibly affected him than all he has ever 'read or thought' about slavery and the slave trade. Put a different way, 'the power of performance, seeing Sambo's lament and his performance of emotion persuades George where written rhetoric could not'.[92] Whether Murdock meant this as a criticism of abolitionist activity is not clear; regardless, the overall effect is to create sympathy for Sambo (and others like him) by helping white audiences to imagine what being a slave actually meant.

But if George Friendly's decision to emancipate Sambo is essentially a sentimental act, it also takes place in a decidedly American context, a point reinforced by the character of Major Manly, a Revolutionary hero who is the mouthpiece for a particularly assertive brand of American exceptionalism. Manly is an enthusiast in the cause of liberty. 'What people on earth, save ourselves, can boast of so free and equal a representation, or of choosing their chief magistrate?' he asks George Friendly. 'What people under heaven enjoy civil and religious liberty with that purity we do?'[93] Liberty, however, is not the same thing as licence. The Whiskey Rebellion, a revolt by farmers in western Pennsylvania, who, in 1794, defied a federal excise tax on whiskey, provokes an angry response from Manly, but his comments might just as well have applied to the slave rebellion in Saint-Domingue, another 'eruption' that hovers menacingly in the background of *The Triumphs of Love*. When George Friendly asks how often 'these things' happen in Europe, Manly can contain himself no longer. 'Why are we eternally confounding our situation with the governments of Europe?' he demands. 'There is no comparison. We are a distinct, heaven-favoured people. The very nature of our government affords us an opportunity of establishing a national character, superior to any people on the face of the earth.'[94] Seen in this light, George Friendly's decision to emancipate Sambo takes on a very different resonance and meaning. Murdock, in effect, reinforced a set of values that invited his audience to view emancipation – here reimagined as a noble act and not in the least subversive or threatening – as a test of America's unique mission to liberate and transform.[95]

Susannah Rowson made a very similar point in her hugely successful play *Slaves in Algiers; or, A Struggle for Freedom* (1794). What

---

[92] Heather S. Nathans, *Slavery and Sentiment on the American Stage, 1787–1861: Lifting the Veil of Black* (Cambridge University Press, 2009), p. 47.
[93] Murdock, *The Triumphs of Love*, pp. 16–17.
[94] Murdock, *The Triumphs of Love*, p. 57.
[95] All of Murdock's plays deal with broadly nationalistic themes. *The Politicians; or, A State of Things* (1798) tackles the disruptive effect of foreign war on American domestic opinion. Similarly, *The Beau Metamorphized; or, The Generous Maid* (1800) deals with a foreigner, Vainly, who ridicules the American character but whose infatuation with an American woman 'metamorphoses' him to the country's 'republican system'.

was sometimes called 'white slavery', in this case the capture of white
Europeans and Americans by Barbary pirates, gave a fresh and, to
many, alarming twist to abolitionist discourse during the 1790s. With
considerable skill and ingenuity, Rowson took the ironies and contradictions inherent in the predicament of these white captives and turned
them into a compelling drama. The plot of *Slaves in Algiers* is easily
told. It concerns a group of Americans, men and women, held captive
in Algiers awaiting the payment of their ransom money. The mood is
tense, angry and increasingly rebellious. None of the American captives
is willing to submit to their condition, and, perhaps more to the point,
their example proves infectious, sowing the seeds of internal rebellion,
reaching as far as the Dey's own daughter, Zorina. When the group try
to escape, they are quickly rounded up and seem certain to pay with
their lives, but then one of them, Olivia, tries to plead with the Dey,
who instead offers her a bargain: that he will release her friends if she
agrees to become his wife. By this stage, however, all of the white slaves
are in a state of rebellion. The Dey, as a result, becomes a prisoner in his
own palace – but still the Americans refuse to take revenge. 'Though
your power over us is at an end', one of them tells him, 'we neither mean
to enslave your person, or put a period to your existence – we are free-
men, and while we assert the rights of men, we dare not infringe the
privileges of fellow-creatures.'[96] Overcome by this display of generosity,
the Dey agrees to free all his slaves and, at the same time, undertakes
'to reject all power but such as my united friends shall think me incapable of abusing'.[97]

What is striking about *Slaves in Algiers* is the play's enthusiastic cel-
ebration of American democratic values. In language that would have
been only too familiar to theatregoers, Frederic, one of the main pro-
tagonists, proclaims that he would rather die than 'live in ignominious
bondage'.[98] 'I am an American', echoes another character, 'and as I
am sure you have often told me, in a right cause the Americans did
not fear any thing.'[99] Emboldened by such rhetoric, the captives finally
take matters into their own hands; once awakened, 'the hope of liberty,
like an electric spark, [runs] instantly through every heart, kindling a

---

Neither of these plays was ever performed but Murdock saw to it that they were published, presumably at his own expense.
[96] Susannah Rowson, *Slaves in Algiers; or, A Struggle for Freedom: A Play Interspersed with
Songs, in Three Acts. As Performed at the New Theatres, in Philadelphia and Baltimore*
(Philadelphia, Pa.: Printed for the Author by Wrigley and Berriman, 1794), p. 70.
[97] Rowson, *Slaves in Algiers*, p. 71.
[98] Rowson, *Slaves in Algiers*, p. 18.
[99] Rowson, *Slaves in Algiers*, pp. 49–50.

flame of patriotic ardour'.[100] But, again, liberty was not to be confused with 'licentiousness'. As Rebecca, one of the female characters, puts it: 'the sons and daughters of liberty take justice, truth and mercy for their leaders, when they enlist under her glorious banner'.[101] Rowson, in other words, enabled her audiences to empathise with the plight of white captives in Algiers by appealing to a set of political values that was still fresh in the minds of many Americans.

Throughout, liberty – defined as a peculiarly American concept – is contrasted with slavery. Sometimes, the obvious intention is to make a point about female equality, as when Selima, a Muslim, says that 'the word slavery sticks in my throat. I wonder how many women of spirit can gulp it down.'[102] At other times, however, Rowson seems to have a wider target in mind. Rebecca, for instance, confesses at one point that slavery is 'so abject that it dyes the cheek with crimson'. 'Let us assert our own prerogatives, be free ourselves', she goes on, 'but let us not throw on another's neck the chains we scorn to wear.'[103] Rowson treads carefully here. On the face of it, she is making a point about white Americans held captive in Algiers; certainly, there is no reference to African slavery or to the plight of those held in bondage in the USA. But American audiences cannot have been unaware of the obvious comparisons, or the unflattering way in which Muslim slaveholders were portrayed in *Slaves in Algiers*. Slavery, Rowson seemed to imply, was inconsistent with American values, and, in case her listeners missed the point, she drew their attention to it again in her epilogue, where she refers to the sad plight of the 'poor captive' (white? black?) borne down by 'slavery's ignominious chains'.[104]

The timing of Rowson's play was hardly accidental. Just months before, the US Congress had passed the Navy Act, which raised the prospect of a possible war with Algeria, the immediate *raison d'être* being the enslavement of American seamen.[105] But there seems little doubt that Rowson meant *Slaves in Algiers* to be read as an abolitionist text. She was, it appears, fully aware of the abuses suffered by blacks, not least in the North, and, as a result, was 'forced by conscience to speak to them, if only indirectly'.[106] (It may not have been a coincidence, either, that

[100] Rowson, *Slaves in Algiers*, p. 22.
[101] Rowson, *Slaves in Algiers*, p. 13.
[102] Rowson, *Slaves in Algiers*, p. 39.
[103] Rowson, *Slaves in Algiers*, p. 70.
[104] Rowson, *Slaves in Algiers*, p. 72.
[105] Benilde Montgomery, 'White Captives, African Slaves: A Drama of Abolition', *Eighteenth-Century Studies*, 27 (summer 1994): 615–30, at pp. 618–19.
[106] Montgomery, 'White Captives, African Slaves', p. 620.

in 1793 Congress had also passed a Fugitive Slave Act, which enabled
Southern slaveholders to reclaim their 'property'.) It made sense, therefore, at this critical juncture in the nation's affairs to remind Americans
of their liberating mission, even if Rowson's underlying message
remained unclear. Did she imagine that in certain circumstances rebellious slaves could also be seen as American patriots, willing to lay down
their lives in a noble cause? Or, as seems more likely, was she suggesting
that slaveholders should voluntarily free their slaves – rather as the Dey
had done – if only as a means of renewing America's commitment to its
revolutionary principles?

Significantly, many American adaptations of foreign stage productions
adopted the same insistent, almost triumphalist tone. A case in point is
Paul and Virginia, a popular musical drama by James Cobb which was
first performed at Covent Garden, London, in May 1800.[107] Adapted
from the 1788 French novel of the same name, *Paul and Virginia* concerns two white orphans who live in the Spanish Caribbean amid scenes
of idyllic contentment, overseen by their two servant-guardians Mary
and Dominique. Paul, it seems, is under the impression that he and
Virginia are brother and sister, but at the outset of the play Dominique
suddenly reveals that they are, in fact, unrelated, a secret that he has
kept from them for over fifteen years. As a result, Paul and Virginia are
recast as lovers, although any hopes they might have of a future together
are rudely interrupted by the appearance of Don Antonio, an emissary
from Virginia's aunt, Donna Lenora, who is clearly intent on taking
Virginia back to Spain and making her his own. With the connivance
of the Governor of the island, Don Antonio succeeds in separating the
couple – Paul is thrown into prison, while Virginia is smuggled on board
a ship lying in the harbour – but this is not quite the end of the story.
Through the intervention of a local planter, Mr Tropick, Virginia's ship
is called back at the last minute, only to find itself engulfed in a terrible
storm. It is widely suspected that Virginia has been lost, along with the
crew and the rest of the passengers. In the final scene, however, she
is rescued, and the couple are reunited amid scenes of great joy and
jubilation.

In many ways, *Paul and Virginia* is a typical nineteenth-century mel-
odrama, featuring two star-crossed lovers, a shipwreck and a villain in
the shape of Don Antonio. But arguably more interesting, certainly for

---

[107] Charles Beecher Hogan, *The London Stage, 1660–1800, Part 5: 1776–1800*
(Carbondale, Ill.: Southern Illinois University Press, 1958), p. 2269. The play
also enjoyed success on the provincial circuit. See Linda Fitzsimmons and Arthur
W. McDonald, *The Yorkshire Stage, 1766–1803* (London and Metuchen, NJ: The
Scarecrow Press, 1989).

our purposes, is the subplot involving Alambra, a runaway slave who seeks refuge in Virginia's cottage. Paul's first instinct is to turn Alambra away, but, after hearing his story – it appears that his only crime is to have tried to defend his sister – he and Virginia decide to take up Alambra's cause with his master, who happens to be Mr Tropick. To their surprise and delight, their mission is successful. One of the reasons, it transpires, is that Tropick is not a Creole but an 'Englishman'. As such, he considers himself to be independent and fair-minded. 'It is the proud boast of Britons', he tells his overseer, Diego, 'that from the moment a slave imprints his footstep on our shore, the moment he breathes the air of our land of freedom, he becomes free.'[108] Interestingly, these sentiments do not lead Tropick to emancipate his slaves or to distance himself from the institution of slavery. Rather, the purpose seems to be to distinguish between freedom-loving Britons, on the one hand, and inhumane and tyrannical Spaniards, on the other. 'Britishness' is also celebrated in the character of Dominique. When in an early scene Diego refers dismissively to Dominique as a 'slave', the latter protests, pointing out that his father was 'an English sailor'. In other words, the circumstances of Dominique's birth – the fact that, as he says, 'I have British blood in my veins'[109] – set him apart: Dominique cannot be a slave because he is British.

What worked on the London stage, however, was hardly likely to work in the USA. In fact, when *Paul and Virginia* was performed for the first time in New York in May 1802, the play was heavily revised.[110] Comparing the two texts, significant differences emerge, most of them involving the subplot. So, when Tropick boasts about his Britishness, Diego dismisses him as a hypocrite, pointing out that 'while you preach freedom and justice at home' you 'send your ships to Africa, provided with fetters for the free-born natives, and doom them to tortures worse than the wrack'.[111] Similarly, Dominique's free status is attributed not to his English father but to the benevolence of his owner. Equally significant, Dominique cannot help pointing out that 'by the wise and unjust laws of Europeans I was doom'd to be a slave and entail slavery on all my descendants, because my mother was born in Africa'.[112] The

[108] James Cobb, *Paul and Virginia: A Musical Drama in Two Acts* (Dublin, 1801), p. 13.
[109] Cobb, *Paul and Virginia* (1801), p. 5.
[110] See George C. D. Odell, *Annals of the New York Stage* (New York: Columbia University Press, 1927), vol. II, pp. 137–8. For an illuminating discussion of the differences between the British and American versions of *Paul and Virginia*, see Nathans, *Slavery and Sentiment on the American Stage*, pp. 54–62.
[111] James Cobb, *Paul and Virginia: A Musical Entertainment in Two Acts* (New York: D. Longworth, 1806), p. 15.
[112] Cobb, *Paul and Virginia* (1806), p. 7.

American version of the play, therefore, denigrated Britons, dismissing their claims to be regarded as a free and enlightened people. If, as a result, Tropick's character is diminished, Paul's stock rises. When Tropick asks Paul by what 'right' he challenges his authority to discipline Alambra, Paul replies, 'By the right which every man has received from nature, to defend his fellow man against oppression.'[113] As New York audiences would have readily appreciated, this was the language of the American Revolution. Tropick eventually relents and pardons Alambra, but that he does so arguably has less to do with his 'Britishness' than the justness of Paul's cause, the same cause that Americans had fought for between 1776 and 1783.

On this evidence, at least, American theatre during the 1790s gave a fresh impetus to debates surrounding slavery and abolition, wrapping them in a nationalistic discourse that played on old antagonisms, while at the same time celebrating the new nation's unique heritage. Another group equally intent on exploring the meaning of the Revolution, certainly as it applied to questions of 'race', were American blacks. As we have seen, the free black community in the North grew rapidly during the 1780s and 1790s, and, as it did so, it developed its own infrastructure and social hierarchy. Pride of place went to the black church. By 1794, there were already two independent black congregations in Philadelphia: St Thomas's African Episcopal Church, led by Absalom Jones, and Bethel Methodist Church, under the care of Jones's close friend, Richard Allen. In the first decade of the nineteenth century, similar initiatives took place in Boston (1805) and in New York (1808).[114] Free blacks also organised their own schools, Masonic lodges and mutual-aid societies.[115] As Julie Winch rightly says, the growth of these institutional frameworks was in part a response to white racial hostility. But it also said something about blacks' desire to have control over their own affairs.[116] More to the point, community organisation facilitated the emergence of a black elite, men such as Absalom Jones in Philadelphia, Prince Hall in Boston and Peter Williams in New York, whose self-appointed task it was to represent blacks' interests and to articulate their grievances.[117]

[113] Cobb, *Paul and Virginia* (1806), p. 18.
[114] Julie Winch, *Philadelphia's Black Elite: Activism, Accommodation, and the Struggle for Autonomy, 1787–1848* (Philadelphia, Pa.: Temple University Press, 1988), pp. 10–12; James Oliver Horton and Lois E. Horton, *In Hope of Liberty: Culture, Community, and Protest Among Northern Free Blacks, 1700–1860* (Oxford University Press, 1997), pp. 142–3.
[115] Horton and Horton, *In Hope of Liberty*, pp. 127–8.
[116] Winch, *Philadelphia's Black Elite*, p. 4.
[117] Winch, *Philadelphia's Black Elite*, especially pp. 4–5.

Largely uncoordinated, black thought and action during the early national period defies easy categorisation. Some, particularly those born in Africa, took a keen interest in African emigration or resettlement, as it was sometimes called, a subject to which we will return later.[118] Others, however, probably the majority, were clearly intent on asserting their rights first and foremost as American citizens. Blacks gave vent to their frustrations through a variety of different genres: autobiographies, newspapers, essays, reprinted sermons and pamphlets.[119] They also made extensive use of petitions, appropriating what was a well-established white tradition of seeking redress and adapting it to their own purposes. Most black petitions were popular in form; that is to say, they were invariably community-based and involved groups of blacks, sometimes quite small groups, rather than formal societies or organisations. Absalom Jones, we know, went through the black community of Philadelphia collecting signatures for the various petitions he organised, and it is reasonable to suppose that other black leaders used petitions in much the same way.[120] In short, the petition was, for Northern blacks, a popular form of protest designed to articulate grievances and, at the same time, to test the limits of American liberty.

Petitioning seems to have been particularly strong in Philadelphia. Here, in 1797, Absalom Jones organised a petition to 'the President, Senate and House of Representatives' of the USA protesting against the unlawful arrest and prosecution of four men, Jupiter and Jacob Nicholson, Joe Albert and Thomas Pritchet, under the terms of the Fugitive Slave Act of 1793.[121] This was followed two years later by another petition to the US Congress, signed by over seventy local blacks, urging the repeal of the Fugitive Slave Act and the end of the foreign slave trade. Jones and Allen were also behind a third petition, organised in 1801, protesting against the kidnapping of free blacks, a practice that for obvious reasons destabilised the black community and caused widespread distress. Meanwhile, at the state level, Philadelphia blacks lobbied the Pennsylvania legislature in 1800, 'stating their willingness to be taxed for the purposes of emancipating slaves within this commonwealth'.[122] As PAS members were quick to point out, this startling

---

[118] See Horton and Horton, *In Hope of Liberty*, pp. 178–9.
[119] See Richard S. Newman, Patrick Rael and Philip Lapansky, eds., *Pamphlets of Protest: An Anthology of Early African-American Protest Literature, 1790–1860* (London and New York: Routledge, 2001), pp. 1–7.
[120] Winch, *Philadelphia's Black Elite*, p. 73.
[121] Sidney Kaplan, *The Black Presence in the Age of the American Revolution, 1770–1800* (Washington, DC: Smithsonian Institution Press, 1973), pp. 231–5.
[122] Quoted in Winch, *Philadelphia's Black Elite*, p. 75.

proposal amounted to compensated emancipation, something that white activists could not and would not agree to. Nevertheless, there was no mistaking either the resolve of the black elite in Philadelphia to rid Pennsylvania of slavery or their determination to make themselves heard, even in the face of strong white opposition.[123]

The language of these petitions is revealing. Citing the Bill of Rights and the Declaration of Independence, Philadelphia blacks presented themselves as fellow citizens and, as such, entitled to 'the liberties and unalienable rights therein held forth'.[124] Their grievances were specific and urgent. Why, they wanted to know, was the kidnapping of free blacks any 'less afflicting or deplorable' than 'the situation of citizens of the Unites States, captured and enslaved through the unrighteous policy prevalent in Algiers'?[125] In the same breath, they charged that the Fugitive Slave Act was 'a Government defect, if not a direct violation of the declared fundamental principles of the Constitution'.[126] Again in 1801, Philadelphia blacks raised what for many legislators was an uncomfortable question, namely 'whether the efforts of Men driven almost to desperation by deprivation of a right implanted by the Author of their existence ... [were] either more atrocious or unjust, than our Struggle with Great Britain for that National Independence to which we concluded ourselves entitl'd'.[127] Blacks, in short, included themselves in the body politic (the use of 'our' and 'we' in this context is particularly significant), while at the same time demanding that 'justice and equity' should be extended 'to all classes'.[128] And, for fear that whites might misinterpret their motives, they insisted that such a policy would undoubtedly 'be a means of drawing down the blessings of Heaven upon this land'.[129]

Gently probing the meaning of the American Revolution, Philadelphia blacks dismissed all talk of slave rebellions, just as they were careful to express their thanks

to our God and Creator and the Government under which we live, for the blessing and benefit extended to us in the enjoyment of our natural right to Liberty, and the protection of our Persons and property from the oppression and violence which so great a number of like colour and National Descent are subjected.[130]

[123] Winch, *Philadelphia's Black Elite*, p. 75.
[124] Winch, *Philadelphia's Black Elite*, p. 74.
[125] Kaplan, *The Black Presence*, p. 234.
[126] Kaplan, *The Black Presence*, p. 234.
[127] Quoted in Winch, *Philadelphia's Black Elite*, p. 74.
[128] Winch, *Philadelphia's Black Elite*, p. 74.
[129] Winch, *Philadelphia's Black Elite*, p. 74.
[130] Kaplan, *The Black Presence*, p. 237.

Yet, in saying this, they could not be

insensible of the conditions of our afflicted Brethren, suffering under curious circumstances in different parts of these States ... believing them to be objects of representation in your public Councils, in common with ourselves and every other class of citizens within the jurisdiction of the USA, according to the declared design of the present Constitution formed by the General Convention and ratified by the different states.[131]

Such claims put members of Congress on their mettle; one angry representative went so far as to suggest that the 1797 petition should be 'sealed up and sent back to the petitioners, not being allowed even to remain on the files of the office'.[132] Nevertheless, they did have an impact. In May 1800, following a protracted and heated debate, Congress passed new legislation greatly strengthening the provisions of the Foreign Slave Act of 1794 – but not before it had censured certain parts of the 1799 petition, which Samuel Dana of Connecticut said 'contained nothing but a farrago of the French metaphysics of liberty and equality'.[133]

In the short term, this struggle took its toll, leading some to reconsider their options. Nevertheless, as Richard Newman has pointed out, the black protest tradition had a lasting impact, not least in re-energising the white abolitionist movement that emerged in the 1830s.[134] Men such as Absalom Jones clearly saw themselves first and foremost as American citizens. Quietly persistent, they were intent on exploring the limits of American liberty while at the same time professing loyalty to its most cherished symbols and institutions: the Declaration of Independence, the Constitution and the Bill of Rights. It was a delicate balancing act but one that Jones seems to have carried off with considerable aplomb, moving easily in abolitionist circles in Philadelphia and winning the support of leading white activists such as James Pemberton and Benjamin Rush. Yet his was essentially an American 'story'. Though his work was known in England, Jones was only marginally a transatlantic figure. For him, the struggle was a national one, the challenge to ensure that the Constitution became a living instrument accessible to all citizens, black as well as white.

Admittedly, these are only vignettes, but together they tell a coherent story. Abolition was clearly still vibrant in the late 1790s, as newspapers, travel accounts, prints and plays attest. In much the same way, we

[131] Kaplan, *The Black Presence*, p. 237. These quotes come from the 1799 petition.
[132] Kaplan, *The Black Presence*, p. 235.
[133] Rappleye, *Sons of Providence*, pp. 320–4; Du Bois, *The Suppression of the African Slave-Trade*, pp. 85–7 (quotation).
[134] Newman, *The Transformation of American Abolitionism*, pp. 86–106.

know that many people on both sides of the Atlantic went on abstaining from the consumption of slave-grown produce. There were also new and insistent voices in these debates, not least in the USA where, as we have seen, free blacks joined white activists in condemning slavery and the slave trade. Increasingly, however, these various discourses looked inward rather than outward. The tense and highly partisan atmosphere of the late 1790s seemed to encourage a narrower mental outlook, a kind of drawing in. This was perhaps most evident in the USA where debates surrounding slavery and abolition became part of an ongoing inquiry into the meaning and future of the American Revolution, both culturally and politically. But in Britain, too, abolition was frequently recast and rearticulated in nationalistic or imperialistic terms. This is not to suggest that international cooperation was no longer considered important; rather, that by the early years of the nineteenth century activists found themselves operating in a very different world and one that demanded they adjust their priorities accordingly.

Part III

A new era

6   Abolition

After eight long years of war, in October 1801 Britain and France signed the Treaty of Amiens, which was ratified the following March. As N. A. M. Rodger points out, for Britain it was 'a peace of financial, political and strategic exhaustion'.[1] Under the terms of the treaty Britain returned most of its overseas conquests, with the exception of Trinidad and Ceylon, in return for assurances of French goodwill. Yet the peace proved short-lived, lasting only until May 1803. Napoleon, it transpired, had no interest in a lasting settlement. The British handover of Malta proved a particular bone of contention. But of greater interest, certainly to British activists, were French ambitions in the Caribbean. These anxieties were brought sharply into focus when in December 1801 a force of some 12,000 men under the command of Charles Leclerc sailed for Saint-Domingue with instructions to disarm the black armies and their leaders, among them Toussaint L'Ouverture. The expedition's long-term objectives, however, remained unclear. Initially, at least, Napoleon seemed to repudiate the idea of restoring slavery. Nevertheless, doubts still lingered, especially after May 1802 when it became obvious that the French intended to impose greater control over their Caribbean colonies, notably those returned to them under the terms of the Treaty of Amiens, even if that meant reversing the changes brought on by emancipation.[2]

British activists watched this unfolding drama with increasing concern. One of them was James Stephen, a lawyer and slavery abolitionist who by 1800 was a key member of Wilberforce's inner circle. As he made

---

[1] N. A. M. Rodger, *The Command of the Ocean: A Naval History of Britain, 1649–1815* (London: Allen Lane, 2004), p. 472.

[2] Dubois, *A Colony of Citizens*, pp. 367–72; Garrigus, *Before Haiti*, pp. 303–5; James, *Black Jacobins*, pp. 292–4. It is worth stressing that British ministers initially supported French efforts to re-establish control of Saint-Domingue. Prime Minister Henry Addington went so far as to suggest that 'the interest of the two governments [Britain and France] is the same: the destruction of Jacobinism and above all that of the Blacks'. Quoted in Dubois, *A Colony of Citizens*, p. 367.

clear in his long treatise on the subject, the aptly titled *The Crisis of the Sugar Colonies* (1802), Stephen was in no doubt about Napoleon's real intentions. He was equally convinced that the French expedition would fail, not simply because of the terrain and the difficulties European troops invariably faced fighting wars in the Caribbean but also because they would face opponents unlikely to give up their hard-won liberty without a struggle. Stephen saw only too clearly that the slave rebellion of 1791 had radically changed black expectations and, at the same time, had created a rising tide of black consciousness. 'It would be no less impossible', he argued, 'to breathe [again] into such men the terrors which kept them in subjection, than it would be to renew in a philosopher the superstitions of the nursery, so that he should again believe in giants and magicians.'[3] The most likely result, to his mind, was that blacks would emerge triumphant – and not just triumphant but also steeled by their fight for independence and eager to export their revolutionary struggle to the rest of the Caribbean. Even if the French attempted conciliation and offered the rebels protection under the French flag, British interests would still be threatened. In that case, France would have at its disposal a fighting force that would have the capability to throw the Caribbean region into turmoil.[4]

Stephen's assessment of the situation in Saint-Domingue proved remarkably prescient. At first, the French made rapid strides, forcing the rebels into the Arbonite hills. Faced by overwhelming forces, some of Toussaint's closest allies, including Henri Christophe and Jean-Jacques Dessalines, defected to the French. Meanwhile, in June 1802 Toussaint himself was seized and shipped to France where he eventually died in prison, a broken and disillusioned man. By this stage, however, the yellow fever was already starting to take its toll, as Stephen and those on the ground had predicted it would. News also reached the rebels that slavery had been reintroduced into Guadeloupe, while under the terms of the Treaty of Amiens Martinique had been returned to France as a slave colony. As distrust of French motives grew, Dessalines again switched sides, emerging as the critical figure in what was now becoming a bitter and protracted struggle for black independence. Increasingly demoralised and decimated by disease, the French were defeated at the battle of Vertières in November 1803, and the following month the last

[3] James Stephen, *The Crisis of the Sugar Colonies; or, An Enquiry into the Objects and Probable Effects of the French Expedition to the West Indies; and Their Connection with the Colonial Interests of the British People. To Which Are Subjoined, Sketches of a Plan for Settling the Vacant Lands of Trinidada* (London: J. Hatchard, 1802), pp. 64–70, 75 (quotation).

[4] Stephen, *The Crisis of the Sugar Colonies*, pp. 82–9.

of the French soldiers left the island. On 1 January 1804, Dessalines went on to declare Saint-Domingue (now renamed Haiti) an independent black republic and installed himself as its first president.[5] Stephen took small comfort in being proved right. As he saw it, the priority now was deciding how Britain should react to Haitian independence. To go on as before was clearly out of the question. Britain could hardly ignore Haiti, any more than it could interdict all commercial intercourse between the two countries. Stephen's solution, which he outlined in *The Opportunity* (1804), was more radical, namely that Britain should acknowledge Haiti and, at the same time, 'enter into federal engagements with [Haitians] as a sovereign and independent people'.[6] Part of the intention here was to check French influence in the Caribbean: Stephen was adamant that Britain 'must not again suffer fifty or sixty thousand French troops to be transported to the West Indies; for we cannot rely that the folly and bigotry of the present, or any future French government, will again deliver us from the jeopardy of such an experiment'.[7] But of equal importance was the need to win over the new republic, thereby guarding 'our sugar colonies so effectively from the evils with which they are menaced'.[8] To do this effectively, however, demanded good faith on Britain's part. In Stephen's view, Haiti could hardly be expected to treat with Britain if it continued with the slave trade. The system would have to go. 'I will freely confess', he went on, 'that I can hope of no good result from the measure here recommended, or from any other precautions of national prudence, while we continue to defy the justice of Omnipotence, by the horrible inequities of the Slave Trade.'[9]

Abolition, in other words, was critical to the future security of Britain's West Indian colonies. Henry Brougham, co-founder of the *Edinburgh Review*, was of the same opinion. In his *Concise Statement of the Question regarding the Abolition of the Slave Trade* (1804), Brougham addressed what he, too, saw as a looming colonial crisis. Like Stephen, Brougham rejected any notion that the slave trade was humane or essential to Britain's national interests; on the contrary, he saw it as a failing trade and one that could be given up with little danger of damaging the British economy.[10] But this was not all. Abolition, he predicted, would lead to

---

[5] James, *Black Jacobins*, pp. 289–377; Garrigus, *Before Haiti*, pp. 303–8.
[6] James Stephen, *The Opportunity; or, Reasons for an Immediate Alliance with St Domingo* (London: J. Hatchard, 1804), p. 10.
[7] Stephen, *The Opportunity*, p. 96.
[8] Stephen, *The Opportunity*, p. 115.
[9] Stephen, *The Opportunity*, p. 146.
[10] Henry Brougham, *A Concise Statement of the Question Regarding the Abolition of the Slave Trade* (London: J. Hatchard, 1804), pp. 33–8.

a natural increase in the slave populations in the Caribbean, much as it had done in the USA, which he held up as an exemplar, drawing particular attention to the 'quiet and obedient' conduct of American blacks, free and enslaved, during 'the whole of the St. Domingo revolution'.[11] Furthermore, Brougham also believed that abolition would improve the manners of 'other classes' in the British Caribbean, check absenteeism ('so much lamented at present') and, just as important, encourage more white women to settle in the region.[12] For Brougham, at least, the incentives were obvious; abolition would not only transform the Caribbean economy, paving the way (in some cases) for the introduction of 'task work', but also create societies that were more akin to 'the compact, firm and respectable communities' of the North American states.[13]

If Brougham saw abolition as essential to the economic success of the Caribbean, he also saw it as crucial to the region's stability. One of the wider lessons of the Saint-Domingue revolt, he suggested, was that 'newly imported slaves [were] more dangerous to the peace of the community than those who [had] been born in the islands'.[14] This was not a new idea (Pitt had raised it in the debates on the foreign slave trade in 1794), but, for obvious reasons, the events of 1801–4 gave it added weight and urgency. In this case, the reliance on fresh imports had led to a revolution, 'complete and in all appearance permanent'.[15] As a result, there was now in

the middle of the slave colonies, almost within the visible horizon of our largest island [Jamaica], a commonwealth of savage Africans ... inspired with irreconcilable enmity to all that bears the name of Negro bondage, and a rooted horror of that subordinate status their efforts have enabled them to shake off.[16]

Brougham drew from this what to him seemed another obvious lesson, namely that abolition was now an urgent necessity. The choice was clear: either to 'surrender the slave trade' or to risk losing everything.[17] 'If we put off doing what every call of duty, and every view of interest so imperiously enjoin', he wrote, 'in all human probability that consummation will have taken place which has already been partially

---

[11] Brougham, *A Concise Statement*, p. 90.
[12] Brougham, *A Concise Statement*, pp. 61–2.
[13] Brougham, *A Concise Statement*, pp. 61–2.
[14] Brougham, *A Concise Statement*, p. 64.
[15] Brougham, *A Concise Statement*, p. 76.
[16] Brougham, *A Concise Statement*, p. 76.
[17] Brougham, *A Concise Statement*, p. 78.

accomplished, and the abolition of the slave trade will have been effected by the utter destruction of the colonial system.'[18]

The French invasion of Saint-Domingue, therefore, re-energised slave-trade debates in Britain, at the same time setting them in a very different context. But it was not only developments in Saint-Domingue that gave abolitionism renewed impetus. There was also the question of what to do about Trinidad and Tobago, which had been acquired by Britain from Spain under the terms of the Treaty of Amiens. These were important strategic gains, but, in the view of many British activists, they only complicated what was already a volatile situation. Stephen, for one, predicted that if Trinidad were allowed to develop as a slave colony, heavily dependent on imports of 'new Negroes', then its defence would only divert forces away from older colonies such as Jamaica, creating even greater instability in the region. Far better, he argued, that the trade should be prohibited, thereby making Trinidad 'a fortress to the rest of our sugar colonies'.[19] The retaking of Dutch Guiana (Demerara, Essequibo and Berbice), following Britain's decision to declare war on France and its allies in May 1803, similarly opened up the possibility of pressing the case for abolition, either directly or through some kind of bargain with the Dutch; interestingly, Brougham, who visited the Netherlands in 1804, contended that the Batavian Republic, established by the French in 1795, would be only too willing to end its involvement in the slave trade, provided it regained control over its American colonies.[20] Clearly, now was the time to act, while Britain had the upper hand. In a few years, Brougham predicted, 'the Dutch Colonies and the French islands will then most likely be restored; [and] the commerce of France and Holland will be in a situation much more favourable to the speculations of the slave trade during peace, than in the present state of hostilities'.[21]

It was against this background that in May 1804 Wilberforce revived the SEAST. Among those present at the first meeting in the Old Palace Yard were Granville Sharp, Samuel Hoare, Richard Phillips and

---

[18] Brougham, *A Concise Statement*, p. 92.
[19] Stephen, *The Crisis of the Sugar Colonies*, pp. 151–3, 160, 187, 202 (quotation). Stephen also favoured setting aside part of the land in Trinidad for free blacks.
[20] See, for instance, Henry Brougham to William Wilberforce, 7 September 1804, Wilberforce Papers, c. 44, fols. 80–1, Bodleian Library, Oxford. Brougham obviously used this visit to try to reach some sort of understanding with the Dutch Government regarding the restoration of Dutch Guiana, although his activities seem to have alienated Wilberforce and Macaulay, who feared that Brougham was out of his depth. See Zachary Macaulay to William Wilberforce, 27 September 1804, Wilberforce Papers, c. 47, fol. 15.
[21] Brougham, *A Concise Statement*, p. 91.

George Harrison, all of them original members of the 'Old Abolition Committee'. The following month, Clarkson came out of retirement, having spent the past ten years in the Lake District.[22] But while there were some important continuities between the old and new societies, there were also some important differences, not least in terms of personnel. Wilberforce brought with him two new faces in James Stephen and Zachary Macaulay. Both men had extensive experience of the Caribbean: Macaulay as a bookkeeper in Jamaica (1784–9), Stephen as a lawyer in St Kitts (1783–8). Macaulay, moreover, had spent almost ten years in Sierra Leone, six of them as governor. They were uniquely placed, therefore, to comment on the scale and enormity of slavery, both in Africa and in the Caribbean, and it was this experience that they brought to bear on the early nineteenth-century abolitionist movement. Perhaps just as important, Stephen and Macaulay were closely identified with Wilberforce, forming an essential part of what was known as the 'Clapham Sect'. Strongly Evangelical in outlook, they shared a common interest not only in abolishing slavery and the slave trade but also in Christianising society, both at home and abroad; hence their involvement in groups such as the British and Foreign Bible Society, the Sunday School Society and the Church Missionary Society.[23]

Kinship ties strengthened these sympathetic connections. In 1800, Stephen had married Wilberforce's sister, Sarah. Macaulay, meanwhile, was introduced to his future wife, Selina Mills, by Hannah More, probably the leading female member of the Clapham Sect and, like Macaulay, closely associated with Wilberforce.[24] The strong bond between Wilberforce, Stephen and Macaulay gave the revived SEAST a very different focus and direction. By and large, these men's vision was imperialistic rather than global in character and was concerned, above all, with Africa, India and the Caribbean, areas ripe for Christianisation yet at the same time vital to Britain's strategic interests. Stephen was a key figure here. As we have seen, he revealed a shrewd sense of how abolition was linked to the security of the British Empire, as well as its morality and purpose. Working behind the scenes, Stephen was to prove invaluable not only in shaping abolitionist strategy but also in drafting legislation, including the Foreign Slave Bill that Parliament

[22] SEAST Minutes, 23 May 1804 and 6 June 1804.
[23] For Macaulay, see Iain Whyte, *Zachary Macaulay: The Steadfast Scot in the British Anti-Slavery Movement* (Liverpool University Press, 2011). For Stephen, see Patrick C. Lipscomb III, 'James Stephen', *Oxford Dictionary of National Biography*, available online at www.oxforddnb.com (accessed 30 April 2012).
[24] Lipscomb, 'James Stephen'; Brown, *Fathers of the Victorians*, p. 72, n. 2. See also Anne Stott, *Wilberforce: Family and Friends* (Oxford University Press, 2012).

passed in 1806.[25] Macaulay, too, brought with him an insider's knowledge of imperial and colonial policy. Together, these two men gave the revived SEAST a much harder edge, one more attuned to parliamentary debates and procedures than to the wider world outside Westminster. Just as important, they had a direct line to Wilberforce, who came to rely on them for ideas, support and, above all, information; indeed, Sir George Stephen would later describe Stephen and Macaulay as Wilberforce's 'two stout crutches'.[26]

The SEAST attracted another important recruit in the shape of Henry Brougham.[27] Following his move to London in 1803, Brougham had identified himself closely with Wilberforce and the other parliamentary supporters of abolition, doubtless hoping thereby to further his political career. Keen to ingratiate himself further, he opened the pages of the *Edinburgh Review* to the abolitionist 'party', pressing them for contributions to his new journal, which, he boasted, already had a circulation of 1,000 in London alone.[28] At this stage, Brougham's loyalties were seemingly with the Government; indeed, Wilberforce was so convinced of this fact that in 1805 he recommended Brougham for a diplomatic posting, presumably with a view to promoting him to a safe Tory seat.[29] Brougham, however, was soon moving in Whig circles and in 1806 would write a damning attack on Pitt's foreign policy, *An Inquiry into the State of the Nation at the Commencement of the Present Administration*, which also set out a Whig programme of reform.[30] Ironically, this web of associations would prove of vital importance to abolitionists, particularly after 1805. Although it would be wrong to describe Brougham as a go-between, he was one of a number of figures, the other being Lord Henry Petty, who later convinced Wilberforce that he might be able to work with the Whigs rather than with Pitt.

---

[25] George Stephen, *Antislavery Recollections: In a Series of Letters Addressed to Mrs Beecher Stowe* (1854; rpt. London: Frank Cass, 1971), pp. 28–9.

[26] Stephen, *Antislavery Recollections*, p. 79.

[27] Brougham was elected a member of the SEAST at its first meeting on 23 May and was a constant presence at meetings throughout 1804. His attendance was sporadic thereafter, but he was clearly in close contact with Wilberforce and his colleagues throughout the period 1805–7. See SEAST Minutes, 23 May 1804, 6 June 1804, 3 July 1804, 17 July 1804, 24 July 1804, 2 August 1804, 23 April 1805, 3 June 1805, 7 March 1806, 2 April 1806, 10 February 1807, 11 February 1807 and 13 February 1807.

[28] Henry Brougham to William Wilberforce, 4 October 1804, Wilberforce Papers, c. 44, fols. 100–1, Bodleian Library, Oxford.

[29] Pollock, *Wilberforce*, p. 190.

[30] Michael Lobban, 'Henry Brougham', *Oxford Dictionary of National Biography*, available online at www.oxforddnb.com (accessed 30 April 2012); Chester William New, *The Life of Henry Brougham to 1830* (Oxford: Clarendon Press, 1961).

The original SEAST established in May 1787 had been conceived primarily as an opinion-building organisation; essentially, its focus was outward-looking and geared towards mobilising public opinion against the slave trade (hence the emphasis on petitions and petitioning). The revived society, however, was more akin to a parliamentary lobby group – that is to say, its aim was to influence the opinions and, ultimately, the votes of key decision-makers. To this end, at its first meeting in May 1804, the SEAST arranged for the distribution of copies of Brougham's *Concise Statement* among the members of the House of Commons. Copies were also circulated among the Lords.[31] Clearly, the intention was to capitalise on the turn of events in the Caribbean and to (re)present abolition not simply as a humanitarian issue – although that was taken as implicit – but also one that touched on pressing national interests, namely the future of Britain's West Indian colonies. Significantly, there was no talk of taking abolition to the country. Wilberforce and his colleagues were obviously intent on making this a 'political' rather than a 'popular' issue, and, to judge from their correspondence, they were confident they could push it through, certainly in the House of Commons. The timing (Wilberforce proposed to bring on his motion in June), not to mention the lack of preparation, all hinted at a new-found confidence and a greater sense of purpose, even urgency, among British activists.

There were also other sources of encouragement, chief among them the fact that many of the Irish MPs newly arrived at Westminster were favourable towards abolition. With a fair wind behind him, Wilberforce's motion for general abolition successfully passed through all three readings in the House of Commons. The votes – ninety-nine to thirty-three on the final reading – hinted at a significant shift in opinion among constituency MPs, not all of which can be attributed to the voting power of the new Irish members. As Roger Anstey points out, the anti-abolition vote (eighty-two on average between 1796 and 1799) had almost halved.[32] But while the Commons vote was secure, the Lords were more unpredictable. Rather than risk a division, Pitt and William Wyndham Grenville recommended postponing the motion till the next session, when it could be 'regarded as a new question, *on the ground of the danger of the colonies*'.[33] Given his close relationship with Pitt, Wilberforce felt compelled to give way, although in doing so he seems to have been

---

[31] SEAST Minutes, 23 May 1804 and 6 June 1804.
[32] Anstey, *The Atlantic Slave Trade*, pp. 343–4.
[33] Robert I. Wilberforce and Samuel Wilberforce, *The Life of William Wilberforce* (London: John Murray, 1838), vol. III, pp. 180–1. My emphasis.

under the impression that abolition might (he could put it no stronger than that) become a government measure in the next Parliament.[34]

Despite this delay, British activists remained buoyant. The prospects of success, they assured their supporters in a circular letter dated 2 August, were 'better than at any former period'.[35] Large majorities in the House of Commons had voted in favour of the proposed Bill, and in both Houses the cause had gained new converts. Activists, of course, had been here before. What was different, however, was their confidence in the strength and validity of their political arguments. Many MPs, they claimed, had had their opinions 'either changed or shaken' by 'new considerations arising out of late events and existing circumstances in the West Indies'.[36] 'The aspect of public affairs in that quarter certainly presents new arguments of great weight against the slave trade', the circular letter went on, 'and since they turn on political as well as moral considerations, it is hoped that they may make the right impression even on those who, from alleged reasons of public expediency, have been hitherto our most determined opponents.'[37] Saint-Domingue had changed everything. The spectre of an independent black republic in the Caribbean, belligerent or otherwise, obviously gave many Britons pause for thought, leading to a greater emphasis on what might possibly be at stake here. Activists pushed hard at these growing anxieties, a ploy that in an interesting reversal of roles enabled them to represent themselves (and not the West India lobby) as the true defenders of Britain's national and imperial interests.

What British activists had been able to do, in other words, was to turn the international situation to their advantage, in effect realigning national and international interests. At the same time, they looked to the USA for support, partly because of the historic ties between the two countries and partly because, according to the US Constitution, the American slave trade would come to an end in 1808. British activists, however, knew enough not to take anything for granted. In 1803, for instance, South Carolina had reopened the Atlantic slave trade for an indefinite period.[38] That same year, the USA had purchased Louisiana from France at a cost of $15 million. While the acquisition of this vast territory, some 900,000 square miles of western land, settled once and for all the vexed question of control over the Mississippi's

---

[34] Anstey, *The Atlantic Slave Trade*, pp. 344–5.
[35] SEAST circular letter, 2 August 1804, 'Anti-Slavery Collection: 18th–19th Centuries from the Library of the Society of Friends' (World Microfilms, 1978), Reel 14.
[36] SEAST circular letter, 2 August 1804.
[37] SEAST circular letter, 2 August 1804.
[38] Drescher, *Abolition*, p. 135.

outlet to the sea, it brought within the orbit of American power a mul-
tiracial and multi-ethnic province that not only had close links with
Saint-Domingue but had also until recently been a port of destination
for both Spanish and French slave ships. The pressing question, therefore, was what action, if any, Congress would take to prohibit the slave
trade into Louisiana and when.[39]

With good reason, the members of the SEAST watched these developments with growing concern, leading Wilberforce to approach James
Monroe, the US Ambassador to Britain, who assured him that there
was 'no doubt whatever' that the American Government would abolish the slave trade, 'as soon as the law permits'.[40] Monroe was also able
to put Wilberforce's mind at rest over Louisiana; significantly, the Act
organising the territory (26 March 1804) had declared the traffic ille-
gal.[41] This was in June. The following month the SEAST re-established
contact with the PAS, although it is revealing that the initiative came
not from Macaulay or Stephen but from William Dillwyn, acting as
Stephen's intermediary. Briefly, Dillwyn set out what he was looking
for. He began by asking for any 'well authenticated facts' concerning
the 'humane and liberal' treatment of slaves in the American states
and the bearing this had on the ability of the black population to reproduce itself.[42] He also asked for information about Saint-Domingue. As
Dillwyn explained, 'events in St. Domingo are likely to have a powerful
influence on our cause next winter – good & early information from
that quarter is therefore very desirable'.[43] Finally, he raised what for him
and for many others was the crucial point at issue, namely the possibility of obtaining a declaration from the American Government that 'so
far from being disposed to take up that part of the slave trade which is
proposed to be relinquished by Great Britain', as the West India lobby
alleged, 'it [was] willing to co-operate with this country in any measures that may be eligible for giving effect to its own existing laws on this

---

[39] See *American State Papers, Miscellaneous*, vol. I, 8th Congress, 1st Session (1804),
pp. 390–1. The American Convention took up this issue at its meeting in January
1804. See *Minutes of the Proceedings of the Ninth American Convention for Promoting the
Abolition of Slavery* (1804), pp. 40–3.
[40] SEAST Minutes, 3 July 1804. See also William Wilberforce to James Monroe, 6 and
7 June 1804, James Monroe Papers, New York Public Library, microfilm edition,
Reel 3.
[41] SEAST Minutes, 3 July 1804; *United States Statutes at Large*, vol. II, 8th Congress, 1st
Session (26 March 1804), Ch. 38, pp. 283–9.
[42] William Dillwyn to James Pemberton, 27 July 1804, PAS Correspondence, microfilm
edition, Reel 11.
[43] Dillwyn to Pemberton, 27 July 1804.

subject'.[44] 'If the friends of the cause could obtain something of this
nature', Dillwyn went on, 'it would be of essential importance.'[45]

Although very little of this correspondence has survived, it is obvious that PAS members set about answering Dillwyn as best they
could (certainly the two societies were in regular contact with each
other throughout 1805), even if they were powerless to influence the
actions of the Federal Government.[46] Following the Pennsylvania society's example, the 1805 American Convention agreed to open a correspondence with the London Committee of the SEAST, welcoming
their erstwhile colleagues back into the fold with 'a bound copy of the
minutes of the Convention, since its commencement'.[47] The opening of
this new phase of Anglo-American cooperation came at an opportune
moment. As we have seen, since the turn of the century the American
movement had been in steep decline. At a national level, at least, the
American Convention had become a truncated organisation dominated by a relatively small group of activists from the old historic centres of Pennsylvania, New York, New Jersey and Delaware. To judge
from the minutes, attendance rarely rose above fourteen and just as
striking was the relatively low turnover of delegates: between 1803 and
1806, for example, half of the New Jersey delegates attended more than
one Convention, while a third attended three.[48] More worrying still,
efforts to revive abolitionism in the South had proved futile. Reporting
from Alexandria in 1805, George Drinker judged that, if anything, the
number of slaves in his district had increased. 'Nothing will contribute to our revival', he concluded, 'but a more thorough conviction of a
divine precept, and tenaciously adhered to; that is, to do unto others as
we would they should do unto us.'[49]

Viewed in this light, the revival of the SEAST, together with the
looming significance of 1808, undoubtedly gave American activists a renewed sense of purpose. In its report to the 1806 American
Convention, the NYMS noted with pleasure the Convention's decision to open a correspondence with the London Committee, adding
significantly that by abolishing the slave trade Britain would not only

[44] Dillwyn to Pemberton, 27 July 1804.
[45] Dillwyn to Pemberton, 27 July 1804. See also SEAST Minutes, 24 July 1804.
[46] SEAST Minutes, 22 January 1805, 29 January 1805 and 9 July 1805.
[47] *Minutes of the Proceedings of the Tenth American Convention for Promoting the Abolition of Slavery* (1805), p. 31.
[48] The figures are extracted from the published minutes of the American Convention, 1803–6.
[49] *Minutes of the Proceedings of the Tenth American Convention for Promoting the Abolition of Slavery* (1805), p. 24.

'improve the condition of her present stock' and 'increase the number by internal population' but also prevent its West Indian colonies from 'falling under the rising empire of the blacks [Haiti]'.[50] Perhaps just as telling, the NYMS referred to the SEAST as 'our sister society', urging the American Convention to assist British activists, if only in the 'smallest degree'.[51] Such support was to prove vital as the British campaign entered its final stages. This was not just a case of aligning British and American interests, or enlisting the help of groups such as the PAS. America also provided incontrovertible proof that, with the right treatment, slave populations in the Americas could reproduce themselves. Wilberforce had made this very point in the Commons debate of 1804, as had Brougham in his *Concise Statement*, and he would return to it time and time again, as his correspondence with Monroe attests.[52]

Convinced of the strength of their arguments – convinced, too, that America was ready to follow Britain's example – the SEAST looked forward to the 1805 parliamentary session with growing confidence. Early in January it appointed a special subcommittee to collect suitable evidence to present at the bar of the House of Lords, which is where most activists thought the real struggle would take place.[53] Understandably, Wilberforce believed he could count on the Commons vote, especially as the House had so decidedly expressed its opinion on the subject in the course of the last session. But when he got up to introduce the second reading of his motion on 28 February, he was met by a barrage of criticism, a lot of it aimed at demonstrating the utter impracticality of abolition (many MPs argued that it would only lead to further uprisings in the Caribbean), or else questioning Wilberforce's motives (some clearly believed that his real aim was not 'abolition' at all but rather 'emancipation').[54] As the debate unfolded, Wilberforce must have quickly realised that he had been ambushed. Many of his most loyal supporters had absented themselves, presumably under the impression that the vote was safe, added to which some of the Irish MPs broke ranks and voted with the opposition.[55] When the House finally divided

[50] *Minutes of the Proceedings of the Eleventh American Convention for Promoting the Abolition of Slavery, and Improving the Condition of the African Race: Assembled at Philadelphia on the Thirteenth Day of January, One Thousand Eight Hundred and Six, and Continued, by Adjournments, Until the Fifteenth Day of the Same Month, Inclusive* (Philadelphia, Pa.: Kimber, Conrad & Co, 1806), pp. 7–8.
[51] *Minutes of the Proceedings of the Eleventh American Convention for Promoting the Abolition of Slavery* (1806), p. 8.
[52] See, for instance, William Wilberforce to James Monroe, 21 August 1806, James Monroe Papers, New York Public Library, Reel 3.
[53] SEAST Minutes, 22 January 1805.
[54] *Parliamentary Debates*, 1st series, vol. III, cols. 641–74 (28 February 1805).
[55] Clarkson, *History*, vol. II, p. 499; Anstey, *The Atlantic Slave Trade*, p. 345.

on Wilberforce's motion, it became clear that he had lost by just seven votes (seventy to seventy-seven). In effect, activists were back to where they had been in 1804.

The Commons vote of February 1805 rocked the movement back on its heels.[56] Undeterred, the SEAST settled in for what it now real-ised would be another long struggle. The first priority was to collect more evidence. To this end, in April Clarkson was asked to undertake another tour of Great Britain. 'I know of no person who on the whole is so fit for this commission as Mr Clarkson', Wilberforce assured his colleagues, 'and his zeal in our great cause continues so unabated that I trust if our Committee should ask him, he would not refuse to resume his labours.'[57] Wilberforce obviously knew his man. Clarkson readily accepted the commission, which seems to have preoccupied him for the rest of the year. By his own account, the tour was a great success. Much to his satisfaction, Clarkson found that the 'ardour of all the former friends of the abolition ... [remained] unabated and that wherever he had been all ranks of people were warm in the cause and desirous of lending their aid'.[58] He was particularly impressed by the enthusiasm of the younger generation, who, he said, professed 'an earnest desire to know more of the subject; and a generous warmth in favour of the injured Africans'.[59] Indeed, everything suggested that the cause 'fur-nished us with endless sources of rallying',[60] although for the moment Wilberforce showed no signs of wishing to rouse the country on the subject.

Eager to carry the fight to their opponents, SEAST members also stepped up their propaganda campaign. In April, for instance, they approved the purchase and circulation of 500 copies of Macaulay's *The Horrors of Negro Slavery* (1805), a damning condemnation of West Indian slavery based on authentic testimony, in this case official documents recently presented to the House of Commons.[61] This short pamphlet, just thirty-two pages in length, made for chilling reading, cataloguing in minute detail a long list

---

[56] See, for instance, SEAST circular letter, 3 June 1805, 'Anti-Slavery Collection: 18th–19th Centuries from the Library of the Society of Friends' (World Microfilms, 1978), Reel 14.
[57] SEAST Minutes, 29 April 1805.
[58] SEAST Minutes, 9 July 1805.
[59] Clarkson, *History*, vol. II, p. 502.
[60] Clarkson, *History*, vol. II, p. 502.
[61] SEAST Minutes, 29 April 1805. The SEAST bought a further 100 copies in May. See SEAST Minutes, 14 May 1805. The final figure, however, was undoubtedly much larger. In July a report was made to the SEAST that 17,000 copies of 'the Horrors of Negro Slavery' had been printed, of which upwards of 11,500 had been forwarded 'free from expence' for distribution. See SEAST Minutes, 9 July 1805.

of crimes ('general inhumanity') that largely went undetected and unpunished. Drawing on this evidence, Macaulay pointed to what he saw as a complete breakdown in the administration of justice in the Caribbean; even Crown officials, he suggested, were complicit in defeating 'the ends of justice'.[62] Here, in other words, was indisputable proof that so far from being humane, as the opponents of abolition alleged, Caribbean planters were vindictive, unruly and lawless; in short, the very antithesis of 'true Britons'. Indeed, Macaulay was at pains to point out that 'the moral perceptions and feelings which prevail in that quarter of the globe [the Caribbean] are wholly different from those which are found on this side of the Atlantic'.[63] This was a familiar trope, but Macaulay marshalled his evidence brilliantly to demonstrate that so far from being fanciful or contrived such claims were all-too-glaringly true.

In the meantime, British activists decided to change tack, returning to the vexed question of the recaptured Dutch colonies (Dutch Guiana). Their thinking was clear: that by playing on the uncertainties of war they could pressurise the Government into abolishing the trade to conquered territories, thereby isolating one part of the wider anti-slave-trade struggle. Here again, important interests were at stake. No one, not least government ministers, was in favour of supplying slaves and capital to colonies that might be restored at the conclusion of war.[64] What is more, many Caribbean planters, already faced by a glut in the British sugar market, seemed to agree. This is not to suggest that overproduction caused abolition; rather, a temporary decline in London sugar prices, triggered by wartime obstacles to the re-exportation of British sugar and competition from producers in Brazil, Cuba and the East Indies, forced those most directly involved to reconsider their priorities, opening up for the first time an important fissure between colonial planters, on the one hand, and African merchants, on the other.[65]

---

[62] Zachary Macaulay, *The Horrors of Negro Slavery Existing in Our West India Islands, Irrefragably Demonstrated from Official Documents Recently Presented to the House of Commons* (London: J. Hatchard, 1805), p. 17.

[63] Macaulay, *The Horrors of Negro Slavery*, p. 16.

[64] Anstey, *The Atlantic Slave Trade*, p. 347.

[65] For London sugar prices, see Joseph Lowell Ragatz, *The Fall of the Planter Class in the British Caribbean, 1763–1783* (New York: Century Co., 1928), p. 351. Ragatz's figures indicate a sharp decline in sugar process around 1804, followed by a period of recovery in 1807. More recently, however, Ryden, using West Indian sugar prices, has argued for a more general decline, stretching from the late 1790s. See David Beck Ryden, *West Indian Slavery and British Abolition, 1783–1807* (Cambridge University Press, 2010). Ryden's work has reopened a long-standing debate about decline in the British West Indian economy. For responses to Ryden, see the exchange of letters in the *New York Review of Books*, 59 (12 January–8 February 2012), pp. 57–8. My

From 1804 onwards, British activists, led principally by James Stephen, sought to play on these increasing tensions while at the same time linking the future of Dutch Guiana to wider British interests.

Wilberforce seems to have first raised the Guiana question with Pitt in July 1804, following the Commons debate on his motion for general abolition. Judging from Wilberforce's correspondence, Pitt's initial response was positive, although it is surely significant that he favoured carrying the measure by Royal Proclamation (effectively an Act of Government) rather than risking a parliamentary vote.[66] By this stage, Pitt seems to have been backtracking on his commitment to abolition. Try as he might, Wilberforce simply could not get him to budge. Writing to James Stephen in November, he confessed that he had been

waiting with more anxiety than anyone but you would conceive in hopes of seeing or hearing of a Proclamation forbidding the slave trade to the conquered colonies & I am so much disappointed in not finding anything about it, even now in the newspapers that I break that great resolution I had made not to mention the matter to you.[67]

At last, Pitt gave way. On 15 August 1805 – after a delay of over twelve months – he issued an Order-in-Council abolishing the trade to Dutch Guiana, reckoned to be about 12,000 slave exports annually. Wilberforce could barely contain his excitement. 'I have so often been disappointed', he confessed to Lord Harrowby, the Foreign Secretary, 'that I rejoice with trembling and shall scarcely dare to be confident till I actually see the Order in the Gazette.'[68]

Having dealt with Dutch Guiana, British activists turned their attention to the foreign slave trade, that is, British involvement in supplying slaves to foreign colonies, territories and dominions. Put simply, British slave merchants were known to be in the habit of supplying slaves to Cuba, Martinique, Guadeloupe and Spanish America via the Danish islands of St Croix and St Thomas, which were, strictly speaking, neutral. As Stephen and others pointed out, such a trade naturally had the effect of aiding Britain's enemies (a related concern was the involvement of neutral flags, especially American, in supplying French and

---

own argument here, which stresses the importance of humanitarian, political and national interests in shaping British slave-trade debates (1804–7), follows closely that first outlined by Roger Anstey in his seminal article, 'A Re-interpretation of the Abolition of the Slave Trade, 1806–1807', *English Historical Review*, 87 (April 1972): 304–32.

[66] Anstey, *The Atlantic Slave Trade*, pp. 348–9; Pollock, *Wilberforce*, pp. 189–91.
[67] William Wilberforce to James Stephen, 10 November 1804, Wilberforce Papers, d. 16, fols. 36–7, Bodleian Library, Oxford.
[68] Quoted in Pollock, *Wilberforce*, p. 189.

Spanish colonies with slaves).[69] The foreign slave trade, in other words, pressed heavily on questions of national interests, especially at a time of war. The larger issue was what could be done about it. Wisely, activists stopped short of attacking the foreign slave trade head-on. Instead, they came up with another solution, which Wilberforce outlined to Grenville on 24 March 1806. In the past, he pointed out, an Act of Parliament had often been found necessary for rendering an Order-in-Council 'really effectual', but in the case of Dutch Guiana it would be 'particularly requisite'.[70] At the same time, Wilberforce offered a further suggestion, namely that the proposed Act should prohibit the foreign slave trade as well. As the present Order-in-Council was supported by those members of the Cabinet 'who were most averse to abolition principles', he explained, 'we thought that a further measure, grounded on the same principles, might probably without difficulty obtain the support of all the members of the present Administration'.[71]

It is a measure of Wilberforce's growing influence among the Whigs (and, it has to be said, their willingness to work with him) that Grenville was prepared to support this proposal, thereby making it a government measure.[72] Steering it through both Houses, however, demanded self-discipline, as well as a fair amount of political skill. Introducing the Bill to the Commons on 31 March, just days after Wilberforce's letter, the Attorney General Sir Arthur Piggott mentioned the word 'humanity' just once. Instead, he stressed the wider political implications of the measure. It was contrary to 'sound policy', he insisted, that under the existing state of affairs Britain should afford its European rivals the means of 'attaining a high degree of commercial prosperity'.[73] Grenville struck the same note in the Lords, arguing that the Bill aimed to prohibit a trade that not only contributed to the wealth of Britain's enemies but also enabled them 'to meet us in the market upon equal

---

[69] *Parliamentary Debates*, 1st series, vol. VI, col. 598 (31 March 1806); Anstey, *The Atlantic Slave Trade*, pp. 349–56.

[70] William Wilberforce to William Wyndham Grenville, 24 March 1806, Dropmore Papers, Add. MS 58978, British Library. The original proposal came from James Stephen, who, at this date, was clearly driving abolitionist policy. See, for instance, William Wilberforce to William Wyndham Grenville, 2 May 1806, 8 May 1806 and 20 May 1806; and William Wyndham Grenville to William Wilberforce, 5 May 1806, Dropmore Papers.

[71] William Wilberforce to William Wyndham Grenville, 24 March 1806.

[72] As the Dropmore Papers reveal, Wilberforce was in constant contact with Grenville between 23 April 1806 and 28 March 1807. Theirs proved a close working relationship, characterised by a high degree of trust on both sides. Indeed, Grenville's crucial role in the abolition of the slave trade has not always been given due credit by historians. See Anstey, *The Atlantic Slave Trade*, p. 379.

[73] *Parliamentary Debates*, 1st series, vol. VI, cols. 597–8 (31 March 1806).

terms of competition, or perhaps to undersell us'.[74] Wilberforce, meanwhile, deliberately kept a low profile, not daring to show his 'suspicious face' in the House of Lords or even the 'avenues to it', presumably for fear he might put off waverers.[75] The subterfuge went deeper than that, however. Privately, Wilberforce confessed to Grenville on 23 April that if the House of Lords got wind of the fact that the Bill rested on 'general abolition principles, or is grounded on justice and humanity', it might prove 'fatal'.[76] The true 'nature' of the measure, he added, a few days later, had 'never been fully stated' in the House of Commons, 'nor the argument in favour of it urged'.[77]

Although, with reason, some members of the West India lobby suspected that the Foreign Slave Bill was a 'scheme to abolish the slave trade', it eventually passed both Houses with comfortable majorities.[78] Irreconcilables such as Banestre Tarleton, MP for Liverpool, put up token resistance, predicting that the Bill would simply throw trade into the hands of the Americans, but in truth their objections were drowned out. One reason for this was that even diehard opponents of abolition supported the measure, as Wilberforce had predicted they might.[79] Sir William Young, for instance, long a thorn in the side of British activists, not only approved of the Bill but also considered it a 'boon' to West India merchants.[80] What is more, Young claimed that he had been at 'a numerous meeting of London merchants, where a majority had agreed with him'.[81] Others took the same line, disputing Tarleton's dire predictions and even questioning whether abolition of the foreign slave trade, which had already been badly disrupted by the Napoleonic Wars, would have any significant impact on British manufactures.[82] Unable to gain any real momentum, the West India lobby was forced to concede defeat. After a short debate on 16 May, the Bill passed the Lords by forty-one

---

[74] *Parliamentary Debates*, 1st series, vol. VII, cols. 32–3 (7 May 1806).
[75] William Wilberforce to William Wyndham Grenville, 8 May 1806, Dropmore Papers.
[76] William Wilberforce to William Wyndham Grenville, 23 April 1806, Dropmore Papers.
[77] William Wilberforce to William Wyndham Grenville, 2 May 1806, Dropmore Papers.
[78] Between its second and third readings, however, the Bill was heavily revised to the point where James Stephen, who had drafted the original Bill, believed that it would be 'ruinous' to weaken its provisions any further. See *Journals of the House of Commons*, vol. LXI (1806), pp. 232, 233, 254–5; William Wilberforce to William Wydham Grenville, 8 May 1806, Dropmore Papers.
[79] See Wilberforce to Grenville, 23 April 1806.
[80] *Parliamentary Debates*, 1st series, vol. VI, col. 806 (18 April 1806).
[81] *Parliamentary Debates*, 1st series, vol. VI, col. 806 (18 April 1806).
[82] *Parliamentary Debates*, 1st series, vol. VI, cols. 917–19 (25 April 1806).

to twenty votes and received the royal assent just a week later. By the spring of 1806, therefore, activists were one step closer to the goal of general abolition.[83]

Flush with success, Wilberforce and his supporters, chief among them Stephen, were minded to press on and raise the 'main question'. Grenville, on the other hand, counselled caution. Much of their recent success, he pointed out, had depended upon being able 'to separate the last measure [the Foreign Slave Act] from the question of immediate and total abolition'.[84] Why, then, risk undoing all their good work? Instead, Grenville proposed introducing two related proposals: one to do something about the Trinidad slave trade, which was likely to prove uncontroversial; the other to set a firm limit on slave imports into the older British Caribbean islands, enough in effect to supply their immediate needs. Grenville was confident that both of these proposals could be carried without difficulty in the present session, leaving 'the rest of the subject' for the future.[85] Eventually, however, Wilberforce and Grenville agreed on a different course of action. As previously arranged, on 10 June Fox rose to propose a resolution binding the House of Commons to take 'effectual measures for abolishing the [slave] trade, in such manner, and at such period, as may be deemed advisable'.[86] Once again, Tarleton voiced his objections, ominously raising the question of compensation. But the most significant intervention came from Lord Castlereagh, who argued that the 'real benefit must be the work of time and gradual progression'.[87] What he had in mind, clearly, was a corrective system, 'something of the nature by which smuggling and other abuses were corrected at home'.[88] More contentious still, however, was his advocacy of a 'prohibitory duty' on the importation of new slaves into the West Indies, which, he predicted, would encourage

[83] Anstey, *The Atlantic Slave Trade*, p. 382. The Foreign Slave Act not only prohibited British vessels and crews supplying slaves to foreign colonies but also banned foreign slave ships from fitting out in Britain or in 'any part of His Majesty's Dominions'. See 46 Geo. II c. 52, sections II and IX.

[84] William Wyndham Grenville to William Wilberforce, 20 May 1806, William Wilberforce Papers, Box 2, William R. Perkins Library, Duke University, North Carolina.

[85] Grenville to Wilberforce, 20 May 1806. Grenville proposed cutting slave exports by up to two-thirds, a figure that he based on estimates provided by his opponents, chief among them the Duke of Clarence, who claimed in the Lords that the Foreign Slave Bill would 'stop' the export from Africa of 22,000 out of 38,000 slaves annually. If this was true, Grenville argued, 'it follows of necessity that one third of the present supply (or a little more) will be equal to the future demand of our People – and if we strike out Trinidad we might I suppose simply take it at one third.'

[86] *Parliamentary Debates*, 1st series, vol. VII, col. 580 (10 June 1806).

[87] *Parliamentary Debates*, 1st series, vol. VII, col. 590 (10 June 1806). The Tarleton reference can be found at col. 587 (10 June 1806).

[88] *Parliamentary Debates*, 1st series, vol. VII, col. 590 (10 June 1806).

'negro population in the islands and [reward] the kindness and encouragement shown to slaves'.[89]

Nevertheless, the House adopted Fox's resolution and with it an address from Wilberforce calling on the king to begin negotiations with foreign powers regarding some international measure or measures against the slave trade.[90] Everything now pointed towards the following parliamentary session. In the meantime, British activists set about closing what they saw as the few remaining loopholes in their arguments. Significantly, one of the first things they did following passage of the Foreign Slave Act was to send a copy to the PAS, at the same time earnestly soliciting its cooperation. Over the course of the next six weeks further approaches were made, both to the PAS and to James Monroe, again requesting information.[91] Wilberforce, too, put pen to paper, pressing Monroe for 'full and minute' details regarding slavery in the USA.[92] He wanted to know, was 'task work' common in the Southern states?[93] How were slaves fed and what quantity of food was allowed them? 'The fact of the American increase is pretty notorious', Wilberforce explained, 'but it might be of great importance for me to be able to adduce undeniable proof of it.'[94] There was one other pressing matter, namely the revival of the slave trade and particularly the extent to which it was carried on from the port of Charleston. Could Monroe shed any light on this matter? Above all, Wilberforce sought reassurances that there was 'no reason to entertain any doubt that Congress as soon as it possesses, will exercise the power of abolishing the slave trade altogether'.[95] As the insistent tone of this correspondence suggests, Wilberforce and his colleagues saw British and American interests as being inextricably intertwined. Wilberforce went further, admitting that America had been 'foremost' in his mind when he had moved his 'address to His Majesty to negotiate with foreign powers for agreeing on a general abolition & mutually assisting each other to carry it into effect'.[96]

Unbeknown to Wilberforce, American activists were already stirring. At its meeting in January 1806, the American Convention had

[89] *Parliamentary Debates*, 1st series, vol. VII, col. 590 (10 June 1806).
[90] *Parliamentary Debates*, 1st series, vol. VII, col. 603 (10 June 1806).
[91] SEAST Minutes, 2 June 1806, 15 July 1806, 30 July 1806.
[92] William Wilberforce to James Monroe, 21 August 1806, James Monroe Papers, New York Public Library, microfilm edition, Reel 3.
[93] Wilberforce to Monroe, 21 August 1806.
[94] Wilberforce to Monroe, 21 August 1806.
[95] Wilberforce to Monroe, 21 August 1806.
[96] Wilberforce to Monroe, 21 August 1806.

urged the various state societies to 'prepare and circulate' memorials to Congress soliciting the passage of a law prohibiting the importation of slaves into the USA after 1808.[97] The response was enthusiastic. In New Jersey, for instance, activists set up a small committee to draft a memorial to this effect, with a view to circulating it 'throughout the state, and to such other persons as they might judge proper'.[98] But, in the event, such memorials proved unnecessary. As we have seen, the slave-trade debates of the early 1790s had imposed strict constitutional limitations on the ability of Congress to end the slave trade, although this had not prevented it from taking some deliberate action, most obviously in the case of the foreign slave trade. Nevertheless, there is little doubt that South Carolina's decision to reopen the trade in 1803 re-energised slave-trade debates, as did the acquisition of the Louisiana territory. Quick to seize the initiative, President Thomas Jefferson, in his annual message to Congress on 2 December 1806, drew attention to the slave-trade clause in the Constitution, in effect inviting Congress to ban all slave imports at the earliest opportunity. The following day, Stephen Bradley of Vermont introduced an Abolition Bill in the Senate, which was passed on 27 January 1807. Concurrently, the House of Representatives reported a similar Bill on 15 December, which was adopted in an amended form the following month. Early in February both Bills were considered in a Committee of the Whole. The upshot was a series of compromises, whereby the Senate Bill replaced the House Bill, but only after several amendments had been made. Following further debate, the Bill was eventually passed by a vote of 113 to five. The 'Act to prohibit the importation of slaves into any port or place within the jurisdiction of the USA, from and after 1 January 1808' received Jefferson's approval on 2 March.[99]

What is remarkable about this turn of events is the seeming spontaneity of America's decision to end the slave trade. As Kenneth Morgan points out, abolition was not the result of a 'sustained abolition campaign', nor was it the result of a protracted legislative struggle.[100] One reason for this was that most states, with the obvious exception of South Carolina, had already banned the importation of slaves. South

---

[97] *Minutes of the Proceedings of the Eleventh American Convention for Promoting the Abolition of Slavery* (1806), p. 26.

[98] Minutes of the New Jersey Abolition Society, 27 September 1806.

[99] Kenneth Morgan, 'Proscription by Degrees: The Ending of the African Slave Trade to the United States', in David T. Gleeson and Simon Lewis, eds., *Ambiguous Legacy: The Bicentennial of the International Slave Trade Bans* (Columbia, SC: University of South Carolina Press, 2012), pp. 1–34, at pp. 22–3.

[100] Morgan, 'Proscription by Degrees', p. 2; Drescher, *Abolition*, pp. 135–6.

Carolina's position, moreover, had invited widespread criticism, not least from its near neighbours. Congress, in other words, was relatively at one on the issue. Just as important, abolition played to important national and sectional interests. If many southerners feared the risk posed by fresh imports of slaves, particularly from the Caribbean, many northerners saw abolition as a means of slowing down the South's population growth and hence checking its political influence. But, above all, abolition was possible 'because a brief constitutional clause [Article I, Section 9, of the Constitution] had separated congressional jurisdiction over its fate from other aspects of slavery'.[101] Put another way, slaveholders – including figures such as Jefferson – could support abolition of the slave trade, safe in the knowledge that the institution of slavery itself remained intact and, to all intents and purposes, unassailable.

It is also worth stressing that the Act of 1807 contained a number of significant flaws and omissions. One of these concerned enforcement of the new legislation. While the law imposed huge penalties – up to $10,000 and jail terms of no less than five years – on those found guilty of participating in the slave trade after January 1808, Congress provided insufficient funding to render it effective; indeed, American slave merchants seem to have evaded the law with impunity.[102] Neither did the Act do anything to curtail the coastal trade, whereby thousands were annually shipped from the Upper to the Lower South or, just as often, smuggled on board vessels leaving Northern ports. More problematic, however, was the law's treatment of those slaves illegally imported into the USA after 1808. Section 4 of the Act made it clear that local courts would have jurisdiction in such cases.[103] In other words, the fate of these men and women would be determined in most instances by those with an interest in enslaving them. Certainly, there was nothing to suggest that they would be freed or sent back to Africa. Jefferson, for one, regarded free blacks as 'pests', and neither he nor his party showed any real interest in treating those illegally imported into the USA as anything other than enslaved people.

Nevertheless, the Act of 1807 was an important victory and one that for obvious reasons gave British activists a huge boost. The news was all the more welcome because attempts to influence other nations, particularly France, had proved futile.[104] Similarly, nothing had come of

[101] Morgan, 'Proscription by Degrees', pp. 23, 25 (quotation).
[102] See http://abolition.nypl.org/content/docs/text/Act_of_1807 (accessed 26 April 2012). For evasions of the 1807 Act, see Chapter 7.
[103] See http://abolition.nypl.org/content/docs/text/Act_of_1807.
[104] Anstey, *The Atlantic Slave Trade*, pp. 382–5.

attempts to ban the Trinidadian slave trade, not least because of disagreements between the relevant law officers over what could be done.[105] More worryingly still, Grenville seemed to be wavering. In August 1806 he had raised with Wilberforce the possibility of abolishing the slave trade by means of 'an increasing duty on the importation of slaves into the islands'.[106] Not surprisingly, Wilberforce had rejected the idea, arguing that duties would not only prove difficult to enforce but would do almost nothing to encourage planters to adopt 'the breeding instead of the buying system'.[107] Wilberforce also feared that the high-duty plan would merely prove a stopgap and that the duties might be 'lessened if political expediency should require it'.[108] For these and other reasons, he favoured pressing the main question, although, as he admitted to William Smith, it was incumbent on British activists to devise some means 'whereby the measure of abolition [might] be practically rendered less injurious in its consequences to West India proprietors'.[109]

Wilberforce clearly believed that Grenville could be won over to total abolition, but in September everything was thrown into the balance following Fox's death and Grenville's decision to call a general election. As it turned out, the result strengthened Grenville's position and, just as important, removed one significant obstacle to abolition, namely the number and strength of Lord Sidmouth's supporters. As Roger Anstey stresses, these internal factors would prove crucial in the final drive towards abolition.[110] Certainly, the election result seems to have settled Grenville's mind, so much so that in November he sent James Stephen the draft of a Bill for Abolition. By now it was also clear that the campaign would be waged first in the House of Lords, where in the past opposition had been strongest. To this end, activists turned their attention to rallying their supporters, including, significantly, the bench of bishops.[111] Belatedly, Wilberforce also began work on an abolitionist tract, his *Letter on the Abolition of the Slave Trade* (1807), hoping thereby

---

[105] See William Wilberforce to William Wyndham Grenville, 25 July 1806 and William Wyndham Grenville to William Wilberforce, 29 July 1806 and 24 September 1806, Dropmore Papers.

[106] See William Wilberforce to William Smith, 18 August 1806, William Smith Papers, Box 2, William R. Perkins Library, Duke University, North Carolina.

[107] Wilberforce to Smith, 18 August 1806.

[108] Wilberforce to Smith, 18 August 1806.

[109] William Wilberforce to William Smith, 5 September 1806, William Smith Papers, Box 2.

[110] Anstey, *The Atlantic Slave Trade*, pp. 391–3.

[111] Anstey, *The Atlantic Slave Trade*, pp. 393–4; William Wilberforce to William Wyndham Grenville, 29 November 1806, 18 December 1806, 15 January 1807 and 31 January 1807, Dropmore Papers; William Wyndham Grenville to William Wilberforce, 2 February 1807, Dropmore Papers.

to win over 'a certain class of readers among the Lords (the Irish, for instance) who hitherto had heard little of the real merits of the case'.[112] Clarkson, meanwhile, published a series of letters on the compensation issue, again with the intention of answering those few remaining objections to an immediate and total abolition of the slave trade.[113]

As we know, these tactics would prove critical in steering abolition through Parliament in 1807 (and here the difference between the British and American campaigns is perhaps most evident). But, at the same time, abolition was possible because activists succeeded in minimising the risks. So, while moral arguments were important (and Grenville made no secret of this in the Lords debate), a lot also depended on demonstrating that ending the slave trade was a safe option ('sound policy' in the language of the day) and one compatible with Britain's national interests.[114] Significantly, Wilberforce addressed this very point in his *Letter on the Abolition of the Slave Trade*, pointing out that the Napoleonic Wars had seriously disrupted the French, Spanish and Portuguese slave trades. Of course, he could not predict what the future conduct of these nations might be but reviving the trade, he claimed, would prove prohibitively expensive. Moreover, Wilberforce was able to confirm the 'welcome tidings' that on the recommendation of the President of the USA, Congress was in the process of 'passing an act for abolishing the slave trade on 1st January 1808'.[115] At a stroke this news removed one of the principal arguments against abolition, just as it raised the possibility of some kind of international action against the slave trade. The timing of these two pieces of legislation, therefore, was hugely significant. It may well be that Grenville could have carried abolition in 1807 without American cooperation but there is little doubt that the news coming out of the USA made his task that much easier.

---

[112] Wilberforce to Grenville, 15 January 1807.

[113] Thomas Clarkson, *Three Letters (One of Which Has Appeared Before) to the Planters and Slave-Merchants, Principally on the Subject of Compensation* (London: Phillips & Farndon, 1807).

[114] Anstey argues that in the final stages of the anti-slave-trade campaign Grenville and Wilberforce placed much less emphasis on matters of national interest, preferring instead to stress moral arguments, if only because the national interest was less apparent than it had been in the case of the foreign slave trade. See Anstey, *The Atlantic Slave Trade*, pp. 385–9. There is some merit in this argument, but Anstey tends to ignore continuing fears over the wider international implications of abolition and the possible dangers involved in surrendering an important advantage to Britain's competitors, not least the USA. In other words, it remained incumbent on abolitionists to prove that quite apart from anything else abolition was 'sound policy', hence the importance of American cooperation.

[115] William Wilberforce, *A Letter on the Abolition of the Slave Trade, Addressed to the Freeholders and Other Inhabitants of Yorkshire* (London: T. Cadell & J. Hatchard, 1807), pp. 390–4.

Though activists remained wary of their opponents, the final struggle turned out to be easier than many had anticipated. In the Lords, the vote on the first reading of Grenville's proposed Bill was 100 to thirty-four, an overwhelming victory that understandably delighted Wilberforce and his supporters. Thereafter, the Bill proceeded smoothly through the committee stages and passed its third reading on 10 February without a division. Much the same thing happened in the House of Commons, where the vote on the second reading of Lord Howick's motion (23 February) was carried by a staggering 267 votes. Nevertheless, there were still some details to sort out, among them the penal provisions and a belated attempt by the West India lobby to postpone the operation of the Bill for five years. Perhaps just as revealing was an unsuccessful attempt made by anti-abolitionists to revise the Bill's preamble so that it made no reference to justice or humanity. But no one, it seems, wished to defeat the Bill. On 23 March it passed the Lords with amendments and two days later received the royal assent. The entire British slave trade was abolished with effect from 1 May 1807.[116]

The dance was over. After a struggle of nearly twenty years, activists had at last succeeded in abolishing Britain's participation in the Atlantic slave trade. While there were undoubtedly long-term factors involved here, among them religious revivalism and the growth of compassionate humanitarianism, victory in 1807 also depended on political contingency (Pitt's sudden death, for instance), as well as skilful political manoeuvring. As Roger Anstey points out, a key element in the abolitionists' success, particularly between 1804 and 1806, was their decision to privilege national interests over humanitarian and moral issues.[117] Equally significant was Wilberforce's willingness to work with the Whigs, thereby allowing figures such as Fox and Grenville to take the lead and push abolition through Parliament. In short, tactical changes, as well as shifting political alliances, helped to engineer a breakthrough. Nevertheless, abolition was never solely a domestic matter. The international context and international concerns were important, too. As we have seen, the French invasion of Saint-Domingue in 1801 and the emergence of an independent black republic in the heart of the Caribbean served to politicise abolition, as did the retaking of Dutch Guiana. American support was also important, along with an evolving international situation that made abolition not only possible but also practicable. Finally, there was the role played by those West Indian planters who believed that some measure of reform was

[116] Anstey, *The Atlantic Slave Trade*, pp. 395–8; Pollock, *Wilberforce*, pp. 210–14.
[117] Anstey, *The Atlantic Slave Trade*, pp. 362–3.

Figure 6.1 James Sayers, *A West India Sportsman*, 1807. © National Maritime Museum, Greenwich, London.

necessary, if only to secure the economic future of the Caribbean. Put another way, slave-trade abolition is best understood as a coalescence of different factors, some of them internal and national, others external and international.[118]

By and large, public opinion was also behind the measure. There appears to have been little sympathy for West Indian planters or, indeed, for a society that seemed too idle and dissolute to reform itself. The point was made rather starkly in a second series of 'West India Prints' published by William Holland in 1807–8 to coincide with the abolition of the British slave trade.[119] In *A West India Sportsman* (Fig. 6.1), a white planter lounges in a chair, his legs up on a small stool, gun at his side, while behind him stands a poorly dressed male servant who protects him from the sun with a large umbrella. Addressing another slave, who approaches balancing a glass of 'sangaree' precariously on a tray,

---

[118] Philip D. Morgan makes a very similar point in his excellent essay, 'Ending the Slave Trade', pp. 120–1.
[119] Holland also took this opportunity to republish or, at least, re-advertise the first series of his 'West India Prints'.

Figure 6.2 James Sayers, *West India Fashionables*, 1807. © National Maritime Museum, Greenwich, London.

he shouts, 'Make haste with the Sangaree, Quashie, and tell Quaco to drive the Birds up to me – I'm ready.' In the foreground are assorted flagons of sangaree, rum and brandy, while at the far left is a table laden with food: a shoulder of lamb, a suckling pig, assorted fish and a round of beef. In the background, another planter reclines lazily on a settee, attended this time by a female servant, while in the middle distance a slave drives birds towards the 'sportsman'. The scene is comical in its absurdity, but is one that at the same time hints at the very 'otherness' of white West Indian society, its idleness and its dissipation.[120]

A similar point is made in *West India Fashionables* (Fig. 6.2), also published in November 1807. The print consists of two designs on one plate. In the first, 'On a Visit in Style', a planter and his wife are being driven in a two-wheeled gig, which is emblazoned with a crest consisting of a goblet and crossed whips. Both figures are shaded from the sun, as is the wife's maid, who sits under the gig's huge canopy holding

---

[120] *Catalogue of Political and Personal Satires Preserved in the Department of Prints and Drawings in the British Museum* (London: Trustees of the British Museum, 1870–1954), vol. VIII, p. 577.

a box. The white party is attended by no fewer than four black servants: two at the front who lead the gig and two others who follow at some distance behind – a man carrying his master's arched-top trunk on his head and a woman carrying her mistress's band-box. The tone is ironic; 'style' here is exposed as a lack of sophistication, as it is in the accompanying image, 'Taking a Ride'. Here, the same couple ride on horseback, each attended by 'running footmen'. The planter and his wife wear a large hat and bonnet that partially or completely obscure their faces, but it is their poses that hint at the faintly ludicrous air of this couple: their saddles are placed very far forward on their horses, the planter's legs are thrust forward beyond his horse's neck, and the belly bands on both horses appear to be loose, perhaps reflecting the dissoluteness of colonial society. The whole spectacle smacks of rudeness or provinciality. One of the footmen wears a long blue coat that is far too big for him while another has torn white trousers. All are barefooted.[121]

West India Fashionables also hinted at something else, namely the transgressiveness of planter society. In both images, the black servants have oddly pointed noses that echo the planter's pointed nose, signifying paternity. The artist, James Sayers, turned to this theme again in *Johnny Newcome in Love in the West Indies*, which was published by Holland in April 1808. Whereas Abraham James had used the Newcome figure to highlight the dangers of the Caribbean climate, Sayers used it to satirise white masculine fantasies and 'colonial lust'. No sooner has he arrived in the West Indies than Johnny falls for the charms of 'Mimbo Wampo', here depicted as a grotesque black woman, who smokes a pipe and wears a hat and large gold earrings. The couple subsequently marry but then Johnny eventually returns to Britain, leaving behind him nine children, among them 'Lucretia Diana Newcome, a delicate girl very much like her Mother only that she has a great antipathy to the pipe' and 'Hector Sammy Newcome, a child of great spirit, [who] can Damnme Liberty and Equality and promises to be the Toussaint of his Country'. *Johnny Newcome in Love in the West Indies* works at a number of different levels. By portraying black women as objects of ridicule, Sayers exaggerated the horror of interracial promiscuity while at the same time hinting at the corruption of West Indian society. But the print also made a wider political point. Johnny's adventures not only challenged metropolitan conventions, hinting, as they did, at the collapse of racial categories, but they also challenged the authority of the British state (the reference to 'Liberty and Equality' is particularly significant in this regard).[122]

[121] *Catalogue of Political and Personal Satires*, pp. 577–8.
[122] *Catalogue of Political and Personal Satires*, pp. 721–2.

If there was more than a hint of opportunism surrounding the publication of Holland's 'West India Prints', there was no mistaking their resonance and meaning. Whether viewed as an attempt to justify or to defend the Abolition Act, such images sought to demonise white Creole planters, thereby setting them and, by implication, slavery and the slave trade at a distance from metropolitan values. Abolition, according to this sentimental discourse, was a benevolent act (a 'gift') that reflected honour on the British nation. Wilberforce was a key figure in the creation of this nascent culture of abolitionism. As Marcus Wood points out, Wilberforce's sanctification began at the very instant of abolition. In Joseph Collyer's *Plate to Commemorate the Abolition of the Slave Trade* (Fig. 6.3), Wilberforce appears not as a living presence but as a relic – 'an impassive neo-Roman monument' – while in the foreground, Britannia, supported by Liberty and Justice, tramples on the 'greed and moral corruption which [had] generated British dominance of the Atlantic slave trade'.[123] The absence of any black figures in this composition is perhaps less remarkable than its self-conscious triumphalism. Here, lest anyone forget, were Britons in heroic mode: independent, freedom loving, idealistic and brave.

Yet, for all that, abolition was not publicly commemorated in Britain, and neither did it create any recognisable commemorative practices. Much the same thing was true in the USA, but with one notable exception. Starting in 1808, blacks in New York, Philadelphia and Boston began to celebrate 'Abolition Day', usually on 1 January, a tradition that seems to have lasted at least until the 1820s.[124] More often than not, these 'services' took place in churches and meeting rooms and consisted of prayers, Bible readings and sermons or orations. Northern blacks also sometimes took to the streets. In 1809, for instance, the New York Wilberforce Philanthropic Society organised two processions that were led by 'the Wilberforce band of music ... [and] the Maritime and Musical Associations, decorated with badges, and accompanied with their appropriate banners'.[125] In these different ways, blacks made 'Abolition Day' their own. Part of the intention, clearly, was to create a continuing tradition. Absalom Jones, for instance, urged his

---

[123] Marcus Wood, 'Popular Graphic Images of Slavery and Emancipation in Nineteenth-Century England', in Douglas Hamilton and Robert J. Blyth, eds., *Representing Slavery: Art, Artefacts and Archives in the Collections of the National Maritime Museum* (Aldershot: Lund Humphries, 2007), pp. 136–51, at p. 141.
[124] Mitch Kachun, *Festivals of Freedom: Memory and Meaning in African American Emancipation Celebrations, 1808–1915* (Amherst, Mass.: University of Massachusetts Press, 2003), pp. 16–53.
[125] Kachun, *Festivals of Freedom*, p. 35.

Figure 6.3 Joseph Collyer, after Henry Moses, *Plate to Commemorate the Abolition of the Slave Trade*, 1808. © National Maritime Museum, Greenwich, London.

congregation to set aside 1 January as 'a day of public thanksgiving'.[126] 'Let the history of our brethren, and of their deliverance, descend by this means to our children', he went on,

and when they shall ask, in time to come, saying, What means the lessons, the psalms, the prayers and the praises in the worship of this day? Let us answer them, by saying, the Lord, on the day of which this is the anniversary, abolished the trade which dragged your fathers from their native country, and sold them as bondsmen in the United States of America.[127]

Significantly, 'Abolition Day' orators made little attempt to distinguish between the British and American campaigns against the slave trade.[128] Often, it was British activists who received the most attention, as well as the most praise. In his 1808 oration, for instance, Peter Williams applauded the 'towering eloquence' of Wilberforce, while at the same time singling out Clarkson 'whose extensive capacities and unremitting zeal, have classed him with the most conspicuous and useful advocates of the cause'.[129] Occasionally, too, Sharp and Dillwyn were included in this pantheon of white abolitionist heroes, taking their place alongside Benezet, Woolman and Rush. Russell Parrott put the case well in 1812:

The pre-eminence which these men [Sharp, Dillwyn, Benezet, Wilberforce, Clarkson and Rush] hold in society is a sufficient test of their virtue and the justice of the cause. What though their names are not recorded on the historic page, in letters of blood; what though their fame is not borne down to distant times, on the groans and sighs of oppressed millions, yet a grateful people, truly sensible of the great blessings resulting from their disinterested exertions, will transmit to the latest posterity their virtuous deeds, engraved in indelible characters.[130]

Black orators, therefore, regarded abolition as an international movement, but just as telling was the fact that they were clearly deeply engaged with the British campaign, were familiar with its leading proponents, both inside and outside Parliament, and had a keen sense of what they as Americans owed them.

[126] Absalom Jones, *A Thanksgiving Sermon, Preached January 1, 1808, in St Thomas', or the African Episcopal Church, Philadelphia: On Account of the Abolition of the Slave Trade on That Day, by the Congress of the United States* (Philadelphia, Pa.: Fry & Kammerer, 1808), p. 19.

[127] Jones, *A Thanksgiving Sermon*, p. 20.

[128] Drescher, *Abolition*, p. 137.

[129] Peter Williams, *An Oration on the Abolition of the Slave Trade: Delivered in the African Church, in the City of New York, January 1, 1808* (New York, 1808), p. 23.

[130] Russell Parrott, *An Oration on the Abolition of the Slave Trade: Delivered on the First of January, 1812, at the African Church of St Thomas* (Philadelphia, Pa.: James Maxwell, 1812), p. 8.

7 The revival of internationalism

One of the reasons British activists made so little fuss over 1807 was that for many of them the Abolition Act represented not an end but a beginning. The immediate priority was to ensure that the new legislation was adequately enforced. In Britain's case, at least, this meant not only careful monitoring and surveillance but also an active policy of slave-trade suppression, involving the Royal Navy, colonial governors and vice-admiralty courts. As we shall see, British activists spent a lot of time perfecting these various instruments, just as they spent a lot of time trying to close the loopholes in the 1807 Act. These activities, however, were merely part of a much wider project. British activists – more than their French or American counterparts – ultimately sought to make abolition of the slave trade 'universal'. The distinction is an important one. In the main, the internationalism of the 1810s, as distinct from the more ideological humanitarianism of the late eighteenth century, was driven by British interests, as well as by British humanitarian zeal. This is not to suggest that other nations were not involved; in fact, quite the contrary. But, more often than not, it was British ministers and activists who took the lead, leaving, as a result, an indelible mark on the slave-trade suppression politics of the early nineteenth century.

Nevertheless, in one important sense 1807 did mark the end of an era. That year, the SEAST was formally disbanded. In its place, Wilberforce, Clarkson, Stephen and others hurriedly organised the African Institution (AI). As its name suggests, the new organisation was designed primarily to aid in the civilisation of Africa. Although the members anticipated that some of their time would be taken up with the slave trade, their real aim was to open up Africa to legitimate trade, something that had preoccupied them since the 1780s.[1] Yet even

---

[1] *Report of the Committee of the African Institution, Read to the General Meeting on the 15th of July, 1807. Together with the Rules and Regulations Adopted for the Government of the Society* (London: J. Hatchard, 1811); Drescher, *The Mighty Experiment*, pp. 93–6.

here there was the potential for misunderstanding. Significantly, the AI shunned any notion of engaging in large-scale commercial enterprises in Africa (or, for these purposes, Sierra Leone) and, perhaps just as telling, dissociated itself from all missionary activity. Instead, it set out to raise awareness of Africa and its potential for economic development while at the same time offering native Africans whatever help it could, whether that meant supplying them with tools and seeds or sponsoring schools and training. In short, the AI's role was akin to that of a modern NGO, an emphasis that reflected the background and experience of its members, who included dukes, MPs and several bishops.[2]

Whatever its original aims and objectives, the AI soon found itself devoting more and more of its attention to the slave trade. Its 1810 report, which was almost entirely given over to this subject, provided details of a new scandal, namely attempts by British and American merchants to evade the Abolition Acts, chiefly through the use of foreign flags. Many slave ships on the west coast of Africa, it transpired, had either cleared from British ports or were owned by British interests that had sold them (and their cargoes) to Spanish, Portuguese or Swedish agents. The worst culprits, however, were the Americans, 'whose ships were now the great carriers of slaves, without any defence against the penalties, to which as Americans they are liable, than is afforded by the flag, and simulated clearances, of some foreign state'.[3] Reports recently received by the directors of the AI suggested the coast was 'crowded' with vessels known to be American, trading in slaves under Spanish and Swedish flags.[4] The cases tried by the Admiralty Court at Sierra Leone told the same story. According to the 1811 report, twenty ships alone had been condemned in the past year on 'satisfactory proof either of their being American or British property, or of their having cleared out from a British port'.[5] The scale of the abuses was so large, indeed, that British activists began to talk despondently of a 'revival' of the international slave trade.[6]

Reacting to this fresh challenge, the members of the AI looked first to stiffen the provisions of the Abolition Act, and, largely through their efforts, in 1811 Parliament passed supplementary legislation making

[2] *Report of the Committee of the African Institution, Read to the General Meeting on the 15th of July, 1807*, pp. 3–5.

[3] *Fourth Report of the Directors of the African Institution, Read at the Annual General Meeting on the 28th of March, 1810* (London: J. Hatchard, 1814), pp. 10–11.

[4] *Fourth Report of the Directors of the African Institution*, p. 3.

[5] *Fifth Report of the Directors of the African Institution, Read at the Annual General Meeting on the 27th of March, 1811* (London: J. Hatchard, 1811), p. 2.

[6] *Fifth Report of the Directors of the African Institution*, p. 1.

slave trafficking a felony and therefore punishable by transportation or imprisonment and hard labour.[7] Simultaneously, they sought to ensure that the new legislation was enforced, not least by the Royal Navy. In 1808, two ships had been sent to the west coast of Africa to help suppress the slave trade, and by 1810 this force had risen to four (what became known as the African Squadron did not come into being until 1819).[8] For obvious reasons, British activists took a close interest in the suppression of the slave trade, circulating abolitionist propaganda among naval officers assigned to the African coast and periodically reminding them of the financial inducements involved, the captors of slave ships being entitled to the forfeiture of both ship and cargo.[9] In the same way, the members of the AI sought to influence colonial governors, consuls and commissary judges, in the process building up an important network that provided not only much needed information but also a valuable link between metropole and colony. Men such as Captain Edward Columbine, one of Wilberforce's close friends who became Governor of Sierra Leone in 1809, were enthusiastic abolitionists and constituted, in Richard Huzzey's words, 'anti-slavers in disguise'.[10]

Although infractions still continued, these various initiatives served as serious deterrents to would-be slave traffickers. America, however, posed a more difficult challenge. As we have seen, British activists were fully aware of the scale of American abuses. But more revealing still was their sense that they could and should do something about them. In 1809, for instance, Zachary Macaulay wrote two long letters to Benjamin Rush, president of the PAS, urging American activists to

[7] 51 Geo. III, c. 23 (1811).
[8] Christopher Lloyd, *The Navy and the Slave Trade: The Suppression of the African Slave Trade in the Nineteenth Century* (London: Longmans, Green & Co., 1949), pp. 61–3. See also William Ward, *The Royal Navy and the Slavers: The Suppression of the Atlantic Slave Trade* (London: George Allen & Unwin, 1969); Keith Hamilton and Patrick Salmon, eds., *Slavery, Diplomacy and Empire: Britain and the Suppression of the Slave Trade, 1807–1975* (Eastbourne: Sussex Academic Press, 2009).
[9] *Fourth Report of the Directors of the African Institution* (1810), pp. 4–5; *Sixth Report of the Directors of the African Institution, Read at the Annual General Meeting on the 25th of March, 1812* (London: J. Hatchard, 1812), p. 9.
[10] *Fourth Report of the Directors of the African Institution* (1810), pp. 7–8; *Sixth Report of the Directors of the African Institution* (1812), pp. 9–11; Richard Huzzey, *Freedom Burning: Anti-Slavery and Empire in Victorian Britain* (Ithaca, NY: Cornell University Press, 2012), pp. 42–51. See also Laidlaw, *Colonial Connections*, especially Part I. After 1812, British activists would also show increasing interest in slave registration as a means of checking the flow of slave imports. That year, an Order-in-Council set up a slave registry in Trinidad, but it was not until 1 January 1820 that all of the British Caribbean islands had a system of public registration, which in each case required regular reports of any changes in slave holdings, whether through births, death, purchases or sales. See Davis, *Inhuman Bondage*, pp. 211–12, 237; Stephen, *Antislavery Recollections*, pp. 24–5, 37–8.

bring the matter before Congress and calling for some form of mutual cooperation, including the right of search of American vessels suspected of being involved in the slave trade.[11] It is safe to say that Macaulay's approach caught Rush off guard. Since 1806, the American movement had become becalmed and increasingly insular in its outlook. Groups such as the PAS and the NYMS still operated and attracted large numbers of members, but, by and large, they focused their attention on issues such as the internal slave trade (kidnapping was still a perennial problem) and the education of free blacks. The American Convention, for its part, was now meeting triennially, partly to save money but partly because of a lack of support and fresh ideas.[12] There had also been a generational shift as figures such as James Pemberton, Miers Fisher and Joseph Bloomfield either died or retired from the cause. One knock-on effect was that British and American abolitionists increasingly operated in two separate spheres; certainly, there was little of the easy familiarity that had existed in the 1780s and 1790s. Rush and Macaulay may well have been aware of each other's existence but they were not friends – at least not in the way that Pemberton and Dillwyn had been friends.

Something else had changed, too. Since 1807, relations between Britain and America had become increasingly fraught, largely because of alleged infringements of America's neutrality (British impressment of American seamen was a particular bone of contention).[13] For this reason, Rush's response was evasive. It was clearly the view of PAS members that they could do little to help the AI, at least 'at present'. In saying this, however, they agreed to carry on a correspondence with the AI and 'to communicate to any of the other abolition societies in the United States such information relative to [the American slave trade] as they may judge proper and useful'.[14] In the circumstances, the PAS's caution was understandable, but, to judge from letters and speeches on the floor of Congress, American abuses were already well known to US politicians. Moreover, an important lead was taken by President James Madison, who, in his annual message to Congress in December 1810, raised the subject of the slave trade, noting that some American citizens were still carrying on the traffic, 'equally in violation of the laws

[11] Zachary Macaulay to Benjamin Rush, 1 August 1809 and 8 November 1809, PAS Correspondence, Reel 12.
[12] Minutes of the Proceedings of the Eleventh American Convention for Promoting the Abolition of Slavery (1806), pp. 12–13, 25.
[13] Wood, Empire of Liberty, pp. 659–700. See also George C. Daughan, 1812: The Navy's War (New York: Basic Books, 2012).
[14] PAS Minutes, 20 October 1809 and 4 December 1809.

of humanity and in defiance of those of their own country', and calling upon Congress to take appropriate measures.[15]

Madison's timely intervention seemed to give American activists fresh impetus. Writing to Roberts Vaux in November 1811, John Murray Jnr. made it clear that it was the intention of the New York society to 'take some steps in order to bring before Congress the revival of the subjects which was [sic] hinted at by the President in his message'.[16] He also hoped to convince the members of the PAS to do likewise.[17] Within a matter of months, however, the nation was at war, which meant that for the moment all talk of petitions was pushed to one side; the 1812 American Convention, for instance, discussed the slave trade but decided against any deliberate action, save to keep a watching brief.[18] Nevertheless, as the war progressed, American activists seem to have had a change of heart. In February 1813, the PAS at last decided to petition Congress, calling for cooperation with Spain and Portugal to put an end to American abuses on the west coast of Africa.[19] Part of the intention here may have been to embarrass the US Government, thereby prompting it into action. If so, the tactic backfired, although in a roundabout way the War of 1812 did engineer a breakthrough. During the peace negotiations that began in August 1814, the British commissioners inserted an article into the treaty that committed both nations to the 'entire abolition' of the slave trade.[20] By the end of the year, therefore, something like normalcy had been restored, even if it remained unclear how Article X of the Treaty of Ghent would be enforced, at least without appropriate congressional action.

---

[15] Du Bois, *The Suppression of the African Slave-Trade*, pp. 112–13.

[16] John Murray Jnr. to Roberts Vaux, 8 November 1811, Roberts Vaux Papers, Box 1, Historical Society of Pennsylvania, Philadelphia.

[17] Murray to Vaux, 8 November 1811.

[18] *Minutes of the Proceedings of the Thirteenth American Convention for Promoting the Abolition of Slavery, and Improving the Condition of the African Race: Assembled at Philadelphia, on the Thirteenth Day of January, One Thousand Eight Hundred and Twelve, and Continued, by Adjournments, Until the Sixteenth Day of the Same Month, Inclusive* (Philadelphia, Pa.: Hamilton-Ville, 1812), pp. 18–20. The delegates clearly felt that Congress could not 'at present' be called upon for 'further measures of prevention'.

[19] For the text of this petition, see PAS Minutes, 29 December 1814.

[20] Wood, *Empire of Liberty*, pp. 695–6. The three British commissioners seem to have raised the issue of the slave trade at a relatively late stage in the negotiations. See Lord Gambier, Henry Goulburn and William Adams to Lord Castlereagh, 10 December 1814 and 13 December 1814, Foreign Office Records, FO5/102. The National Archives, London. It is not clear from the Foreign Office records whether this initiative came from Castlereagh or from the commissioners themselves. For the American response, see John Quincy Adams, J. A. Bayard, Henry Clay, Jonathan Russell and Albert Gallatin to the British Plenipotentiaries, 14 December 1814, Foreign Office Records, FO5/102. The National Archives.

While the USA was clearly important to the AI's strategic aims, its chief focus was understandably Europe. In 1807, Britain had adopted an advanced position with respect to the slave trade. The problem for government ministers was to ensure that, as a result, Britain was not damaged, or, worse, ruined by what it had done. Though the French Revolutionary and Napoleonic Wars had seriously disrupted the international slave trade, Spanish and Portuguese merchants were still trafficking on the west coast of Africa and, just as important, were willing to provide a protecting arm to other nations.[21] Then there was France. Here, again, long years of war had taken their toll; in fact, the French slave trade had all but come to a halt. But British activists worried that with the return of peace French merchants would want to revive the slave trade, thereby putting British interests at risk. Put a different way, the European situation remained extremely volatile, which is why government ministers were willing to share information with abolitionists and to consider their advice. However, this did not mean that groups such as the AI had complete control over government policy. Rather, theirs was a symbiotic relationship; each needed and, to some extent, depended on the other. As Paul Kielstra puts it, 'Abolition was an accomplished fact. Its proponents had to be dealt with civilly.'[22]

British fears became a reality when in 1814 Napoleon abdicated and the Bourbons were restored (1814–15). With the war seemingly over, thoughts naturally turned to the peace settlement that would follow. Anticipating these negotiations, early in May both Houses of Parliament passed resolutions calling on the Prince Regent to use all his influence with the Allied Powers to secure the 'general abolition' of the slave trade.[23] Lord Castlereagh's instructions could not have been clearer, but early indications suggested that the French were in no mood to accede to Britain's demands. Louis XVIII, it was reported in the British press, had refused to agree to the abolition of the slave trade on the grounds that it would interfere with the internal government of the French colonies, a position that many editors clearly found untenable.[24] Rumours of French intransigence proved well founded. What Castlereagh managed to negotiate at Paris amounted to a compromise. While Louis XVIII and his ministers agreed to do everything in their power to promote

---

[21] See the various published reports of the African Institution, 1807–15.
[22] Paul Kielstra, *The Politics of Slave Trade Suppression in Britain and France, 1814–48: Diplomacy, Morality and Economics* (Basingstoke: Palgrave-Macmillan, 2000), pp. 14–15.
[23] *Morning Chronicle*, 29 April 1814 and 4 May 1814; *Leeds Mercury*, 7 May 1814.
[24] *Morning Chronicle*, 23 May 1814 and 24 May 1814; *Trewman's Exeter Flying Post*, 26 May 1814.

the general abolition of the slave trade at the forthcoming Congress of Vienna, on the central question of French trafficking they effectively obtained a stay of execution; under the terms of the Treaty of Paris it was agreed that it would continue for another five years.[25]

When news of this fudge finally reached Britain in June there was widespread alarm and consternation. The peace treaty represented to many not only a national insult but also an insult to the memory of all those who had fought so valiantly to bring the slave trade to an end. As an editorial in the *Bury and Norwich Post* exclaimed,

No one can read or hear of such an article as this without a religious veneration for the names of Wilberforce and Clarkson and those other heroes of human-ity who so long and so strenuously laboured, both in and out of Parliament, to wipe away the deep spot from the character of our nation and of our race.[26]

Few, it seems, trusted France's intentions or its commitment to procur-ing a total abolition of the slave trade. To the *Morning Chronicle*, such a 'subterfuge' made 'a mockery of our humane wishes ... for at the end of that time [five years] how can the promise be enforced? By no means but [by] going to war'.[27] Up and down the country there were similar protests against the Government's actions, hinting at a depth of feeling that took even many activists by surprise. 'We have been told that the compliance was necessary to satisfy the needs of commercial men in France', complained the *Leeds Mercury*. 'Let the French yet be told, that non-compliance on the part of the British Government is indispensable to satisfy the people of England.'[28]

Almost immediately, leading activists, among them Wilberforce, Brougham, Macaulay and Stephen, called a public meeting at London's Freemasons' Hall on 17 June. The outcome was a series of resolutions criticising Castlereagh's handling of the negotiations and calling on the Government to do all in its power to effect the total abolition of the slave trade at the forthcoming Congress of Vienna.[29] Significantly, it was left to the Board of Directors of the AI to carry these resolutions into effect, the upshot being that on 20 June a small committee consisting

---

[25] Kielstra, *The Politics of Slave Trade Suppression*, pp. 23–5.
[26] *Bury and Norwich Post*, 8 June 1814.
[27] *Morning Chronicle*, 11 June 1814.
[28] *Leeds Mercury*, 18 June 1814.
[29] For details of this meeting, see *Morning Post*, 18 June 1814 and 20 June 1814. Those present were also concerned that the French treaty would set a dangerous precedent, insisting that 'no colony yet remaining in the possession of Great Britain, wherein slavery exists, should be ceded to any other power, without requiring an express stip-ulation for relinquishing the slave trade immediately and for ever'. See *Morning Post*, 20 June 1814.

of Clarkson and William Allen, a Quaker chemist and fellow member of the AI, was set up and given the task of orchestrating a nationwide petition campaign.[30] From their headquarters in the Freemasons' Tavern, the two men worked from ten in the morning till ten at night in a desperate and ultimately successful attempt to rally their supporters. Allen noted in his diary on 24 June that in just four days they had posted 'above two thousand' letters.[31] The scale of this undertaking was enormous, dwarfing even the earlier campaigns of 1788 and 1792. When they were not writing or answering letters, Clarkson and Allen were collecting signatures and receiving petitions; indeed, together they seem to have driven the whole campaign, which, given the short lead-in time, makes their achievement all the more remarkable.

As had been the case in 1788 and 1792, the 1814 campaign also acquired its own visual culture. Copies of the *Brookes*, for instance, were printed and circulated, as were copies of George Morland's two prints *Execrable Human Traffic* (1788) and *African Hospitality* (1799).[32] Through these various means, activists succeeded in forcing the slave trade once again to the forefront of political debate in Britain, although in truth many Britons seem to have needed very little prompting. The results exceeded even their wildest expectations. In all, over 800 petitions were presented to both Houses of Parliament carrying nearly 2 million signatures.[33] The London petition alone was signed by nearly 40,000 petitioners; Clarkson claimed that if it had 'lain three days longer' the figure would have been closer to 100,000.[34] The numbers were, by any estimate, staggering. Equally telling was the way the campaign crossed party lines. Time and time again, petitioners stressed that abolition was not a partisan issue. The *Leeds Mercury* noted that the British nation had 'risen up as one man against the continuance of the slave trade; that all distinctions of political party, of religious sects, and even of rank, [had] been forgotten, and that she [had] with one voice of her collective population proclaimed aloud "Let there be no slave trade"'.[35] 'The call will vibrate through Europe', the paper went

[30] See *Morning Post*, 28 June 1814 and 29 June 1814; *Leeds Mercury*, 9 July 1814.
[31] Thomas Clarkson to Catherine Clarkson, 21 June 1814 (CN41), 28–9 June 1814 (CN42), and 30 June 1814 (CN43), Thomas Clarkson Papers, Huntington Library, San Marino, California (Anon.), *Life of William Allen*, vol. I, p. 152.
[32] Hamilton and Blyth, *Representing Slavery*, pp. 274–5, 281.
[33] Drescher, *Abolition*, p. 229. For a full list of these petitions, see *Eighth Report of the Directors of the African Institution, Read at the Annual General Meeting on the 23rd of March, 1814* (London: J. Hatchard, 1814), pp. 40–7.
[34] Thomas Clarkson to Catherine Clarkson, 28–9 June 1814, Thomas Clarkson Papers, CN42, Huntington Library, San Marino, California.
[35] *Leeds Mercury*, 9 July 1814.

on. 'It will reach to the shores of Africa and it will ultimately prevail, for it is the voice of God.'[36]

Reacting to this public outcry, in late June the Lords and the Commons both passed addresses directing ministers to reopen negotiations with the French, ideally with a view to ending the slave trade or, failing that, pressing for some kind of restriction. The same addresses also demanded action at the forthcoming Congress of Vienna.[37] Not without reason, activists claimed an important victory. Clarkson, for one, thought the Commons address 'the best thing Wilberforce ever did', not least because it would hold the Government to account.[38] No longer would ministers be able to neglect abolitionists or to take their support for granted. On the contrary, 'future governments would have to meet exacting standards of behaviour defined by the religious attitude to the traffic or face a worse attack than that of 1814'.[39] In this sense, the importance of the petition campaign cannot be underestimated. As Kielstra neatly puts it, 'Universal abolition had joined control of the seas and a select few other goals as fundamental, unnegotiable interests of British foreign policy.'[40]

Not content with putting pressure on government ministers, British activists also set themselves the task of trying to convert Europeans to abolition, thereby effecting a revolution from within. This was not a new idea – after all, it had been at the heart of the internationalism of the 1780s – but, as we shall see, following Napoleon's abdication, it rapidly regained impetus. An important marker was set down at the meeting at the Freemasons' Tavern in June 1814. The sixth resolution urged British activists 'to use their utmost endeavours, as well in France, as in all other countries where that trade still subsists, to diffuse authentic information, and excite just sentiments and feelings on this great subject'.[41] The challenge, as many saw it, was to educate Europeans about the slave trade. Arthur Wellesley, the Duke of Wellington, Britain's ambassador to Paris, was of the same mind. Partly out of self-interest, Wellington willingly aided activists in their efforts to win over the French, who, he believed, were woefully ignorant about slavery and inclined to see abolition as a British plot.[42] In this sense, again, 1814 marked the opening

---

[36] *Leeds Mercury*, 9 July 1814.
[37] Kielstra, *The Politics of Slave Trade Suppression*, p. 32; *Morning Chronicle*, 1 July 1814.
[38] Quoted in Kielstra, *The Politics of Slave Trade Suppression*, p. 32.
[39] Kielstra, *The Politics of Slave Trade Suppression*, p. 32.
[40] Kielstra, *The Politics of Slave Trade Suppression*, p. 33.
[41] *Morning Post*, 20 June 1814.
[42] See, for instance, Thomas Clarkson to William Wilberforce, 27 August 1814, Wilberforce Papers, c. 45, fols. 45–6, Bodleian Library, Oxford.

of a new era. The steady flow of information back and forth across the Channel testified to the growing importance attached to Anglo-French cooperation, not least because to many it seemed to hold the key to international action against the slave trade.

British activists took up this challenge with renewed energy and purpose, none more so than William Wilberforce. As early as April 1814, Wilberforce had approached Thomas Harrison, a fellow member of the AI, with a view to setting up a committee to oversee the 'composition and translation of abolitionist tracts into different [European] languages'.[43] The expense would be considerable, he went on, especially if the translations were properly done, but he was in no doubt that some initiative of this kind was necessary if Europeans were to be converted to abolition.[44] Privately, Wilberforce went further, blaming himself for not 'having foreseen this conjuncture [Napoleon's abdication and the restoration of the Bourbons] and been prepared with works in all the modern languages against the slave trade'.[45] Keen to make up for lost ground, over the next twelve months he would spend more and more of his time trying to mobilise European leaders and, by extension, European public opinion. Wilberforce even took up the pen himself. His first thought had been to draft a letter to Tsar Alexander, now considered the 'great man' of Europe and generally thought to be sympathetic to abolition, but by the summer of 1814 he was immersed in a more ambitious project, a letter to the French minister, Talleyrand, which was published simultaneously in English and French later that year.[46]

Running to over eighty printed pages, Wilberforce's letter rehearsed in detail the many considerations that had led the British to abolish the slave trade. Britain's cause, he was at pains to point out, was a noble one, motivated less by economic or political gain than by a profound sense of national guilt. (Wilberforce even went so far as to suggest that Britain was guilty of drawing other nations, including the French, into

---

[43] William Wilberforce to Thomas Harrison, 26 April 1814, William Wilberforce Papers, Box 2, William R. Perkins Library, Duke University, North Carolina.

[44] Wilberforce to Harrison, 26 April 1814.

[45] Wilberforce and Wilberforce, *The Life of William Wilberforce*, vol. IV, p. 177.

[46] William Wilberforce, *A Letter to His Excellency the Prince of Talleyrand Périgord, etc.,* on the Subject of the Slave Trade (London: Printed for J. Hatchard, Piccadilly; and Cadell & Davies, 1814). The French edition was published under the title *Lettre à son excellence Monseigneur Le Prince de Talleyrand Périgord, Ministre et Secrétaire d'état de SMTC au Département des Affaires Étrangères, et son Plénipotentiaire au Congrès de Vienne, au sujet de la traite des nègres. Par Wm. Wilberforce, Écuyer, Membre du Parlement Britannique. Traduite de l'anglais* (London: Schulze & Dean and Paris: Normand, 1814).

the trade.[47]) Setting aside the animosities of the past twenty years, Wilberforce approached Talleyrand in a spirit of 'mutual cooperation'.[48] With the return of peace, he said, he had hoped that the French would not only join Britain in calling for 'an immediate and universal' abolition of the slave trade but that they would also support Britain's civilising efforts in Africa (meaning presumably Sierra Leone).[49] What he had not anticipated was that France would resist these overtures, least of all that 'any considerable number of people could so far misconstrue the invitation to concur with us in [these] benevolent designs ... as to have imagined that we were assuming a tone of moral superiority, or wishing in some way to defraud or injure you'.[50]

Understandably, Wilberforce regarded French intentions to revive the slave trade as a retrograde step. To his mind, this would be tantamount to beginning 'a new slave trade', especially as 'not one solitary vessel, not a single seaman, not a *livre* of [French] capital is now employed in the slave trade; not a single manufacturer or artisan is occupied in fabricating goods for it'.[51] The trade, he could not help pointing out, was 'uncertain' and 'fluctuating'.[52] Moreover, once it had been re-established, it would be all the more difficult to abolish, particularly after an interval of five years.[53] Wilberforce was equally sceptical about the wisdom of reintroducing slavery into Saint-Domingue, reminding Talleyrand of the fateful results of the last French expedition. Such an enterprise, he predicted, was sure to end in disaster, especially given the determination of Saint-Dominguan blacks to resist the 'abhorred yoke' of slavery.[54] Nevertheless, Wilberforce stopped short of questioning France's liberality of spirit or the wisdom of its leaders. The problem, as he saw it, was 'a want of information'.[55] Once the French nation had become familiar with the true horrors and inequities of the slave trade – hence the importance of pamphlets such as his own – then he predicted the effects would be the same as they had been among the British.[56]

Simultaneously, Clarkson also took up the challenge of influencing French public opinion in favour of reform. In June he had come up with the idea of writing a short pamphlet on the subject, *A Summary View of*

[47] Wilberforce, *A Letter to His Excellency*, p. 56.
[48] Wilberforce, *A Letter to His Excellency*, p. 50.
[49] Wilberforce, *A Letter to His Excellency*, p. 48.
[50] Wilberforce, *A Letter to His Excellency*, p. 49.
[51] Wilberforce, *A Letter to His Excellency*, pp. 43, 54.
[52] Wilberforce, *A Letter to His Excellency*, p. 43.
[53] Wilberforce, *A Letter to His Excellency*, p. 58.
[54] Wilberforce, *A Letter to His Excellency*, pp. 40–1.
[55] Wilberforce, *A Letter to His Excellency*, p. 51.
[56] Wilberforce, *A Letter to His Excellency*, p. 61.

*the Evidence Delivered Before the Committee of the English House of Commons
on the Subject of the Slave Trade,* which he addressed to European leaders, pleading with them to abolish the slave trade in 'every quarter
of the globe'.[57] Once he had completed the thirty-two-page pamphlet, which also included plans and sections of the slave ship *Brookes,*
Clarkson arranged for it to be translated into French and German,
with the intention of distributing it among the European leaders about
to convene in Vienna, among them Tsar Alexander, the Emperor of
Austria and the King of Prussia. Copies were also sent to the Italian
deputies at Vienna, as well as Cardinal Consalvi, the Pope's Nuncio
to the Congress.[58] Subsequently, the Duke of Wellington prevailed
upon Clarkson to publish a second French edition of the *Summary,*
this time for circulation in and around Paris. According to Clarkson's
own estimates, over 500 copies were sent to the 'Houses and Peers and
Commons', sixty to French officials, including the Ministers of War
and Finance, and scores to the French journals and members of the
French Academy. In all, over 1,000 copies of the *Summary* were distributed in this way, not to mention those already sent to Vienna, making
it one of the most instantly recognisable and ubiquitous publications in
this second British invasion.[59]

According to Clarkson, Wellington also persuaded him to republish the French edition of his *Essay on the Impolicy of the Slave Trade.*[60]
Here, again, the pamphlet was distributed in and around Paris, 'and

---

[57] Thomas Clarkson, *Résumé du témoignage donné devant un comité de la Chambre des
Communes de la Grand Bretagne et de l'Irlande, touchant la traite des nègres: adresse dans
cette crise particulière aux différentes puissances de la chrétienté* (London: Richard &
D'Artus Taylor, 1814).
[58] Thomas Clarkson to (probably) Zachary Macaulay, 1814, Thomas Clarkson Papers,
CN34, Huntington Library, San Marino, California. Clarkson had originally hoped
to distribute copies of his pamphlet in person but when Castlereagh blocked the idea
of his going to Vienna he was forced to rely on his diplomatic contacts, among them
Sir Robert Wilson and Tsar Alexander's ambassador at Paris. See Thomas Clarkson
to William Wilberforce, 11 August 1814, 13 August 1814 and 15 August 1814,
Wilberforce Papers, c. 45, fols. 37–44, Bodleian Library, Oxford.
[59] Clarkson to (probably) Macaulay, 1814. The second edition of Clarkson's pamphlet
was published in Paris by Adfrien Egron, printer to the Duke of Angoulême. Clarkson
indicates that Egron was also given permission to print 1,000 copies of his *Summary*
for sale in Paris at his own expense. See Clarkson to (probably) Macaulay, 1814.
Another edition of Clarkson's pamphlet appears to have been published in Geneva by
Luc Sestie.
[60] Thomas Clarkson to William Wilberforce, 27 August 1814 and 2 September 1814,
Wilberforce Papers, c. 45, fols. 45–8, Bodleian Library, Oxford; Thomas Clarkson,
*Essai sur les désavantagés politiques de la traite des nègres. Traduit de l'anglais sur la dern-
ière édition qui a paru à Londres en 1789* (Paris: Adfrien Egron, 1814).

put into the same hands, number for number, as the Summary had been before'.[61] Works such as these relied for the most part on old arguments, many of which, like the horrors of the Middle Passage, had been first formulated in the late 1780s. But if British activists trusted to the justness of their cause, based as it was on universal humanitarian values, they were not above appealing to national interests or to national pride. Wilberforce implored Talleyrand to 'Take that lead in this generous and politic enterprise which becomes the character of an enlightened and liberal people. Act in a manner worthy of the antiquity and greatness of your Empire'.[62] 'It was formerly customary', he went on,

for princes to celebrate the birth of a son, or any other acceptable event, by some act of mercy and munificence. So let the era of the restoration of your sovereign to the throne of his ancestors be marked, in the page of history, as the era, also, at which Africa was delivered from her tormentors.[63]

This was the challenge. The question was whether France, or other European powers for that matter, would meet it.

If Talleyrand's response was cool and non-committal, British activists were encouraged by what they saw as a revival of interest in abolition, especially among European intellectuals. By and large, abolitionism in France had been stifled between 1799 and 1814. Napoleon's defeat and abdication, however, gave activists grounds for greater optimism.[64] A key figure here was the French writer Anne-Louise-Germaine Necker, better known as Madame de Staël, whose undisguised hostility to Napoleon had forced her into exile, first in Switzerland and later in Germany. In 1813, she arrived in Britain, ostensibly to publish two works, *De l'Allemagne*, which had been banned by Napoleon, and *Dix années d'exil*. Staël quickly became a sensation, by turn captivating and antagonising her British hosts, among them Lord Holland, Sir James Mackintosh and Elizabeth Barrett Browning.[65] One of those she sought out, interestingly enough, was William Wilberforce. Staël clearly knew about the British campaign to end the slave trade and was keen to meet its chief parliamentary spokesman – more, it was said, 'than any other person'.[66] At first, Wilberforce resisted Staël's pressing invitations,

[61] Clarkson to (probably) Macaulay, 1814.
[62] Wilberforce, *A Letter to His Excellency*, p. 63.
[63] Wilberforce, *A Letter to His Excellency*, p. 64.
[64] Jennings, *French Anti-Slavery*, pp. 4–5.
[65] See Angelica Goodden, *Madame de Staël: The Dangerous Exile* (Oxford University Press, 2008), especially pp. 222–65.
[66] Gooden, *Madame de Staël*, p. 256.

pleading indisposition, but eventually, in March 1814, after days of ago-
nising deliberations, he agreed to dine with her at Bowood House in the
company of Lord Harrowby and Lord and Lady Lansdowne.[67]
    Despite his initial reservations about being drawn into her 'magic
circle', Wilberforce warmed to Staël, finding in her a serious friend to
abolition and one who would prove an important ally. It was Staël, for
instance, who proposed a French translation of Wilberforce's *Letter to
the Freeholders of Yorkshire*, originally published in 1807; indeed, she
even offered to write a stirring preface.[68] But, more than that, Staël gave
British activists access to European intellectuals, among them the Swiss
economist Charles Léonard de Sismondi. Best known for his *History of
the Italian Republics in the Middle Ages* (1807–18), Sismondi became an
increasingly important figure in slave-trade debates, particularly after
1814. That year he published *De l'intérêt de la France à l'égard de la traite de
nègres*, a painstaking analysis that set out to prove that the revival of the
French slave trade (which he adamantly opposed) would cost the nation
somewhere in the region of 288 million francs, or £12 million sterling.
Moreover, Sismondi predicted that it would be two years at least before
any returns could be expected. Put simply, the whole enterprise was too
risky, particularly at a time when France needed to 'husband and cher-
ish the remains of her capital'.[69] Sismondi was equally sceptical about
the merits of retaking Saint-Domingue. To his mind, France could not
re-enter colonial production without setting up restrictive monopolies
that would prove ruinous to its trade with Britain, the USA, South
America, Asia and the whole of the Mediterranean.[70]
    In essence, these were the same arguments put forward by Wilberforce
in his letter to Talleyrand, but the difference was that in this case they
came not from outside but from within European intellectual circles.
Understandably, British activists seized on this opening. Wilberforce,
for instance, arranged for extracts from Sismondi's essay to be published in the French émigré newspaper *L'Ambigu*, edited by Jena-Gabriel
Peltier. There was more than a hint of opportunism in this move. As
Wilberforce explained, Peltier's paper had

---

[67] Goodden, *Madame de Staël*, pp. 254–60. See also Robert I. Wilberforce and Samuel
    Wilberforce, eds., *The Correspondence of William Wilberforce* (London: John Murray,
    1840), vol. II, p.160.
[68] Goodden, *Madame de Staël*, p. 259. Apparently, nothing came of this project, although
    Staël's preface survives. See 'Préface pour la traduction d'un ouvrage de Monsieur
    Wilberforce sur la traite des nègres', in Madame de Staël, *Oeuvres complètes* (Paris:
    Treuttel and Wurtz, 1820–1), vol. XVII, pp. 369–75.
[69] J. C. L. Simonde de Sismondi, *De l'intérêt de la France à l'égard de la traite des nègres*
    (Geneva: J. J. Paschoud, 1814), pp. 24–5.
[70] Sismondi, *De l'intérêt de la France*, pp. 23–35, 40–9.

suffered of late from the return to France of a great number of emigrants who used to take it [and] on this account Peltier will be the more sensible of the value of any support just now, as well as because the line he has taken regarding St. Domingo and the slave trade has alienated many of his former friends.[71]

Be that as it may, Wilberforce's actions reflected the growing importance attached to European (specifically, French) cooperation. Echoing these sentiments, William Allen pointed out in his lengthy review of Sismondi's essay that 'there was now an action and re-action between the intellects of the two countries – an action and re-action which [was] growing stronger and stronger every day'.[72] It was not a matter of indifference to the people of France, he went on,

what are the mental pursuits of the people of England; but completely the reverse. They have the highest curiosity to know them, and ambition to imitate them; and those sentiments are the strongest in the classes who have received the best education, and the state of whose mind is the most highly improved. They know that, during the last twenty years, England has enjoyed advantages of which in the turbulent state of France she has been deprived. They are eager, therefore, to observe the modes of thinking in England and well disposed to take lessons.[73]

What Allen envisaged, in other words, was a reinvigorated internationalism, a community of values that would help to shape a new era. 'A larger proportion of the ideas of each nation will have a powerful influence upon the mode of thinking in the other', he predicted, 'and it will not be easy for a French book to become highly popular in England, without exciting a degree of curiosity in France.'[74]

It was in this same spirit of cooperation that Wilberforce approached the Prussian scientist and explorer Alexander von Humboldt, who had become famous for his expeditions through the Spanish colonies in South America (1799–1804). Liberal in outlook, Humboldt consistently stressed the importance of racial and economic equality, 'emphatically rejecting the assumed existence of superior and inferior people'.[75] He

[71] William Wilberforce to unknown recipient, 12 October 1814, William Wilberforce Papers, Box 3, William R. Perkins Library, Duke University, North Carolina; L'Ambigu, 46 (30 September 1814), pp. 737–53. For Peltier and the French émigré press, see Simon Burrows, 'The Cosmopolitan Press, 1760–1815', in Hannah Barker and Simon Burrows, eds., Press, Politics and the Public Sphere in Europe and North America, 1760–1820 (Cambridge University Press, 2002), pp. 23–47.
[72] William Allen, review, The Philanthropist; or, Repository for Hints and Suggestions Calculated to Promote the Comfort and Happiness of Man, 5 (1815), p. 38.
[73] Allen, review, p. 38.   [74] Allen, review, p. 39.
[75] Sandra Rebok, 'Enlightened Correspondents: The Transatlantic Dialogue of Thomas Jefferson and Alexander von Humboldt', The Virginia Magazine of History and Biography, 116 (4) (2008): 328–69, at p. 334.

made no secret of his opposition to the slave trade (he described the South Carolina law of 1803 as 'abominable'), and, in his *Essai politique sur le royaume de la Nouvelle-Espagne* (1808–11), he set out to prove that free labour was more productive and ultimately more beneficial than slavery.[76] It was these convictions, as well as Humboldt's warm interest in abolition, that brought him to the attention of British activists. No less important, Humboldt was a transatlantic figure whose correspondents included Thomas Jefferson, the architect William Thornton and Jefferson's Secretary of the Treasury, Albert Gallatin. Like Jefferson, Humboldt believed in the importance of large-scale intellectual networks as well as the open exchange of ideas and information.[77] In short, he was ideally placed to help abolitionists and, in doing so, to influence slave-trade debates in Europe.

Certainly this was Wilberforce's view of the matter. What he seems to have had in mind was a 'little committee' made up of Humboldt and others that would 'draw up and circulate intelligence respecting our cause'.[78] On paper, at least, this must have seemed like a good idea. Since the restoration of the Bourbons there had been growing interest in abolition, as evidenced by Sismondi's essay. Staël had also contributed a short pamphlet, as had old friends such as the Abbé Grégoire.[79] Given all of this activity, not to mention the works produced by Wilberforce and Clarkson, it was understandable that British activists should have thought that now was the time to press home their advantage. Yet all was not quite as it seemed. In truth, abolitionist literature went unread and unnoticed. Grenville told Clarkson that only one copy of Sismondi's essay 'had been sold by the bookseller at Paris, tho' many had I believe been given away'.[80] Just as worryingly, prejudice against abolitionists remained as strong as ever. Humboldt frankly admitted to Wilberforce that any attempt to set up an abolitionist committee would only do the cause harm. 'Everyone would protest against this society', he went on.

---

[76] Rebok, 'Enlightened Correspondents', p. 368, n. 79.

[77] Rebok, 'Enlightened Correspondents', p. 363, n. 15. See also Vera M. Kutzinski, 'Alexander von Humboldt's Transatlantic Personnae', *Atlantic Studies*, 7 (2) (2010): 100–12.

[78] William Wilberforce to Alexander von Humboldt, 16 September 1814, Wilberforce Papers, c. 46, fol. 112, Bodleian Library, Oxford. See also Wilberforce and Wilberforce, *The Life of William Wilberforce*, vol. IV, p. 214.

[79] For Staël, see *Appel aux souverains réunis à Paris pour en obtenir l'abolition de la traite des nègres*, in *Oeuvres complètes*, vol. XVII, pp. 376–82; for Grégoire, see *De la traite et de l'esclavage des noirs et des blancs: par un ami des hommes de toutes les couleurs* (Paris: Adfrien Egron, 1815).

[80] William Wyndham Grenville to Thomas Clarkson, 31 December 1814, Thomas Clarkson Papers, CN 105, Huntington Library, San Marino, California.

'Memories of the Amis des Noirs would be reawakened.'[81] The implication was clear: in the minds of many French people abolition was still
associated with Jacobinism and the threat of the mob.

No one understood the depth of these feelings better than the Duke
of Wellington, who had been sent to Paris with instructions to try again
for complete abolition, thereby reversing the terms of the Treaty of
Paris. Progress was slow and halting. Clarkson, who was in Paris at
this time, suspected that the French were holding out for some kind of
compensation, preferably in the form of 'a Colony as an equivalent'.[82]
Where this rumour came from is not entirely clear but the proposal was
certainly considered serious enough to be raised in Parliament. Louis
XVIII, however, was not about to give up the slave trade; to have done
so would have alienated some of his strongest supporters. But he was
willing to agree to restrictions. Finally, in November 1814, following
long and protracted negotiations, Wellington was able to report success
in the shape of a decree prohibiting French trafficking in north-west
Africa as far down as Cape Formoso.[83] This was not the complete victory that British activists had been hoping for. Nevertheless, as Zachary
Macaulay explained to his son, Thomas Babington Macaulay, the
French decree did mean that henceforth 'Senegal, Gorée, Sierra Leone,
the Gold Coast and all the places where we have been carrying on our
improvements [would be] exempted from the calamity which threatened them.'[84]

Attention now turned to the Congress of Vienna (September 1814 to
June 1815). Once again, Lord Castlereagh, the chief British negotiator,
repeated Wellington's demand for immediate abolition or, failing that,
collective agreement 'to shorten the period by which the slave trade
should be carried on by France, Spain and Portugal'.[85] He also proposed setting up permanent international commissions, in London and
Paris, to monitor the slave trade and to report abuses.[86] The delegates,
however, were in no mood to accede to British demands. While they
issued a joint declaration condemning the slave trade as 'the desola-
tion of Africa, the degeneration of Europe, and the afflicted scourge of

[81] Wilberforce and Wilberforce, *The Life of William Wilberforce*, vol. IV, pp. 213–14.
[82] Thomas Clarkson to William Wilberforce, 27 August 1814, 2 September 1814,
3 September 1814 and 5 September 1814, Wilberforce Papers, c. 45, fols. 45–52,
Bodleian Library, Oxford.
[83] Kielstra, *The Politics of Slave Trade Suppression*, pp. 39–50.
[84] Zachary Macaulay to Thomas Babington Macaulay, 17 November 1814, Zachary
Macaulay Papers, MY569, Huntington Library, San Marino, California.
[85] *Ninth Report of the Directors of the African Institution, Read at the Annual General Meeting
on the 12th of April, 1815* (London: J. Hatchard, 1815), p. 18.
[86] *Ninth Report of the Directors of the African Institution*, pp. 18–19.

humanity', they refused to make an example of France or to agree to any abridgement of the Treaty of Paris.[87] No agreement, either, was reached on restricting the international slave trade, despite British attempts to have the equator recognised as the line of demarcation to the north. For these reasons, Vienna turned out to be a grave disappointment to British activists, although, as Paul Kielstra points out, the Congress did at least recognise that abolition was an 'issue of international concern, specifically because it was of humanitarian interest'.[88]

Understandably, post-Vienna, British activists continued to fret about the revival of the French slave trade. But they could hardly have anticipated the course of events that saw Napoleon's return from exile and then, following his defeat at Waterloo, a second Bourbon restoration. Napoleon was hardly well disposed towards abolition. In March 1815, however, he issued a decree declaring the immediate abolition of the French slave trade, presumably in an attempt to placate domestic and international opinion.[89] Whatever the reason, the decree set down an important marker and one that Napoleon's Bourbon successors could hardly ignore. Certainly, British ministers assumed that Louis XVIII would confirm the abolition of the French slave trade, and, privately at least, Talleyrand gave them every indication that he would do so. In the same spirit, in November 1815, France signed an additional article to the Treaty of Paris that effectively committed it (and the other contracting parties) to the 'complete and universal abolition of the slave trade'.[90] British activists concluded that this was the end of the matter. The 1816 AI report adopted a self-congratulatory tone, noting with satisfaction Talleyrand's assertion that British propaganda had helped to undermine French prejudices, thereby allowing Louis to 'follow, without reserve, the dictates of his inclination'.[91] Here, it seemed, was incontrovertible proof that British tactics worked and that, with the help of government ministers, groups such as the AI could effect meaningful political change.

By 1817, however, it was clear that French promises counted for little. While Louis XVIII had signalled his intentions to abolish the slave trade, he had issued no public or authoritative ordinances to that

---

[87] *Ninth Report of the Directors of the African Institution*, p. 2.
[88] *Ninth Report of the Directors of the African Institution*, pp. 17–19; Kielstra, *The Politics of Slave Trade Suppression*, pp. 52–3.
[89] Kielstra, *The Politics of Slave Trade Suppression*, pp. 56–7; *L'Ambigu*, 49 (10 April 1815), p. 76.
[90] *Tenth Report of the Directors of the African Institution, Read at the Annual General Meeting on the 27th of March, 1816* (London: J. Hatchard, 1816), pp. 2–8.
[91] *Tenth Report of the Directors of the African Institution*, pp. 10–11.

effect, save for an ordinance of 1817 prohibiting the importation of slaves into the French colonies. To all intents and purposes, the foreign trade remained unmolested.[92] What made this situation all the more frustrating was the fact that British suppression efforts elsewhere had proved relatively successful. By 1818, both Spain and Portugal had signed agreements abolishing the slave trade north of the equator. Spain, moreover, had committed itself to 'final and universal' abolition by 30 May 1820. Admittedly, doubts still remained over the likely termination of the Portuguese trade, but British activists confidently predicted it would not extend beyond 1823.[93] Viewed in this light, French obduracy seemed all the more culpable. In March 1818, however, the French Chambers finally bent to mounting British pressure and passed an abolition law, which made participation in the trade by Frenchmen anywhere an indictable offence, punishable by confiscation of the vessel and cargo involved.[94] Once again, British activists could breathe more easily. Yet, for all that, they remained wary of French motives, especially as it was unclear how the new legislation would be enforced.

One important feature of the Spanish and Portuguese treaties was that they both provided for the right of mutual search. British activists had increasingly come to the conclusion that this was the only effective way of making suppression work. They were equally keen that the principle should be 'universally recognised'.[95] It was with this in mind that in June 1818 Lord Castlereagh approached Richard Rush, the American ambassador to Britain, with a view to enlisting the aid of the USA.[96] Since 1814, abolition in America had followed an erratic course. Despite the lofty aims of the Treaty of Ghent, US legislators had done little to reform American abuses on the west coast of Africa. However, in his final message to Congress in December 1816, James Madison once again referred to the subject, noting the progress 'made by concurrent efforts of other nations toward a general suppression of so great an evil'.[97] Responding to this message, in 1817 Congress passed

---

[92] *Twelfth Report of the Directors of the African Institution, Read at the Annual General Meeting on the 9th of April, 1818* (London: J. Hatchard, 1818), pp. 8–15; Kielstra, *The Politics of Slave Trade Suppression*, pp. 69–71.

[93] *Twelfth Report of the Directors of the African Institution* (1818), pp. 21–30; Drescher, *Abolition*, pp. 187, 199–202. It is also worth noting that by this date nearly every mainland country in Spanish America, including Chile, Venezuela and Argentina, had prohibited further slave imports. See Drescher, *Abolition*, pp. 186–7.

[94] Kielstra, *The Politics of Slave Trade Suppression*, pp. 76–7.

[95] *Twelfth Report of the Directors of the African Institution*, p. 7.

[96] *Thirteenth Report of the Directors of the African Institution, Read at the Annual General Meeting on the 24th of March, 1819* (London: J. Hatchard, 1819), pp. 11–14.

[97] Du Bois, *The Suppression of the African Slave-Trade*, p. 255.

a joint resolution authorising the President to 'consult and negotiate' with foreign nations on the 'means of effecting an entire and immediate abolition of the traffic in slaves'.[98] The Senate returned to the subject again early in 1818, this time with a view to amending the Abolition Act of 1807. The result was a sweeping new Act that shifted the burden of proof in all prosecutions to the defendant. Henceforth, anyone caught in possession of an African-born slave would have to prove that the person involved had been in the USA at least five years before any prosecution.[99]

As of 1818, therefore, American legislators had gone some way towards stiffening the provisions of the original Abolition Act. Castlereagh's approach to Rush, however, hinted at something altogether more ambitious and potentially threatening. Attractive though the right of mutual search might sound, at least to the British, Americans considered it at odds with their 'circumstances and institutions'.[100] Central to their concerns was the idea of mixed courts, which under the British proposals would have responsibility for handling all prosecutions and disposing of the ships and cargoes involved. Such courts, Rush argued, would be not only impracticable but also unconstitutional, all judicial power in the USA being vested in the Supreme Court.[101] But if this were the case, and Americans were serious about slave-trade suppression, then they would have to come up with a viable alternative. These considerations were all the more important given the fact that American activists were stirring themselves. Between December 1818 and February 1819, the Senate received memorials from citizens in New York, Rhode Island, Connecticut, Massachusetts, New Jersey and Pennsylvania, all calling for some further revision of existing legislation, if only to close the loophole that allowed state legislatures to dispose of anyone brought into the USA in contravention of the Abolition Act.[102]

[98] Du Bois, *The Suppression of the African Slave-Trade*, pp. 255–6. See also *History of Congress*, 14th Congress (1815–17), House, 2nd Session, col. 941.
[99] *United States Statutes at Large*, vol. III, 15th Congress, 1st session (20 April 1818), ch. 90, pp. 450–3.
[100] *Thirteenth Report of the Directors of the African Institution* (1819), p. 42.
[101] *Thirteenth Report of the Directors of the African Institution* (1819), pp. 42–4.
[102] *History of Congress*, 15th Congress (1817–19), Senate, 1st Session, cols. 77 (New York and Philadelphia), 88 (Carlisle, Pennsylvania), 90 (Philadelphia), 97 (Newport, Rhode Island), 113 (Hartford, Connecticut), 162 (New Bedford, Massachusetts), 167 (New Jersey), 176 (Trenton, New Jersey), 189 (Lancaster, Pennsylvania and Chester County, Pennsylvania), 197 (Middletown, Connecticut). American abolitionism seems to have enjoyed a revival around this period. The American Conventions of 1817 and 1818, for instance, received communications from societies in Easton (Maryland), Kent County (Delaware), Columbia (Philadelphia) and Kentucky. See *Minutes of the Proceedings of the Fifteenth American Convention for Promoting the Abolition of Slavery, and Improving*

Memorialists were in no doubt what was at stake here. Presenting their case to the Senate in December 1818, PAS members pointed out that if nothing was done to check American abuses then the USA would not be able 'to keep pace with the recent efforts of some of the principal nations of Europe'.[103] 'While the unhappy African ... will hail with delight the flag of Europe, which restores him to freedom', they went on, 'he will tremble at the approach of the American banner which transfers him from one set of masters to another.'[104] National pride and honour, if nothing else, demanded that Congress should act. This relentless pressure seems to have had its desired effect. In March 1819, Congress passed another supplementary Act that authorised the President to send armed cruisers to the west coast of Africa to interdict slave traders. The Act also provided that all captives should be returned to Africa, rather than sold in the USA.[105] In effect, the 1819 Act provided an answer to two related questions: on the one hand, how to close the remaining loopholes in the original Abolition Act; on the other, how to respond to British demands over the right of mutual search. Congress explicitly stated that the USA would rise to these different challenges but would do so in its own way and in its own time.[106]

If nothing else, American suppression debates exposed the limits of international cooperation, at least in so far as the right of mutual search was concerned. British activists (and their ministerial allies) ran into similar difficulties at the Congress of Aix-la-Chapelle in 1818. With good reason, the Congress was seen as an opportunity (perhaps the last opportunity) to gain broad European agreement on abolition. Activists prepared themselves accordingly, writing and circulating tracts and working closely with government ministers to present what they hoped would be a coherent case for suppression.[107] Clarkson was again at the centre of these different activities. He even made the long journey to

the Condition of the African Race, Assembled at Philadelphia, on the Fifth Day of August 1817, and Continued, by Adjournments, Until the Eighth of the Same Month, Inclusive (Philadelphia, Pa.: Merritt, Printer, 1817), p. 22; Minutes of the Proceedings of a Special Meeting of the Fifteenth American Convention for Promoting the Abolition of Slavery, and Improving the Condition of the African Race, Assembled at Philadelphia, on the Tenth Day of December 1818, and Continued, by Adjournments, Until the Fifteenth of the Same Month, Inclusive (Philadelphia, Pa.: Hall & Atkinson, 1818), pp. 20, 41.

[103] PAS Minutes, 3 December 1818.
[104] PAS Minutes, 3 December 1818.
[105] United States Statutes at Large, vol. III, 15th Congress, 2nd session (3 March 1819), ch. 101, pp. 532–4.
[106] In 1820, Congress passed a further Act, this time declaring participation in the African slave trade piracy and therefore punishable by death. See United States Statutes at Large, vol. III, 16th Congress, 1st session (15 May 1820), ch. 113, pp. 600–1; Du Bois, The Suppression of the African Slave-Trade, pp. 123–5, 261–2.
[107] Kielstra, The Politics of Slave Trade Suppression, pp. 86–9.

Aix-la-Chapelle with the specific aim of talking to Tsar Alexander of Russia (long considered a friend of abolition) and pushing the case for sweeping reform.[108] What Clarkson and his colleagues now had in mind was a multilateral right-of-search convention. Privately, they also hoped the Allied Powers might be persuaded to declare the slave trade piracy, a move intended to deter would-be traffickers once and for all. For their part, Castlereagh and Wellington seemed only too keen to accommodate these various demands, receiving Clarkson with 'great civility and politeness'.[109] Certainly, there was no doubt about the resolve of British ministers, or their determination to promote abolition.[110]

The Congress, however, proved another grave disappointment. Tellingly, debate stalled over the right of mutual search. France strongly opposed the measure, as did Prussia. Tsar Alexander, while sympathetic, put forward a rival scheme involving the creation of an independent agency based in Africa.[111] Activists could barely contain their frustration. Why, they wanted to know, should Russia, Austria and Prussia 'unnecessarily postpone taking some measure for the suppression of the slave trade for an indefinite period, and until Portugal shall have universally abolished [it]', when 'there are now more than two thirds of the Coast of Africa, which might be as beneficially operated upon as if that much wished for era had already arrived'?[112] As for France's objections that the right of mutual search would delay French ships frequenting the coast of Africa and give rise to disputes between France and other foreign powers, they were frankly incredulous.[113] Yet the truth of the matter was that, like the Americans, European leaders were not prepared to agree to international conventions of this kind, at least not while they could try to suppress the slave trade themselves, by either setting up slave registries (as France proposed to do in 1818) or sending naval patrols to the west coast of Africa. So far from producing a breakthrough, Aix-la-Chapelle seemed only to have resulted in a dead end.

Nevertheless, there were still grounds for optimism. The Americans had redoubled their efforts to suppress the slave trade.[114] Progress had

[108] Wilson, *Thomas Clarkson*, pp. 147–9; Thomas Clarkson, *Interviews with the Emperor Alexander I of Russia at Paris and Aix-la-Chapelle in 1815 and 1818* (London: Slavery and Native Races Committee of the Society of Friends, 1930); Thomas Clarkson to William Wilberforce, 18 October 1818, Wilberforce Papers, c. 45, fols. 71–2, Bodleian Library, Oxford.
[109] Kielstra, *The Politics of Slave Trade Suppression*, p. 89.
[110] Kielstra, *The Politics of Slave Trade Suppression*, pp. 88–9.
[111] *Thirteenth Report of the Directors of the African Institution* (1819), pp. 18–22.
[112] *Thirteenth Report of the Directors of the African Institution* (1819), pp. 32–3.
[113] *Thirteenth Report of the Directors of the African Institution* (1819), p. 35.
[114] Drescher notes that by the 1820s American penalties against slave trading were 'among the harshest in the world'. See Drescher, *Abolition*, p. 138.

also been made with Spain and Portugal. The real problem was France. Despite the 1818 law prohibiting the trade, French trafficking continued unabated. The AI report of 1821, which was almost entirely given over to this subject, noted despondently that 'the slave trade is carried on under the French flag, not only from Senegal and Gorée, but along the whole extent of the African coast'.[115] In July 1820 alone, five vessels had been reported at Gallinas bearing the French flag, and a further three had been intercepted by the British, either in the Caribbean (Antigua) or on the west coast of Africa.[116] Attempts to check these abuses were met by promises and denials. Repeatedly, the Minister of the Marine, the marquis de Clermont-Tonnerre, assured the British that further action, including the possibility of supplementary legislation, would be taken to suppress French trafficking, and yet still the French Chambers prevaricated.[117] British activists, however, refused to give up hope. The king and the nation, they assured their supporters, 'sincerely desire [abolition]'.[118] It was not so much the French people who stood in the way of reform but 'subaltern agents' whose conduct 'had been manifestly, either corrupt, or, at the very least, criminally negligent'.[119]

Faced with the scale of these abuses, British activists turned to the tried-and-tested method of attempting to reform French society from within. Since 1814, Wilberforce and his colleagues had been endeavouring to create a network of European activists, and, to a large extent, they had succeeded. Staël, Sismondi and Humboldt had all at different times lent their names to the cause, even if they had stopped short at formal organisation. Grégoire had also re-entered the fray, providing an important, if sometimes controversial, link with the activism of the late eighteenth century. Over the decade these associations grew closer while, at the same time, new ones took root. Zachary Macaulay, for instance, was friendly with both Staël's son, Baron Auguste de Staël, and her daughter, Albertine, who was married to the 3rd duc de Broglie.[120] He also remained

[115] *Fifteenth Report of the Directors of the African Institution, Read at the Annual General Meeting on the 28th of March, 1821* (London: J. Hatchard & Son, 1821), p. 21.
[116] *Fifteenth Report of the Directors of the African Institution* (1821), pp. 4–22.
[117] *Fifteenth Report of the Directors of the African Institution* (1821), pp. 22–5; Kielstra, *The Politics of Slave Trade Suppression*, pp. 103–7. If anything, Kielstra notes a stiffening of French resolve between 1818 and 1822. François-René Chateaubriand, the newly appointed French ambassador to London, privately admitted that 'a French ministry will never become unpopular, for having been attacked in the British Parliament, on a subject which touches ... the interests of our commerce'. Quoted in Kielstra, *The Politics of Slave Trade Suppression*, p. 106.
[118] *Fifteenth Report of the Directors of the African Institution* (1821), p. 24.
[119] *Fifteenth Report of the Directors of the African Institution* (1821), p. 24.
[120] Margaret Jean Holland, Viscountess Knutsford, *Life and Letters of Zachary Macaulay* (London: E. Arnold, 1900), pp. 356–8; Whyte, *Zachary Macaulay*, pp. 154–9.

in close contact with Grégoire, who, following Madame de Staël's death in 1817, 'served as the chief intermediary between the London and Paris abolitionists'.[121] Macaulay almost certainly channelled financial assistance to French activists through Grégoire and, in return, looked to him to 'publish anti-slave trade pamphlets and issue petitions'.[122] Meanwhile, Macaulay's brother, General Colin Macaulay, provided an important link between Paris and London, not least because he enjoyed the ear of the Duke of Wellington. Others, too, gravitated towards these circles, among them Joseph Morénas and the Abbé Giudicelli.[123]

Through these channels, activists continued to distribute a wide range of abolitionist propaganda: AI reports, newspapers, books and pamphlets. French abolitionists also played their part, editing British texts (in effect, repackaging them for French audiences) and sometimes adding stirring and highly complimentary prefaces.[124] By common consent, this activity intensified after 1819, partly in response to French initiatives, among them Morénas's two petitions (1820 and 1821) to the French Chambers protesting against slave trafficking in Senegal. Morénas's revelations sparked a fresh pamphlet campaign (Grégoire and Giudicelli both produced pamphlets during this period), details of which filtered back to Britain, fuelling a loud chorus of disapproval against continued French abuses.[125] Anglo-French cooperation was also strengthened by face-to-face contacts. Clarkson, for instance, visited Paris in 1819 and again in 1820. Macaulay was also a regular visitor, using these opportunities to renew his acquaintance with leading French activists while at the same time offering them his support and encouragement. As William Allen had predicted in 1814, the return of peace in Europe resulted in much greater fraternisation between French and British abolitionists as well as a greater sense of common purpose.[126]

A further development occurred in December 1821 when a group of French activists, led by the duc François Alexandre Frédéric de La Rouchefoucauld-Liancourt, the comte Alexandre de Laborde, the baron

---

[121] Jennings, *French Anti-Slavery*, pp. 7–8.
[122] Jennings, *French Anti-Slavery*, p. 8.
[123] Kielstra, *The Politics of Slave Trade Suppression*, p. 35.
[124] Kielstra, *The Politics of Slave Trade Suppression*, pp. 95–6.
[125] Kielstra, *The Politics of Slave Trade Suppression*, pp. 96–8; Grégoire, *Des peines infamantes à infliger aux négriers* (Paris: Baudion Frères, 1822); Abbé Juge Giudicelli, *Observations sur la traite des noirs, en réponse au rapport de M. Courvoisier sur la pétition de M. Morénas* (Paris: Les Marchands de Nouveautés, 1820). Morénas's two petitions were also published in 1820 and 1821.
[126] Wilson, *Thomas Clarkson*, p. 150; Kielstra, *The Politics of Slave Trade Suppression*, pp. 96, 98–9; Whyte, *Zachary Macaulay*, pp. 154–9.

Joseph Marie Degerando and the comte Charles Philibert de Lasteyrie du Saillant – all of them liberal Catholics – organised the Société de la Morale Chrétienne.[127] As its name suggests, the new society had broad philanthropic aims, but chief among its nine committees (there were others on prison reform and the suppression of the death penalty) was the slave-trade committee, organised in 1822 and presided over by Baron Auguste de Staël. Like the Société des Amis des Noirs before it, the committee maintained close links with British activists and shared many of the same priorities – certainly when it came to the relative merits of 'abolition' and 'emancipation'. For the moment, at least, its members stopped short of attacking slavery head-on, simply because it was 'considered too essential for the survival of the colonies'.[128] Instead, they looked to attack the slave trade, confident that in this way they could force colonial planters to reform the system from within.

The appearance of this new society gave the French campaign renewed impetus. In 1822, for instance, George Schulze published a French translation of Wilberforce's speech on the slave trade in the House of Commons (27 June 1822), together with his *Lettre à l'Empereur Alexandre sur la traite des noirs*.[129] That same year, a French translation of Clarkson's *The Cries of Africa to the Inhabitants of Europe*, a reworking of his earlier *Summary*, was published simultaneously in London and in Paris.[130] Not to be outdone, the slave-trade committee of the Société de la Morale Chrétienne sponsored its own publication programme, working closely with Henri Servier, described in 1829 as the leading Protestant bookseller in Paris.[131] It was Servier, for instance, who published extracts from one of the duc de Broglie's addresses before the Chamber of Peers, *Cruautés de la traite des noirs* (1822), which, significantly, appeared with an ornate title page depicting the figure of a kneeling slave, together with the motto 'Ne suis-je pas un homme [et]

[127] Strictly speaking, the society was interdenominational. As Jennings points out, many of the members (perhaps 33 per cent) were Protestants. See Jennings, *French Anti-Slavery*, pp. 9–11.
[128] Jennings, *French Anti-Slavery*, p. 13.
[129] (William Wilberforce), *Résumé du discours prononcé par M. Wilberforce dans la Chambre des Communes, le 27 juin 1822, sur l'état actuel de la traite des nègres* (London: G. Schulze, 1822); (William Wilberforce), *Lettre à l'Empereur Alexandre sur la traite des noirs* (London: G. Schulze, 1822).
[130] (Thomas Clarkson), *Le cri des africains contre les européens, leurs oppresseurs, ou coup d'oeil sur le commerce homicide appèlé traite de noirs* (Paris: De L. T. Cellot, 1822). Another French edition published by 'les Marchands de Nouveautés (Paris)', again in 1822, contains a preface by Grégoire. The London edition was published by Harvey and Darton and W. Phillips.
[131] *Gentleman's Magazine*, 99 (1829), p. 257.

un frère?' More revealing still, the same pamphlet also contained advertisements for Wilberforce's *Lettre à l'Empereur Alexandre* and Clarkson's *Le cri des africains*, further evidence of the strength of international abolitionist networks during this period.[132]

It is easy to be sceptical about the impact of these initiatives. In practical terms, French abuses continued, as did British efforts to bring them to an end.[133] But this is to miss the point. Together, British and French activists succeeded in creating an abolitionist culture in France, evident in the increasing number of poems, plays and novels that dealt directly or indirectly with slavery and the slave trade. The emergence of women writers tackling these themes, among them Claire de Duras and Sophie Doin, is particularly striking, hinting at a much broader engagement with slavery not just as a colonial issue but also as a domestic issue that blighted the lives of innocent women and children.[134] On this evidence, at least, abolition was slowly seeping into the manners and mores of French society, in the process helping to mould popular attitudes. Some have attributed this quiet revolution to Madame de Staël, who returned to France in 1815.[135] A more likely explanation, however, is the continued efforts of British and French activists to educate the French public about slavery, a project that occupied them throughout the 1820s and beyond.[136]

---

[132] Achille-Léonce-Victor-Charles, 3rd duc de Broglie, *Cruautés de la traite des noirs; ou relation des horreurs commises sur les nègres à bord des vaisseaux le Rôdeur et l'Estelle extraite du discours de M. le Duc de Broglie, prononcé à la Chambre des Pairs le 28 mars 1822* (Paris: Henri Servier, 1822).

[133] Kielstra, *The Politics of Slave Trade Suppression*, pp. 108–37.

[134] Kadish, 'The Black Terror', pp. 668–80; Claire de Duras, *Ourika* (Paris: Chez Ladvocat, 1823); Sophie Doin, *La famille noir* (Paris: Henri Servier, 1825).

[135] Edith Lucas, *La littérature antiesclavagiste au dix-neuvième siècle* (Paris: Boccard, 1930), p. 15.

[136] There were other manifestations of this nascent culture of abolition. Around 1817, for instance, Frédéric Feldtrappe produced a roller-printed design for a Rouen cotton printer based on Morland's two prints, *Execrable Human Traffic* and *African Hospitality*. Evidence suggests that roller-printed cottons of this kind were mass-produced, usually in a variety of colours, and intended as furnishings or, occasionally, decorations. Whitworth Art Gallery in Manchester has in its collections a quilt made up of three lengths of 'Le Traite des Nègres', interlined with cotton wadding and quilted all over in running stitches, the whole measuring 1,808 millimetres by 1,180 millimetres. Judging by the pinholes in the border, at some stage this item was probably used as a wall hanging, perhaps in a bedroom or even a parlour. See Whitworth Art Gallery, T.2003.54. Other examples can be found at the Metropolitan Museum in New York and the International Slavery Museum in Liverpool. Probably produced for the export market, we cannot rule out the possibility that 'Le Traite des Nègres' was also intended to mobilise French public opinion against the slave trade.

As we have seen, Wilberforce and his colleagues invested a huge amount of time and effort in these activities. They did so because they believed that ultimately public opinion would prove the decisive factor in bringing the international slave trade to an end. The British example, after all, testified to the efficacy (indeed, the necessity) of building a constituency for anti-slavery. At different times, Wilberforce and Clarkson both came back to this point, stressing that victory in 1807 would not have been possible if public opinion had not been behind the measure.[137] Rightly or wrongly, Wilberforce assumed that Britain's example – and British methods – could be exported. In this sense, groups such as the AI never entirely lost their faith in a set of values that transcended narrow national boundaries. Important as suppression politics were – and British activists worked hard to secure international agreement on the abolition of the slave trade – the real challenge was to make people believe in abolition. Diplomatic activity and opinion-building, therefore, were two sides of the same coin, an emphasis that gave the internationalism of the early nineteenth century its own distinctive and surprisingly modern quality.

Nevertheless, initiatives of this kind were costly and time-consuming. It was also easy to lose sight of their ultimate purpose. Suppression had never been an end in itself but a means to put pressure on colonial planters to 'ameliorate' slavery and, in doing so, to prepare the ground for some kind of scheme of voluntary emancipation. As late as 1845, Lord Palmerston, Britain's Foreign Secretary, told the House of Commons that the slave trade was 'the root which gives life, and spirit, and stability to the condition of slavery'.[138] 'Seek to upheave a vast living tree, whose mighty roots are strong, vigorously, and deeply embedded in the soil', he went on, '[and] it will baffle the utmost exertions of your strength; but lay the axe to the root, cut off the supply of nourishment, and the tree will sicken and die, and you will no longer find difficulty in bringing it to the ground.'[139] At least, that was the theory. The problem was that, while many planters in the British Caribbean supported amelioration, if by that was meant efforts to improve the economic efficiency of plantation slavery, most of them strenuously opposed anything they thought would threaten either their property

[137] Wilberforce, *A Letter to His Excellency*, pp. 2–3; Zachary Macaulay Papers, MY155 (copy of memorandum written by Clarkson, September 1814).
[138] *Parliamentary Debates*, 3rd series, vol. LXXXII, col. 143 (8 July 1845).
[139] *Parliamentary Debates*, 3rd series, vol. LXXXII, col. 143 (8 July 1845).

or basic white principles of authority and subordination.[140] No one, it seems, wished to abandon suppression. But by the early 1820s it was apparent to many activists that this indirect approach (attacking slavery through the slave trade) was not really working. Something more was needed. The question was what.

---

[140] Davis, *Inhuman Bondage*, pp. 214–21; William A. Green, *British Slave Emancipation: The Sugar Colonies and the Great Experiment, 1830–1865* (Oxford University Press, 1991), pp. 104–10. See also J. R. Ward, *British West Indian Slavery, 1750–1834: The Process of Amelioration* (Oxford University Press, 1988).

8   Colonisation debates

Another issue that preoccupied activists after 1807 was black colonisation. As we shall see, colonisation – both as an idea and as a process –
aroused considerable controversy. Yet, between 1810 and 1820, it gained
increasing momentum, in the process re-energising debates about the
viability of free-labour experiments and their potential to undermine
slavery and the slave trade. What was noteworthy about these international debates, moreover, was the lead taken by blacks – figures such
as Paul Cuffe, whose plans to carry Christianity, legitimate trade and
'civilised' ways to Africa galvanised abolitionist activity on both sides
of the Atlantic. Similarly, Haitian emigration, which emerged with
renewed force after 1819, forged important links between black and
white activists, among them Prince Saunders, an African-American
traveller who moved easily in white abolitionist circles. The result was
a web of associations that spanned the Atlantic world, from Britain to
Africa, from Africa to America and from America to the Caribbean.
This chapter delineates the contours of these expanding abolitionist
networks while at the same time charting the origins and fates of the
various colonisation schemes that emerged in the early years of the
nineteenth century.

The idea of resettling blacks had been debated by American slaveholders since the 1780s and would resurface at regular intervals until
the 1820s and beyond. In the immediate aftermath of the Gabriel slave
rebellion in Virginia in 1801, figures such as George Tucker began
openly to advocate black colonisation, either to the interior of the country or to West Africa or the Caribbean.[1] The Virginia Assembly also
took up the issue, recommending that free blacks and those likely to
be emancipated in the future should be relocated 'as soon as possible'.[2]
Simultaneously, President Thomas Jefferson pursued another option,
that of sending troublesome blacks to the British colony of Sierra Leone

---

[1] For the Gabriel slave rebellion, see Chapter 4.
[2] Whitman, *Challenging Slavery in the Chesapeake*, p. 91.

on the west coast of Africa. When that project failed (British authorities were understandably wary of admitting more 'rebels' to Sierra Leone), the Virginia legislature returned to the idea of colonising blacks in the American West, beyond the limits of white settlement, pressing Jefferson with more resolutions in 1804 and 1805, by which time the USA had acquired the Louisiana territory. But, again, nothing came of the idea, largely because Jefferson feared the possible dangers of establishing a black colony within America's territorial limits. As a result, white interest in colonisation slowly faded away, although, as we shall see, it re-emerged with even greater force in the years immediately following the War of 1812.[3]

Coincidentally, some African Americans also showed an interest in leaving America, even if they baulked at the idea of being compelled to do so.[4] In January 1787, for instance, a group of black Bostonians petitioned the General Court, asking for assistance in resettling in Africa. There were similar initiatives in Newport, Rhode Island, where the African Union Society, organised in 1780, actively pursued the idea of planting its own settlement in Africa. By and large, these efforts were uncoordinated, but, during the early 1790s, blacks in Boston, Newport and Providence joined forces to promote an expedition to Sierra Leone, led by James Mackenzie, who later entered into a contract (never taken up) to receive twelve families into the British settlement.[5] Behind these different initiatives was a growing sense of alienation, particularly among those blacks who had been born in Africa.[6] But if Africa held out the prospect of escaping American oppression, it also offered an opportunity to give something back. As Floyd Miller notes, many of these early black emigration schemes were often as much about Africa (and the regeneration of Africa) as they were about African Americans themselves.[7] Alternatively, the idea of establishing a black nationality in Africa was promoted as a means of abolishing slavery and the slave trade, a view endorsed by a number of early white abolitionists, among

---

[3] Whitman, *Challenging Slavery in the Chesapeake*, pp. 89–92.
[4] As we shall see, blacks drew an important distinction between 'colonisation', which they associated with forcible removal from the USA, and 'emigration', which they embraced as a voluntary movement, depending on choice and circumstances.
[5] Floyd J. Miller, *The Search for a Black Nationality: Black Colonization and Emigration, 1787–1863* (Urbana, Ill.: University of Illinois Press, 1975), pp. 3–20; Winch, *Philadelphia's Black Elite*, pp. 27–9; Horton and Horton, *In Hope of Liberty*, pp. 178–81.
[6] Interestingly, Winch notes that in Philadelphia, where very few 'Africans' were members of the black elite, there was much less interest in emigration. See Winch, *Philadelphia's Black Elite*, pp. 28–9.
[7] Miller, *The Search for a Black Nationality*, pp. 4–7, 12–13.

them Samuel Hopkins, the influential minister of Newport's First Congregational Church.[8]

By 1800, black interest in emigration was 'moribund'.[9] A decade later, however, the situation was very different, thanks largely to the efforts of Paul Cuffe. Born in 1759, Cuffe came from a free black family that owned land in southern Massachusetts. While his brother John took care of the family farm, Cuffe went to sea, first on a whaling voyage to the Gulf of Mexico and then to the West Indies. Some time later he built his own open boat and began plying the coastal trade, from Massachusetts to Cape Cod, Newfoundland, Philadelphia and Maryland. By 1806, he had part shares in two vessels, the *Traveller* and the *Alpha*, a 268-ton ship that he sailed from America to Sweden. Cuffe clearly was a man of means, yet, as Miller points out, he 'could never forget his heritage or his black brethren'.[10] He seems to have bitterly resented the way he and other free blacks were treated, not least by local courts, and to have harboured ambitions to raise black consciousness by aiding in the civilisation of Africa. In a further stage in his steady advancement, in 1808 Cuffe joined the Westport Monthly Meeting of the Society of Friends, thereby establishing close relationships with figures such as James Pemberton, whom he had met in Philadelphia. Cuffe, in other words, was not only a man of property, he was also resourceful, ambitious and, perhaps most important of all, well connected.[11]

As his business expanded, Cuffe's thoughts turned more and more towards Africa. Clearly, what excited him was the possibility that American blacks might help to regenerate the continent, offering, as it were, an example for others to follow. Cuffe, it should be stressed, was not in favour of mass emigration. Rather, what he favoured was the transportation of small groups of settlers, invariably people with property and of good moral character, who would 'serve as midwives of a new order'.[12] But an equally important part of Cuffe's vision, and one that undoubtedly attracted interest among Northern blacks, was the prospect of setting up legitimate trade with Africa. What he appears to have had in mind was a 'Pan-African triangular trade' between

---

[8] Miller, *The Search for a Black Nationality*, pp. 6–7.
[9] Miller, *The Search for a Black Nationality*, p. 21.
[10] Miller, *The Search for a Black Nationality*, p. 24.
[11] Most of these biographical details are taken from Miller, *The Search for a Black Nationality*, pp. 22–5. See also Lamont D. Thomas, *Rise to a People: A Biography of Paul Cuffe* (Urbana, Ill.: University of Illinois Press, 1986); Rosalind Cobb Wiggins, *Captain Paul Cuffe's Logs and Letters, 1808–1817: A Black Quaker's 'Voice from Within the Veil'* (Washington, DC: Howard University Press, 1996); (Anon.), *Life of William Allen*, vol. I, pp. 99–100.
[12] Miller, *The Search for a Black Nationality*, p. 25.

the USA, Britain and Sierra Leone that 'would lead to economic and social improvement in Africa and perhaps stimulate new international involvement in this just cause'.[13] To this extent, Cuffe's plans differed from those of many white and black evangelicals. As Lamont Thomas puts it, 'his Quaker-influenced civilizing mission remained one of promoting a way of life, not a religion'.[14] And, of course, with his own ships, Cuffe was in a unique position to encourage such a transformation. Nevertheless, as he came to realise, to move his plans forward he needed the cooperation of others, particularly those on both sides of the Atlantic who had access to Government and to government officials.

By 1808, Cuffe was resolved, as a first step, to make a voyage to Sierra Leone, which had only recently been taken over by the British Crown. One of those who encouraged him in this endeavour was James Pemberton, then in his eighties but still, it seems, as committed as ever to the abolitionist cause.[15] Keen to offer Cuffe any help he could, Pemberton brought Cuffe's plans to the attention of his old friend William Dillwyn, who, in turn, discussed them with Zachary Macaulay, secretary to the newly established AI, which cast 'a benevolent eye' over the black colony at Sierra Leone.[16] Macaulay's response was favourable, although he seems to have been under the mistaken impression that Cuffe proposed to 'migrate' to Sierra Leone. The best plan, he suggested, 'would be to run across a small vessel of from 70 to 90 or 100 tons burthen and satisfy himself on the spot with respect to all those local advantages and disadvantages which ought to enter into the decision of such a question'.[17] Macaulay even proposed a suitable cargo, principally flour, pitch, Virginia tobacco, 'pine boards and planks and scantling from 4 to 10 inches square', all of which he thought would find a ready market at Sierra Leone 'or in its neighbourhood'.[18] Equally important, Macaulay was willing to provide Cuffe with letters of introduction to the Governor of Sierra Leone, representing him as 'a person of great worth and who has objects in view which may prove of great eventual benefit to Africa'.[19]

[13] Thomas, *Rise to a People*, pp. 59, 109.
[14] Thomas, *Rise to a People*, p. 109.
[15] Pemberton did not live to see what became of Cuffe's plans for Sierra Leone. He died the following February at the age of eighty-five.
[16] James Pemberton to Paul Cuffe, 8 June 1808 and 27 September 1808, in Wiggins, *Captain Paul Cuffe's Logs and Letters*, pp. 77–80.
[17] Zachary Macaulay to William Dillwyn, 29 August 1809, in Wiggins, *Captain Paul Cuffe's Logs and Letters*, p. 84.
[18] Macaulay to Dillwyn, 29 August 1809, in Wiggins, *Captain Paul Cuffe's Logs and Letters*, p. 84.
[19] Macaulay to Dillwyn, 29 August 1809, Wiggins, *Captain Paul Cuffe's Logs and Letters*, p. 85.

For the moment, the main obstacle in Cuffe's way was the Non-Intercourse Act of 1809, which effectively banned American ships from trading with Britain or its colonies. When the Act expired in the summer of 1810, however, he began to plan a trip to Sierra Leone, eventually arriving in Freetown in March 1811.[20] During his short stay, Cuffe set about assessing the social, religious and commercial prospects of the colony, meeting with black settlers as well as native chieftains. He also took steps to try to stimulate the commercial development of Sierra Leone. Before he left he organised a group of settlers into 'The Friendly Society of Sierra Leone', the idea being that the society would buy up local produce for export and, in so doing, help to create a commercial network that integrated Africa into the wider Atlantic world.[21] Cuffe's original plan had been to return to the USA. But while he was in Sierra Leone he received word that he had been granted a special trading licence to continue his voyage to Britain, an idea that had first been floated by some of his American backers. Eager to make the most of this opportunity, Cuffe and his all-black crew – a rare and unexpected sight in British waters – finally arrived in Liverpool on 12 July, only to be greeted by a press-gang that seized one of his crew, Aaron Richards, under the mistaken impression that he was a British citizen.[22]

The Richards affair proved an unwelcome distraction (with the help of British activists, Cuffe eventually secured his release), but, ironically, it brought Cuffe into close contact with British abolitionists, among them Zachary Macaulay, Thomas Clarkson and William Allen.[23] Cuffe evidently made a strong impression. A tall and imposing figure, he spoke enthusiastically about the prospects of Sierra Leone, in terms of both trade and civilisation. Appearing before the Directors of the AI on 27 August, Cuffe predicted that American blacks would settle in the colony, 'if the channels could be kept open' and urged the necessity of special trading privileges from the USA to Sierra Leone and Britain.[24] 'On the whole it was a most gratifying meeting', Allen noted in his diary, 'and fully answered, and even exceeded all we could have hoped.'[25] The

---

[20] Miller, *The Search for a Black Nationality*, pp. 26–7.
[21] Winch, *Philadelphia's Black Elite*, p. 31.
[22] Miller, *The Search for a Black Nationality*, pp. 29–40; John James and Alexander Wilson to William Dillwyn, 21 June 1809, in Wiggins, *Captain Paul Cuffe's Logs and Letters*, pp. 81–2; (Anon.), *Life of William Allen*, vol. I, pp. 101–3.
[23] For Cuffe's time in England, see Wiggins, *Captain Paul Cuffe's Logs and Letters*, pp. 132–53; (Anon.), *Life of William Allen*, vol. I, pp. 102–5.
[24] Thomas, *Rise to a People*, p. 61. See also (Anon.), *Life of William Allen*, vol. I, p. 104; *Sixth Report of the Directors of the African Institution* (1812), pp. 26–8.
[25] (Anon.), *Life of William Allen*, vol. I, p. 104. See also *Sixth Report of the Directors of the African Institution* (1812), pp. 26–8.

Directors immediately set up a committee to review Cuffe's proposals. In the meantime, Allen and others worked tirelessly to secure him another trading licence, this time to allow him to return to Sierra Leone and 'to be protected from British cruisers in his passage from thence to America'.[26] The sense of excitement was palpable. Allen believed that 'if proper use' were made of Cuffe's 'disposition and abilities', then 'more [would] be done towards the civilisation of Africa in one year, than in all the time which [had] elapsed since the first attempts were made'; Cuffe seemed 'made on purpose for the business'.[27]

By the time he left Britain in September 1811, Cuffe had 'reached the most instrumental policy-making segment of British society – [those] sympathetic to Sierra Leone and the abolition movement, elected and appointed government officials, and the leading philanthropists for the African cause'.[28] Of particular significance was his growing relationship with William Allen. The two men seem to have hit it off immediately. To judge from his diaries and letters, Allen was clearly excited by Cuffe's descriptions of Sierra Leone, the fertility of the soil and the potential for growing a range of cash crops, including sugar cane, coffee, indigo and rice. Equally, he came to see that the black settlers wanted 'only a stimulus to their industry, that they were looking to us for it, and that we can afford it without the slightest inconvenience to ourselves'.[29] Allen, as a result, was to emerge as one of the chief advocates for 'Africans under British rule', not only underwriting the activities of groups such as the Friendly Society of Sierra Leone but also offering to be their agent. But if Cuffe opened Allen's eyes to the economic potential of Sierra Leone, he also opened his eyes to the abuses suffered by black settlers, not least at the hands of government officials. Again, it is symptomatic of these concerns that in 1812 Allen reminded members of the Friendly Society of Sierra Leone to report their economic grievances directly to him rather than to take matters into their own hands.[30]

Cuffe eventually reached Sierra Leone on 12 November, immediately making contact with many of the settlers he had met on his previous visit to the colony. Eager to push his plans forward, he 'examined conditions for cotton production and surveyed for a sawmill, gristmill and a rice-processing factory'.[31] Early in December he also called a

---

[26] (Anon.), *Life of William Allen*, vol. I, p. 103.
[27] *The Philanthropist*, 2 (6) (1812), p. 200.
[28] Thomas, *Rise to a People*, p. 64.
[29] (Anon.), *Life of William Allen*, vol. I, p. 107. See also Drescher, *The Mighty Experiment*, p. 95.
[30] Thomas, *Rise to a People*, p. 81.
[31] Thomas, *Rise to a People*, p. 70.

meeting of the Friendly Society of Sierra Leone, breathing new life
into an organisation that had been largely inactive during his absence.
Allen's offer of assistance was critical to these discussions, presenting
black settlers with what amounted to a 'new beginning'. True to his
word, the following year Allen sent a consignment of goods, amount-
ing to £70, to the Friendly Society of Sierra Leone, with permission
for them to 'return the amount' in rice, cotton, tobacco, Indian corn
or any other crops that the settlers could produce. He also engaged the
services of merchants W. and R. Rathbone of Liverpool to act on their
behalf.[32] In other words, what Allen and Cuffe were trying to do was
to create the means whereby black settlers could market their goods on
favourable terms, thus breaking the monopoly enjoyed by local British
agents. (It is also reasonable to suppose that most of these crops would
have been transported in Cuffe's own ships or, failing that, in ships
owned by British and American investors friendly to Africa's economic
interests.)

Cuffe's biggest challenge, however, was to extend this commercial
nexus to black communities in the USA, which, of course, had been part
of his original vision. Things could not have got off to a worse start. On
his return to America in 1812, customs officials at Westport seized his
ship, the *Traveller*, and Cuffe himself was charged with trading illegally
with the British, an accusation he vigorously denied.[33] The case dragged
on for weeks and was only finally resolved in May 1813, after Cuffe
had made personal representations to Secretary of the Treasury Albert
Gallatin. On his way back from Washington, DC, however, he was able
to stop off in Baltimore, Philadelphia and New York to discuss his plans
with black leaders. The response was enthusiastic. In Philadelphia,
Cuffe spoke to a meeting of the 'African Association', helping to organise what would become the Philadelphia African Institution, 'for the
purpose of aiding, assisting and communicating with the Sierra Leone
Friendly Society, as well as with the African Institution in London for
Africa's good'.[34] Similarly, in New York a society was formed to unite
'with that of Philadelphia, Baltimore, etc. for the future promotion of
Africa ... of which Sierra Leone at present seems to be the principal
established colony'.[35] The hectic activity of these summer months was
a vital stage in the realisation of Cuffe's plans for Africa. In little more
than a year he had succeeded in creating a transatlantic network, a

---

[32] (Anon.), *Life of William Allen*, vol. I, p. 116.
[33] Miller, *The Search for a Black Nationality*, p. 33; *The Philanthropist*, 2 (7) (1812), p. 308.
[34] Thomas, *Rise to a People*, p. 77.
[35] Thomas, *Rise to a People*, p. 77.

complex web of associations that stretched from 'England to America and to Sierra Leone and from thence to England'.[36] It was a remarkable achievement and one that spoke volumes about Cuffe's ambitions, as well as his energy and perseverance.

For the moment, at least, Cuffe's plans were thwarted by the outbreak of hostilities between Britain and the USA. Undeterred, in June 1813 he petitioned the US Congress – unsuccessfully, as it turned out – to be allowed to trade with Africa, albeit on a limited scale.[37] Similar efforts were made by Cuffe's British friends, who pressed his case with government ministers, as well as with members of the Privy Council. As Lamont Thomas observes, what was interesting about this campaign was its deliberate attempt to link Cuffe 'with the best interests of British colonial development and settler harmony'.[38] By this stage, Cuffe had become, in the minds of many British activists, an important catalyst. He would bring to Sierra Leone not only 'a spirit of industry', chiefly through the example set by 'exemplary' American settlers, but also much-needed technological innovation. With this in mind, British activists redoubled their efforts to clear the obstacles in Cuffe's path, among them the uncertainty over land grants (the periodic renewal of land grants, not to mention the vexed issue of 'quit-rents', created understandable settler anxiety) and the deeply unpopular Militia Act of 1810, which appeared to grant the Governor of Sierra Leone authority to 'separate [settlers] from their wives and families and to employ them at their leisure in any part of Africa'.[39] Yet government ministers remained unmoved, many of them fearing that 'embarrassing consequences' might result if Cuffe were granted a special licence to trade with Africa, particularly as Britain and America were at war. Nevertheless, the case was left open, 'with an indication that the lords [of the Privy Council] might reverse themselves' if circumstances changed.[40]

One unforeseen consequence of all this activity was that the AI found itself under increasing scrutiny. In the summer of 1813, William Allen's periodical *The Philanthropist* published a damning review, probably written by Allen himself, of the AI's seventh annual report, which accused the organisation of allowing the abolition of the slave trade to 'engross' too much of its attention. What little was said about

---

[36] Thomas, *Rise to a People*, p. 59.
[37] Thomas, *Rise to a People*, pp. 82, 88–9.
[38] Thomas, *Rise to a People*, p. 87.
[39] *The Philanthropist*, 5 (19) (1815), pp. 246–7.
[40] Thomas, *Rise to a People*, p. 88; *Seventh Report of the Directors of the African Institution, Read at the Annual General Meeting on the 24th of March, 1813* (London: J. Hatchard, 1813), p. 32.

Sierra Leone, moreover, seemed to point to an obvious inconsistency, namely that while those entrusted with its management consistently earned high praise the colony itself was failing. The conclusion was inescapable: either the 'managing hands [had] not been good ones'; or 'the plan upon which they [had] been made to work [was] a bad one'.[41] Significantly, Allen refused to believe that the task was hopeless. As he put it, 'That a people advanced in civilisation may do much towards accelerating the progress of civilisation among a barbarous people is a proposition which we cannot hesitate one moment in adopting.'[42] The problem to his mind was mismanagement, a lot of it systemic. It was common knowledge that mistakes had been made in the past. Allen himself made it his business to ferret out information of this kind, using his contacts to build up a picture of what was really going on in Sierra Leone. But others, too, had raised concerns about the colony, among them Captain Philip Beaver, who described it as an 'ill-selected spot'.[43] Allen's point was simple: that it behoved the AI to look into these various reports and to make them 'a proper line of inquiry'.[44] 'They are before the public', he insisted, 'let the truth or falsehood of them be explored.'[45]

Convinced that the AI was failing in its duty to Sierra Leone, Allen pressed the case for an official inquiry and, with Wilberforce's backing, eventually forced the Directors' hands. According to his own account, the hearings began on 15 December when a special committee examined Robert Thorpe, a former Chief Justice of Sierra Leone who later published a vicious attack on the AI. Other witnesses followed, among them John Clarkson, a former Governor, and Zachary Macaulay. Very quickly it became clear

that the people were discontented about their lands, and that a surveyor was much wanted; that on account of one governor revoking what a former one had granted, confidence in the security of property was weakened, and this had proved a discouragement to cultivation; that the colony from mismanagement and neglect had certainly gone back in morals, etc.[46]

In all, the investigations occupied more than twenty long sittings. At the end of them, Allen concluded that 'the principle attended to by the white people of Sierra Leone, at least by many of them, has been getting

---

[41] *The Philanthropist*, 3 (12) (1813), p. 304.
[42] *The Philanthropist*, 3 (12) (1813), p. 303.
[43] *The Philanthropist*, 3 (12) (1813), p. 322.
[44] *The Philanthropist*, 3 (12) (1813), p. 322.
[45] *The Philanthropist*, 3 (12) (1813), p. 324.
[46] (Anon.), *Life of William Allen*, vol. I, p. 138.

money, and that in the shortest way'.[47] In the meantime, the black settlers had retrograded, education had been neglected, and discontent
had become widespread. It was a bleak picture, but one that seemed to
point to an obvious and urgent conclusion: what the settlers needed,
more than anything else, was economic stimulus.[48]

It was with this in mind that in January 1814 Allen and some of his
closest friends, among them Thomas Clarkson, Samuel Hoare and
George Harrison, all members of the 'original Abolition Committee'
(SEAST), organised 'The Society for the Purpose of Encouraging the
Black Settlers at Sierra Leone, and the Natives of Africa Generally, in
the Cultivation of Their Soil, and by the Sale of Their Produce'. The
aim of the new society was to raise a fund (membership was fixed at
£20) in order to open a 'mercantile connection' with black settlers 'upon
easy terms'; in effect, to extend Allen's own efforts to help the Friendly
Society of Sierra Leone.[49] By these means, it was hoped to stimulate the
settlers to become 'industrious cultivators of the soil' and to raise the
natives to 'like industry through their medium'.[50] Significantly, it was
not the intention to make the settlers into 'general merchants', a matter
of some concern to those who worried about the wider moral and social
impact of commercial enterprise, but rather to 'encourage them in raising exportable produce'.[51] The appearance of this society marked a new
phase in attempts to 'civilise' Africa, one more attuned to the economic
needs of the settlers. While many of its members, including Allen, were
also members of the AI and professed a desire to work 'in unison' with
a body that had 'contributed in a variety of ways to the protection and
welfare of the inhabitants of Africa', it is difficult not to see it as a direct
challenge to the AI or, at least, as an implied criticism of its 'fixed determination' not to engage in 'commercial speculations' in Africa.[52]

'The Society for the Purpose of Encouraging Black Settlers at Sierra
Leone' set trade with Africa on a new and more secure foundation.

---

[47] (Anon.), *Life of William Allen*, vol. I, p. 138.
[48] (Anon.), *Life of William Allen*, vol. I, p. 138.
[49] 'Prospectus of the Society for the Purpose of Encouraging the Black Settlers at Sierra
Leone, and the Natives of Africa Generally, in the Cultivation of Their Soil, and
by the Sale of Their Produce, Instituted 24 January 1814', London, The National
Archives, Colonical Office Records, CO267/41.
[50] 'Prospectus of the Society for the Purpose of Encouraging the Black Settlers at Sierra
Leone'.
[51] 'Prospectus of the Society for the Purpose of Encouraging the Black Settlers at Sierra
Leone'. For contemporary debates surrounding trade and the civilisation of Africa,
see *The Philanthropist*, 1 (2) (1811), pp. 177–82; 1 (3) (1811), pp. 223–8; 1 (4) (1811),
pp. 291–302; 5 (19) (1815): 243–50.
[52] 'Prospectus of the Society for the Purpose of Encouraging the Black Settlers at Sierra
Leone'.

Writing to his close friend Richard Reynolds in October 1814, Allen reported enthusiastically that 'our little plan for the settlers promises very fair'.[53] 'The *Enterprise*', he went on,

just arrived, has brought us a remittance of above three thousand pounds, in camwood, rice, palm oil, and coffee; this, together with what they sent before, if sold, as I hope it will be, will make a balance in their favour; they have also sent a list of articles wanted, which will, perhaps amount to seven or eight hundred pounds, and we are preparing to ship them in the *Wilding*.[54]

Simultaneously, Allen and others worked hard to ensure that Sierra Leone produce, with the exception of sugar, was put on the same footing with all other British colonies with respect to duties, a proposal that won the support of the Chancellor of the Exchequer, Nicholas Vansittart, only to be rejected by the House of Lords.[55] There was also talk of chartering or purchasing a small ship so as to 'keep up a constant intercourse between these poor people and their friends in England'.[56] By May 1815, the society had a working capital of £500, and there were increasing signs that trade between Britain and Africa was starting to gain momentum.[57]

Nevertheless, it is clear that a lot still depended on Paul Cuffe. As Clarkson pointed out to Earl Bathurst, the Secretary of State for the Colonies, in June 1815, many of the problems facing Sierra Leone, such as the Militia Act and the uncertainty over property rights, could be quickly dealt with by the minister's 'own fiat'. But, as regards the 'want of stimulus' among the settlers, this could only be remedied through outside help. For ease of reference, Clarkson appended a series of short notes, among them one that

Captain Paul Cuffe [should] bring over from America to Sierra Leone a few respectable black settlers, who from their own experience should be able to teach those now there the cultivation and cleaning of rice, the cultivation and dressing of cotton, the cultivation, harvesting and curing and preserving [of] tobacco, etc.[58]

Allen echoed these sentiments. He also had another request to make, namely that the Government should 'renew the privilege it granted to Cuffe about three years ago, permitting him to make one voyage from

[53] (Anon.), *Life of William Allen*, vol. I, p. 160.
[54] (Anon.), *Life of William Allen*, vol. I, p. 160.
[55] (Anon.), *Life of William Allen*, vol. I, pp. 168–74.
[56] *The Philanthropist*, 5 (19) (1815), p. 250.
[57] (Anon.), *Life of William Allen*, vol. I, p. 168.
[58] Thomas Clarkson to Earl Bathurst, 22 June 1815, Colonical Office Records, CO267/41, The National Archives, London.

America to Sierra Leone in his vessel and from thence to some port in England in the same manner as a British subject'.[59] Cuffe, he added, was 'highly respected wherever he [was] known'.[60] Moreover, 'from the experience which the African Institution had had of his disposition and abilities they [were] fully persuaded that he [would] materially assist in promoting the prosperity of the colony'.[61] Allen offered Bathurst one final inducement. He was convinced, he said, that, given the right incentives, cotton and many other 'very valuable articles of commerce' could be raised in such quantities 'in the neighbourhood of Sierra Leone' as to 'render Great Britain independent in these respects of North America'.[62]

Despite all these efforts, the Government refused to give Cuffe a trading licence, although Bathurst did write to Sierra Leone's Governor, Charles McCarthy, asking him to afford Cuffe all the assistance he could.[63] Whether Cuffe knew of this decision before he left the USA is unclear. Throughout the late summer of 1815 he had been working hard to gather together a group of suitable emigrants and, by September, had identified eight families who were willing to accompany him, most of them from Boston. After further delays, Cuffe finally set sail on 10 December, eventually reaching Freetown early in February 1816.[64] Here, at last, were the first visible signs of the outside stimulus that Cuffe, Allen and Clarkson had all agreed was so important if Sierra Leone was to realise anything like its full potential. Yet, as Cuffe quickly realised, the voyage had proved a financial disaster. Unpaid passenger expenses alone were in excess of $2,900, added to which Cuffe was forced to sell his cargo at a loss.[65] To compound his problems, McCarthy had proved unfriendly, even obstructive, although he had allowed the emigrants to disembark. In all, Cuffe remained in Sierra Leone for two months while the thirty-eight American settlers acclimatised and adjusted to their new surroundings, but it was already clear to him that without more help from British activists, as well as the cooperation of the British Government, he could not go on carrying more settlers to Africa.[66]

---

[59] William Allen to Earl Bathurst, 27 May 1815, Colonical Office Records, CO267/41, The National Archives, London.

[60] Allen to Bathurst, 27 May 1815.

[61] Allen to Bathurst, 27 May 1815.

[62] Allen to Bathurst, 27 May 1815.

[63] Miller, *The Search for a Black Nationality*, pp. 39–40.

[64] Miller, *The Search for a Black Nationality*, pp. 40–1; *Eleventh Report of the Directors of the African Institution, Read at the Annual General Meeting on the 26th of March, 1817* (London: J. Hatchard, 1817), pp. 39–41.

[65] Thomas, *Rise to a People*, pp. 100–3. Thomas estimates that Cuffe's outstanding debts, 'in regard to both old and new settlers', probably amounted to more than $8,000.

[66] Miller, *The Search for a Black Nationality*, pp. 41–3; Thomas, *Rise to a People*, p. 106.

By this date, moreover, debates over emigration had started to take a different and, to some, a more worrying turn. While Cuffe's chief motivation had always been the regeneration of Africa, many whites, particularly those in the South, began to advocate relocating blacks as a means of addressing internal domestic problems. In truth, there was nothing new about this idea – as we have seen, colonisation had been openly discussed since at least the 1780s – but charges of black disloyalty during the War of 1812, together with growing concerns about the rise in the number of blacks, free and enslaved, seem to have given it added momentum.[67] As tensions mounted, the free black population came under increasing scrutiny. Variously dismissed as being 'lazy' and 'mischievous', free blacks were widely suspected of corrupting slaves 'by rendering them idle, discontented and disobedient'.[68] Behind these fears, of course, lay the threat of slave insurrection. Indeed, by 1816, many white slaveholders had come to the conclusion that the only way of securing their property was by relocating thousands of free blacks. Colonisation was also promoted by some southerners as a means of attracting more whites into the slave states, thereby stimulating greater industry and enterprise.[69] At stake here, therefore, was not only the security of the slave South but also its social and economic future.

It is a measure of just how important these debates had become that colonisation dominated the proceedings of the 1816 American Convention, the first that had met since 1812. The mood of the delegates was expectant, buoyed up by the course of events in Europe, as well as a sense that in the USA there was a growing disposition, 'even amongst those who possess their fellow beings in bondage', to meliorate their condition and, if possible, 'purify themselves from an offence which violated the great obligations of Christianity'.[70] During the proceedings several letters were read from slaveholders in the Southern and South-western states who professed to want to free their slaves, if only they could find a means of doing so that did not abrogate state manumission laws. Colonisation, it was conceded, provided one possible solution, although at this stage the delegates seem to have favoured setting apart a portion of the unappropriated land of the South and

[67] See Whitman, *Challenging Slavery in the Chesapeake*, pp. 97–101.
[68] Whitman, *Challenging Slavery in the Chesapeake*, p. 109.
[69] Whitman, *Challenging Slavery in the Chesapeake*, p. 110.
[70] *Minutes of the Proceedings of the Fourteenth American Convention for Promoting the Abolition of Slavery, and Improving the Condition of the African Race, Assembled at Philadelphia on the Ninth Day of January 1815, on the Eighth Day of January 1816, and Continued by Adjournments, Until the Twelfth Day of the Same Month, Inclusive* (Philadelphia, Pa.: W. Brown, 1816), pp. 22–3.

West, 'on which to establish a colony of blacks protected and guaranteed by the [US] government, and regulated by suitable provisions'.[71] Interestingly, there was no mention of African colonisation, either to Sierra Leone or to any other part of the African coast, and no mention of the Caribbean or South America. Indeed, as the Convention's subsequent memorial to the US Congress made clear, the choice before the delegates seemed to be between some scheme of 'gradual emancipation and general improvement', leading to 'all the rights and privileges of [American] citizens', or settlement within the continental limits of the USA, preferably west of the Mississippi.[72]

Keen to build on what they saw as a shift in attitudes among Southern slaveholders, the delegates also proposed publishing an abridged version of Thomas Clarkson's *History of the Rise, Progress and Accomplishment of the Abolition of the African Slave-Trade*, with a view to giving it a wide circulation through the Southern states.[73] The driving force behind this project appears to have been Evan Lewis, a delegate from Delaware who was also a member of the Convention's Committee of Arrangements. To judge from the minutes, the original intention was that the Convention should publish the *History* at its own expense but, when this fell through, Lewis, who proposed to do the work of abridgement himself, was forced to rely on subscriptions. The 1817 Convention reported that over 1,500 copies of the work had been printed, 750 of which had been subscribed and paid for by the NYMS and a similar number (635) by the PAS. Moreover, considerable progress had been made in distributing them, principally through the Kentucky Abolition Society, which had been organised in 1809, and sympathisers in South Carolina, Maryland and Tennessee. In an interesting precursor of the pamphlet campaigns of the 1830s, therefore, Clarkson's *History*, a British work by a British author, became an important vehicle in rousing Southern white opinion against slavery and the slave trade.[74]

Although many American activists had decided views about colonisation, for and against, they were clearly intent on soliciting the views of others. It was with this in mind that in June 1816 Evan Lewis approached

[71] *Minutes of the Proceedings of the Fourteenth American Convention for Promoting the Abolition of Slavery* (1816), pp. 28, 32; Evan Lewis to Thomas Clarkson, 12 June 1816, Thomas Clarkson Papers, CN122, Huntington Library, San Marino, California.
[72] Lewis to Clarkson, 12 June 1816.
[73] *Minutes of the Proceedings of the Fourteenth American Convention for Promoting the Abolition of Slavery* (1816), pp. 12, 24, 39–40.
[74] *Minutes of the Proceedings of the Fifteenth American Convention for Promoting the Abolition of Slavery, and for Improving the Condition of the African Race* (1817), p. 20. See also PAS Minutes, 4 April 1816, 27 June 1816, 27 September 1816, 26 December 1816, 27 March 1817 and 25 December 1817.

Thomas Clarkson, enclosing a copy of the Convention's memorial to Congress and asking him for his thoughts on a scheme that in his (Lewis's) view 'would be attended with almost insuperable difficulty'.[75] By the time Clarkson got round to answering this letter in March 1817, a new factor had emerged in the shape of the American Colonisation Society (ACS). Organised in December 1816, the ACS was made up of a number of prominent white colonisationists who included Francis Scott Key, Henry Clay and John Randolph of Virginia. Put simply, the aim of the new organisation was to secure government backing for a scheme to settle a colony in Africa that would absorb large numbers of free blacks and emancipated slaves, thereby 'serving the needs of Africa as well as enabling whites to rid themselves of an alien and discordant people'.[76] The scheme had little if anything to do with abolitionist principles. Though ACS members professed that their activities would help to suppress the slave trade, they were intent, by and large, on protecting slavery; indeed, Randolph argued that the society 'must materially tend to secure the property of every master in the United States over his slaves'.[77] For these and other reasons, American activists, black and white, viewed the ACS with growing suspicion. Yet, at the same time, the new society, together with its emphasis on African colonisation, posed a challenge that could not be ignored.

To help it realise its plans, the ACS sought the advice of British activists, among them Clarkson, who was well known to have an interest in African trade and emigration. How much Clarkson knew about the ACS at this stage is open to question. It seems unlikely, however, that he had any inkling of its real intentions or, indeed, its pro-slavery bias. If anything, Clarkson assumed that these different approaches, the one from Evan Lewis and the other from the ACS, were somehow linked and part of the same wider inquiry.[78] For this reason, he was prepared to give the ACS all the help he could. The most promising site for an African colony, he suggested, was the Sherbro region, south of Sierra Leone, where the natives were reputed to be 'kind and friendly' and unlikely 'to do any great injury to a colony upon a proper scale'.[79] Clarkson also offered advice about provisions, clothing, seeds and 'proper instruments both

[75] Lewis to Clarkson, 12 June 1816.
[76] Miller, *The Search for a Black Nationality*, p. 45. For the ACS, see Philip J. Staudenraus, *The African Colonization Movement, 1816–1865* (New York: Columbia University Press, 1961); Archibald Alexander, *The History of Colonization on the Western Coast of Africa*, 2nd edn (Philadelphia, Pa.: W. S. Martien, 1849).
[77] Quoted in Thomas, *Rise to a People*, p. 111.
[78] See Thomas Clarkson to Francis Scott Key, 18 March 1817, Thomas Clarkson Papers, CN58, Huntington Library, San Marino, California.
[79] Clarkson to Key, 18 March 1817.

for horticulture and husbandry'.[80] Before they did anything, however, he advised the members of the ACS to consult his friend Paul Cuffe, 'who was intimately acquainted with the Sherbro people, their land, customs, languages, etc.'[81] Furthermore, he suggested that they might employ John Kizell, an American ex-slave based on the west coast of Africa, who 'would be of eminent use to the new colony, in explaining matters and in doing away with misunderstandings'.[82]

As it happened, Cuffe was already in contact with the ACS. Since his return to America in 1816, he had started to rethink his commitment to Sierra Leone. Frustrated by the unwillingness of the British Government to issue him with a trading licence and conscious of the fact that the various black African Institutions had become largely inactive, 'either for the want of spirit or property', he began to consider the possibility of setting up a colony in another part of Africa, even sounding out John Kizell about the idea.[83] Cuffe's initial response to the ACS, therefore, was enthusiastic. Like Clarkson, he warmly recommended the Sherbro region, but he also suggested that the US Government should explore other sites, among them the Gambia river delta, the Congo river basin and the Cape of Good Hope. Nevertheless, Cuffe was not quite ready to turn his back on America. On the contrary, he stressed the importance of offering free blacks a choice, including, significantly, an alternative site in the USA. Perhaps just as important, Cuffe strongly advised the ACS to contact the members of the New York and Boston African Institutions, so as to win their cooperation, and even suggested that Peter Williams Jnr., president of the New York society, should lead the Government's survey team to Africa.[84]

For once, however, Cuffe found himself out of step with the mood among Northern blacks. The sticking point was the issue of 'consent'. Many free blacks clearly believed that the ACS was intent on forcibly removing them from the USA, thereby strengthening the institution of slavery. Such fears only fostered a growing sense of black solidarity. As a protest meeting in Philadelphia in January 1817 put it: 'They [slaves] are our brethren by the ties of consanguinity, of suffering and of wrong;

[80] Clarkson to Key, 18 March 1817.
[81] Clarkson to Key, 18 March 1817.
[82] Thomas Clarkson to Francis Scott Key, 18 March 1817, Clarkson Papers, CN58, Huntington Library, San Marino, California. For Kizell, see Kevin G. Lowther, *The African American Odyssey of John Kizell: A South Carolina Slave Returns to Fight the Slave Trade in His African Homeland* (Columbia, SC: University of South Carolina Press, 2011).
[83] Miller, *The Search for a Black Nationality*, pp. 43–5; Thomas, *Rise to a People*, pp. 110–11.
[84] Thomas, *Rise to a People*, p. 111.

and we feel there is more virtue in suffering privations with them, than fancied advantages for a season.'[85] If anything, opposition to the ACS increased as time went on. At a second meeting in August 1817, Philadelphia blacks protested that African Americans were unsuited to life in Africa, that the proposed colony would soon degenerate into 'the abode of every vice and the home of every misery' and that emigration on the scale envisaged by the ACS would only delay emancipation.[86] In saying this, however, blacks did not necessarily reject colonisation per se. A protest meeting in Richmond, Virginia, for instance, called upon Congress to consider the wisdom of granting blacks 'a portion of their territory, either on the Missouri river, or any other place that may seem to them most conducive to the public good and our future welfare, subject, however, to such rules and regulations as the government of the United States may think proper to adopt'.[87] For this group, at least, the problem was not so much colonisation itself as African colonisation and the ACS.

White activists monitored these developments closely. The 1817 American Convention, which met in August, devoted another session to colonisation, before referring the subject to a special committee of seven to determine what further steps it might be proper for the delegates to take. In its formal report, the committee members noted that 'some project of colonization appears to occupy the minds of a great multitude of our fellow citizens, but [that] as yet, opinions are varied and unsettled'.[88] As for the ACS, while admiring 'the dignified and benevolent intention' of its members, they could not help expressing their hope that no such plan would go into effect 'without an immutable pledge from the slaveholding states of a just and wise system of gradual emancipation'.[89] In effect, what the committee was insisting upon was that emancipation should *precede* colonisation.[90] By 1817, therefore, clear differences were beginning to emerge between white activists (as represented by the American Convention) and the members of the ACS. This became even more apparent in 1818, when the delegates met again, this time at a special meeting called to discuss, among other

---

[85] Quoted in Winch, *Philadelphia's Black Elite*, p. 35.
[86] Winch, *Philadelphia's Black Elite*, p. 35.
[87] Quoted in Herbert Aptheker, *A Documentary History of the Negro People in the United States*, (New York: The Citadel Press, 1969), vol. I, p. 71.
[88] *Minutes of the Proceedings of the Fifteenth American Convention for Promoting the Abolition of Slavery* (1817), p. 30.
[89] *Minutes of the Proceedings of the Fifteenth American Convention for Promoting the Abolition of Slavery* (1817), p. 31.
[90] *Minutes of the Proceedings of the Fifteenth American Convention for Promoting the Abolition of Slavery* (1817), pp. 30–1.

things, the issue of African colonisation. In the view of PAS members, 'the period [had] arrived when a serious investigation of the probable result of this measure ought to be no longer avoided'.[91] 'We forbear all comment upon the subject', they went on, urging the Convention into action, 'but we ask your solemn attention to the enquiry whether such colonization will subserve the interests of humanity or whether it will have the effect to perpetuate slavery in the US?'[92]

The report subsequently approved and adopted by the Convention began by tracing the history of African colonisation, from Tucker's influential pamphlet on the subject (1801), through to the organisation of the ACS in 1816. It then turned to the ACS's 'proceedings', before concluding that it could find nothing in them, 'or in the avowed sentiments of its members', 'friendly to the abolition of slavery in the United States'.[93] For many activists, this would have been enough to condemn the whole project, but the report went on to dismiss the ACS's plans as 'impracticable'.[94] It was not just that Northern blacks were against the idea, although that was undoubtedly important. The west coast of Africa was unhealthy, inhospitable and 'occupied by a bold and martial race, entirely addicted to war; many of them of a large size, strong and well proportioned; their courage intrepid'.[95] Securing a foothold in such a region, let alone making a success of it, would be extremely difficult. If proof were needed, the report pointed to the 'failure' of the European nations to establish successful colonies in Africa. Sierra Leone was reported to be 'languishing', and much the same was true of the settlements established by the Swedes at Gorée and the Danes at Aquapin. The scheme, in short, would hardly warrant the expense. Britain, France, Spain, Denmark and Sweden had each 'exerted themselves to colonize there, and they [had] all, in a great measure, failed in their efforts'.[96]

As if that were not enough, the report questioned the wisdom of forming a plan of colonisation, 'in the bosom of the slaveholding states, for other purposes than those connected with the abolition of slavery'.[97] The effect, it predicted, would be to 'eternize' the bondage of

---

[91] PAS Minutes, 19 November 1818.
[92] PAS Minutes, 19 November 1818.
[93] *Minutes of the Proceedings of a Special Meeting of the Fifteenth American Convention for Promoting the Abolition of Slavery* (1818), p. 49.
[94] *Minutes of the Proceedings of a Special Meeting of the Fifteenth American Convention for Promoting the Abolition of Slavery* (1818), p. 49.
[95] *Minutes of the Proceedings of a Special Meeting of the Fifteenth American Convention for Promoting the Abolition of Slavery* (1818), p. 52.
[96] *Minutes of the Proceedings of a Special Meeting of the Fifteenth American Convention for Promoting the Abolition of Slavery* (1818), p. 50.
[97] *Minutes of the Proceedings of a Special Meeting of the Fifteeenth American Convention for Promoting the Abolition of Slavery* (1818), p. 52.

those left behind, thus 'defeating the slow but certain progress of those principles, which, if uninterrupted, [would] produce their universal emancipation'.[98] There were similar concerns about the impact of the scheme on free blacks in the South, who were already objects of 'fear and hatred'.[99] It seemed only too likely that undue pressure would be placed on these men and women to emigrate, and, when that did not work, that 'other measures' might be resorted to, such as heavy poll taxes 'levied exclusively on the free people of colour'.[100] 'The option of voluntary emancipation, and the protest which has always been avowed against the employment of compulsory means to increase the numbers of colonists', the report concluded, 'will avail nothing, if measures of this kind are adopted by those states, when a disposition to get rid of the free people of colour prevails.'[101] It was a damning commentary and a damning verdict. Convinced that the ACS's plans were not only impracticable but also positively 'injurious', the Convention joined black activists in publicly condemning African colonisation (at least, as envisaged by the ACS), thereby signalling an important rupture that in many ways anticipated Garrison's attacks on those colonisationists who supported 'mandatory deportations'.[102]

Yet, in rejecting the ACS, American activists did not turn their backs on colonisation altogether. The 1819 Convention, for instance, discussed at length the idea of relocating blacks west of the Mississippi, preferably under 'a territorial or provincial form of government' that would guarantee the protection of their 'property and personal rights'.[103] At the same time, the delegates showed an increasing interest in Haitian emigration.

---

[98] *Minutes of the Proceedings of a Special Meeting of the Fifteenth American Convention for Promoting the Abolition of Slavery* (1818), p. 53.

[99] *Minutes of the Proceedings of a Special Meeting of the Fifteenth American Convention for Promoting the Abolition of Slavery* (1818), p. 53.

[100] *Minutes of the Proceedings of a Special Meeting of the Fifteenth American Convention for Promoting the Abolition of Slavery* (1818), p. 54. These concerns seem to have been widespread among American activists. Writing to Roberts Vaux in September 1817, Samuel Emlen expressed his fear that 'a Colony, or even the semblance of one, formed on the African Coast [might] furnish the Legislatures of Southern States with a pretext for the enactment of laws prohibiting the residence of free blacks among them, this then would be banishment without any crime alleged; & to the hardened slaveholder it would be of little moment whether they perished on the voyage or [lived] a few years longer in misery on a desert Coast'. See Samuel Emlen to Roberts Vaux, 19 September 1817, Vaux Papers, Box 1, Folder 13.

[101] *Minutes of the Proceedings of a Special Meeting of the Fifteenth American Convention for Promoting the Abolition of Slavery* (1818), p. 54.

[102] *Minutes of the Proceedings of a Special Meeting of the Fifteenth American Convention for Promoting the Abolition of Slavery* (1818), p. 54. For Garrison, see Mayer, *All On Fire*, pp. 72–3.

[103] *Minutes of the Proceedings of the Sixteenth American Convention for Promoting the Abolition of Slavery, and Improving the Condition of the African Race. Held at Philadelphia, on*

Since the removal of Jean-Jacques Dessalines in 1807, Haiti had effectively become two coexisting nations: the 'black' Kingdom of Haiti under Henri Christophe's rule in the north of the island and the southern Republic of Haiti presided over first by Alexandre Pétion (1807–18), a mulatto who had formerly been head of the Haitian Congress, and later by Jean-Pierre Boyer. Though these two regimes – one a monarchy, the other a republic – were very different in political outlook, they shared a common set of problems: a devastated economy, rural depopulation, the crippling cost of maintaining large standing armies and, above all, what amounted to diplomatic isolation.[104] The 'recognition issue' (frustratingly, no other nation would recognise Haiti's sovereignty, for fear of antagonising the French) made the work of economic recovery all the more important. As Sara Connors Fanning writes, all of Haiti's early leaders, from Dessalines to Boyer, 'assumed that once they [had] established and made Haiti a stable, well-regarded, and commercially invaluable state, then diplomats and important allies would rally round'.[105]

Britain figured largely in these calculations. At different times, both Pétion and Christophe approached the British about the recognition issue, hoping thereby to legitimise one or other of their respective governments.[106] British support became all the more imperative following the defeat of Napoleon and his abdication on 31 March 1814. It soon became apparent that the new French government intended to re-establish control over Haiti, initially by trying to intimidate Pétion and Christophe and, when that did not work, by offering them bribes, in the form of either money or titles.[107] Both leaders successfully resisted these blandishments, but the wider lesson to Christophe, at least, was that he 'needed friends abroad who would advise him concerning the internal and external affairs of his kingdom, who would recognize his achievements and publicly announce them to the world, and who would present his case to the European powers'.[108] So it was that he made contact with the members of the AI. By 1814, Christophe was already in touch with Wilberforce, who evidently saw in the Kingdom of Haiti

the *Fifth of October and the Tenth of November, 1819* (Philadelphia, Pa.: William Fry, 1819), pp. 50–2.
[104] See Sara Connors Fanning, 'Haiti and the US: African American Emigration and the Recognition Debate', unpublished Ph.D. dissertation, University of Texas at Austin, 2008, Chapter 2.
[105] Fanning, 'Haiti and the US', p. 26.
[106] Fanning, 'Haiti and the US', pp. 40–1.
[107] See Earl Leslie Griggs and Clifford H. Prator, eds., *Henry Christophe and Thomas Clarkson: A Correspondence* (Berkeley: University of California Press, 1952), pp. 56–61.
[108] Griggs and Prator, *Henry Christophe and Thomas Clarkson*, pp. 61–2.

an opportunity 'of sowing the seeds of civilization, and still more of Christian faith'.[109] Not content with lending Christophe what personal support he could, Wilberforce also brought Haitian affairs to the attention of his friends and associates, among them Thomas Clarkson.

Clarkson would go on to become one of Christophe's most trusted advisers. In many ways it was an unlikely alliance, not least given the two men's backgrounds, experiences and political loyalties. For once, however, Clarkson was prepared to compromise his republican principles. Christophe's government was 'certainly monarchical', he conceded, but that was more a matter of 'necessity than of choice', particularly given the state of Haiti (interestingly, Clarkson thought that the bulk of the population, especially ex-slaves, were 'unfit for a pure republic').[110] What seems to have impressed Clarkson was Christophe's obvious commitment to long-term reform, particularly educational reform. To his mind, 'King Henry' was not resistant to change; rather, he was 'preparing his subjects gradually for it'.[111] In this sense, Christophe's enlightened despotism was merely a (necessary) phase in Haiti's social, political and economic development. Clarkson, therefore, was willing to give Christophe the benefit of the doubt. Either way, he argued, the king's wide-ranging reforms would surely effect change. As Clarkson explained in March 1819, 'the streams of knowledge which must be daily pouring in [to Haiti] cannot fail in the end to overwhelm despotism of every kind'.[112]

Excited by the example that a successful black nationality in the Caribbean would set to the rest of the world, Clarkson worked tirelessly to help Christophe realise his plans for the Kingdom of Haiti. Besides offering the king advice, not least about Haiti's diplomatic position, he also arranged for teachers to be sent to the island, among them William Wilson, who became tutor to Chistophe's son, the Prince Royal.[113] Clarkson was aided in these efforts by his old friend William Allen, who was deeply involved in educational reform, largely through his work with the British and Foreign School Society, which promoted Joseph Lancaster's monitorial system (what we would now call 'peer learning'). Allen even arranged for teachers to be sent out to the Republic of Haiti, boasting in September 1817 that the 'whole island of Haiti is

---

[109] Griggs and Prator, *Henry Christophe and Thomas Clarkson*, p. 62.
[110] Thomas Clarkson to Roberts Vaux, 8 March 1819, Thomas Clarkson Papers, CN63, Huntington Library, San Marino, California.
[111] Clarkson to Vaux, 8 March 1819.
[112] Clarkson to Vaux, 8 March 1819.
[113] For details, see King Henri Christophe to Thomas Clarkson, 18 November 1816, and Thomas Clarkson to King Henri Christophe, 24 January 1820, in Griggs and Prator, *Henry Christophe and Thomas Clarkson*, pp. 97–8, 186–7.

now provided with teachers on our school plan'.[114] But if Haiti excited Clarkson and Allen and took up an increasing amount of their time, this did not mean that they had turned their backs on Africa; on the contrary, Allen's journal makes it clear that he was able to juggle these competing demands, which in his own mind were part of the same bigger abolitionist project.[115] What did change, however, was their interest in and commitment to African colonisation. Paul Cuffe's sudden death in 1817 was an important factor here but so, too, was the negative reaction to the ACS. What had once seemed an exciting opportunity (that is, the relocation of American blacks to Sierra Leone) increasingly looked impossible, even futile.[116]

With the help of men such as Clarkson and Allen, Christophe set about turning the Kingdom of Haiti into an 'English' state, even toying with the idea of making English rather than French the official language.[117] Yet, despite these efforts, the British still refused to acknowledge Haiti. Understandably, Christophe vented his frustration on Clarkson. Without British recognition, he argued, it would be impossible to push forward his 'favourite plan, that of returning the soldiers of the army to agricultural pursuits'.[118] Haitians desperately needed assurances that such a measure would not endanger their safety. 'When I read your letters and those of our mutual friends', Christophe went on,

when I see that our ideas are in perfect harmony and understand that these ideas – concerning the necessity of devoting ourselves wholly to agriculture, morality, public instruction, and religion – are capable of great extension, I cannot but bewail and deplore this imperious necessity which prevents the execution of my projects in their entirety.[119]

Christophe grew increasingly insistent, demanding that Britain should recognise Haitian independence or, failing that, 'take some equivalent steps such as promising that the French will undertake no expedition to blockade our ports and harass our territory, and also that Spain will not

---

[114] (Anon.), *Life of William Allen*, vol. I, p. 242.
[115] For details, see (Anon.), *Life of William Allen*, vol. I, pp. 197, 223–4, 225, 228–9, 231–4, 242, 246.
[116] In 1820, Clarkson went further, admitting that Africa was 'unfit' for free blacks. See Thomas Clarkson to Roberts Vaux, 31 January 1820, Thomas Clarkson Papers, CN64, Huntington Library, San Marino, California.
[117] Fanning, 'Haiti and the US', pp. 42–3.
[118] King Henri Christophe to Thomas Clarkson, 26 April 1818, in Griggs and Prator, *Henry Christophe and Thomas Clarkson*, p. 108.
[119] Christophe to Clarkson, 26 April 1818, in Griggs and Prator, *Henry Christophe and Thomas Clarkson*, p. 108.

be permitted to cede her part of this island to our enemies, thus leaving the latter established at our rear'.[120]

Clarkson knew that the British were unlikely to give way to Christophe's demands. Nevertheless, he did offer another solution to the King's fears about Haiti's security – American emigration. Initiatives of this kind had been tried in the past, notably by Dessalines, but, as we shall see, the idea of attracting American blacks to Haiti gained wider currency after 1818, principally as an alternative to African colonisation.[121] A key figure here was Prince Saunders, a free black from Vermont and a close confidant of King Henry, who in 1818 visited the USA to promote his *Haytian Papers*, a translation with historical commentary of Christophe's 'Code Rural'. During his short visit, Saunders met with local blacks, exciting wide interest in Haiti and impressing them with 'a most favourable idea of [the king's] character'.[122] Significantly, Saunders also spoke before the American Convention, which in response passed a resolution calling on its acting committee to open a correspondence with the AI, with a view to effecting some kind of 'pacification' between the 'two independent governments' in Haiti and promoting 'such arrangements as [would] render that island a safe asylum for [those] people of color in the United States and elsewhere, as [might] *choose* to emigrate to it'.[123]

Several weeks later, Saunders contacted Thomas Clarkson to solicit his thoughts on the subject. Clarkson's response was measured, probably reflecting his earlier experiences with the ACS. Any scheme of emigration, he pointed out, would need the consent of those principally concerned, that is, free blacks, as well as a pledge from Southern slaveholders 'that they would prepare gradually for sending away those, whom they now hold in slavery', which, of course, was the position endorsed by the American Convention.[124] If these points could be satisfied, then Clarkson thought that some kind of colonisation scheme might be feasible, although by this stage he had clearly rejected the idea of sending free blacks to Africa. As for Haiti, the real question to his mind was whether Christophe or Boyer would take American emigrants and on what terms.[125] Clarkson, however, was interested enough to raise the issue with King Henri, pointing out that an influx

---

[120] Christophe to Clarkson, 26 April 1818, in Griggs and Prator, *Henry Christophe and Thomas Clarkson*, p. 108.

[121] For Dessalines and emigration, see Fanning, 'Haiti and the US', pp. 30–2.

[122] Griggs and Prator, *Henry Christophe and Thomas Clarkson*, pp. 45, 125.

[123] *Minutes of the Proceedings of a Special Meeting of the Fifteenth American Convention for Promoting the Abolition of Slavery* (1818), p. 55 (my emphasis).

[124] Thomas Clarkson to Prince Saunders, 3 February 1819, Thomas, Clarkson Papers, CN61, Huntington Library, San Marino, California.

[125] Clarkson to Saunders, 3 February 1819.

of American immigrants, 'if it consisted of persons of character, would very much add to your population, and of course to the security of your dominions'.[126] He also held out one further inducement. 'If the American Government were to apply to you on this subject', he went on, 'you might stipulate to receive them, *provided the American Government would purchase the Spanish part of the Island* and cede it to you, but upon no other terms.'[127] That way, Christophe would have 'no fear of France, either by a direct invasion of Hayti, or by the settlement of Frenchmen on the Spanish part of the Island'.[128] What Clarkson was proposing, in short, was that King Henri should use American interest in Haiti as a bargaining tool to secure his country's borders.

Simultaneously, Clarkson approached Roberts Vaux, a member of the PAS. Here again, he was careful to distance himself from the ACS. Clarkson even admitted that if given a free choice he would favour relocating blacks west of the Mississippi, an indication that he was much more conversant with American colonisation debates than might have been imagined. All of this was by way of a prelude to the real purpose of his letter, namely to offer what advice he could on the practicability of Haitian emigration, taking as his point of departure the resolution recently adopted by the American Convention. Clarkson favoured two possible schemes: to send blacks to Haiti either 'as an independent people under the protection of the United States, or as subjects to be equally divided between King Henri and General Boyer'.[129] (Interestingly, Clarkson thought Boyer would only grow nervous if Christophe gained an undue advantage, and vice versa.) Whichever scheme they chose, he insisted that Congress would have to buy the Spanish part of the island. Clarkson went further. He had it on good authority, he said, that the 'free people of colour now settled in the United States would not be received as subjects by either of the governments mentioned but upon these terms'.[130]

Clarkson, as a result, found himself at the very heart of emerging debates about Haitian emigration. More than that, he seemed to be dictating official policy, assuming responsibility for shaping the future of US–Haitian relations. Not for the first time, however, Clarkson had

---

[126] Thomas Clarkson to King Henri Christophe, 20 February 1819, in Griggs and Prator, *Henry Christophe and Thomas Clarkson*, p. 124.
[127] Clarkson to Christophe, 20 February 1819, in Griggs and Prator, *Henry Christophe and Thomas Clarkson*, p. 125 (emphasis in original).
[128] Clarkson to Christophe, 20 February 1819, in Griggs and Prator, *Henry Christophe and Thomas Clarkson*, p. 125.
[129] Thomas Clarkson to Roberts Vaux, 8 March 1819, Thomas Clarkson Papers, CN62, Huntington Library, San Marino, California.
[130] Clarkson to Vaux, 8 March 1819.

allowed his enthusiasm to run away with him. In reality, there was never much likelihood that the USA would purchase Santo Domingo, added to which growing tensions with Spain over the cession of the Floridas rendered any such scheme unworkable. Clarkson accordingly was forced to narrow his sights. Privately, he conceded in January 1820 that any prospect of a US-sponsored programme of mass emigration, involving not only those blacks already freed but also those likely to be freed in the future, was now out of the question. What he proposed, instead, was something different, not a 'public undertaking' but a limited emigration scheme, perhaps involving only a few thousand free blacks.[131] As for the recognition issue, Clarkson felt that this might be settled through diplomatic negotiation. France at this time was 'trying' King Henri on the subject of a treaty. Moreover, 'all' the members of the House of Deputies were seemingly in favour of the idea, having accepted, so Clarkson said, that the reconquest of Haiti was impossible. One, in particular, L'Aisne de la Villeveque, had even gone as far as to suggest that France 'might be a great gainer by acknowledging the independence of Haiti'.[132] So confident was he that an agreement might at last be possible that Clarkson offered the French his services as a mediator, 'so as to bring the parties together, should a few conditional outlines be previously approved'.[133]

By 1820, therefore, the debate over Haitian emigration had taken an unexpected turn. In effect, what Clarkson was now proposing was that King Henri – and not the US Government – should subsidise the whole 'adventure'. This was not an open-door policy, however. As Clarkson explained to Roberts Vaux, Christophe would take no Haitians, 'because they had traitorously left their country', neither would he take those of 'bad and abandoned character'.[134] Nevertheless, if these conditions could be met then he was confident that King Henri would give 'a very handsome sum towards the payment of their passage'.[135] For American activists, in particular, this development cast Haitian emigration in an entirely different light. Yet still they hesitated. The sticking point, it seems, was their doubts over the suitability of Haiti – long associated with bloody revolution – as an asylum for free blacks. Clarkson worked tirelessly to allay these fears and suggested that, rather than take his

---

[131] Thomas Clarkson to Roberts Vaux, 31 January 1820, Thomas Clarkson Papers, CN64, Huntington Library, San Marino, California.
[132] Clarkson to Vaux, 31 January 1820.
[133] Clarkson to Vaux, 31 January 1820.
[134] Clarkson to Vaux, 31 January 1820.
[135] Clarkson to Vaux, 31 January 1820. Christophe was later reported to have set aside a ship and $25,000 to cover the incidental expenses of transporting American blacks to Haiti. See Prince Saunders to Thomas Clarkson, 14 July 1821, in Griggs and Prator, *Henry Christophe and Thomas Clarkson*, p. 226.

word for it, they go and see for themselves. Clarkson had originally raised this idea in 1819.[136] It was not until 1820, however, that American activists finally resolved to do something about it. In May of that year, Roberts Vaux reported that Evan Lewis was eager to undertake such a mission; all that was needed was for the American Convention's acting committee to approve the measure. Significantly, Vaux's tone was upbeat. If Lewis did go to Haiti, he wrote, he had 'no doubt of his being enabled to make an arrangement with the King, & procure such information in respect to that country as will induce many of the free people of colour to emigrate thither'.[137]

At last, Clarkson's plans seemed to be coming together. But then disaster struck. On 15 August 1820, King Henri was seized with a fit of apoplexy that left his whole right side paralysed. News of Christophe's increasing indisposition was the signal for widespread revolt. By early October, the king's own palace at Sans-Souci was under siege. When his own guards joined the insurgents, he decided to take his own life, bringing to an end a regime that had lasted thirteen years.[138] Christophe's death and the confusion that followed it effectively called a halt to Haitian emigration. (Evan Lewis never did get to visit the island.) Perhaps just as significant, Clarkson's attempts to establish a relationship with the king's successor, Jean-Pierre Boyer, who reunited the two parts of Haiti in 1820, fell on stony ground. Haitians, Boyer implied, could and would take care of themselves.[139] With that, Clarkson's active involvement with Haiti came to an end. Yet, in a curious way, his efforts to build a constituency for Haitian emigration bore fruit in Boyer's subsequent plans to promote the Republic as 'an emigrant destination' for free and enslaved blacks. As is well documented, between 1824 and 1826 some 6,000 African Americans, most of them from Boston, Philadelphia and New York, settled in Haiti.[140] Theirs was not always a happy lot – in fact, many of them subsequently returned to the USA – but that they made the trip at all is in some measure an indication of just how important figures such as Clarkson and Saunders were in raising awareness about Haiti and in bringing together disparate parts of the Atlantic world into what would later become a coherent movement.

---

[136] See Thomas Clarkson to Richard Peters, 14 June 1819, Thomas Clarkson Papers, CN62, Huntington Library, San Marino, California.
[137] Roberts Vaux to Thomas Clarkson, 1 May 1820, Roberts Vaux Papers, Box 5, Folder 10.
[138] Griggs and Prator, *Henry Christophe and Thomas Clarkson*, pp. 73–6; Fanning, 'Haiti and the US', pp. 46–7.
[139] Griggs and Prator, *Henry Christophe and Thomas Clarkson*, p. 78.
[140] Fanning, 'Haiti and the US', especially Chapter 5 and Appendix; Miller, *The Search for a Black Nationality*, pp. 74–82.

During the first two decades of the nineteenth century, therefore, activists on both sides of the Atlantic found common cause in 'colonisation' and the associated idea of a black nationality, whether in Africa, the USA or the Caribbean. British abolitionists seem to have been particularly excited by the potential of these projects. As we have seen, men such as Clarkson and Allen were part of extensive networks that spanned the Atlantic world, from Britain to Africa, from Africa to America and from America to the Caribbean. In an important sense, these were again communication networks, but, at the same time, they involved the movement of people, goods and money. Crucially, they also involved the participation of blacks. If Paul Cuffe relied heavily on whites for assistance, he nevertheless was responsible for promoting a new vision of the (black) Atlantic, one based on a triangular trade that linked Britain, Africa and America and that, to a large extent, was run by and for the benefit of blacks. Prince Saunders, too, was a transatlantic traveller who moved easily between Britain, Haiti and America, helping to build important links between black communities on both sides of the Atlantic. What we are dealing with here, in other words, is a series of overlapping networks that revolved around a number of key individuals, black and white: Clarkson, Allen, Cuffe and Saunders.

This web of associations was at its height between 1810 and 1820. These were the years that witnessed the emergence of friendly societies in Africa, African Institutions in the USA and the realisation of Cuffe's plans for the regeneration of Africa. Once again, however, there proved to be limits to this particular brand of internationalism, some of them internal (black opposition to colonisation, for example), others external. Cuffe's death in 1817, ongoing problems in Sierra Leone and the 1820 crisis in Haiti all contributed to a greater wariness about the practicability of colonisation projects, particularly when the results were so disappointing. Even enthusiasts such as William Allen grew disillusioned. For all his efforts to 'civilise' Africa, Allen was forced to admit in 1818 that it was impossible to induce black settlers in Sierra Leone 'to turn their attention to the raising of produce, as cotton &c', even though the benefits were obvious for all to see.[141] Perhaps the wider lesson was that these types of endeavour did not really work, if by that was meant furthering the cause of abolition. For over thirty years British activists had pursued the idea of a black nationality in Africa. By 1820, however, many of them were clearly beginning to question the wisdom of this strategy, just as they were

[141] (Anon.), *Life of William Allen*, vol. I, pp. 251–2.

beginning to question the efficacy of slave-trade suppression, at least as a means of ending colonial slavery. If they had not quite reached a dead end, the time was ripe for a fresh approach and one more suited to the demands of a new era.

Epilogue

By the early 1820s, European and American reformers had been struggling to suppress the international slave trade for over thirty years. During that time they had won some notable successes, among them the Abolition Acts of 1807, but, as the British discovered, enforcing this legislation proved costly and time-consuming. Neither had suppression done much to improve the treatment of enslaved Africans, which, of course, had been the expectation. On the contrary, information coming out of the Caribbean suggested that little had changed since 1807. Not only did much publicised and sometimes horrific abuses continue, but more damaging was the evidence that the rate of natural population increase in the West Indies was still relatively low, certainly when compared with the USA.[1] The failure of Sierra Leone as a free-labour experiment further compounded the sense – in Britain, at least – that suppression tactics had proved a blunt instrument, if by that was meant their success in putting pressure on colonial planters to reform the institution of slavery from within.

By 1823, if not before, British activists were already beginning to rethink their priorities. That year they organised the Anti-Slavery Society or, to give it its full title, the Society for the Mitigation and Gradual Abolition of Slavery Throughout the British Dominions. This emphasis was important. As Howard Temperley stresses, the new society 'did not demand the immediate overthrow of slavery, merely the adoption of measures to protect slaves from wanton mistreatment, together with a plan for gradual emancipation leading ultimately to complete freedom'.[2] In other words, British activists set themselves modest aims. Theirs was essentially a pragmatic approach, designed to appeal to a broad section of the British public. Coincidentally, French activists were moving in the same direction. Despite its early preoccupation with the slave trade, by 1823 the slave-trade committee of the

[1] Howard Temperley, *British Antislavery, 1833–70* (London: Longman, 1972), p. 9.
[2] Temperley, *British Antislavery*, pp. 9–10.

Société de la Morale Chrétienne was already stressing the importance of amelioration in the French colonies, espousing a gradual process that would 'achieve slave liberation without upheaval'.[3] Like their British counterparts, the members of the committee favoured 'salutary regulations to improve the conditions of blacks'.[4] Here again, the approach was pragmatic, even to the extent of recognising the rights of colonial planters.

By the early 1820s, therefore, British and French activists had moved closer to their American counterparts. Yet, at the same time, American abolitionism was also undergoing a transformation. Since the 1780s, 'gradualism' had become an American orthodoxy. Conservative in outlook, groups such as the PAS and the NYMS proceeded cautiously, using legal devices to chip away at the institution of slavery. Up to a point, these tactics worked. As John Stauffer points out, they led to the abolition of slavery in the Northern states, the voluntary manumission of thousands of slaves (mainly in the South) and the end of the international slave trade.[5] Yet, as the colonisation debates of 1816–19 demonstrated, there were clear limits to how far American activists could push gradualism. The appearance of the ACS, in particular, signalled a subtle shift in American pro-slavery debates, as Southern slaveholders sought to tighten their grip on an institution they increasingly saw as a positive good.

What was at stake here became apparent in 1819 when American activists found themselves facing a new challenge in the shape of a proposed Bill to allow Missouri to enter the Union as a slave state. The emerging debate sharply divided political opinion, precipitating what became known as the 'Missouri Crisis'. Eventually, Henry Clay came up with a compromise whereby Missouri entered the USA as a slave state on the condition that the spread of slavery was prohibited north of the 36° 30′ parallel within the former Louisiana Purchase territory. In retrospect, it is easy to see that this fudge changed the terms of political debate in America. Some have gone so far as to suggest that 'after the Missouri Compromise, the basic agreement between the North and the South over the future of slavery became untenable'.[6] Certainly, the events of 1819–20 left activists pondering their future. As Southern

[3] Jennings, *French Anti-Slavery*, p. 14.
[4] Jennings, *French Anti-Slavery*, p. 15.
[5] Stauffer, 'Fighting the Devil with His Own Fire', p. 70.
[6] Stauffer, 'Fighting the Devil with His Own Fire', p. 72. For the Missouri Compromise, see Robert Pierce Forbes, *The Missouri Compromise and Its Aftermath: Slavery and the Meaning of America* (Chapel Hill, NC: University of North Carolina Press, 2007).

slaveholders started to talk expansively of 'an empire of slavery', appeals to gradualism began to seem hollow and, in truth, impractical.

During the 1820s, in other words, transatlantic abolitionism underwent a transformation – or, to be more precise, a series of transformations. Of course, there were important continuities. The British, for instance, would go on trying to suppress the slave trade on the eastern and western coasts of Africa until the 1880s and beyond.[7] Nevertheless, the anti-slavery politics of the 1820s and 1830s rested on a very different set of assumptions. They were also more uncompromising. Firebrands such as William Lloyd Garrison, whose newspaper the *Liberator* appeared in January 1831, demanded the immediate abolition of slavery, as did many black activists (among them James Forten and Robert Purvis), whose anti-colonisationist stance re-energised American anti-slavery debates, pushing them in more radical directions.[8] How this particular transformation came about lies outside the scope of the present study. Suffice it to say that by 1832 gradualism had given way to 'immediatism' – in Britain and the USA, at least – a development that significantly opened a new chapter in the history of transatlantic abolitionism.

---

[7] Robert Blyth, 'Britain, the Royal Navy and the Suppression of Slave Trades in the Nineteenth Century', in Douglas Hamilton and Robert J. Blyth, eds., *Representing Slavery: Art, Artefacts and Archives in the Collections of the National Maritime Museum* (Aldershot: Lund Humphries, 2007), pp. 76–91.

[8] For black activism, see especially Newman, *The Transformation of American Abolitionism*, Chapter 4; John Stauffer, *The Black Hearts of Men: Radical Abolitionists and the Transformation of Race* (Cambridge, Mass.; Harvard University Press, 2002); Manisha Sinha, 'Did Abolitionists Cause the Civil War?', in Andrew Delbanco, John Stauffer, Manisha Sinha, Darryl Pinckney and Wilfred M. McClay, *The Abolitionist Imagination* (Cambridge, Mass.: Harvard University Press, 2012), pp. 81–108, at pp. 88–90, 102.

Bibliography

PRIMARY SOURCES

ARCHIVES

Archives Nationales, Le Marais, Paris
Minutes ('Registre') of the Société des Amis des Noirs, 1788–91, microfilm.

Bodleian Library, Oxford
Wilberforce Papers.

British Library, London
Dropmore Papers, Add. MS 58978.
Minute books of the Society for Effecting the Abolition of the Slave Trade, 1787–1819, Add. MS 21254–6.

Friends House Library, London
Biographical files.

Haverford College, Haverford, Pennsylvania
Minutes of the New Jersey Society for the Abolition of Slavery, 1793–1809.
Robert Pleasants Letterbook, 1754–97.

Historical Society of Pennsylvania, Philadelphia
Dreer Collection.
Etting Collection.
Fisher Family Papers.
Pemberton Papers.
Pennsylvania Abolition Society Papers, microfilm edition, minutes and correspondence.
Roberts Vaux Papers.

Huntington Library, San Marino, California
Thomas Clarkson Papers.
Zachary Macaulay Papers.
Elizabeth Montagu Papers.
Robert Pleasants Papers.

254

La Bibliothèque de Port-Royal, Paris
Abbé (Henri) Grégoire Papers. These papers contain the loose minute books (really notes) of the Société des Amis des Noirs et des Colonies, 1796–9.

Lewis Walpole Library, Yale University, Farmington, New Haven, Connecticut
Prints and drawings.

Liverpool Record Office, Liverpool
William Roscoe Papers.

National Library of Wales, Aberystwyth
Benjamin Flower Papers.

New-York Historical Society, New York
New York Manumission Society Papers, Quarterly Committee Minutes, 1785–97.
New York Manumission Society Papers, Quarterly Committee Minutes, 1798–1814.
New York Manumission Society Papers, Standing Committee Minutes, 1791–1807.

New York Public Library
James Monroe Papers.

St John's College, Cambridge
Thomas Clarkson Papers.

Shropshire Record Office, Shrewsbury
Diaries of Katherine Plymley.

The National Archives, London
Colonial Office Records, CO267/41.
Foreign Office Records, FO5/102.

Whitworth Art Gallery, Manchester
'Le Traite des Nègres', T.2003.54.

William R. Perkins Library, Duke University, North Carolina
William Smith Papers.
William Wilberforce Papers.

NEWSPAPERS AND PERIODICALS

Bury and Norwich Post
Cambridge Intelligencer
Flower's Political Review and Monthly Register

Freeman's Journal
Friends' Miscellany
Gentleman's Magazine
L'Ambigu
Le Patriote Français
Leeds Mercury
Lloyd's Evening Post
Morning Chronicle
Morning Post
New-Haven Gazette, and the Connecticut Magazine
(New York) *Independent Journal*
New York Review of Books
Pennsylvania Gazette
Pennsylvania Mercury and Universal Advertiser
Pennsylvania Packet
Pennsylvania Packet, and Daily Advertiser
Providence Gazette and Country Journal
The London Chronicle
The Philanthropist; or, Repository for Hints and Suggestions Calculated to Promote the Comfort and Happiness of Man
Trewman's Exeter Flying Post

BOOKS AND PAMPHLETS PRINTED BEFORE 1900

Alexander, Archibald, *The History of Colonization on the Western Coast of Africa*, 2nd edn (Philadelphia, Pa.: W. S. Martien, 1849).

(Anon.), *Life of William Allen, with Selections from His Correspondence*, 2 vols. (Philadelphia, Pa.: Henry Longstreth, 1847).

Brissot de Warville, Jacques-Pierre, *A Discourse, Upon the Necessity of Establishing at Paris, a Society to Co-operate with Those of America and London, Towards the Abolition of the Trade and Slavery of the Negroes. Delivered the 19th of February 1788, in a Society of a Few Friends, Assembled at Paris, at the Request of the Committee of London* (Philadelphia, Pa.: Francis Bailey, 1788).

New Travels in the United States of America, 1788, ed. Durand Echeverria (Cambridge, Mass.: The Belknap Press of Harvard University, 1964).

(Broglie, Achille-Léonce-Victor-Charles, 3rd duc de), *Cruautés de la traite des noirs; ou relation des horreurs commises sur les nègres à bord des vaisseaux le Rôdeur et l'Estelle extraite du discours de M. le Duc de Broglie, prononcé à la Chambre des Pairs le 28 mars 1822* (Paris: Henri Servier, 1822).

Brougham, Henry, *A Concise Statement of the Question Regarding the Abolition of the Slave Trade* (London: J. Hatchard, 1804).

Clark, James, *A Treatise on Yellow Fever, As It Appeared in the Island of Dominica, 1793–6* (London: J. Murray & S. Highley, 1797).

Clarkson, Thomas, *Essai sur les désavantages politiques de la traite des nègres. Traduit de l'anglais sur la dernière edition qui a paru à Londres en 1789* (Paris: Adfrien Egron, 1814).

Essay on the Comparative Efficiency of Regulation or Abolition, As Applied to the Slave Trade (London: James Phillips, 1789).

The History of the Rise, Progress, and Accomplishment of the Abolition of the African Slave-Trade by the British Parliament, 2 vols. (London: Longman, Hurst, Rees & Orme, 1808).

Résumé du témoignage donné devant un comité de la Chambre des Communes de la Grand Bretagne et de l'Irlande, touchant la traite des nègres: adresse dans cette crise particulière aux différentes puissances de la chrétienté (London: Richard & D'Artus Taylor, 1814).

Three Letters (One of Which Has Appeared Before) to the Planters and Slave-Merchants, Principally on the Subject of Compensation (London: Phillips & Farndon, 1807).

(Clarkson, Thomas), *Le cri des africains contre les européens, leurs oppresseurs, ou coup d'oeil sur le commerce homicide appèlé traite de noirs* (Paris: De L. T. Cellot, 1822).

An Inquiry into the Causes of the Insurrection of Negroes in the Island of St Domingo. To Which Are Added, Observations of M. Garron-Coulon on the Same Subject (London: J. Johnson, 1792).

Cobb, James, *Paul and Virginia: A Musical Drama in Two Acts* (Dublin, 1801).

Paul and Virginia: A Musical Entertainment in Two Acts (New York: D. Longworth, 1806).

Coleridge, Henry Nelson, *Six Months in the West Indies in 1825* (London: John Murray, 1826).

Condorcet, Marie Jean Antoine Nicolas de Caritat, marquis de, *Réflexions sur l'esclavage des nègres* (Neuchâtel: Chez la Société Typographique, 1781).

Cugoano, Quobna Ottobah, *Thoughts and Sentiments on the Evil of Slavery*, ed. Vincent Carretta (1787; rpt. London: Penguin Books, 1999).

Doin, Sophie, *La famille noir* (Paris: Henry Servier, 1825).

Dunlap, William, *A History of the American Theatre from Its Origins to 1832* (1832; rpt. Urbana, Ill.: University of Illinois Press, 2005).

Duras, Claire de, *Ourika* (Paris: Chez Ladvocat, 1823).

Edwards, Bryan, *An Historical Survey of the Island of Saint Domingo, Together with an Account of the Maroon Negroes in the Island of Jamaica; and a History of the War in the West Indies, in 1793 and 1794* (London: John Stockdale, 1801).

Flower, Benjamin, *National Sins Considered, in Two Letters to the Rev. Thomas Robinson, Vicar of St Mary's, Leicester, on His Serious Exhortation to the Inhabitants of Great Britain, with Reference to the Fast* (Cambridge, 1796).

The Proceedings of the House of Lords in the Case of Benjamin Flower, Printer of the Cambridge Intelligencer, for a Supposed Libel on the Bishop of Llandaff (Cambridge: Printed by and for B. Flower, 1800).

Fox, William, *A Defence of the Decree of the National Convention of France, for Emancipating the Slaves in the West Indies* (London, 1794).

Frossard, Benjamin, *La cause des esclaves nègres et des habitants de la Guinée, portée au tribunal de la justice, de la religion, de la politique*, 2 vols. (Lyon, 1789).

Gillespie, Leonard, *Advice to the Commanders and Officers of His Majesty's Fleet Serving in the West Indies, on the Preservation of the Health of Seamen* (London: J. Cutrell, 1798).

Gilpin, Thomas, *Exiles in Virginia; with Observations on the Conduct of the Society of Friends During the Revolutionary War, Comprising the Official Papers of the Government Relating to That Period, 1777–1778* (Philadelphia, Pa.: Published for the Subscribers, 1848).

Giudicelli, Abbé Juge, *Observations sur la traite des noirs, en réponse au rapport de M. Courvoisier sur la pétition de M. Morénas* (Paris: Les Marchands de Nouveautés, 1820).

Grégoire, Henri, *Lettre aux citoyens de couleur et nègres libres de Saint-Domingue, et des autres isles françoises de l'Amérique. Par M. Grégoire, député à l'Assemblée Nationale, evêque du Département de Loir et Cher* (Paris: De L'Imprimerie du Patriote Français, 1791).

Des peines infamantes à infliger aux négriers (Paris: Baudion Frères, 1822).

De la traite et de l'esclavage des noirs et des blancs: par un ami des hommes de toutes les couleurs (Paris: Adfrien Egron, 1815).

Henderson, Stewart, *A Letter to the Officers of the Army under Orders for, or That May Hereafter Be Sent, to the West Indies, on the Means of Preserving Health, and Preventing That Fatal Disease the Yellow Fever* (London: John Stockdale, 1795).

Jones, Absalom and Allen, Richard, *A Narrative of the Proceedings of the Black People, During the Late Awful Calamity in Philadelphia, in the Year 1793: and a Refutation of Some Censures Thrown Upon Them in Some Late Publications* (Philadelphia, Pa.: William W. Woodward, 1794).

A Thanksgiving Sermon, Preached January 1, 1808, in St Thomas', or the African Episcopal Church, Philadelphia: On Account of the Abolition of the Slave Trade on That Day, by the Congress of the United States (Philadelphia, Pa.: Fry & Kammerer, 1808).

Lemprière, William, *Practical Observations on the Diseases of the Army in Jamaica* (London: Longmans, 1799).

McKinnen, Daniel, *A Tour through the British West Indies, in the Years 1802 and 1803, Giving a Particular Account of the Bahama Islands* (London: J. White, 1804).

Macaulay, Zachary, *The Horrors of Negro Slavery Existing in Our West India Islands, Irrefragably Demonstrated from Official Documents Recently Presented to the House of Commons* (London: J. Hatchard, 1805).

Murdock, John, *The Beau Metamorphized; or, The Generous Maid* (Philadelphia, Pa.: Printed by Joseph C. Charles for the Author, 1800).

The Politicians; or, A State of Things (Philadelphia, Pa: Printed for the Author, 1798).

The Triumphs of Love; or, Happy Reconciliation. A Comedy in Four Acts. Written by an American and a Citizen of Philadelphia. Acted at the New Theatre, Philadelphia (Philadelphia, Pa.: R. Fowell, 1795).

Parrott, Russell, *An Oration on the Abolition of the Slave Trade: Delivered on the First of January, 1812, at the African Church of St Thomas* (Philadelphia, Pa.: James Maxwell, 1812).

Pinckard, George, *Notes on the West Indies, Written During the Expedition under the Command of the Late General Sir R. Abercrombie, Including Observations on the Island of Barbadoes, and the Settlements Captured by the British Troops, Upon the Coast of Guiana; Likewise Remarks Relating to the Creoles and Slaves of the Western Colonies, and the Indians of South America; with Occasional Hints, Regarding the Seasoning or Yellow Fever of Hot Climates*, 3 vols. (London: Longman, Hurst, Rees & Orme, 1806).

Raimond, Julien, *Observations adressée a l'Assemblée Nationale par un député des colons américains* (Paris, 1789).

Observations sur l'origine et les progrès du préjugé des colons blancs contres les hommes de couleur (Paris: Belin, Desenne & Bailly, 1791).

Roscoe, William, *General View of the African Slave-Trade, Demonstrating Its Injustice and Impolicy: With Hints Towards a Bill for Its Abolition* (London: R. Faulder, 1788).

Rowson, Susannah, *Slaves in Algiers; or, A Struggle for Freedom: A Play Interspersed with Songs, in Three Acts. As Performed at the New Theatres, in Philadelphia and Baltimore* (Philadelphia, Pa.: Printed for the Author by Wrigley and Berriman, 1794).

Sharp, Granville, *The Law of Retribution; or, A Serious Warning to Great Britain and Her Colonies, Founded on Unquestionable Examples of God's Temporal Vengeance Against Tyrants, Slaveholders, and Oppressors* (London: B. White & E. and C. Dilly, 1776).

Simonde de Sismondi, J. C. L., *De l'intérêt de la France à l'égard de la traite des nègres* (Geneva: J. J. Paschoud, 1814).

(Société des Amis des Noirs), *Adresse à l'Assemblée Nationale pour l'abolition de la traite des noirs par la Société des Amis des Noirs de Paris* (Paris: L. Poitier de Lille, 1790).

Règlement de la Société des Amis des Noirs (Paris, 1788).

Seconde adresse à l'Assemblée Nationale, par la Société des Amis des Noirs, établie à Paris (Paris: De l'Imprimerie du Patriote Français, 1790).

Staël, Madame de, *Oeuvres complètes*, 17 vols. (Paris: Treuttel & Wurtz, 1820–1).

Stephen, George, *Antislavery Recollections: In a Series of Letters Addressed to Mrs Beecher Stowe* (1854; rpt. London: Frank Cass, 1971).

Stephen, James, *The Crisis of the Sugar Colonies; or, An Enquiry into the Objects and Probable Effects of the French Expedition to the West Indies; and Their Connection with the Colonial Interests of the British People. To Which Are Subjoined, Sketches of a Plan for Settling the Vacant Lands of Trinidada* (London: J. Hatchard, 1802).

The Danger of the Country; by the Author of War in Disguise (London: J. Butterworth & J. Hatchard, 1807).

The Opportunity; or, Reasons for an Immediate Alliance with St Domingo (London: J. Hatchard, 1804).

Trollope, Anthony, *The West Indies and the Spanish Main* (1860; rpt. New York: Carroll & Graf, 1999).

Wilberforce, William, *A Letter on the Abolition of the Slave Trade, Addressed to the Freeholders and Other Inhabitants of Yorkshire* (London: T. Cadell & J. Hatchard, 1807).

A Letter to His Excellency the Prince of Talleyrand Périgord, etc., on the Subject of the Slave Trade (London: Printed for J. Hatchard, Piccadilly; and Cadell & Davies, 1814).

A Practical View of the Religious System of Professed Christians Contrasted with Real Christianity (London: T. Cadell & W. Davies, 1797).

(Wilberforce, William), *Lettre à l'Empereur Alexandre sur la traite des noirs* (London: G. Schulze, 1822).

Résumé du discours prononcé par M. Wilberforce dans la Chambre des Communes, le 27 Fuin 1822, sur l'état actuel de la traite des nègres (London: G. Schulze, 1822).

Wilberforce, Robert I. and Wilberforce, Samuel, *The Life of William Wilberforce,* 5 vols. (London: John Murray, 1838).

eds., *The Correspondence of William Wilberforce,* 2 vols. (London: John Murray, 1840).

Williams, Peter, *An Oration on the Abolition of the Slave Trade: Delivered in the African Church, in the City of New York, January 1, 1808* (New York, 1808).

OFFICIAL PUBLICATIONS

(African Institution), *Reports of the Directors of the African Institution,* 1807–21 (London: J. Hatchard, 1807–21).

(American Convention), *Minutes of the Proceedings of a Convention of Delegates from the Abolition Societies Established in Different Parts of the United States, Assembled at Philadelphia, on the First Day of January, One Thousand Seven Hundred and Ninety-Four, and Continued, by Adjournments, Until the Seventh Day of the Same Month, Inclusive* (Philadelphia, Pa., Zachariah Poulson, Junior, 1794).

Minutes of the Proceedings of the Second Convention of Delegates from the Abolition Societies Established in Different Parts of the United States, Assembled at Philadelphia, on the Seventh Day of January, One Thousand Seven Hundred and Ninety-Five, and Continued, by Adjournments, until the Fourteenth Day of the Same Month, Inclusive (Philadelphia, Pa., Zachariah Poulson, Junior, 1795).

Minutes of the Proceedings of the Third Convention of Delegates from the Abolition Societies Established in Different Parts of the United States, Assembled at Philadelphia, on the First Day of January, One Thousand Seven Hundred and Ninety-Six, and Continued, by Adjournments, Until the Seventh Day of the Same Month, Inclusive (Philadelphia, Pa., Zachariah Poulson, Junior, 1796).

Minutes of the Proceedings of the Fourth Convention of Delegates from the Abolition Societies Established in Different Parts of the United States, Assembled at Philadelphia, on the Third Day of May, One Thousand Seven Hundred and Ninety-Seven, and Continued, by Adjournments, Until the Ninth Day of the Same Month, Inclusive (Philadelphia, Pa., Zachariah Poulson, Junior, 1797).

Minutes of the Proceedings of the Fifth Convention of Delegates from the Abolition Societies Established Different Parts of the United States, Assembled at Philadelphia, on the First Day of June, One Thousand Seven Hundred and Ninety-Eight, and Continued, by Adjournments, Until the Sixth Day of the Same Month, Inclusive (Philadelphia, Pa., Zachariah Poulson, Junior, 1798).

Minutes of the Proceedings of the Sixth Convention of Delegates from the Abolition Societies Established in Different Parts of the United States, Assembled at Philadelphia, on the Fourth Day of June, One Thousand Eight Hundred, and

Continued, by Adjournments, Until the Sixth Day of the Same Month, Inclusive (Philadelphia, Pa., Zachariah Poulson, Junior, 1800).

Minutes of the Proceedings of the Seventh Convention of Delegates from the Abolition Societies Established in Different Parts of the United States, Assembled at Philadelphia, on the Third Day of June, One Thousand Eight Hundred and One, and Continued, by Adjournments, Until the Sixth Day of the Same Month, Inclusive (Philadelphia, Pa., Zachariah Poulson, Junior, 1801).

Minutes of the Proceedings of the Eighth Convention of Delegates from the Abolition Societies Established in Different Parts of the United States, Assembled at Philadelphia, on the Tenth Day of January, One Thousand Eight Hundred and Three, and Continued, by Adjournments, Until the Fourteenth Day of the Same Month, Inclusive (Philadelphia, Pa., Zachariah Poulson, Junior, 1803).

Minutes of the Proceedings of the Ninth American Convention for Promoting the Abolition of Slavery and Improving the Condition of the African Race: Assembled at Philadelphia, on the Ninth Day of January, One Thousand Eight Hundred and Four, and Continued, by Adjournments, Until the Thirteenth Day of the Same Month, Inclusive (Philadelphia, Pa., Solomon W. Conrad, 1804).

Minutes of the Proceedings of the Tenth American Convention for Promoting the Abolition of Slavery, and Improving the Condition of the African Race: Assembled at Philadelphia, on the Fourteenth Day of January, One Thousand Eight Hundred and Five, and Continued, by Adjournments, Until the Seventeenth Day of the Same Month, Inclusive (Philadelphia, Pa., Kimber, Conrad & Co, 1805).

Minutes of the Proceedings of the Eleventh American Convention for Promoting the Abolition of Slavery, and Improving the Condition of the African Race: Assembled at Philadelphia, on the Thirteenth Day of January, One Thousand Eight Hundred and Six, and Continued, by Adjournments, Until the Fifteenth Day of the Same Month, Inclusive (Philadelphia, Pa., Kimber, Conrad & Co., 1806).

Minutes of the Proceedings of the Twelfth American Convention for Promoting the Abolition of Slavery, and Improving the Condition of the African Race: Assembled at Philadelphia, on the Ninth Day of January, One Thousand Eight Hundred and Nine, and Continued, by Adjournments, Until the Twelfth Day of the Same Month, Inclusive (Philadelphia, Pa., J. Bouvier, 1809).

Minutes of the Proceedings of the Thirteenth American Convention for Promoting the Abolition of Slavery, and Improving the Condition of the African Race: Assembled at Philadelphia, on the Thirteenth Day of January, One Thousand Eight Hundred and Twelve, and Continued, by Adjournments, Until the Sixteenth Day of the Same Month, Inclusive (Philadelphia, Pa., Hamilton-Ville, 1812).

Minutes of the Proceedings of the Fourteenth American Convention for Promoting the Abolition of Slavery, and Improving the Condition of the African Race: Assembled at Philadelphia, on the Ninth Day of January, 1815, on the Eighth Day of January, 1816, and Continued, by Adjournments, Until the Twelfth Day of the Same Month, Inclusive (Philadelphia, Pa., W. Brown, 1816).

Minutes of the Fifteenth American Convention for Promoting the Abolition of Slavery, and Improving the Condition of the African Race: Assembled at Philadelphia, on the Fifth Day of August 1817, and Continued, by Adjournments, Until the Eighth of the Same Month, Inclusive (Philadelphia, Pa., Merritt, 1817).

Minutes of the Proceedings of a Special Meeting of the Fifteenth American Convention for Promoting the Abolition of Slavery, and Improving the Condition of the African Race: Assembled at Philadelphia, on the Tenth Day of December 1818, and Continued, by Adjournments, Until the Fifteenth of the Same Month, Inclusive (Philadelphia, Pa., Hall & Atkinson, 1818).

Minutes of the Sixteenth American Convention for Promoting the Abolition of Slavery, and Improving the Condition of the African Race. Held at Philadelphia, on the Fifth of October and the Tenth of November, 1819 (Philadelphia, Pa., William Fry, 1819).

Minutes of the Seventeenth Session of the American Convention for Promoting the Abolition of slavery, and Improving the Condition of the African Race. Convened at Philadelphia, on the Third Day of October, 1821 (Philadelphia, Pa., 1821).

American State Papers, Miscellaneous

Cobbett's Parliamentary History

History of Congress

Journals of the House of Commons

Journals of the House of Lords

Memorials Presented to the Congress of the United States of America by the Different Societies Instituted for Promoting the Abolition of Slavery, Etc. in the States of Rhode-Island, Connecticut, New-York, Pennsylvania, Maryland, and Virginia. Published by Order of the 'Pennsylvania Society for Promoting the Abolition of Slavery, and the Relief of Free Negroes Unlawfully Held in Bondage, and for Improving the Condition of the African Race' (Philadelphia, Pa.: Francis Bailey, 1792).

Parliamentary Debates

Philadelphia City Directory

United States Statutes at Large

SECONDARY SOURCES

BOOKS AND ARTICLES

Alexander, David, *Richard Newton and English Caricature in the 1790s* (Manchester University Press, 1998).

Anstey, Roger, *The Atlantic Slave Trade and British Abolition, 1760–1810* (London: Macmillan, 1975).

'A Re-interpretation of the Abolition of the Slave Trade, 1806–1807', *English Historical Review*, 87 (April 1972): 304–32.

Aptheker, Herbert, *A Documentary History of the Negro People in the United States*, 2 vols. (New York: The Citadel Press, 1969).

Armitage, David, 'Three Concepts of Atlantic History', in David Armitage and Michael J. Braddick, eds., *The British Atlantic World, 1500–1800* (Basingstoke: Palgrave Macmillan, 2002), pp. 11–27.

Bailyn, Bernard, *Atlantic History: Concept and Contours* (Cambridge, Mass.: Harvard University Press, 2005).

Bailyn, Bernard and Denault, Patricia L., eds., *Soundings in Atlantic History: Latent Structures and Intellectual Currents, 1500–1830* (Cambridge, Mass.: Harvard University Press, 2009).

Barker, Hannah, *Newspapers, Politics and Public Opinion in Late Eighteenth-Century England* (Oxford: Clarendon Press, 1998).

Barrell, John, 'Radicalism, Visual Culture, and Spectacle in the 1790s', *Romanticism on the Net*, 46 (May 2007), available online at www.erudit. org/revue/ron/2007/v/n46/01613ar.html (accessed 16 August 2011).

Barringer, Tim, Forrester, Gillian, and Martínez-Ruíz, Barbara, *Art and Emancipation in Jamaica: Isaac Belisario and His Worlds* (London and New Haven, Conn.: Yale Center for British Art in association with Yale University Press, 2007).

Batten, Jnr., Charles L., *Pleasurable Instruction: Form and Convention in Eighteenth-Century Travel Literature* (Los Angeles: University of California Press, 1978).

Belanger, Claude, Godechot, Jacques, Guiral, Pierre, and Terrou, Fernand, eds., *Histoire générale de la presse français*, 5 vols. (Paris: Presses Universitaires de France, 1969–76).

Berlin, Ira, *Slaves Without Masters: The Free Negro in the Antebellum South* (Oxford University Press, 1974).

Best, G. F. A., 'The Evangelicals and the Established Church in the Early Nineteenth Century', *Journal of Theological Studies*, new series, 10 (April 1959): 68–78.

Blackburn, Robin, *The American Crucible: Slavery, Emancipation and Human Rights* (London: Verso, 2011).

The Overthrow of Colonial Slavery, 1776–1848 (London: Verso, 1987).

Blyth, Robert, 'Britain, the Royal Navy and the Suppression of Slave Trades in the Nineteenth Century', in Douglas Hamilton and Robert J. Blyth, eds., *Representing Slavery: Art, Artefacts and Archives in the Collections of the National Maritime Museum* (Aldershot: Lund Humphries, 2007), pp. 76–91.

Bolster, W. Jeffrey, *Black Jacks: African American Seamen in the Age of Sail* (Cambridge, Mass.: Harvard University Press, 1997).

Braidwood, Stephen J., *Black Poor and White Philanthropists: London's Blacks and the Foundation of the Sierra Leone Settlement, 1786–1791* (Liverpool University Press, 1994).

(British Museum), *Catalogue of Political and Personal Satires Preserved in the Department of Prints and Drawings in the British Museum*, 11 vols. (London: Trustees of the British Museum, 1870–1954).

Brown, Christopher Leslie, 'Empire without America: British Plans for Africa in the Era of the American Revolution', in Derek R. Peterson, ed., *Abolitionism and Imperialism in Britain, Africa, and the Atlantic* (Athens, OH: Ohio University Press, 2010), pp. 84–100.

Moral Capital: Foundations of British Abolitionism (Chapel Hill, NC: University of North Carolina Press, 2006).

Brown, Ford K., *Fathers of the Victorians: The Age of Wilberforce* (Cambridge University Press, 1961).

Buckley, Roger N., 'The Frontier in the Jamaican Caricatures of Abraham James', *Yale University Library Gazette*, 58 (April 1984): 152–62.

Burnard, Trevor, 'Powerless Masters: The Curious Decline of the Jamaican Sugar Planters in the Foundational Period of British Abolitionism', *Slavery and Abolition*, 32 (June 2011): 185–98.

Burrows, Simon, 'The Cosmopolitan Press, 1760–1815', in Hannah Barker and Simon Burrows, eds., *Press, Politics and the Public Sphere in Europe and North America, 1760–1820* (Cambridge University Press, 2002), pp. 23–47.

Burton, Antoinette, *Empire in Question: Reading, Writing, and Teaching British Imperialism* (Durham, NC: Duke University Press, 2011).

Calvert, Monte A., 'The Abolition Society of Delaware, 1801–1807', *Delaware History*, 10 (4) (1963): 295–320.

Cannon, John, *Parliamentary Reform, 1640–1832* (Cambridge University Press, 1973).

Canny, Nicholas P., 'Atlantic History: What and Why?' *European Review*, 9 (4) (October 2001): 399–411.

'Writing Atlantic History; or, Reconfiguring the History of Colonial British America', *Journal of American History*, 86 (3) (1999): 1093–114.

(Clarkson, Thomas), *Interviews with the Emperor Alexander I of Russia at Paris and Aix-la-Chapelle in 1815 and 1818* (London: Slavery and Native Races Committee of the Society of Friends, 1930).

Cranfield, G. A., *The Development of the Provincial Newspaper, 1700–1760* (Oxford University Press, 1962).

Darnton, Robert, 'An Early Information Society: News and Media in Eighteenth-Century Paris', *American Historical Review*, 105 (February 2000): 1–35.

The Forbidden Best-Sellers of Pre-Revolutionary France (New York and London: W. W. Norton, 1995).

Daughan, George C., *1812: The Navy's War* (New York: Basic Books, 2012).

Davis, David Brion, *Inhuman Bondage: The Rise and Fall of Slavery in the New World* (Oxford University Press, 2006).

The Problem of Slavery in the Age of Revolution, 1770–1823 (Ithaca, NY: Cornell University Press, 1975).

The Problem of Slavery in Western Culture (London: Penguin Books, 1970).

Degenne, Alain and Forse, Michel, *Introducing Social Networks*, trans. Arthur Borges (London: Sage Publications, 1999).

Delbanco, Andrew, 'The Abolitionist Imagination', in Andrew Delbanco, John Stauffer, Manisha Sinha, Darryl Pinckney and Wilfred M. McClay, *The Abolitionist Imagination* (Cambridge, Mass.: Harvard University Press, 2012), pp. 1–55.

Delbanco, Andrew, Stauffer, John, Sinha, Manisha, Pinckney, Darryl, and McClay, Wilfred M., *The Abolitionist Imagination* (Cambridge, Mass.: Harvard University Press, 2012).

Ditz, Toby L., 'Formative Ventures: Eighteenth-Century Commercial Letters and the Articulation of Experience', in Rebecca Earle, ed., *Epistolary Selves: Letters and Letter-Writers, 1600–1945* (Aldershot: Ashgate, 1999), pp. 59–78.

Dorigny, Marcel, and Gainot, Bernard, *La Société des Amis des Noirs, 1788–1799: Contribution a l'histoire de l'abolition de l'esclavage* (Paris: UNESCO, 1998).

Doyle, William, *The French Revolution: A Very Short Introduction* (Oxford University Press, 2001).

Drescher, Seymour, *Abolition: A History of Slavery and Antislavery* (Cambridge University Press, 2009).

Capitalism and Antislavery: British Mobilization in Comparative Perspective (London: Macmillan, 1986).

The Mighty Experiment: Free Labor versus Slavery in British Emancipation (Oxford University Press, 2002).

Du Bois, W. E. B., *The Suppression of the African Slave-Trade to the United States of America, 1638–1870* (1896; rpt. New York: Library of America, 1986).

Dubois, Laurent, *A Colony of Citizens: Revolution and Slave Emancipation in the French Caribbean, 1787–1804* (Chapel Hill, NC: University of North Carolina Press, 2004).

Dubois, Laurent, and Garrigus, John D., *Slave Revolutions in the Caribbean, 1789–1804: A Brief History with Documents* (New York: Palgrave Macmillan, 2006).

Dun, James Alexander, 'Philadelphia Not Philanthropolis: The Limits of Pennsylvanian Antislavery in the Era of the Haitian Revolution', *The Pennsylvania Magazine of History and Biography*, 145 (1) (2011): 73–102.

Echeverria, Durand, *Mirage in the West: A History of the French Image of American Society to 1815* (Princeton University Press, 1968).

Egerton, Douglas R., *Gabriel's Rebellion: The Virginia Slave Conspiracies of 1800–1802* (Chapel Hill, NC: University of North Carolina Press, 1993).

Ellery, Eloise, *Brissot de Warville: A Study in the History of the French Revolution* (Boston, Mass.: Houghton Mifflin, 1915).

Feather, John, 'Cross-Channel Currents: Historical Bibliography and l'*histoire du livre*', *The Library*, 6th series, 2 (March 1980): 1–15.

Feldman, David, 'The New Imperial History', *Journal of Victorian Culture*, 9 (2) (2004): 235–9.

Ferguson, Moira, *Subject to Others: British Women Writers and Colonial Slavery, 1670–1834* (London and New York: Routledge, 1992).

Fitzsimmons, Linda, and McDonald, Arthur W., *The Yorkshire Stage, 1766–1803* (London and Metuchen, NJ: The Scarecrow Press, 1989).

Fladeland, Betty, *Men and Brothers: Anglo-American Antislavery Cooperation* (Urbana, IL: University of Illinois Press, 1972).

Forbes, Robert Pierce, *The Missouri Compromise and Its Aftermath: Slavery and the Meaning of America* (Chapel Hill, NC: University of North Carolina Press, 2007).

Furstenberg, François, 'Atlantic Slavery, Atlantic Freedom: George Washington, Slavery, and Transatlantic Abolitionist Networks', *The William and Mary Quarterly*, 3rd series, 68 (April 2011): 247–86.

Garrigus, John D., *Before Haiti: Race and Citizenship in French Saint-Domingue* (Basingstoke: Palgrave Macmillan, 2006).

'The Free Colored Elite of Saint-Domingue: The Case of Julien Raimond, 1774–1801', available online at http://users.ju.edu/jgarrig (accessed 14 June 2011).

Geggus, David, 'British Opinion and the Emergence of Haiti, 1791–1805', in James Walvin, ed., *Slavery and British Society, 1776–1846* (London: Macmillan, 1982), pp. 123–49.

'The Cost of Pitt's Caribbean Campaigns, 1793–1798', *The Historical Journal*, 26 (September 1983): 699–706.

Slavery, War and Revolution: The British Occupation of Saint Domingue, 1793–1798 (Oxford: Clarendon Press, 1982).

ed., *The Impact of the Haitian Revolution in the Atlantic World* (Columbia, SC: University of South Carolina Press, 2001).

Gilje, Paul A., *Liberty on the Waterfront: American Maritime Culture in the Age of Revolution* (Philadelphia, Pa.: University of Pennsylvania Press, 2004).

Glaisyer, Natasha, 'Networking: Trade and Exchange in the Eighteenth-Century British Empire', *Historical Journal*, 47 (2) (2004): 451–76.

Goodden, Angelica, *Madame de Staël: The Dangerous Exile* (Oxford University Press, 2008).

Gough, Hugh, *The Newspaper Press in the French Revolution* (London and New York: Routledge, 1988).

Gould, Eliga H., 'Atlantic History and the Literary Turn', *Early American Literature*, 43 (1) (2008): 197–203.

Graham, Jenny, 'Revolutionary in Exile: The Emigration of Joseph Priestley to America, 1794–1804', *Transactions of the American Philosophical Society*, 85 (2) (1995): 1–213.

Green, James, 'The Publishing History of Olaudah Equiano's *Interesting Narrative*', *Slavery and Abolition*, 16 (3) (1995): 362–75.

Green, William A., *British Slave Emancipation: The Sugar Colonies and the Great Experiment, 1830–1865* (Oxford University Press, 1991). First published 1976.

Greene, Jack D. and Morgan, Philip D., eds., *Atlantic History: A Critical Appraisal* (Oxford University Press, 2009).

Griggs, Earl Leslie, and Prator, Clifford H., eds., *Henry Christophe and Thomas Clarkson: A Correspondence* (Berkeley: University of California Press, 1952).

Hall, Catherine, *Civilising Subjects: Metropole and Colony in the English Imagination, 1830–1867* (Cambridge: Polity Press, 2002).

Hall, Catherine, and Rose, Sonya, eds., *At Home with the Empire: Metropolitan Culture and the Imperial World* (Cambridge University Press, 2006).

Hamilton, Douglas, 'Local Connections, Global Ambitions: Creating a Transoceanic Network in the Eighteenth-Century British Atlantic Empire', *International Journal of Maritime History*, 23 (2) (December 2011): 1–17.

Hamilton, Douglas, and Blyth, Robert J., eds., *Representing Slavery: Art, Artefacts and Archives in the Collections of the National Maritime Museum* (Aldershot: Lund Humphries, 2007).

Hamilton, Keith, and Salmon, Patrick, eds., *Slavery, Diplomacy and Empire: Britain and the Suppression of the Slave Trade, 1807–1975* (Eastbourne: Sussex Academic Press, 2009).

Hancock, David, *Citizens of the World: London Merchants and the Integration of the British Atlantic Community, 1735–1785* (Cambridge University Press, 1995).

Hawke, David Freeman, *Benjamin Rush: Revolutionary Gadfly* (Indianapolis, Ind.: Bobbs-Merrill, 1971).

Hill, Peter P., *French Perceptions of the Early American Republic, 1783–1793* (Philadelphia, Pa.: University of Pennsylvania Press, 1988).

Hind, R. J., 'Wilberforce and Perceptions of the British People', *Historical Research*, 60 (143) (1987): 321–35.

Hogan, Charles Beecher, *The London Stage, 1660–1800, Part 5: 1776–1800* (Carbondale, Ill.: Southern Illinois University Press, 1958).

Holland, Margaret Jean, Viscountess of Knutsford, *Life and Letters of Zachary Macaulay* (London: E. Arnold, 1900).

Holmes, Richard, *Coleridge: Early Visions* (London: Penguin Books, 1990).

Horton, James Oliver, and Horton, Lois E., *In Hope of Liberty: Culture, Community, and Protest Among Northern Free Blacks, 1700–1860* (Oxford University Press, 1997).

Huzzey, Richard, *Freedom Burning: Anti-Slavery and Empire in Victorian Britain* (Ithaca, New York: Cornell University Press, 2012).

James, C. L. R., *Black Jacobins: Toussaint L'Ouverture and the San Domingo Revolution* (1938; rpt. London: Virgin Publishing, 1991).

Jasanoff, Maya, *Liberty's Exiles: The Loss of America and the Remaking of the British Empire* (London: HarperCollins, 2011).

Jennings, Judith, *The Business of Abolishing the British Slave Trade, 1783–1807* (London and New York: Routledge, 1997).

Jennings, Lawrence C., *French Anti-Slavery: The Movement for the Abolition of Slavery in France, 1802–1848* (Cambridge University Press, 2000).

Kachun, Mitch, *Festivals of Freedom: Memory and Meaning in African American Emancipation Celebrations, 1808–1915* (Amherst, Mass.: University of Massachusetts Press, 2003).

Kadish, Doris Y., 'The Black Terror: Women's Responses to Slave Revolts in Haiti', *French Review*, 68 (4) (1995): 668–80.

Kaplan, Sidney, *The Black Presence in the Age of the American Revolution, 1770–1800* (Washington, DC: Smithsonian Institution Press, 1973).

Kielstra, Paul, *The Politics of Slave Trade Suppression in Britain and France, 1814–48: Diplomacy, Morality and Economics* (Basingstoke: Palgrave-Macmillan, 2000).

Kilduff, Martin, and Tsai, Wenpin, *Social Networks and Organizations* (London: Sage, 2006).

Knight, Frida, *The Strange Case of Thomas Walker* (London: Lawrence & Wishart, 1957).

Kutzinski, Vera M., 'Alexander von Humboldt's Transatlantic Personnae', *Atlantic Studies*, 7 (2) (2010): 100–12.

Laidlaw, Zoë, *Colonial Connections, 1815–45: Patronage, the Information Revolution and Colonial Government* (Manchester University Press, 2005).

Lewis, Simon, and Gleeson, David T., eds., *Ambiguous Legacy: The Bicentennial of the International Slave Trade Bans* (Columbia, SC: University of South Carolina Press, 2012).

Lipscomb, Patrick C., III, 'James Stephen', *Oxford Dictionary of National Biography*, available online at www.oxforddnb.com (accessed 30 April 2012).

Litwack, Leon F., *North of Slavery: The Negro in the Free States, 1790–1860* (University of Chicago Press, 1961).

Lloyd, Christopher, *The Navy and the Slave Trade: The Suppression of the African Slave Trade in the Nineteenth Century* (London: Longmans, Green & Co., 1949).

Lobban, Michael, 'Henry Brougham', *Oxford Dictionary of National Biography*, available online at www.oxforddnb.com (accessed 30 April 2012).

Lowther, Kevin G., *The African American Odyssey of John Kizell: A South Carolina Slave Returns to Fight the Slave Trade in His African Homeland* (Columbia, SC: University of South Carolina Press, 2011).

Lucas, Edith, *La littérature antiesclavagiste au dix-neuvième siècle* (Paris: Boccard, 1930).

Matthewson, Tim, 'Jefferson and Haiti', *Journal of Southern History*, 61 (May 1995): 209–48.

Mayer, Henry, *All On Fire: William Lloyd Garrison and the Abolition of Slavery* (New York: St Martin's Press, 1998).

Midgley, Clare, *Women Against Slavery: The British Campaigns, 1780–1870* (London and New York: Routledge, 1994).

Miller, Floyd J., *The Search for a Black Nationality: Black Colonization and Emigration, 1787–1863* (Urbana, Ill.: University of Illinois Press, 1975).

Montgomery, Benilde, 'White Captives, African Slaves: A Drama of Abolition', *Eighteenth-Century Studies*, 27 (summer 1994): 615–30.

Morgan, Kenneth, 'Proscription by Degrees: The Ending of the African Slave Trade to the United States', in David T. Gleeson and Simon Lewis, eds., *Ambiguous Legacy: The Bicentennial of the International Slave Trade Bans* (Columbia, SC: University of South Carolina Press, 2012), pp. 1–34.

Morgan, Philip D., 'Ending the Slave Trade: A Caribbean and Atlantic Context', in Derek R. Peterson, ed., *Abolitionism and Imperialism in Britain, Africa, and the Atlantic* (Athens, OH: Ohio University Press, 2010), pp. 101–28.

Murphy, Michael J., *Cambridge Newspapers and Opinion, 1780–1850* (Cambridge: The Oleander Press, 1977).

Nash, Gary B., *First City: Philadelphia and the Forging of Historical Memory* (Philadelphia, Pa.: University of Pennsylvania Press, 2006).

'Reverberations of Haiti in the American North: Black Saint Dominguans in Philadelphia', *Pennsylvania History*, 65 (5) (1998): 44–73.

Nash, Gary B., and Soderlund, Jean R., *Freedom by Degrees: Emancipation in Pennsylvania and Its Aftermath* (Oxford University Press, 1991).

Nathans, Heather S., *Early American Theatre from the Revolution to Thomas Jefferson: Into the Hands of the People* (Cambridge University Press, 2003).

Slavery and Sentiment on the American Stage, 1787–1861: Lifting the Veil of Black (Cambridge University Press, 2009).

Necheles, Ruth F., *The Abbé Grégoire, 1787–1831: The Odyssey of an Egalitarian* (Westport, Conn.: Greenwood, 1971).

New, Chester William, *The Life of Henry Brougham to 1830* (Oxford: Clarendon Press, 1961).

Newman, Richard S., *The Transformation of American Abolitionism: Fighting Slavery in the Early Republic* (Chapel Hill, NC: University of North Carolina Press, 2002).

Newman, Richard S., Rael, Patrick, and Lapansky, Philip, eds., *Pamphlets of Protest: An Anthology of Early African-American Protest Literature, 1790–1860* (London and New York: Routledge, 2001).

Newman, Simon P., *Parades and the Politics of the Street: Festive Culture in the Early American Republic* (Philadelphia, Pa.: University of Pennsylvania Press, 1997).

O'Shaughnessy, Andrew, *An Empire Divided: The American Revolution and the British Caribbean* (Philadelphia, Pa.: University of Pennsylvania Press, 2000).

Odell, George C. D., *Annals of the New York Stage*, 15 vols. (New York: Columbia University Press, 1927).

Oldfield, J. R., '2007 Revisited: Commemoration, Ritual and British Transatlantic Slavery', in David T. Gleeson and Simon Lewis, eds., *Ambiguous Legacy: The Bicentennial of the International Slave Trade Bans* (Columbia, SC: University of South Carolina Press, 2012), pp. 192–207.

'Chords of Freedom': Commemoration, Ritual and British Transatlantic Slavery (Manchester University Press, 2007).

Popular Politics and British Anti-Slavery: The Mobilisation of Public Opinion Against the Slave Trade, 1787–1807 (Manchester University Press, 1995).

Pasley, Jeffrey L., *'The Tyranny of Printers': Newspaper Politics in the Early American Republic* (Charlottesville, Va.: University of Virginia Press, 2001).

Peabody, Sue, *'There Are No Slaves in France': The Political Culture of Race and Slavery in the Ancien Régime* (Oxford University Press, 1996).

Pearsall, Sarah M. S., *Atlantic Families: Lives and Letters in the Later Eighteenth Century* (Oxford University Press, 2008).

Peterson, Derek R., ed., *Abolitionism and Imperialism in Britain, Africa, and the Atlantic* (Athens, OH: Ohio University Press, 2010).

Petley, Christer, 'Gluttony, Excess and the Fall of the Planter Class in the British Caribbean', *Atlantic Studies*, 9 (1) (2012): 85–106.

Pollock, John, *Wilberforce* (London: Lion Publishing, 1986). First published 1977.

Quinney, Valerie, 'Decisions on Slavery, the Slave Trade and Civil Rights for Negroes', *Journal of Negro History*, 55 (April 1970): 118–27.

Ragatz, Joseph Lowell, *The Fall of the Planter Class in the British Caribbean, 1763–1783* (New York: Century Co., 1928).

Rappleye, Charles, *Sons of Providence: The Brown Brothers, the Slave Trade and the American Revolution* (New York: Simon & Schuster, 2006).

Rebok, Sandra, 'Enlightened Correspondents: The Transatlantic Dialogue of Thomas Jefferson and Alexander von Humboldt', *The Virginia Magazine of History and Biography*, 116 (4) (2008): 328–69.

Resnick, Daniel P., 'The Société des Amis des Noirs and the Abolition of Slavery', *French Historical Studies*, 7 (4) (1972): 558–69.

Rodger, N. A. M., *The Command of the Ocean: A Naval History of Britain, 1649–1815* (London: Allen Lane, 2004).

Royle, Edward, *Revolutionary Britannia? Reflections on the Threat of Revolution in Britain, 1789–1848* (Manchester University Press, 2000).

Ryden, David Beck, *West Indian Slavery and British Abolition, 1783–1807* (Cambridge University Press, 2010).

Schama, Simon, *Rough Crossings: Britain, the Slaves and the American Revolution* (London: BBC Books, 2005).

Scrivener, Michael, *The Cosmopolitan Ideal in the Age of Revolution and Reaction, 1776–1832* (London: Pickering & Chatto, 2007).

Seeber, Edward Derbyshire, *Anti-Slavery Opinion in France during the Second Half of the Eighteenth Century* (New York: Burt Franklin, 1971). First published 1937.

Shaffer, Jason, *Performing Patriotism: National Identity in the Colonial and Revolutionary American Theater* (Philadelphia, Pa.: University of Pennsylvania Press, 2007).

Sidbury, James, *Ploughshares into Swords: Race, Rebellion, and Identity in Gabriel's Virginia, 1730–1810* (Cambridge University Press, 1997).

Sinha, Manisha, 'Did Abolitionists Cause the Civil War?', in Andrew Delbanco, John Stauffer, Manisha Sinha, Darryl Pinckney and Wilfred M. McClay, *The Abolitionist Imagination* (Cambridge, Mass.: Harvard University Press, 2012), pp. 81–108.

Staudenraus, Philip J., *The African Colonization Movement, 1816–1865* (New York: Columbia University Press, 1961).

Stauffer, John, *The Black Hearts of Men: Radical Abolitionists and the Transformation of Race* (Cambridge, Mass.: Harvard University Press, 2002).

'Fighting the Devil with His Own Fire', in Andrew Delbanco, John Stauffer, Manisha Sinha, Darryl Pinckney and Wilfred M. McClay, *The Abolitionist Imagination* (Cambridge, Mass.: Harvard University Press, 2012), pp. 57–79.

Steele, Ian K., *The English Atlantic, 1675–1740: An Exploration of Communication and Community* (Oxford University Press, 1986).

Stott, Anne, *Wilberforce: Family and Friends* (Oxford University Press, 2012).

Swaminathan, Srividhya, *Debating the Slave Trade: Rhetoric of British National Identity, 1759–1815* (Farnham: Ashgate, 2009).

Sydenham, M. J., *The Girondins* (London: The Athlone Press, 1961).

Tabili, L., 'Colony and Metropole: The New Imperial History', *The Historian*, 69 (1) (2007): 84–6.

Temperley, Howard, *British Antislavery, 1833–70* (London: Longman, 1972).

Thomas, Lamont D., *Rise to a People: A Biography of Paul Cuffe* (Urbana, IL: University of Illinois Press, 1986).

Thompson, E. P., *The Romantics: England in a Revolutionary Age* (The New York Press, 1997).

Walvin, James, Unwin, Melanie, and Farrell, Stephen, eds., *The British Slave Trade: Abolition, Parliament and People* (Edinburgh University Press, 2007).

Ward, J. R., *British West Indian Slavery, 1750–1834: The Process of Amelioration* (Oxford University Press, 1988).

Ward, William, *The Royal Navy and the Slavers: The Suppression of the Atlantic Slave Trade* (London: George Allen & Unwin, 1969).

Wasserman, Stanley and Faust, Katherine, *Social Network Analysis: Methods and Application* (Cambridge University Press, 1994).

White, Shane, *Stories of Freedom in Black New York* (Cambridge, Mass.: Harvard University Press, 2002).

Whitman, T. Stephen, *Challenging Slavery in the Chesapeake: Black and White Resistance to Human Bondage, 1775–1865* (Baltimore, Md.: Maryland Historical Society, 2007).

Whyte, Iain, *Zachary Macaulay: The Steadfast Scot in the British Anti-Slavery Movement* (Liverpool University Press, 2011).

Wiggins, Rosalind Cobb, *Captain Paul Cuffe's Logs and Letters, 1808–1817: A Black Quaker's 'Voice from Within the Veil'* (Washington, DC: Howard University Press, 1996).

Wilson, Ellen Gibson, *Thomas Clarkson: A Biography* (London and New York: Macmillan, 1990).

Wilson, Kathleen, ed., *A New Imperial History: Culture, Identity and Modernity in Britain and the Empire, 1660–1840* (Cambridge University Press, 2004).

Winch, Julie, *Philadelphia's Black Elite: Activism, Accommodation, and the Struggle for Autonomy, 1787–1848* (Philadelphia, Pa.: Temple University Press, 1988).

Wood, Gordon S., *Empire of Liberty: A History of the Early Republic, 1789–1815* (Oxford University Press, 2009).

Wood, Marcus, *Blind Memory: Visual Representations of Slavery in England and America, 1780–1865* (Manchester University Press, 2000).

'Packaging Liberty and Marketing the Gift of Freedom: 1807 and the Legacy of Clarkson's Chest', in James Walvin, Melanie Unwin and Stephen Farrell, eds., *The British Slave Trade: Abolition, Parliament and People* (Edinburgh University Press, 2007), pp. 203–23.

'Popular Graphic Images of Slavery and Emancipation in Nineteenth-Century England', in Douglas Hamilton and Robert J. Blyth, eds., *Representing Slavery: Art, Artefacts and Archives in the Collections of the National Maritime Museum* (Aldershot: Lund Humphries, 2007), pp. 136–51.

Zilvermit, Arthur, *The First Emancipation: The Abolition of Slavery in the North* (University of Chicago Press, 1967).

UNPUBLISHED THESES

Bliss, Jane, 'The Idea of Providence in Eighteenth-Century Abolitionist Discourse and Its Impact on the British Campaign to Abolish the Slave Trade', unpublished M.Res. thesis, University of Southampton, 2004.

Fanning, Sara Connors, 'Haiti and the US: African American Emigration and the Recognition Debate', unpublished Ph.D. dissertation, University of Texas at Austin, 2008.

Finlay, Cheryl, 'Committed to Memory: The Slave Ship Icon in the Black Atlantic Imagination', unpublished Ph.D. thesis, Yale University, 2002.

Scott, Julius Sherrard, III, 'The Common Wind: Currents of Afro-American Communication in the Era of the Haitian Revolution', unpublished Ph.D. thesis, Duke University, 1987.

WEB RESOURCES

Abolition Act of 1807 (USA), http://abolition.nypl.org/content/docs/text/Act_of_1807

American National Biography Online, www.anb.org

Biographical Directory of the United States Congress, http://bioguide.congress.gov

English Short-Title Catalogue, http://est.bl.uk

Minutes of the New Jersey Society for the Abolition of Slavery, http://triptych.brynmawr.edu/cdm4/document.php?CISOROOT=/HC_QuakSlav&CISOPTR=12257&CISOSHOW=12143

Oberg, Barbara B. and Looney, J. Jefferson, ed., *The Papers of Thomas Jefferson, Digital Edition,* http://rotunda.upress.virginia.edu/founders/TSJN-01-29-02-0273

Oxford Dictionary of National Biography, www.oxforddnb.com

Quakers and Slavery, http://trilogy.brynmawr.edu/speccoll/quakersandslavery/commentary/people

Robert Pleasants Letterbook, http://triptych.brynmawr.edu/cdm4/document.php?CISOROOT=/HC_QuakSlav&CISOPTR=11435&REC=10

Index

Page numbers with 'n' are notes; in italics are illustrations.

demise of, 117
and Dillwyn, 37
disbanded, 195
government hostility, 106–7
letter from 'Leicestrensis', 80
and Necker, 85
and PAS, 117
revival of, 169–77
and Saint-Domingue uprising, 94, 96–9
and Wedgwood, 59–60
and Wilberforce, 40
see also African Institution
Society for the Purpose of Encouraging
    Black Settlers at Sierra Leone,
    232–3
Soderlund, Jean, 15–16
Sons of Africa, 64–6
Sonthonax, Léger-Félicité, 104, 118, 120,
    122
South (American), 120, 129, 175, 185,
    252–3
and colonisation debates, 235
South Carolina, slave trade, 173, 183,
    184–5
Spain, slave trade, 200, 213
Speech of Mr Beaufoy, 58
Staël, Baron Auguste de, 217, 219
Staël, Madame de, 51, 207–8, 210,
    217–18, 220
Stanfield, James, 58
Stauffer, John, 9, 252
Stephen, James, 4, 165–7, 169, 179–80
    Crisis of the Sugar Colonies, The, 166
    criticism of Castlereagh, 201
    Opportunity, The, 167
    and SEAST revival, 170–1
Stephen, Sir George, 171
Sterett, Samuel, 110
sugar, 178–9
    boycott, 96
Summary View of the Evidence, A
    (Clarkson), 205–6
Summary View of the Slave Trade
    (Clarkson), 58
Swaminathan, Srividhya, 80

Talleyrand, 212
    letter from Wilberforce, 204–5, 207
Tarleton, Banestre, 181, 182
'task work', 168, 183
Temperley, Howard, 251
Terror, see French Revolution
theatre, American, 150–7
Thelwall, John, 108–9
Third Civil Commission to
    Saint-Domingue, 118–20

Thomany, Pierre, 122
Thomas, Lamont, 226, 230
Thornton, William, 210
Thorpe, Robert, 231
Thoughts and Sentiments (Cugoano), 65
Thoughts Upon the African Slave Trade
    (Newton), 58
Todd, James, 112
Tooke, Horne, 108–9
Torrid Zone, The (print) (James), 145–8,
    146
Tour through the West Indies, A
    (McKinnen), 140–3
Toussaint L'Ouverture,
    François-Dominique, 122–3, 165,
    166
Tracy, Uriah, 24, 110
trade, Sierra Leone, 226, 228–9, 233
Treaty of Amiens, 165, 169
Treaty of Ghent, 199, 213
Treaty of Paris, 211, 212
Trinidad, 165, 169, 186
    slave registration, 197n.10
Triumphs of Love, The (play) (Murdock),
    151–2
Tucker, George, 125, 223

Unitarians, 22
USA, 5–6, 13–15, 252–3
    abolition, 173–6, 183–5, 252–3
    abuses after Act, 196–200, 213–15
    abolition societies, 15–16, 22–7, 70,
        72–3, 115–17, 126–7
    see also American Conventions; New
        York Manumission Society;
        Pennsylvania Abolition Society
    American Revolution, 14–15, 20, 69
    colonisation debates, 223–30, 235–41
    emigration to Haiti, 245–8
    condition of freed slaves, 70–2
    and France, worsening situation, 120–1
    and French freeing slaves in
        Caribbean, 105
    French Revolution effect on, 109–10
    legislation, 121
        Abolition Act (1807), 184–5, 215
        against abolitionists, 115
        against freed slaves, 114–15
        Foreign Slave Trade Act (1794), 160
        Fugitive Slave Act, 155, 158, 159
        Navy Act, 154
        Non-Intercourse Act (1809), 227
        slave trade, 72–7, 81, 112, 213–14
        slavery, 46, 69, 128
    newspapers, 53, 56–9
    theatre in, 150–7

Vansittart, Nicholas, 233
Vaux, Roberts, 246, 247–8

Wadstrom, Charles, 117–18
  Observations on the Slave Trade, 50
Walker, Thomas, 22, 29, 109
War of 1812, 199, 235
war
  Britain and France, 110, 165, 169
  Britain and USA (1812), 199, 235
  France and USA, 120–1
Watson, Richard, 131
Wedgwood, Josiah, 29, 59–60
Wellington, Arthur Wellesley, Duke of,
    203
  and Clarkson's publications, 206
  in Paris, 211
Wells, Daniel, 36
West India Fashionables (print) (Sayers),
    190–3, *190*
West India lobby, 6, 82, 174–5, 181–2,
    188
'West India Prints', 145–50, 189–92
West India Sportsman, A (print) (Sayers),
    189–90, *189*
West Indies, *see* Caribbean
'white slavery', 153–5
white West Indian society, 142–4,
    147–50, 189
Wilberforce Philanthropic Society, 192
Wilberforce, William, 2, 17, 40, 82, 96,
    98, 194, 219, 221
  and abolition legislation, 176–7,
    179–83, 186–8
  in Collyer's print, 192

criticism of Castlereagh, 201
Flower on, 133–7
and Haiti, 242–3
and Humboldt, 209–10
letter to Talleyrand, 204–5, 207
revives SEAST, 169–74
and Sismondi's essay, 208–9
and Staël, 207–8
writings
  *Letter on the Abolition of the Slave
    Trade*, 186–7
  Letter to the Freeholders of Yorkshire,
    208
  Lettre à l'Empereur Alexandre, 219, 220
  Practical Christianity, 136
Wilkinson, Thomas, 107
Williams, Helen Maria, 51, 122
Williams, Peter, 157, 194, 238
Wilson, David, 16
Wilson, William, 243
Winch, Julie, 157
Wistar, Caspar, 16
women
  and abolitionist societies, 18, 74
  abolitionist writers, 51, 220
Wood, Marcus, 192
Woodfall, William, 55
Woods, Joseph, 17
Woolman, John, 13

Yearsley, Ann, 51
yellow fever, 139–40, 166
Young, Sir William, 105, 181

Zilversmit, Arthur, 128–9

Milton Keynes UK
Ingram Content Group UK Ltd.
UKHW021307041023
429933UK00022B/674